SOCIO-ECONOMIC PROFILE OF RURAL INDIA

Volume Three

NORTH-CENTRAL & WESTERN INDIA

Socio-Economic Profile of Rural India

Vol. I : SOUTH INDIA
Andhra Prades, Karnataka, Kerala, Tamil Nadu

Vol. II : NORTH-EAST INDIA
Assam, Manipur, Tripura, Nagaland

Vol. III : NORTH-CENTRAL & WESTERN INDIA
Punjab, Haryana, Himachal Pradesh, Gujarat, Maharashtra

Vol. IV : EASTERN INDIA
Bihar, West Bengal, Orissa, Uttar Pradesh

About the editor

Rajendra Vora is presently Lokmanya Tilak Professor and Head of the Department of Politics and Public Administration, University of Pune. He has three books to his credit—*Indian Democracy: Meanings and Practices* (co-edited with Suhas Palshikar); *Adhunikta ani Parampara: Ekonisavya Shatakateel Maharashtra;* and *Home, Family and Kinship in Maharashtra* (co-edited with Irina Glushkova. Also, Prof. Vora has published a good number of research and occasional papers.

SOCIO-ECONOMIC PROFILE OF RURAL INDIA

VOLUME THREE

NORTH-CENTRAL & WESTERN INDIA

(Himachal Pradesh, Punjab, Haryana, Gujarat, Maharashtra)

Edited by

RAJENDRA VORA

Lokmanya Tilak Professor and Head, Department of Politics and Public Administration, University of Pune, Poona

Published for

Centre for Rural Studies

L.B.S. National Academy of Administration, Mussoorie

by

CONCEPT PUBLISHING COMPANY, NEW DELHI-110 059

Cataloging in Publication Data—DK
Courtesy: D.K. Agencies (P) Ltd. <docinfo@dkagencies.com>

Socio-economic profile of rural India / edited by
V.K. Agnihotri.
v. 3 cm.
Includes bibliographical references.
Includes indexes.
Contents: v. 3. North-central & western India (Himachal Pradesh, Punjab, Haryana, Gujarat, Maharashtra) / edited by Rajendra Vora.
ISBN 8170227429 (set)
ISBN 818069206X (v. 3)

1. India—Social conditions. 2. India—Economic conditions. 3. India—Rural conditions. 4. Rural development projects—India. I. Agnihotri, V. K. (Vivek Kumar), 1945- II. Lal Bahadur Shastri National Academy of Administration. Centre for Rural Studies.

DDC 330.954 21

ISBN 81-8069-206-X (Vol. 3)
ISBN 81-7022-742-9 (Series)

First Published 2005

Published and Printed by
Ashok Kumar Mittal
Concept Publishing Company
A/15-16, Commercial Block, Mohan Garden,
New Delhi (INDIA)

Phones : 25351460, 25351794
Fax : 091-11-25357103
Email : publishing@conceptpub.com

FOREWORD

Since the time of independence, alleviation of poverty has been one of the chief aims of India's policy. India has seen a variety of anti-poverty programmes and evolving strategies in more than 50 years of its existence as an independent nation. The statistics reveal that, though there has been a relative decline in poverty figures, in absolute terms we have more poor people than at the time of independence. This reveals a serious shortcoming in poverty alleviation efforts over the past decades.

There has been an increased degree of focus on poverty alleviation after the reforms initiated in the country in 1991. With the opening up of the economy and a larger area being taken over by markets, there is a concern for the vulnerable, marginalized and the poor as they do not have the wherewithal to take advantage of the opportunities being offered in a growing economic environment. Such persons would be excluded from any growth process, which is based on market institutions. Current trends also shows that there is a large disparity in the growth rate of different states and the poor are largely getting concentrated in the fewer number of states. In a recent study, (Ahluwalia 2000), Ahluwalia has stated that the degree of this regional disparity increased significantly during 1990s indicating a widening of the gap in economic performances across states.

India has had one of the largest number of poverty alleviation programmes and rural development schemes, but, from the figures available, these have not made any significant difference. The schemes suffer from policy lacunae and also infirmities in their implementation. There have been numerous progressive steps like 73rd Amendment Act, which has empowered the Panchayats and given them a higher role in poverty alleviation. However, there is still need for an effective structure and liaison between bureaucrats and the politicians at that level. The government agenda regarding poverty alleviation can be realized through free primary education, adequate health care, basic services and infrastructure in rural areas, employment generation and increased access to credit for the rural population. Recently, the government has come up with a number of initiatives to give a fillip to the agrarian sector. There is increased attention to improve productivity in the agricultural sector and to come out of what is termed as "agrarian crisis". As a large number of rural poor depend on agriculture, more rapid growth of agriculture will ensure higher incomes to them. An Act to ensure right to work is also being contemplated. An adult in a poor family will get assured employment for 100 days in a year. This will not only act as a security net but also ensure work for those who are extremely poor and for whom physical labour is the only source of their livelihood.

Global experience has shown that countries require not more than two decades for transition from a developing economy to a developed one. The South East Asian tigers and recently China's example corroborate this. India too can tread the same path. However, it would require concentrated efforts from all concerned including the stakeholders, administrators, politicians, academicians and NGOs and also a lucid understanding of the issues involved in tackling poverty.

This book is the third volume of the series 'Socio-Economic Profile of Rural India'. The book is mainly based on the studies carried out by Officer Trainees during their village attachment, which forms a part of their district training. This book is based on grassroots study of poverty. The Western and North-Central volume of Socio-economic Profile of Rural India is a collection of papers of the states of Gujarat, Madhya Pradesh, Maharashtra, Rajasthan, Punjab, Haryana and Himachal Pradesh. The States are varied in terms of their socio-economic profile and present interesting differences in their development scenarios.

The authors of different state papers of this volume are senior bureaucrats and academicians. Many of the authors are directly involved in policy formulation at different levels of

Government of India. Undoubtedly, the state papers prepared by them are of high quality being enriched by inputs from long experiences in the field of rural development. I express my thanks for their contributions.

The task of publishing the volumes of Socio-Economic series was initiated by the Village Study Unit (VSU), later merged with Land Reforms Unit to form Centre of Rural Studies (CRS). The efforts of Manoj Ahuja, IAS, the Coordinator of Centre for Rural Studies and Shri Subhransu Tripathy, Assistant Professor, Centre for Rural Studies to bring out this book are worthy of praise. I look forward to the publication of the remaining volumes in this series.

LBS National Academy of Administration
Mussoorie

D.S. Mathur
Director

CONTENTS

LIST OF TABLES

PROFILE OF THE CONTRIBUTORS

Ashok Thakur

Shri Ashok Thakur is an IAS Officer of 1977 Batch and belongs to Himachal Pradesh cadre. During his career as Indian Administrative Officer, he has been posted in several important Government Departments. He was posted as Deputy Director in the Lal Bahadur Shastri National Academy of Administration and was deeply involved in Research and Training activities of the Academy. At present he is the Principal Secretary, Department of Language, Art & Culture. He is also Principal Secretary, Department of home and Department of Tourism & Civil aviation, Government of Himachal Pradesh.

Brij Pal Singh

Professor Brijpal Singh was the Vice Chairman/Coordinator of Village Study Unit, Lal Bahadur Shastri National Academy of Administration. He was also Professor of Economics in Lal Bahadur Shastri National Academy of Administration. During his career as an eminent Academician, he has been associated with many Institutions, organizations. He has also served as Director of Mahant Gopal Singh Institute of Competitions and Employment, Patiala. His in-depth knowledge and keen interest on developmental issues of India are supported by several publications, projects undertaken by the author. After retirement presently, he is deeply involved in other academic activities.

Padamvir Singh

Shri Padamvir Singh is an IAS Officer of 1977 Batch and belongs to Madhya Pradesh cadre. During his career as Indian Administrative Officer, he has been posted in several important Government Departments. He was posted as Director of Deputy Director in the Lal Bahadur Shastri National Academy of

Administration and was deeply involved in Research and Training activities of the Academy. He was also posted as Secretary, Indian Institute of Advanced Study, Shimla. He has significant contributions to Research activities and author of many books/ papers. Presently, he is the Managing Director, M.P. Warehousing & Logistics Corporation, Government of Madhya Pradesh.

C. N. Ray

Dr. C. N. Ray is an eminent Academician and earlier he was assistant Professor in the Centre for Environmental Planning and Technology (CEPT), Kasturbhai Lalbhai campus Ahemedabad. Later on he became the Reader in Sociology in CEPT. His in-depth knowledge on socio-economic issues of rural India is manifested in the form of many qualitative publications. Presently, he is involved in the academic activities.

Harsh Mander*

Shri Harsh Mander started his career as an IAS officer of Madhya Pradesh cadre. Later on he resigned from the Indian Administrative Service and concentrated on social welfare programmes. He was the Country Director of Action Aid India, a reputed international organization. Rarely does development literature capture the stark human face of poverty, let alone give it a voice. Harsh Mander does both brilliantly in his book *Unheard Voices: Stories of Forgotten Lives.* He received Rajiv Gandhi Sadbhavna Award 2002, jointly with Teesta Setalvad in August 2002. He is also visiting professor of many Universities.

Ajay Sinha*

Shri Ajay Sinha was working as a Research Associate in the Land Reforms Unit, Lal Bahadur Shastri National Academy of Administration. Later on he has also worked as Research Officer in the village Study Unit of Lal Bahadur Shastri National Academy of Administration. He has several publications on Rural Development, poverty and Land Reforms. Presently, he is posted as Assistant Project Officer in UNICEF, India.

---

* Implies he/she is one of the authors, who have prepared the State Paper on Maharasthra.

1

INTRODUCTION

RAJENDRA VORA

India is a country of villages. According to 2001 census 72 per cent of her population lives in villages. After more than fifty years of economic planning 742 million people still live in rural areas. The proportion of rural population has declined from 74.29 in 1991 to 72 per cent in 2001. Agriculture provides employment to around 60 per cent of the total workforce in the country. Therefore whoever wants to study and understand India has to direct his/her attention to what is happening and is not happening in the villages. Colonial masters realised that they should better know villages if they want to rule over this land. Since the land revenue was one of the important sources of income the British revenue officers were the first to encounter society and economy of the Indian villages. A village became a focus of study when census operations were started especially after 1901. Some of the earliest political actions against the policies of the colonial government were organised not in urban areas but in villages. Farmers indebtedness, higher rates of land revenue and inadequate famine relief were the causes around which these actions were organised in 1870s. Justice M. G. Ranade, the founder of Indian Economics had argued that India's economic problem was two-fold as (a) phenomenal poverty and (b) dependence on agriculture and its solution lied in industrialisation and commercialisation of agriculture. Mahatma Gandhi was the first Indian leader who realised what place a village occupies in the life of Indian nation. He believed that India's soul lived in her village and thought that if the village perished India will perish too. "It will be no more India: her own mission in the world will get lost". Gandhi argued that cities have exploited the villages. The blood of the villages is the edifice on which the cities are built. He wanted the blood that is inflating the arteries of the cities to run again in the blood vessels of the villages. (O'Leary: 1994: 143)

Unfortunately strategy of economic development adopted after independence did not reflect this view. Even though around 72 per cent population lives in rural area that agriculture provides employment to about 60 per cent of our workforce the share of agriculture sector in the national income has gone down from 55.4 per cent in 1950-51 to 30.9 per cent in 1990-91 and 26.1 per cent in 2001-02. Declining share of agriculture sector in country's national income is considered an indication of development. But the fact remains that the proportion of Indian population dependent on agriculture has not declined in that quantity. Very low plan outlay on agriculture in last nine plans is the most important reason for such a state of affairs. The plan outlay on agriculture has remained as low as 20 to 24 per cent in last fifty years except in the first plan (1951-56) when it was 31 per cent. This lop-sidedness has resulted into a considerable gap between the development of urban and rural areas both in economic and social sectors. Minhas, Jain and Tendulkar have shown that incidence of poverty is greater in rural area by 8.3 per cent. In 1987-88 for instance population living below poverty line was 44.8 per cent in rural as against 36.5 per cent in urban India.

Instead of looking at percentages if looked at actual number of poor people we come to know the real gravity of the problem. In urban areas this number in 1987-88 was 77 million while it was as high as 284 million in rural area. (Minhas, Jain, Tendulkar: 91: 6-13)

The gap between the rural and urban is glaringly seen also with respect to the growth rate of employment. It was around 1.41 to 1.96 per cent between 1983-94 (see Table 1.1).

Table 1.1: Growth Rates of employment

(Annual compound rates per cent)		
Period	Rural	Urban
1983 to 1987-88	1.36	2.77
1987-88 to 1993-94	2.3	3.34

Source: Frontline, June 18, 2004: 118).

On human development side also we get the similar picture. The birth (30.9), death (10.6) and infant mortality rates (87) are higher in rural area than in urban area (24.3, 7.1 and 54 in that order) (Government of Maharashtra: 1996: 114). With respect to literacy, schools, employment, infrastructure and such other indices of economic and human development the gap between village and cities is quite wide and it is no doubt an outcome of our strategy of development.

The efforts to restore the balance between the two were done by the union and also the state governments. The first such attempt was in the form of the community development programme started on 2nd October 1952. The land reforms of fifties were meant to rationalise the land holding patterns. But the most decisive step in restoring the balance between the rural and the urban was the green revolution a package of programmes for the intensive development of agriculture sector. It was undertaken during the third plan period (1961-66).

In the seventies the emphasis was given on eradication of poverty (1971) especially in the rural sector and then came the policy package named rural development, which included number of programmes of employment generation, self employment promotion, as well as housing for poor and agriculture development. During the Janata Party's rule (1977-79) a rural bias was perceptible since the rich peasantry leadership of the north had come to power (Rudolph and Rudolph: 1987: 314-32). The multiple programmes of the rural development were eventually brought under one umbrella of the Integrated Rural Development Programme (IRDP). It was started in all the 5011 blocks in the country on 2nd October 1980. When the inadequacies both in its planning and implementation were revealed the government launched new and improved schemes such as Rural Landless Employment Guarantee Programme (1983), National Rural Employment Programme (1980), Jawahar Rozgar Yojana (1989), Million Wells Schemes (1988-89), Indira Awaas Yojana (1985-86), Employment Assurance Scheme (1993) etc. for the benefit of the rural area and specially for the rural poor.

These schemes and programmes have certainly benefited the villages but one fact which has come to the fore in last fifty years is that these schemes have not benefited the target groups to the extent they were intended to and it is mainly because of the social and economic inequalities and resultant uneven distribution of political power in the villages. The study conducted in forty eight villages in Maharashtra has indicated that the land owing clans belonging to dominant caste of the village monofilise the power positions at the local level (Vora: 1999: 199-218). These clans control the resources and power in such a way that any programme of by-passing them fall on the ground. The cooperatives and panchayati raj institution have not been able to do much in Maharashtra due to these stumbling blocks. Studies carried out in other states also point at almost identical conditions (Gough: 1989: 10-20). The village studies while assessing the rural development programmes will have to take into account these factors which are in a way internal to the village system.

Idea of village studies which had its origin in the colonial period was brought into practice by social scientist, policy makers, and activists in post-independent period basically for the purpose of locating the impact of economic planning on the rural society. A rapid survey of literature on these studies suggest that the most of the studies belong to the category of case study in which an in-depth study is done of a single village. We also find that many scholars make a study of the same village after some years to record the transformation. There are few sample surveys of villages to either understand the impact of development programmes or to analyse the socio-political structure into rural areas. Most of the observations about villages are mainly based on a case study of a particular village.

The present volume makes a departure from the earlier studies in many ways. It brings together case studies of 170 villages from five states to present generalisations and to give across—state comparison. Thus it is not a report of a case study of a single village or a sample survey of the villages. The studies are done by the Indian Administrative Service officer trainees and not by social scientist or policy makers. Lal Bahadur Shastri National Academy of Administration at Mussoorie makes each IAS officer trainee to stay in a village during the field training in the district and do a socio-economic survey of a village. Out of two years of training period of these trainees one year is spent in the district. One of their assignment during this year is to do a socio-economic study of a village in that district. The main purpose of these studies is to sensitise and educate the officer-trainees. The trainees present their reports during the Phase II at the Academy. The guidelines regarding conducting the studies are given by the Course Coordinator and the Centre for Rural Studies (earlier known as the Village Study Unit). The trainees are required to examine the social structure of the village, the economic conditions of the villagers and the state of attains with regard to agriculture, village industries, land reports, the panchayati raj, cooperative institutions, irrigation and land revenue administration. They are supposed to study the impact of multiple government schemes and programmes about employment, education, health, family welfare and also the agriculture development. The villagers are not selected according to the method of random sampling. The officer trainees are not the trained researchers. The observations presented here are basically those of the fresh entrants to the administrative cadre. The micro-studies done by the trainees are brought together in systematic manner to present a general picture of the rural economy and the society of a particular state by the senior officers at the Academy or the academicians. While preparing the state reports these scholars have provided the secondary data about the district or the state in order to contextualise the village studies. The aim of the state reports is to give an overall picture of the state's villages rather than throwing light on a village X or Y.

The five states covered in this volume belong to the central and western India and they are Himachal Pradesh, Punjab, Haryana, Gujarat and Maharashtra. The studies from 170 villages belonging to 65 districts of the above five states are brought together in this volume to give a profile of central and western Indian villages (see Table 1.2).

Table 1.2: Number of Villages Studies (State wise)

Sl. No.	*State*	*Period of Study*	*Districts*	*Villages*
1.	Himachal Pradesh	1985-1994	8 (12)	15 (16997)
2.	Punjab	1983-1993	10 (12)	25 (12428)
3.	Haryana	1983-1994	13 (16)	50 (6759)
4.	Gujarat	1983-1994	13 (19)	39 (18028)
5.	Maharashtra	1987-1992	21 (36)	41 (40412)
Total:			65 (89)	170 (94624)

Note : Figures in brackets show total number.

The state of Himachal Pradesh is located in the hilly areas and geographically differs from the states with respect to the land use pattern, the size of the villages and their spread. The population of the villages in this state is very small and these villages are dispersed over a large hilly areas. The proportion of urban population there is only 8.69 per cent. Even though the per capita income is Rs. 1948 which is much lower than that of other states, the percentage of population living below poverty line is only 15.46 per cent. So here is a state where almost 91 per cent population lives in villages and even then the proportion of poverty is very low compared to all India population or that of Maharashtra and Gujarat the 'developed states'. The foodgrain yield per hectare is also higher than these two developed states.

Social indicators of Himachal Pradesh also show that the conditions are certainly better than what you find in many of the developed studies. On the count of literacy; school going children, sex ratio, infant mortality rate, life expectancy and female worker participation rate Himachal Pradesh is either doing better than the other states or is at par with these states. It is the only state in this group which is known for its horticulture specially the apple production.

In the vicinity are two states Punjab and Haryana which are also covered by this volume. Both are famous for their success stories of green revolution. If one takes into consideration the economic indicators these two states are among the top five states in the country and in our groups they excel all others. The per capita income of these two states is the highest and the population below poverty line is between 12 to 16 per cent only. It shows at least from these two figures that the economic disparity in Punjab and Haryana is not very high. This observation makes more sense if we compare these two states with Maharashtra and Gujarat where population of poor is quite high even though these two states are considered as the developed states in the country. And the interesting feature of Punjab and Haryana is that the urban population is small compared to Gujarat and Maharashtra. Both Maharashtra and Gujarat are known for the contribution of their industrial sector rather than the agriculture. In case of Punjab and Haryana it is the agriculture or rural sector which has performed exceedingly well and that is secret of their economic development as well as that of lower proportion of poverty. Does it mean that the states where villages perform well perform better so far as two crucial factors: disparity and per capita income are concerned. It is true that the percentage of irrigated land is between 77.9 to 94.6 per cent in Punjab and Haryana and therefore their agriculture production is the highest in the country. In Maharashtra and Gujarat on the other hand, proportion of irrigation is between 16.2 to 27.4 per cent. Both are cases of regional imbalance and also sectoral imbalance. Whatever water is available is not being used rationally. In Maharashtra for instance almost 60 per cent water is used for sugarcane farming when there are around 148 drought-prone tehsils and 14000 villages with drinking water shortage (Dastane: 1992). The contribution of agriculture sector to the state income has come down from 28.1 to 21.2 per cent in last decade when the state still has 60 per cent rural population which mainly depends on agriculture. The percentage of poor population in Maharashtra is about 40 per cent. These figures suggest that the

Table 1.3: Comparative Picture of Five States

State	Urban population (1991)	Literacy Percentage (1991)			No. of Students in Primary/ Secondary schools per thousand population (1994-95)	Sex Ratio No. of females per thousand males (1991)	Life expectancy at birth (year) (1988-92)	Infant Mortality Rate (1994)	Percentage of gross irrigated area to gross cropped area (1991-92)	Total foo grain yield per hectare in Kg (1991-94)	Female worker participation rate (1991)	Per capita income (1988-89) at constant prices (1980-81)	Percentage of population living below poverty line (1987-88)
		Male	Female	Total									
Himachal Pradesh	8.69	75.36	52.13	63.86	232	976	63.3	63	17.8	1555	34.81	1948	15.46
Haryana	24.63	69.10	40.47	55.85	194	865	62.5	67	77.9	2586	10.76	3160	16.63
Punjab	29.55	65.66	50.41	58.51	162	882	66.6	53	94.6	3560	4.40	3421	12.70
Gujarat	34.49	82.01	66.99	61.29	206	934	59.5	64	27.4	1029	25.96	2631	32.33
Maharashtra	38.69	76.56	52.32	64.87	210	934	63.4	54	16.2	1267	33.11	2026	40.10
All India	25.71	64.13	39.29	52.21	183	927	58.7	73	35.0	1442	22.25	2078	39.34

Source: Economic Survey of Maharashtra, 1996.

development does not reach the large section of the state population. Does it mean that the model of development Maharashtra or for that matter Gujarat has adopted is responsible for such lopsidedness and inequality? The villages in these states are not performing to the expectation.

Punjab and Haryana as the Table 1.3 shows are trailing behind on the human development front. We come to know this fact if we look at number of school going children, the sex ratio, the female worker participation and female literacy rate. When it comes to gender dimension of development Punjab and Haryana do fall behind the states such as Gujarat and Maharashtra. Is it because the rate of urbanisation is lower in Punjab and Haryana? Can we argue that the green revolution and rural development may not necessarily help women and that in Punjab and Haryana villages everything is not that fine?

The state reports in this volume do discuss the issues and questions raised above. The village studies reported here were done between 1983 to 1994 and therefore they do not take into consideration the impact of the 73rd amendment which radically changed the panchayati raj institutions in rural areas. Since early 1990s was too early to judge the effect of new economic reforms these studies also do not sufficiently touch this aspect.

There are these and other limits mentioned earlier. In spite of these limits we think that the academicians, administrators and social activists would find the state chapters useful not only for the overall perspective but also for the insights about the Indian village given by the officer trainees on the basis of their first hand experience of the reality. And we hope that this volume would provide to its readers a profile of rural India.

REFERENCES

Census of India: 1991, State Profile: 1991: India.

Dastane, Santosh, (ed.), *Maharashtra: 1992,* Dastane Ramchandra and Co. Pune, 1992 .

Frontline, June 18, 2004.

Gough, Kathleen, *Rural change in Southeast India: 1950s to 1980s,* Oxford University Press, Delhi, 1989.

Government of Maharashtra, Directorate of Economics and Statistics, Economic Survey of Maharashtra; 1995-96, Mumbai, 1996.

Lloyd, I. Rudolph and S. H. Rudolph, In *Pursuit of Laxmi: The Political Economy of the Indian State,* The University of Chicago Press, 1987.

Madan, Vandana, (ed.), *The village in India,* Oxford University Press, New Delhi, 2002.

Minhas, B. S., L. R. Jain and S. D. Tendulkar, "Declining Incidence of Poverty in 1980s", *Economic and Political Weekly,* July 6-13, 1991.

O'Leary, Basil, An Approach to Gandhian Economics, in S. Mukherjee and S. Ramswamy (eds.), *Facets of Mahatma Gandhi,* Vol. III, Deep and Deep, New Delhi, 1994.

Vora, Rajendra, Dominant Lineages and Political Power in Maharashtra, in Irina. Glushkova and Rajendra Vora (eds.), *Home, Family and Kinship in Maharashtra,* Oxford University Press, New Delhi, 1999.

2

HIMACHAL PRADESH

Ashok Thakur

Himachal Pradesh came into being with the merger of several princely hill states on 15th April, 1948. It underwent a series of metamorphic changes, both politically and administratively, till it became the Eighteenth State of Indian Union on 25th January, 1971. Subsequently, the re-organisation of districts in 1972 gave Himachal Pradesh the shape as it exists today.

Himachal Pradesh is predominantly rural. In the Central Government notification regarding categorisation of inhabitations in the country, even Shimla is put in the category of a semi- urban locality. In this sparsely populated state, even a cluster of a few houses is classified as a village. This fact has been pointed out by most of the studies. One has come across villages in Himachal with a population of no more than 20-30 people.

The difficult terrain, the lack of available habitable land and the capacity of the land to support inhabitations has been limited. Hence people have settled in remote and distant places and that too in numbers just enough to be able to eke out a living from land available to them. Taking the case of Mandi, Rajpal in his report points out that "it has a population of about 6 lakhs and the total number of villages about 3000 (2806 to be precise). Assuming that 60, 000 people in the district live in urban areas, the average population per village comes to 180. In comparison, the corresponding figures for a comparable district in the plains is close to 550. Nor is there enough plain contiguous land available where people can develop and build clusters of houses. Also, the capacity of the land to sustain a high density of population being limited, the people have found it expedient to build their houses in a scattered manner." (Mandi/Rajpal/1990)

Himachal Pradesh is striking because are law abiding and peaceful. Very few major crimes are reported in the State. There is amity amongst the various religious communities which is rooted in history. As Anil Khachi states in his report "1947 did not witness any communal riots in the village. Not one Muslim family emigrated from this village. There is no mosque in the village and none of the Muslim families appeared to be the fundamentalist kind. They live quite happily here in the village and the grievances they had, were not against any community. The lone Sikh family was also happy to be around. He had not suffered any loss during the Nov'84 riots; and in fact was concerned about terrorism in Punjab as the other communities." (Bilaspur/Khachi/1988)

Rajpal writes about his village in Mandi "Here in Kehanwal (and it is true of most villages in HP), I have come across dispersed houses within a village as well. Unlike Punjab and Haryana, the people here never felt the need to stay closely huddled together since there is no threat of dacoits or organized gangs of thieves in this area."

Although Himachal Pradesh is surrounded by states where the law and order situation is/has been rather tense, it continues to be a haven of peace and tranquillity as is observed by Prabodh Kumar in his report on Kangra in the year 1990. "Although Kangra district borders the terrorist infested Gurdaspur district of Punjab, there seems to be very remote possibility of terrorism coming here because in hills the exit routes are limited and secondly the population is so scarce that any outsider can be noticed immediately and further there is no chance of any support from the local population. (Kangra/Prabodh/1990) It is interesting to note the response of the terrorists when asked as to why they do not attempt to disturb Himachal. Their response as told to an IPS officer of HP during interrogation was " Himachal is our rest house. When we are tired of getting hounded by Punjab Police we come here to relax and recuperate. Why should we disturb it". So much so for the effectiveness of Himachal Police!

The severest comment that one could cull from the reports regarding law and order and communal strains is, "Talking to the Muslims gave an insight into the minority syndrome suffered by them. Nuru, an old man of 65 years said that his brother Bagru was asking him to run away from the village a few months back on the plea that he would be killed by the Hindus. Nuru found this quite absurd as he said he has been living in the village for more than twenty years and no Hindu had ever posed a threat to him. This incident was probably during the Babri Masjid-Ramjanamabhoomi controversy. On talking to SDM, Jogindernagar I found that Muslim Gujjars were quite afraid during the Mandir-Masjid controversy phase, and eleven families from the sub-division had actually migrated. He had personally brought back the nine families. Two of the families had refused to come back at that time but they came back in the last week of February." (Mandi/Anita/1989)

The original people or the aboriginals are now represented by various scheduled caste which form a considerable part of the population (25% of the population in HP is SC). These people could be such castes as Kolis, Holis, Chamars, Darains, Rehars, Chanals, Lohars, Baris, Dagis, Dhakis and Turis. These people are mostly artisans and work/worked as cobblers, basket makers, iron smiths, tailors and weavers. The second and perhaps the more important aspect in the origin of the people of Himachal Pradesh is a tribe called the Khasha. They are said to be originally an Aryan tribe of Central Asia which entered West Himalaya through the north-west. But with the passage of time and alien influence they split into numerous sub-clans and clans. Kanet is one of the important clans. The Rajputs and Brahmins were later entrants to Himachal Pradesh. They came from the Indian plains from time to time for a number of reasons. Sometime as an adventurer or at times in search of security. The location of holy places in and around Himachal attracted high caste Hindus like Khatris, Mahajans, Kaisthas, Vohras and Karars who migrated to the hills during the Muslim invasions of north India from the twelfth to sixteenth century.

The Gaddis are the descendants of the Khatris of the Punjab who migrated to the high hills due to persecution by the Muslim rulers. They are a semi-nomadic, semi-pastoral and semi-agricultural tribe. They reside mainly on the slopes of the Dhauladhar and its spurs covering the Districts of Kangra, Chamba and Mandi. In summer they move to the high hills in search of grass and fodder for their herds and in the winter season to the low valleys of Kangra and adjoining plains. Gaddis are also divided into different castes. The reports from Kangra, Chamba and Mandi mention about them.

The Gujjars are pastoral and nomadic. They wander throughout the year in search of grazing pastures for their cattle which mostly consists of buffaloes and cows. Gujjars are Hindus as well as Muslims though the bulk of them are Muslims. Muslim Gujjar is a nomad and therefore, has no settled home in any part of Himachal Pradesh. Today Hindu Gujjars mostly lead a settled life. Although, there is no caste system among Gujjars as we find among Hindus, yet, there are four communities within it, namely, Gujjar, Kashmiri, Julaha and Teli. It is interesting to note that all the people of these four communities frequently get together and also dine together, but, no marital relations are discouraged between any two of these communities. (Chamba/Subramanyam/1986)

Anita writes about the Gujjars in Mandi District "Now they have started settling and can be said to be in a transition phase. They have some land and have also built houses. So they leave the old and the women folk behind and migrate. When winter is over and greenery returns to the villages, they come back to the same village, though normally they would have moved to some new village. Gujjars are gradually taking up the settled agricultural practices. Earlier they used to own only buffaloes and sold milk and milk products wherever grazing land was available. They still own buffaloes and derive major portion of their income from them. Their children mostly spend their time on the pastures with the buffaloes and are rarely ever sent to school." (Mandi/Anita/1989)

The people of the upper reaches of Kinnaur, Lahaul and the whole of Spiti, are perhaps the descendants of those who migrated under adverse political conditions from Tibet in the ninth and tenth centuries. There exists evidence of the migration of people from Zanskar and other parts of Ladakh to Spiti. The Spitians are Buddhist by religion while the people of Lahaul and Kinnaur are half Buddhist and half Hindu. The people of Kinnaur, Lahaul and Spiti used to migrate their livestock to the lower hills in the cold months and ascend to high altitude pastures in the summer months. This has now been greatly reduced. (Unfortunately there are no reports on any of these areas, and therefore, they will not form part of this study).

GENERAL OBSERVATIONS

Some of the aspects observed and commented upon by the OTs have been highlighted below :

Sudhir Rajpal writes that "contrary to the normal image of the hills i.e. the sparkling streams, birds chirping in dense forests, happy people singing and dancing in cool air of the mountains, the way a hill person views his own life is quite different: in fact many of them feel that they are leading a tough isolated life, wherein they are trapped in their small world full of hardship and drudgery".

The inhabitants of the area of Kehanwal seemed utterly dissatisfied with their fate. They blame Mother Nature the most for reducing them to their present plight. The cultivable land around them is quite infertile, hard and rocky and extracts a lot of labour from them before it is willing to yield any crop to them in return. (Mandi/Rajpal/1990)

(He further writes about the other aspect of their characteristics which is much attributed to the people of the hills i.e. their being gentle and not ambitious). Rajpal writes that "the people are gentle and calm and not at all ambitious or outgoing. This has perhaps proved to be their undoing. Lack of interaction with outsiders has led to a stagnation of ideas and a consequent lack of will to strive hard to improve their fate. People are happy and contented if their basic needs of 'Roti, Kapda and Makan' are provided for alongwith the mandatory bottle of liquor every evening." (Mandi/Rajpal/1990)

Because of adverse geographical conditions everyone has to work for survival. "There is no stigma against manual work. Every one whether Brahmin, Rajput or Harijan is prepared to take even wage employment no vested interest based on caste or class are working in the village." (Mandi/Agarwal/1985)

But Nisha Singh and Sushil Negi observe the other aspect of the people in Bilaspur and Una.

"The common man of our village is very conscious of his rights and of the government servants duties towards them. This welcome symbol of a democratic India, though progressive in giving a greater status to women, in educating children etc. is conservative too" (Bilaspur/Nisha/1987). This aspect is particularly true for the districts of Bilaspur and Una as Sushil Negi writes :

Mostly people in this village are less educated but are well aware of revenue laws and are highly litigating types, as most of the money is wasted in court case and litigation due to land disputes and minor problems. Almost every family has the distinction of having a family lawyer for which they feel proud, and consider it as a prestige symbol. Country liquor is very prevalent in this village, many people are addicted to it and this is one of the factors for their slow progress and people being quarrelsome. People are generally humble with government officials and are selfish nature, they try all means to get favours. (Una/Negi/1985)

Slowly and slowly the villagers are introduced to new items of "comforts and luxuries". Tooth paste is used by the younger generation. Even shampoo is found at one of the shops. Women spend money on items of cosmetics though many of them are imitation of the popular brands. Many other luxury items have made inroad from the town market. In families where there are people working in government service, these things are more in use than the other families. (Kangra/Prabodh/1990)

"Given the terrain and climatic conditions outdoor activities are rather limited. Under the influence of television, children are picking up games like cricket. However, the facilities for playing there are virtually non-existent. Simple living is still the rule, as few can afford anything better!" (Solan/Rizvi/1988)

CASTE AND UNTOUCHABILITY

Kangra Division

Dhiman made a detailed break-up of the people of his village in Kangra District and show how the traditional caste based occupations are no longer valid in rural Himachal and also how their situation once there is economic activity? The village which was surveyed by him has developed a rich area due to the Slate Mining industry which on the social side seems to have literally wiped out caste structure yet so damaging to the environment and nature. Such are the dilemmas of development. Out of the total of 385 families, 136 were SCs which included the sub-castes of Halli, Batwal, Chamar, Jogi, Chhimbas, Doomnas, Sippy and Dhogri. There were 66 families of Gurkhas, 64 families of Gaddies. Following is detail of each caste:

Table 2.1 : Traditional Caste based occupations

Sl. No.	*Name of Caste*	*No of Families*	*Whether SC*	*Traditional Occupation*
1.	Halli	1	Yes	Removing dead animals
2.	Ghirth	3	—	Agriculture
3.	Batwal	60	Yes	Labour class
4.	Batare (Mason)	4	—	Mason
5.	Chamar	6	Yes	Cobbler/leather work
6.	Jogi	6	Yes	Beggars
7.	Chhimba	4	Yes	Tailoring/dyeing and washing cloths
8.	Rajput	23	—	Warriors
9.	Doomna	5	Yes	Bamboo work
10.	Carpenter	3	—	Wood work
11.	Gaddi	64	—	Pastoral, weaving

contd.

Table 2.1 (contd.)

Sl. No.	*Name of Caste*	*No of Families*	*Whether SC*	*Traditional Occupation*
12.	Nath	3	-	Pooja-path
13.	Sippy	34	Yes	Weaving wool harvest sewing of chogas.
14.	Gurkhas	66	-	Service to Rulers
15.	Mahajan	9	-	Business community
16.	Barber (Hazam)	1	-	Hair-cutting
17.	Dhogri	20	Yes	Black smithy, charcoal, work in forests.
18.	Muslims	13	-	-
19.	Brahamin	31	-	Purohits, family priests
20.	Bhatt (Gaddi)	29	-	Gaddi Purohits.

Speaking in general, for the whole of the State of HP, caste feelings is not as intense as in the plain areas, but its existence cannot be denied. During festivals or marriages, food for Brahmins and high castes are cooked and served by Brahmins and high castes. Apart from this mild precautions about pollution and purity, caste feelings are not dominant.

With the decline of the traditional caste-based occupations, and decline of agriculture as the mainstay of economic activity, most of caste/most of the families in each caste were no more engaged in these occupations.

"Slate mining is an important activity in the Ghaniara Panchayat area. Today most of the people belonging to sippys, atwals, muslims, chamar, gaddis are engaged in the slate mining industry as contractors/labourers. Out of 28 families 3 are contractors and 11 families have their main occupation as labour in slate mining, and which includes people from all castes and communities. Muslims, most of whom are landless, are employed as labourers in slate mining industry. Most of the chamars, having stopped the traditional leather work, upper caste people face difficulty when some animal dies, and in most of the cases, owners irrespective from any caste have to remove the dead animals (indication enough to the dying caste system). Similarly, Dhobis and Chhimbas no more do the washing and dyeing business, a few of them are engaged in tailoring. Gurkhas were mainly employed in the army, though people from other castes also have representation in the army. Similarly Dhogris are employed as labourers in the slate mining industry.

The economy is fast getting monetised and the jajmani system is becoming a thing of the past. The Jajmani System refers to the economic system where payments for the services rendered are made in kind at the rates settled long before traditionally and in most of the cases payments made in kind not necessarily correspond to the services rendered. As local Doomna (engaged in bamboo works) said that traditionally people used to give 1-2 kg of foodgrains for each item, where now 1-2 kg of foodgrains cost around Rs 2/-4/- but in market, they get Rs 7/-8/- for same item, and hence they prefer to get the payments in cash." (Kangra/ Dhiman/1988)

The general impression about caste system is that the domain of Brahmin and upper caste is getting weaker by the year. Some of the other observations are :

"Although traditionally, the Brahmins command respect and hold a pre-eminent position in this village, there is no domination of one caste over the other. Peaceful co-existence is the general principle." (Chamba/Subramanyam/1986)

"No doubt the Brahmins are at the top of caste hierarchy, but castism in its extreme form is not practised here in this village. As Brahmins maintained that there was a time when chamars were outcastes, they could not enter the hamlets of Brahmins without informing in advance and taking off the shoes outside, but now, ideas of pollution and purity have weakened. The locations of houses of various castes are completely mixed, at the same time social intercourse among all the castes has increased. Yet the traces are there and so-called lower caste are equally concerned about their rights and express their resentment when such attitudes are displayed. Now chamars and muslims are invited on occasions like marriage etc. where they are served food either in separate utensils, and cooks or they are given the uncooked food items like—rice, dal etc. Though they come for dining, they cannot mix with the people of other castes. Chamars and Surariras are reluctant to attend such occasions, and feel hurt if somebody refers to them as harijans. As far as economic conditions are concerned, Harijans are not that worse off as compared to other castes, as I observed during my house to house survey, they are very conscious and sensitive to their caste positions, and feel strongly if somebody asks them about the certain attributes traditionally associated with Harijans." (Kangra/Dhiman/1988)

Added to this is the fact that in this village there is not much of caste distinction because barring three brahmin families, the rest of the village does not belong to the so called category of "upper caste Hindus". (Kangra/Prabodh/1990)

What is remarkable is the fact that there is no demonstration of feudal tendencies. I suppose the reason is that the land was always limited and secondly land reforms have. The result is that there is no widespread discrepancy in landholding pattern. Another reason is that nobody requires agricultural labour. In the hills because of difficult living conditions everyone has to inculcate the sense of dignity of labour especially for domestic purposes. A villager who serves outside is expected to do all the activities if he happens to be in the village particularly in the sowing and the harvesting season." (Kangra/Prabodh/1990)

And this is what happens in villages when the Scheduled Caste population is more than the upper castes as Prabodh writes; "This is a village where the Scheduled Caste population is in numerical superiority but even otherwise the villagers tell us that there is no untouchability. In the adjoining villages within the Panchayat, there is no evidence of the fact that the Harijans are treated as untouchables. The village taps are open for use by all the communities. There is no caste wise division of the bowlies also. The village temple is looked after by a Brahmin but everyone can worship there". (Kangra/Prabodh/1990)

The Brahmin families do not feel any discrimination as such in spite of being a microscopic minority. They get the customary respect and they also do not consider any untouchability. After all they are the major trading community of Padher and how can they afford to treat their customers as untouchables. The caste distinction was prominent at one time but now it is on its way out here. It is a matter of time before it becomes insignificant in social relations though it will stay in politics. One ex-serviceman who belonged to Batawal caste and was trained in nursing has contributed remarkably towards better relation of the different communities through his professional skills." (Kangra/Prabodh/1990)

However Baldi met with Harijans in their hamlet in Una District and asked them whether any form of untouchability is practised in their village and whether they are put to some disadvantage due to this. In reply, most of them said that "as far as socio-economic conditions of Harijan are concerned, they are at par with other communities of the village. Their land holdings can be compared with the land holdings of the Brahmins. In fact two of the members of Panchayat belong to Harijan community. In general no social disability is faced by Harijan in this village." (Una/Baldi/1985)

Mandi Division

Caste considerations continue to linger on in all forms of social interaction through strong in others just a trace of it.

"I did not come across even a single instance of inter-caste marriage in the village. Inter-caste rivalry and antagonism keeps simmering below the surface. But since this inter-caste antagonism is not backed by intense economic disparities (of Bihar and UP variety) there is no threat of it assuming any violent form. Before tap water appeared on the scene owing to a drinking water scheme of the Irrigation Public Health Department, there used to be separate bowlies for the Harijans and upper caste people. The upper caste continue to refuse to drink or eat at a Harijan household though I saw Harijans visiting their hearths and partaking of meals prepared in the upper caste houses." (Mandi/Rajpal/1990)

Untouchability exists but not in the vicious form. Higher caste people still refuse to eat alongwith the Harijans but the demands of the modern times are leading to a gradual removal of such restrictions. (Mandi/Rajpal/1990)

In the village though there is outwardly no discrimination against the other Harijans, but a deeper look shows that they are kept separate from main social events and considered low. Most of the Harijans live in a hamlet called 'Makrana' which incidentally is also the least developed region of the village. Most of them have been helped through IRD programme and given Nautor land in land to landless drive. (Bilaspur/Nisha/1987)

Although the scheduled castes do not suffer from any apparent prohibitions imposed by the higher castes, the people are yet to get completely rid of casteist feelings. Even today inter-caste marriages are frowned upon, in spite of open government encouragement. I did not come across any such marriages in the village during my survey work. The upper castes may invite the scheduled caste people on social function such as marriages but their food is separately cooked and they sit away from the upper castes while eating. The Rajputs and Brahmins of the village even today will not accept food or water from a SC family openly (what happens surreptitiously is entirely different!).

However, the SCs cannot be treated with the contempt they were dealt with in the pre-independence days, and apart from eating and drinking, there is a lot of social interaction amongst the various castes. The kind of tensions which rupture the social fabric of rural society every now and then in Bihar and Eastern U.P. is conspicuous by its absence. (Bilaspur/Khachi/1988)

The lower castes are not allowed to enter the houses of upper caste. (Mandi/Anita/1989)

A Rajput living in higher hill had cut the water supply to these houses. Intervention by IPH officials had proved to be futile and now it had become an active caste issue and gone to District office. Many Harijans alleged that even after having good jobs (outside the area) they were looked down upon and their milk etc. kept separate viz., the milk from their cattle is not purchased by prominent sweet shops. Though this discrimination is there, yet there is no exploitation as such, and there has been no case of direct confrontation between different caste groups. (Bilaspur/Nisha/1987)

In fact Anita notes a very interesting aspect of casteism in the survey village where she found casteism being practised amongst the upper castes themselves; "there is no restriction in mixing or even sitting together in Gram Sabha meeting. In fact the feeling of caste was more obvious in the case of Khatris and Rajputs. These two are not on good terms with each other. This can be attributed to the fact that the Khatris think themselves to be of the same status as the Rajputs whereas the Rajputs are not ready to accord equal status to them. Khatris in general, are equal in economic status to the Rajputs. So wherever they are in larger number than Rajputs, they dominate the Panchayat." (Mandi/Anita/1989)

Shimla Division

Similar sentiments and feelings are recorded from the other villages in Solan and Sirmaur District.

Discrimination against the Harijans is fast disappearing in such things as access to drinking water taps, temples and public places. However, people still live in pockets of their own castemen and the ritual purity of the house kitchen is strictly enforced by the housewives. (Solan/Rizvi/1988)

This village is peculiar in the sense that the scheduled castes people far out-number the caste Hindus. "Besides this, there are three scheduled tribe families and one Muslim family. Dhiggars form the majority of scheduled caste population and the lone Muslim family has mingled well with the caste Hindus—so much so that the typical Muslim customs that are witnessed in parts of western and central UP were nearly absent in this family." (Nahan/Sanjeev/1993)

Yet some of the Officer Trainees did find that all is not well in these quiet villages as there was an under-current of casteist feeling and tension still lingering in the background, though not, so intense as seen in UP or Bihar (mercifully!) In Kangra region there have been references to the practice which are not so flattering:

Intercaste marriages, are, therefore, very rare. Even in the case of love marriages also, the partners will first ensure that both of them belong to the same caste, before they proceed and advance in their love-relationship. (Chamba/Subramanyam/1986)

It seems that the government schemes for the districts is a cause for tension as reported from Una and Kangra by S. Baldi and Prabodh. "When I enquired about untouchability from caste Hindus, they mentioned that untouchability is not followed in this area and harijans mix with them without any hitch. However the special benefits like reservation in employment and more subsidy in IRDP to Harijan etc. were troubling their mind and they were quite against these policies. One poor carpenter told me that why they should get extra benefits when they do not face any disability or disadvantage in this area." (Una/Baldi/1985)

"This has obviously caused jealous among the non-antodaya families. A major reason of resentment is the cheap ration provided to these families. Not only is the ration cheap but there are strict government instructions that in case of shortage the first preference should be given to the antodaya families and only when each of them have been supplied with the quota, then the rest of the families can avail of the public distribution system and such occasions are not rare. When people are not convinced about the fairness of the system, such discrimination is irritating for them. They believe that instead of extending the political base of the ruling party, such a scheme will restrict their voters to that category only. Such an assessment must be taken with a pinch of salt and it may be more particularly true of this village only as the Panchayat is dominated by Congress." (Kangra/Prabodh/1990)

There are differences of commensality and consanguinity in the village. The distinction of "roti and beti" is maintained. "No two communities in the village eat together though as one of the senior villager said " Jab Dharamshala jate hain to whan chai saat saat pee lete hain" (When we go to Dharamshala there we take our tea together)." (Kangra/Prabodh/1990)

Another interesting situation has been reported by Pramod Kumar from Kangra. He finds out that "there is a discrimination among Scheduled Castes themselves and they have their own hierarchy in which Batawal are the highest and the Dumna are the lowest. Such discrimination is not so acute among the backwards. The backwards are looking forward for the acceptance and implementation of Mandal Commission Report even when Himachal has rejected it." (The BJP Government of Shanta Kumar has the unique distinction of being the only government to officially oppose the Mandal Commission in the Supreme Court!).

Spatial Segregation

One important indicator of the practice of caste system is whether there is segregation in habitation amongst the lower and upper caste people. The picture that has emerged is a mixed one as the following paragraphs indicate:

"The site locations for the dwelling show a definite trend. On the crest are houses of the Rajputs, surrounded by small kutcha dwellings of Kolies (S.C.) who used to work for them in the past Brahmins lived together at the western end of the village. There are separate small hamlets of Ramdasias (S.C.) who were cobblers by profession and Kabir Panthis (S. C.) who are weaver by profession. Most remotely situated are the dwellings of ceiling surplus and government land allottees which lie on the other side of the Raro Pend nallah." (Solan/Vivek/1989)

Dwelling in this village is very peculiar in the sense that not only scheduled castes but all the different communities of the village are living in separate hamlets.

The following different hamlets exist in this village:

1. Bhatar proper (Brahmins)
2. Chanoria (Rajput)
3. Muhalla Mirad (Brahmin)
4. Naian (barber)
5. Muhalla Harijan (Scheduled Caste)
6. Muhalla Tarkhan (carpenter)
7. Muhalla Manhanta (carpenter)
8. Muhalla Padhya (Brahmin)
9. Muhalla Vadhmania (Rajput)
10. Muhalla Mandava (Brahmin)

11. Muhalla Amavlanar (Brahmin)
12. Muhalla Upaldwar (Brahmin)
13. Muhalla Jingaldwar
14. Kaludi-Bar

"Thus we see that a small population of 1200 is spread over in fourteen hamlets and all the different caste and sub-caste dwell at different places. However, this caste based segregation is not due to the practice of untouchability or due to any hierarchy in caste ladder but wholly because of undulating hilly terrain of this area (how far this is true is doubtful!).The different communities have settled down wherever they got some land to cultivate as the cultivable land and flat land is very scarce in hilly area. When I enquired into more depth I came to know that the resident of a hamlet have descended from a common ancestor and therefore have some relationship with one another. As they are connected with blood or marriage, therefore the relationship among them is generally cordial. As far as caste rivalry is concerned, it is completely missing in this village mainly because different castes are living in different hamlets and their interaction is limited to meeting in some fair and festivals. (Uma/Baldi/1985)

The Behdala village has mainly Rajput and Brahmin population. Though there is no rigid caste practices followed but still lower caste people are living concentrated in one corner of the village and are by and large poor and having very small holding. (Una/Negi/1985)

In the village there is a definite pattern of settlement on the basis of the subset though in recent years this is not strictly followed in case of change in land due to any transaction of property. The Brahmins live on the periphery perhaps due to proximity to the road." (Kangra/Prabodh/1990)

"As harijans, backward classes and Brahmins live in the same village, which has a very compact residential area, there is really no need of any road to link the different "colonies" for the simple reason that though residential pattern are different yet the colony is the same. The entire village has small "pagdandis" built of stones under JRY. Need determines the settlement and not caste." (Kangra/Prabodh/1990)

"Distribution of households in the villages is guided more by necessity than caste feelings. In hills, there is generally paucity of open space and so abadis settle down wherever some space is available. The households tend to settle at a place where there is at least one shop which can meet their daily requirements and there is at least one source of water (a spring or bawdi). In abadi Darbed of village Batheri a Muslim and a Rajput household live quite close by mainly because both have to use the Khud water. The Muslim for his buffaloes and the Rajput for his flour mill. So, the location of households is guided more by the necessity than any other feeling." (Mandi/Anita/1989)

WOMEN

The sturdy and self-reliant women of the Pradesh enjoy a greater degree of freedom than their sisters in the plains. The striking feature of the women here is their heavy costumes and jewellery. They enjoy a greater variety of fashion and usually have a bigger wardrobe than men. Jewellery is an essential article of dress. Their styles vary from village to village. The Division- wise notes by the Officer Trainees on the role and status of women in their villages give a good insight into this important aspect.

Kangra Division

Writing about village Jaddera in Chamba district, Subramaniam observes about Chamba and Gujjar women :

It is felt that Jaddera is a village, "where male domination is imperceptibly very high. Almost all the women are illiterate, except the present generation who are studying in schools. It is, therefore, quite natural, that in such a society, it is the male members of the family who come forward to be covered under the development programmes. It is also seen that the women of Jaddera have also not been adequately motivated to seek coverage under these development oriented programmes."

The Hindu Succession Act is in force except in the case of the Scheduled Tribes, and, under it, daughters can also inherit property. The full effect of this law, which has to reckon with the lingering influence of custom and tradition, are gradually coming into play.

A girl of tender age is regarded sacred and worshipped on different occasions such as birthdays and navratris. A married woman is regarded lucky. Certain auspicious works are initiated through the hands of a married woman. At the time of certain religious ceremonies such a *yagya, dan,* and *puja,* a married woman is given due share and is seated on the left side of her husband. The women of all castes and communities command the same respect. A married woman may command respect in her family according to her intellectual power or common sense. As the majority of women is illiterate, they generally receive instructions from their husbands, mothers -in-law or fathers-in-law and other elders.

She is generally looked down upon if she fails to maintain chastity. All women freely participate in singing, dancing and merrymaking on certain occasions such as marriages and meals, etc. A widow refrains from putting on such ornaments as nose-ring and chak, as also coloured cloths.

On being asked with hesitation, whether their women are beaten up by their husbands, a very interesting reply came— "Whenever differences crop up between the husband and wife, it is quite possible that the latter are beaten up by the former, but, yet, since they are husband and wife, who enjoy the most intimate relationship, the differences will subside and pale away for love".

Despite biting cold, the women among Gujjars do not smoke cigar (probably he means beeri!) nor do they consume liquor.

"It may also be pointed out, that no Gujjar woman, has ever become a member of the Panchayat so far since 1978, when the first elections to Panchayat took place.

Frequent divorcing of women is not uncommon among the Gujjars. Whenever any husband or wife decides to live apart and seeks to divorce, they have to approach the Committee which consists of elder members of their community. There are 6 members and one Chairman. The Committee hears both parties and decrees grant of divorce. The party moving the Committee for grant of divorce is required to give some amount, as determined by the Committee, to the other party. Unilateral seeking of divorce is not at all possible. The consent of both the parties is a must. The proceedings of divorce are written down and kept as a record. The Committee, before granting divorce to the parties, shall also endeavour to bring about rapprochement and conciliation between the parties. Complicated cases, however, are filed in the regular court." (Chamba/Subramanyam/1986)

The comments from district Kangra are as follows:

"There is no differential wage for men and women. But this is not significant as the women folk do not offer casual labour and it is only the men who offer their labour in construction works." (Kangra/Murti/1989)

"There is one widow who weaves woollen shawls and blankets on a loom which is locally called as "khaddi". She has received assistance under IRDP. She receives wool from the consumer and weave the shawl or the blanket for Rs. 35 in little more than two days. She does not weave anything to market it. The villagers purchase wool from Gaddis who come to this district in the winter months. These shawls and blankets are fairly warm. Some girls of the village are keen to take up weaving on a commercial scale. It can be organized under DWACRA." (Kangra/Prabodh/1990)

"Prostitutions; Gambling; Traffic in women are not known in this village. However, on some festive occasions, some women drink liquor. It is also understood that some times, women are beaten by their husbands, in case of differences between them." (Chamba/Subramanyam/1986)

"The elders of the village and the women are most worried about the significant increase in drinking in the men of the village in the last decade or so. They are more worried because of the tendency among the youngsters to take to drinking heavily. The domestic problems have increased, particularly misbehaviour with the female and quarrel over the household budget. Minor scuffles due to influence of liquor is another result. The elders recall that earlier such incidents were very rare. Some of them hold the government policy of setting up of liquor shops at very conceivable point as the major contributing factor. But still most of the villagers consume illegally distilled liquor available in Gaggal. There is no local brewery in the village. (probably he means an illegal still!)" (Kangra/Prabodh/1990)

Mandi Division

The report on Mandi division seems to be full of women's concern about drunkenness and maltreatment at the hands of their husbands.

"Most of the farm work is done by women and agriculture labour is rare. A major work of the people in monsoons is to cut the hired grass, dry it, and store it for the winters. In monsoons- all members of a family work in the farms. The women in the house are very hard working and tend to the cattle, the housework, cut grass and many also raise crop as their husbands serve outside. Men in the village drink heavily and in the afternoon groups of men sit under a banyan tree, playing cards and smoking beedis. The general village gossip is exchanged here. The elder folks are fond of 'Chilam'. This pastime has now become a custom." (Bilaspur/Nisha/1987)

"One social evil that has spread its ugly wings over Kehanwal is the habit of excessive drinking by its menfolk. Throughout my stay at Kehanwal, I did not notice any instance of a woman also taking to the bottle. Despite the harsh and inclement winters, the men have retained the habit of drinking as solely their own prerogative." (Mandi/Rajpal/1990)

"Excessive drinking is sapping the energy of this area possessing a lot of latent, untapped potential. Drinking is a deep-rooted social custom and I found women and children reluctantly acquiescing in this vice of their menfolk. Drunken revelries take place not just during the night when people can be legitimately trying to unwind themselves after a hard days' labour but in the day time as well. This social malaise has been upsetting the budgets and tranquillity of many a family in the area." (Mandi/Rajpal/1990)

Shimla Division

Consumption of alcohol is very common among the adult male population and no stigma is attached to it. Illicit distillation of liquor appears to be quite prevalent. The women folk are worried about this and in some parts of the district a voluntary organisation by the name of Sutra is doing excellent job by organising the women in the form of a movement forcing the government to close the liquor vends. (Sol/Rizvi/1989)

MAHILA MANDALS

The story of women in Himachal Pradesh would only be half told without mentioning the Mahila Mandals. Every village has a Mahila Mandal, some active and others not as much. With the introduction of 73rd Constitutional Amendment and greater involvement of the women, these bodies have become more meaningful and effective. The remarks which have been highlighted are interesting and, some, encouraging.

"A Mahila Mandal exists in the area. Its meeting was scheduled on one of the days. Gram Sevika came on the day but only three women came to the meeting place. The Gram Sevika had to go to call the women who were closeby. They sat in the meeting and later said that they prefer not coming to the meetings since they have lots of work to do at home. It seems that the disinterest on the part of the women has led to the failure of such groups." (Mandi/Anita/1989)

It is heartening to note that the following activities, which really help the women folk of their village, are being vigorously undertaken by the Mahila Mandal:—i) Popularising Family Planning Programme; Smokeless Chullahas; ii) Educating the women about maintenance of kitchen; bringing up children maintenance of cleanliness; iii) Organising cultural programmes; iv) Making women aware of their rights and obligations etc.

"It is also understood that they are collecting some amount every month, which is kept in a Bank as a fund to organize the activities of the Mahila Mandal." (Chamba/Subramanyam/1986)

A large number of women of the upper castes are members of Mahila Mandal; **S/Cs women are not well represented**. Meeting of the Mandal is held as and when President decides. But on 20th of every month, Lady Village Development Coordinator (LVDC) convenes the meeting and monitors its activities. Its meetings are held in the Mahila Mandal Bhavan which was constructed out of Block grant and Panchayat assistance. Its activities are mainly confined to kitchen gardening, family planning, hygiene awareness and sanitation.

"Better quality of seeds for vegetables and fruit trees are provided by LVDC. In this village, it is common to see beautiful kitchen gardens in every house. LVDC frequently organizes the visit to each house and advises the women to improve kitchen gardens. Also she contributes a lot to propagate the family planning techniques and about personal hygiene. Mahila Mandal also owns a number of items needed during marriages such as, tents, trunks, durries, glasses, degchies and other brass utensils which are given on rental basis to the villagers." (Kangra/Dhiman/1988)

"The village Mahila Mandal, which was formed about 3 years ago has about 15 active members. The Pradhan Smt. Nikkoo is a semi-literate woman while the Secretary Smt.Vimla is educated upto matriculation. Formed with the laudable objective of creating awareness amongst the women of the village on issues such as health and hygiene, kitchen gardening, promoting small savings and family welfare programme evils such as dowry, campaigning against liquor, teaching simple crafts to the women to supplement family incomes, the Mandal has been unable to rise above personal feuds and ego problems, and today is more of a political forum for the political parties to garner votes for themselves. The responsibility of the failure of this Mahila Mandal must also be shared by the Block agency, which failed to provide effective leadership and motivation to the women of the village, and took no steps to prevent the degeneration of the Mahila Mandal into a political lobby." (Bilaspur/Khachi/88)

Marriage and Dowry

The marriages in rural HP take place mostly along castelines and are all arranged except a few. The evil of dowry is not as severe as in the plains but exists none the less.

The marriages are on caste basis and are usually solemnised within the district, in a village 4-5 kms. away. The bridegroom's party consists of, on an average, 40-50 persons and marriage is a simple affair, though dowry is given to the best of capacity. The attendance of other castes in an SC marriage is negligible. The feast at the marriage and other occasions is called *'Dham'*. This consists of small quantities of rice being served 4 times with different kinds of pulses each time. This has layers of fat floating above it and is rich and spicy. Most of the people are non-vegetarians. The marriage practices are reported in the villages from Bilaspur, Solan, Una and Chamba. Their observation are as follows:

"Marriage ceremonies are generally simple and exchange of gifts takes place. The practice of dowry is virtually non-existent. Marriage is generally the time for the whole village to get together and people co-operate the families in making arrangements for the marriages. Arranged marriage is the norm, and elaborate caste and gotra considerations go in to decide matches." (Sol/Rizvi/1988)

"None of them would like to take up lowly professions such as shoe making and scavenging. And none of them wants to marry out of their caste also. Mostly marriage are of arranged, dowry is not prevalent in this village and are simple and inexpensive." (Una/Negi/1985)

"Practice of dowry as such is not in practice. Only in rich families, the girl after marriage, is given some money at the time of going to in-law's place." (Chamba/Subramanyam/1986)

It may be mentioned here that, generally, such love marriages (does he mean mutual consent?) are approved by parents, without much ado. (Chamba/Subramanyam/1986)

Religion

The majority of the population of Himachal Pradesh are Hindus but Buddhists, Jains, Sikhs, Muslims and Christians also exist. The people of all groups live in harmony and pursue their own way of life, customs, conventions and beliefs. Perhaps here we find the best example of mutual cooperation and religious tolerance. Apart from some incidents during the 1984 riots, the State has never witnessed any serious law and order problem. Every village has a temple where people congregate for worship. The village gods, locally called *Devtas* are carried in palanquins, on a number of occasions, to the places of religious interest or village fair. When in trouble, the people go to the village deities to seek their guidance and help. The village god is supposed to watch over the destiny of the village. He protects, rewards, threatens and punishes the people, while they in turn, worship him by singing and dancing.

The muslims in the State are very few and the remarks made in one of the reports is interesting.

"There are 13 Muslim families in Ghaniara, who migrated to this place around 50 years back. Due to fear of Hindu on slaughts, in 1947, they changed their names to Hindu names like Jaisi Ram, Hari Ram etc. but now they are well settled here and gone back to Muslim names. As I talked to old people, they appear to be converts, and do not know their place in muslims hierarchy of sayeeds, pathans etc. and their knowledge of Islam is negligible. People know a little bit of the Quran. The younger generation is completely unaware of Islam religion. Nobody except one old man knows the 'Qlma', who is also their Maulvi and performs various rites. For all practical purposes they are Hindus except that they bury the dead and names are Muslims. They speak in Pahari, dress like others, and there is no Mosque in the village, they do not go for Haj and are mostly employed as labourers in the slate mining industry." (Kangra/Dhiman/1988)

Daily Routine and Entertainment

Anil Khachi gives a good description about their daily routine.

"Generally, the people get up around 5 a.m. in summers and 6 to 6.30 a.m. in winters. The women set about milking animals, and preparing food. The older children and the men fetch the water from the tap. After a light breakfast, the men head for their work. If it is sowing and harvesting time, they work all day in the fields and their lunch (mid-day meal) is brought to them there. Many a times the children also accompany their parents to the fields. In winters the men-folk bask in the sun and gossip, unless they are employed somewhere. The women, once free from the hearth, fetch fire-wood and fodder from the forest or fields. Bed-time is normally between 9 p.m. to 10 p.m. Early mornings, they have some maize or wheat roti, left over from the last meal, with tea. This constitutes their breakfast. The mid-day meal consists of maize or wheat roti with dal or vegetable. In the evening, rice is taken if one can afford it, otherwise it is the same diet of roti and dal or vegetables. Though 95 per cent of the population is non-vegetarian, yet not many of the villagers cannot afford meat even once a week. An effort was made some years ago to rear poultry birds but it failed to last long". (Bilaspur/Khachi/1988)

The Officer Trainees have also made some notings regarding the distractions and entertainment indulged in by the villagers in their otherwise routine life. The drudgery and boredom in the villages is reduced and life becomes lighter when traditional practices, and more so the modern technological interventions become part of their lives.

A huge banyan tree with a platform erected around it serves as a sort of a 'choupal' for all village gatherings. Even in the day time, menfolk are found here indulging in their favourite pastime of idle chatter and smoking. *Hookah* (water-pipe) serves as another excuse for the people to get together. The activity of playing cards is also increasing, particularly among the young. Even in the month of October, the early morning sun is warm and mellow while it continues to be uncomfortably cold in the shade. This encourages the men and the women to troop out into the sun and while the women gather in front of their homes, the men prefer to assemble at the traditional public places." (Mandi/Rajpal/1990)

"Otherwise the only recreation available in the village for youngsters is the game of *kabbadi and volleyball* which they play in the ground of the school after the school closes. Sometime they see movies in Video parlour at Gaggal." (Kangra/Prabodh/1990)

"One of the most frequent form of recreation in the village is performing the roles of *Ramayan, Mahabharat* and *Bhagwat Gita* by a group of singers. They use a musical instrument known as *Khanjari* and a *Dhol* etc. Generally, wide publicity is given in advance about this activity. All the villagers on that day assemble at a particular place and this cultural activity goes on throughout the night." (Chamba/Subramanyam/1986)

"There are about fifteen black and white television sets in the village. There is no community television set in the village. If one such set can be installed in the office of the Panchayat Secretary, then it will not just break the monotony of the village evening but will also be greatly educative. At present the evenings are totally dull and the menfolk generally spend it in drinking country made liquor and also gambling." (Kangra/Prabodh/1990)

"TV and radio are making inroads. There are about 90 B/W TV sets in the village though there is no community or common TV. In the more well-off families, a refrigerator and a washing machine are the items of luxury that are becoming popular, especially as dowry items." (Mandi/Rajpal/1990)

DWELLING HOUSES

In the lower hills, houses are usually single storied with thatched roofs while in the upper regions, there are generally two storied with slate roofs. In the highlands, however, the houses are three storied, the ground floor or basement being used for keeping cattle. But the traditional architecture is being replaced by RCC. Timber is getting scarcer by the year, RCC seems to be the most acceptable and practical material. Whoever makes some money now pulls down his ancestral home and builds these structure which have become a status symbol in rural Himachal as elsewhere.

Kangra Division

"Almost all the houses have sloping roofs made of locally available slate. These slates are supported with bamboo poles which are available free of cost because every family has rights in the Chil forest. The walls are made of clay, sand and even cement. There are no attached latrines in the village houses. There are just 6-7 houses which are pucca with RCC. The Upadhaya households are pucca houses but 2-3 Batawal families also live in concrete houses. Though the families do feel that there is a need to extend the built up area there is scarcity of land. That is the reason why hardly 2-3 families in the entire village have an adjoining garden to their houses. But by and large there is no homelessness as such in the village. The maximum distance of the cultivated land from the home of the cultivator does not exceed one kilometre." (Kangra/Prabodh/1990)

"Practically every house is double storied with sloping roofs made of slates. Roof at first floor is constructed generally of wooden battens and planks which support earthfilling. But now angle irons are replacing the wooden battens and clay tiles are replacing planks, due to ban on cutting of trees and general increase in the prices of wood work. Here people are fancy by latest designs of houses, practically every house is having verandah covered with slates, there is small courtyard, a place of worship, a small kitchen garden, as a part of the house. People earning enough in slate mining business, locally, there are 46 fully *Pucca* houses with RCC slabs, 75 houses are semi-pucca type with slate roofing and rest are katcha houses with slate roofing. Caste wise, generally Gorkhas are having very good, large ornamental houses with a separate place of worship like Tulsi-platform etc. General condition of housing is much better in the village and there is not even a single thatched house." (Kangra/Dhiman/1988)

Mandi Division

"Since the construction costs are very high owing to inaccessibility of the area, most of the people continue to live in their Kutcha slate-topped houses made out of locally available materials. The houses are low-roofed and their door and window frames are small in order to keep out the cold in the winters." (Mandi/Rajpal/1990)

"The structure of houses in the village consists of stone houses covered by tinshed. These are mostly double storied and only 10 per cent of the houses have 'Kuccha' structure. Large stone slabs are used instead of bricks. At places decorative floral painting (mostly in the houses of Rajputs) is done on the slabs at the top. The pattern of houses is quite similar with two three rooms in each floor. The most characteristic part of the household is the cattle house *'Maveshikhana'* where fodder is kept and cattle live. It is a pucca building. In this room dried grass is also kept. In many houses the kitchen is also an 'annexe' sort to this building." (Bilaspur/Nisha/1987)

"Every household has a house of their own and in case of any damage to house the economically weaker sections are provided with financial assistance for construction of the house by the government. The houses are mostly *Katcha* and use of wood is very high." (Mandi/Jagdish/1991)

"The majority of houses in the village are typically constructed with sun-dried bricks (though the more modern houses have kiln-baked bricks). A house normally has 2 storeys the lower one is used as a dwelling place by the inmates and the upper part as a lumber room or store room for grains. The roof is generally sloping and thatched with bomboo leaves or grass. The more modern houses, belonging to affluent people in the village use slates or RCC slabs. The walls are plastered with red or light coloured clay. The courtyard is kept clean but the cleanliness does not extend beyond that. In most households of the village, furniture consists of stringed cots, mats made from rice straw, a chair or two and a quilt like mattress stuffed, with pieces of old rags and clothes. Household utensils are usually of brass and earthen jars. One or two trunks or wooden boxes, used for keeping clothes and valuables, are tucked away in one corner of the living room complete the household possessions. Of course, the more affluent people possess sofa-sets, a transistor set or a two in one radio cassette player and sometimes a television set (during my survey I came across 15 such households)." (Bilaspur/Khaci/1988)

Shimla Division

Most of the houses are *partly pukka* as some walls have cement plastering. This area traditionally has an altogether different type of wall construction called *"Thaji Walls"*. Wood pillars and cross beams are used to construct the basic structure. Then the walls are filled in using stones and mud. This was done because wood was quite cheap and this kind of houses are quite warm. Gradually some walls started being plastered with cement. The old type of houses were all three storied, the top floor for human dwelling, the middle floor for storage of grains and the bottom floor for cattle. Now all the houses being constructed are only two storeys high. The first floor is used for housing the human and the ground floor usually for cattle and storage. In some cases now cattle sheds are separately constructed and both the floor are used for living. The buildings are usually quite large with about 5-10 rooms in each building but usually 2/3 or even more families reside in each building. This is usually because of gradual splitting up of joint families. (Shimla/Tarun/1987)

Joint-Family System

Like in the rest of rural India, in the sphere of social relations, an important feature is the strong family affinities and the joint family system though it is on the decline. Some glimpses into this important social system is provided in some of the reports.

In the village Jaddera joint family system is quite prevalent. Even when their children are married, they continue to live with their parents, inas much as, it is a costly affair to construct a new house, after buying a piece of land. All the family members eat and live under the same roof. Sometimes, it so happens that due to paucity of space, the cattle as well as all the family members live under the same roof, which poses a great threat to the hygiene of the House and health of the family members. All these are the consequences of poverty. (Chamba/Subramanyam/1986)

Traditionally the entire district with few exceptions lived in joint family. Of late, it has been disintegrating because of the economic stress and strain of living. The urge to break-up the family and to establish separate household springs mainly from the desire and longing for freedom and privacy. Another contributory factor is the explosion of population. One more factor is the displacement of families due to the construction of Dam. In the Manwa village I found only 3 joint families that can be called nuclear family. Village Manwaa had the same joint family system as elsewhere among the Hindus, but the economic stress and strain of living and a rapidly rising population has led to its near disappearance. The displacement of families, owing to the construction of Bhakra Dam, has also been a contributory factor. In my survey, I could identify only 9 such joint families in the village. (Bilaspur/Khachi/1988)

The area is generally hilly and the agricultural occupation is predominantly the main stay of the people who are constantly in need of more hands to work in the fields, and this situation has been responsible in the past, for holding together various individual families and thus for the prevalence of the joint family system almost without exception. The joint family system is still prevalent although exceptions have crept in and are gradually on the increase. It is estimated that seventy out of hundred live jointly in the village. (Nahan/Prasad/1986)

ECONOMIC OVERVIEW

Himachal Pradesh has an area of 55,673 square kilometres with a population of 51.70 lakh according to 1991 Census. The density of population is 93 persons per square kilometre as compared to 267 at the all-India level. Himachal Pradesh is predominantly rural in character as 91.31 per cent of the population lives in rural areas and the remaining 8.69 per cent is located in 58 towns. According to 1991 Census Scheduled Castes form 25.34 per cent of population while Scheduled Tribes account for 4.22 per cent. The population has shown a net decline of 2.92 per cent between the period 1981-91 from 23.56 per cent to 20.79 per cent.

Human Resources

The main workers and marginal workers constitute 22.14 lakh

which forms 42.82 per cent of the total population. The following Table 2.2 gives the distribution of main workers, marginal workers and non-workers as classified in 1991 Census.

Out of the total population of 51.70 lakh, main workers are 17.79 lakh, marginal workers 35 lakh and non-workers 29.56 lakh, which comes to 34.41 per cent, 8.42 per cent and 57.17 per cent respectively.

Table 2.2 : Distribution of Total population and main workers

Sl. No.	*Item*	*Unit*	*Particulars*
1.	Total Population	Lakh Persons	51.70
2.	Main Workers:	Lakh Persons	17.79
	(a) Cultivators	Lakh Persons	11.25
	(b) Agricultural Labourers	Lakh Persons	0.59
	(c) Livestock, Forestry, Fisheries,	Lakh Persons	0.44
	Plantation and Allied Activities		
	(d) Mining and Quarrying	Lakh Persons	0.05
	(e) Manufacturing, Processing,	Lakh Persons	0.92
	Servicing and Repairs		
	(f) Construction	Lakh Persons	0.86
	(g) Trade and Commerce	Lakh Persons	0.78
	(h) Transport, Storage and	Lakh Persons	0.34
	Communication		
	(i) Other Services	Lakh Persons	2.56
3.	Marginal Workers	Lakh Persons	4.35
4.	Non-Workers	Lakh Persons	29.56

Source: Annual Plan Document 1993 -94.

Growth of State Economy

The estimates of State Domestic Product (State Income) is the most commonly used economic indicator for measuring the general economic health of the State. The study of inter-sectoral distribution of State Domestic Product shows the cumulative effect of development efforts made in various sectors of the economy. After the release of the new series of National Accounts Statistics by Central Statistical Organisation in February, 1989 which is based on 1980-81 prices, this State also brought-out a new series of estimates on similar lines. According to these estimates, the State income of the Pradesh during 1980-81 to 1991-92 period increased from Rs. 794.04 crore to Rs. 3096.70 crore at current prices and to Rs. 1198.09 crore at constant prices (1980-81). The per capita income at current prices increased from Rs. 1871 in 1980-81 to Rs. 5926 in 1991-92 while at constant prices, it rose to Rs. 2293 during the same period.

The economy of Himachal Pradesh has been able to achieve an impressive growth rate of 8.16 per cent during the Seventh Five Year Plan. The following table 2.3 shows that in the matter of economic growth, Himachal Pradesh has always kept pace with the all India Scenario of economic growth:

Table 2.3 : Himachal Pradesh and All India Scenario of economic growth

Period / Year	*Average Annual Growth Rate (Percentage)*	
	Himachal Pradesh	*All India*
1985-86	(+) 13.80	(+) 4.80
1986-87	(+) 7.00	(+) 3.60
1987-88	(+) 0.90	(+) 3.50
1988-89	(+) 8.80	(+) 11.10
1989-90	(+) 10.30	(+) 6.00
1990-91	(+) 1.01	(+) 5.20
1991-92	(-) 1.19	(+) 1.20
Average 1985-90	(+) 8.16	(+) 5.80
Average 1985-92	(+) 5.80	(+) 5.06

Source: Annual Plan Document 1993-94.

Himachal being a hilly state it is only fair to compare it with the other such states, therefore, the data on the per capita income of the Pradesh vis-à-vis other Special Category States which are all hilly, as also all India average, is depicted in the following Table 2.4:

Table 2.4 : Per Capita income of Himachal Pradesh

Sl. No.	*State*	*Per Capita Income (In Rs.)*		
		1981	*1985-86*	*1989-90*
1.	Arunachal Pradesh	1561	3274	4176
2.	Sikkim	1571	3023	4396
3.	Himachal Pradesh	1698	2630	4005
4.	Mizoram	1289	2658	4077 (87-88)
5.	Nagaland	1383	2800	3464 (88-89)
6.	Manipur	1430	2354	3502
7.	Assam	1200	2313	3179
8.	Jammu and Kashmir	1649	2716	3420 (88-89)
9.	Tripura	1323	2108	2866
10.	Meghalaya	1361	2250	3250
	All India	1630	2726	4252

Source: Annual Plan Document 1993 -94.

Sectoral Profile

An examination on the sectoral profiles of growth is necessary to arrive at some inference about the manner in which the economy has been responding to the policy programmes. Broadly the sectors have been divided in three parts namely (i) Primary sector (Agriculture, Animal Husbandry, Forests, Fishing and Mining), (ii) Secondary sector (Manufacturing, Construction, Electricity and Gas and Water supply), and (iii) Tertiary Sector (Transport, Communication, Trade, Finance, Real Estate and Community and Personal Services). The contribution by way of these broad sectors of the economy to State Domestic Product (State Income) during 1980-81 to 1991-92 at selected Years is depicted in the following Table 2.5:

Table 2.5 : Sectoral profile of growth

(*In Percentage*)

S. No.	*Sector*	*1980-81*	*1984-85*	*1985-86*	*1989-90*	*1990-91*	*1991-92*
1.	Primary	47.22	42.14	44.78	40.70	39.89	39.88
2.	Secondary	19.70	19.72	21.65	18.93	19.88	17.43
3.	Tertiary	33.08	38.14	33.57	40.37	40.23	42.69

Source: Annual Plan Document 1993 -94

It would be seen from the above table that the Primary sector which consists of Agriculture, Animal Husbandry, Fisheries, Forests etc. is showing the sign of constant decline whereas Secondary and Tertiary sector is showing an upward increase. This augurs well for the structural changes introduced in the economy over the decade and promises better diversification in future potential.

Land Systems

Land systems assume a very important role in Himachal Pradesh as more than 91.30 per cent of the population is rural (all India 74%). It employs 75 per cent of the total working population (all India 67%) and accounts for 37.31 per cent of the total State Domestic Product (all India 30%).

Size of Land Holdings

The fascinating aspects is that the distribution of land is very even and in fact majority of the farmers are small and marginal as evident from the Table 2.6 which pertains to the year 1985-86:

Table 2.6 : Majority of farmers distribution of lands

Size of	*Category Size*	*No. of Holdings (ha)*	*Area of Holdings*	*Average Holdings (in '00s)*
Below 1.0	Marginal	4634 (61.5%)	2006 (20.4%)	0.4
1.0 - 2.0	Small	1553 (20.6%)	2226 (22.7%)	1.4
2.0 -4.0	Semi- Medium	922 (12.4%)	2547 (26.0%)	2.8
4.0- 10.0	Medium	364 (4.8%)	2077 (21.2%)	5.7
10 and above	Large	56 (0.7%)	946 (9.7%)	16.8
Total		5729 (100.9%)	9802 (100.o%)	1.3

Source: Annual Plan Document 1993 -94.

From the reports of the Officer Trainees, the following information pertaining to the land holdings have been shown in Table 2.7 on the bases of which some observations have been made. Adding or averaging the figures culled below from 22 odd villages over different time periods may not necessarily be relevant for the entire State, yet it is surprising to note that on many issues/ parameters the results are the same.

Table 2.7 : Information pertaining to the land Holdings

S. No.	*District*	*Village*	*Year*	*Land-less*	*<5 Bgs*	*5-25 Bgs*	*25-5 Bgs*	*>50 Bgs*	*Total*
1	Kangra	Rehlu	1989 Hh	0	97	67	6	0	170
			Area	0	NA	NA	NA	0	
2	Kangra	Ganyara	1988 Hh	0	310	27	1	0	338
			Area	0	NA	NA	NA	0	NA
3	Kangra	Padher	1990Hh	0	70	30	20	0	120
			Area	0	NA	NA	NA	0	NA
4	Una	Behdala	1985Hh	0	430	73	102	7	612
			Area	0	NA	NA	NA	NA	NA
5	Una	Bhater	1985Hh	0	44	96	36	29	204
			Area	0	44	288	252	535	1022
6	Chamba	Jhedera	1986Hh	30	20	41	7	0	98
			Area	NA	NA	NA	NA	0	NA
7	Mandi	Batheri	1989 Hh	NA	NA	NA	NA	NA	NA
		etc.							
			Area	NA	NA	NA	NA	NA	NA
8	Mandi	Kathayari	1988 Hh	NA	NA	NA	NA	NA	NA
			Area	NA	NA	NA	NA	NA	NA
9	Mandi	Bardana	1985 Hh	0	13	25	4	0	42
			Area	0	56	349	120	0	525
10	Mandi	Kehanwal	1990 Hh	NA	NA	NA	NA	NA	NA
			Area	NA	NA	NA	NA	NA	NA
11	Mandi	Meyot	1991 Hh	0	9	16	5	0	30
			Area	0	NA	NA	NA	0	NA
12	Bilaspur	Janduta	1987 Hh	NA	NA	NA	NA	NA	NA
			Area	NA	NA	NA	NA	NA	NA

contd.

Table 2.7 (contd.)

S. No.	District	Village	Year	Land-less	<5 Bgs	5-25 Bgs	25-5 Bgs	>50 Bgs	Total
13	Bilaspur	Panthera	1987 Hh	NA	158	43	8	0	209
			Area	NA	38%	44%	18%	0	100%
14	Bilaspur	Manwa	1988Hh	1	55	44	0	0	90
			Area	NA	NA	NA	0	0	NA
15	Shimla	Senji etc	1987 Hh	0	94	55	41	1	191
			Area	0	NA	NA	NA	NA	NA
16	Shimla	Shogi	1987 Hh	0	56	82	20	1	159
			Area	0	NA	NA	NA	NA	NA
17	Solan	Raro Pind	1989 Hh	0	0	22	7	3	32
			Area	0	0	NA	NA	NA	NA
18	Solan	Topkiber etc.	1988 Hh	6	27	88	11	0	126
			Area	NA	NA	NA	NA	0	NA
19	Sirmaur	Trilokpur	1986 Hh	1	NA	NA	NA	NA	NA
			Area	NA	NA	NA	NA	NA	NA
20	Sirmaur	Mohalia	1987 Hh	0	20	91	5	0	116
			Area	0	NA	NA	NA	0	NA
21	Sirmaur	Majra	1989 Hh	NA	35	141	12	10	198
			Area	NA	NA	NA	NA	NA	NA

There are very few landless in the state (Those that exist can be counted on fingers in every village). Out of the above 21 villages reported upon, 11 have categorically denied that there was any landlessness in the village; 6 have not reported at all and only 4 have said that there are landlessness in the village. In Kangra Division only Chamba (Jaddera) has reported that there are 30 landless people. In Mandi Division only one village (Manwa) has pointed out that there is 1 landless. In Shimla Division two villages, namely Topkiber in Solan District and Trilokpur in Sirmour have shown 6 and 1 landless respectively.

There is equitable distribution of land throughout the State. In spite of the fact that the pressure on land is very acute in the hills, thanks to the land reforms the big landlords are unheard of.

Prabodh Kumar remarks that in his village "the average size of holdings is 6-7 Kanal. There is no remarkable distinction in the average size of holding between Scheduled Castes and Non Scheduled Castes if we exclude the three brahmin families who have land exceeding 2 hectare in the name of different family members. Even two Batawal families have land exceeding 2 hectares. On a rough estimate it can be said that about 70 families have land between 0-1 acres whereas about 30 families have land between 1-5 acres. How equitable?" (Kangra/Prabodh/1990)

A Division wise break up of the percentage of households on the bases of land holdings works out as follows :-

	Kangra	*Mandi*	*Shimla*
>5 beghas	59.80%	49.25%	23.30%
5-25 beghas	26.34%	43.25%	61.20%
25-50 beghas	10.66%	7.50%	12.82%
>50 beghas	3.20%	0.00%	2.68%

There is an element of skewedness in the land ownership pattern though not as acute as in the other States. In Kangra Division, village Bather of Una District the imbalance is the most. 21 per cent of the house-holds with holdings of less than 5 beghas own only 4 per cent of the land in contrast to 14 per cent of the house-holds with holdings more than 50 beghas owning more than 48 per cent of the land available. In Panthera, District Bilaspur, 75 per cent of the population own only 38 per cent of the land whereas less than 4 per cent have more than 18 per cent of it. In Bardana village, district Mandi, 31 per cent of the population own less than 10 per cent of the land whereas 10 per cent of the upper layer possess more than 25 per cent of the lands.

The comments of the Officer Trainees on their own villages of study on this issue are as follows :

B.K. Aggarwal writes that "ownership of land is skewed as is expected in every rural society. There are only 11 farmers i.e. 26 per cent of the total who own land more than 1.5 hectare but together they account for nearly 50 per cent of total land. As against this 60 per cent farmers account for only 33 per cent of total land." (Mandi/Aggarwal/1985)

Srikant Baldi writes that "if we analyse the data, we can see that 140 land owners are holding only 332 acre whereas rest 65 land-owners are holding 792 acre. It means that 70% of the land owners are holding an area less than 5 acres whereas 30 per cent of the land owners are controlling 75 per cent of the village area. Thus the difference between the land holdings is very acute. Moreover out of the total holding only 25 per cent of that is cultivable thus the average cultivable holding in this village comes out to be only one acre per person which is not enough to provide both ends meet to a family." (Una/Baldi/1985)

Caste-wise Holdings

Manoj Kumar has tried to analyse the caste -wise break-up of ownership and power equation in the village.

Caste	*No. of owners*	*Holding Bigha—Biswa*
Rajput	47	359-01
Brahman	11	73-19
Jat	3	28-12
Khatri	6	3-02
Jheevar	11	51-00
Muslims	19	55-02
Harijans	74	115-12

"The above data shows that more than one fourth of the land is under Rajputs. But their population is less than 1/4 of the total population. They are also very powerful. They have been maintaining their high position in the power structure due to their strong hold on the village land." (Mandi/Manoj/1988)

Rizvi finds in his village in District Solan, that "while 15 caste Hindu families hold 4 to 5 acres of land and 9 others hold over 5 acres of land, the respective figures for the schedule castes is 4 and 2. Thus in spite of the comprehensive land reform measures inequalities as to access to landed property do exist. However the problem is not that acute and small peasant proprietorship is by far the most common tenurial system." (Solan/Rizvi/1988)

On the other hand Murti and Dhiman find the situation just the opposite in District Kangra "Also the average size of holdings of the scheduled castes households does not differ significantly from the average holdings of the other castes. But the holdings of the scheduled castes households is mostly unirrigated land. About 25 per cent of their holdings is irrigated. The holdings of the non S. C. households have about 60% irrigated land of the total land owned by them". (Kangra/Murti/1989)

The average size of holdings of scheduled caste household does not differ significantly from the average holding of other caste though among the landless category, scheduled castes and muslims are in majority". (Kangra/Dhiman/1988)

Land Reforms

Himachal Pradesh is perhaps one of the very few states where land reforms have been seriously enacted and enforced. One of the important reasons stated by some of the senior IAS officers was rather interesting. One was told that Himachal being a Union Territory at that time, the Government of India was able to experiment and push the laws more effectively in the absence of a vocal representative government. Another reason for the smoother implementation of the land reform laws has been the absence of intermediaries and the serious confrontation between the land owners and the tenants. Rizvi writes " the agrarian structure differed in a major way from that existing in the plains. The class of intermediaries between the state and the tillers of the land, was neither that well entrenched nor did it command the sort of control it did over rural property as in the plains. The hill states never witnessed the agrarian unrest that was a regular feature in the plains. To that extent the work of amelioration of the position of the landless, and abolishment of zamindari system became easier."

Till 1953, the condition of the farmers was very bad as nearly 80 per cent of total tillers were landless who ploughed others' lands, received only a small share of the produce and lived at the mercy of the landlords. The Punjab Tenancy (Himachal Pradesh Amendment) Act, 1952 and Himachal Pradesh Tenants Rights and Restoration Act, 1952 were first enacted. These Acts limited the rent payable by tenant to landlord to one fourth of the produce. The Himachal Pradesh Abolition of Big Landed Estates and Land Reforms Act, 1953 conferred proprietary rights on the tenants. Land owners whose land revenue was more than Rs 125 had to surrender their lands which was in excess of the limit. Resumption of land by land owners (from their tenants) was permitted for personal cultivation subject to a maximum area of 5 acres, provided further that no tenant could be ejected from more than 1/4 of the area held by him. The Act further provided security of tenure to the tenancies, by making the provisions of ejectment very stringent. In this way proprietary rights were given to 4.75 lakh families who were tilling other's land. Under the Himachal Pradesh Ceiling on Land Holding Act, 1972 ceiling on the holdings of the land-owner beyond the following extent was imposed:

(a) land under assured irrigation capable of growing two crops in a year -10 acres
(b) land under assured irrigation capable of growing one crop in a year—15 acres
(c) land other than described in (a) and (b) above including land under orchards -30 acres

Himachal Pradesh Tenancy and Land Reforms Act, 1972 conferred proprietary rights on occupancy tenants and non-occupancy tenants. However the Act made two exceptions. Small land owners were entitled to reserve land for personal cultivation upto 3/2 acres irrigated and 3 acres unirrigated land. Secondly persons serving in the armed forces, widows, unmarried women, divorced or separated women, a person permanently or temporarily disabled were permitted to create tenancies over land. Finally the

Himachal Pradesh Village Common Land Vesting and Utilization Act, 1974 placed Shamlat land at the disposal of the Government for allotment to agricultural labourers and landless persons. Area not less than 50 per cent of the total vested land was earmarked to be used for grazing and other common purposes of the inhabitants and the remaining was allotted to the landless persons those whose holding was less than one acre. The Government framed a scheme and a number of persons were provided relief under it. The above legislation was strengthened with the framing of two schemes namely the Surplus Area Utilisation Scheme and the Nautor Rules. Under Nautor Rules government land upto 20 bighas brought under cultivation for the first time was granted to the cultivator. The Surplus Area Utilisation Scheme transferred to landless or to those having less than 5 bighas of land the land vested in government under the Ceiling on Holding Act. After enforcement of the above Acts and Rules, the number of operational land holdings increased in almost all the districts of the State; for e.g. Lahaul-Spiti 38.70 per cent, Sirmaur 22.00 per cent, Una 11.10 per cent, and Shimla 0.11 per cent.

Feudal Systems of the Past

From the study of Rizvi of the State in general and Solan District in particular it is evident that there were no really big landlords even prior to independence and that the Tenancy system was not back breaking or hopeless for the tenant after all. He quotes the Superintendent of Hill States in 1859 as writing:

"A purely ryotwar system prevails in these hills. The Government is the direct landlord of the present tenants, who maintain themselves, and pay the Government demand from the portions of land each cultivates. Here there are neither capital nor capitalists, nor large landed proprietors who can act as agents between the Government and the actual cultivators. Every man who cultivates the land, however insignificant his possessions are, is termed a zamindar. The settlement is made direct with each zamindar for the lands he cultivates. Each receives a patta or lease from the Government officer."

The bulk of the land was, however, held by the peasantry, which paid revenue directly to the chief or ruler. In some of the bigger States "Jagirdars" did emerge, however they were entitled only to the land revenue due from the area assigned to them. In the areas where the native rulers continued to rule, conditions were not much different. In theory the Raja or Thakur was the lord of the land. In practice the cultivator though not exactly a free peasant proprietor, had the right to cultivate the land he held and could bequeath this right also. To this right were attached liberal rights of user in the adjacent waste. In lieu of this the cultivator paid rent to the state and was also required to contribute `begar' or forced labour. By the 1930s the latter was already restricted to the following:-

(a) begar for large camps and the Raja's touring.
(b) begar on the occasions of deaths and marriages in Raja's family.
(c) begar for repair of roads.

"The incidence of land revenue or rent charged was also not very high. Thus in the state of Nalagarh (district Solan) the gross charge on the cultivations was less than 25% of the produce. To assert as I have done above is not to say that no large zamindaries existed. In the native states, apart from the Raja and his relatives there were the state officials or jagirdars who held land in excess of what their family labour could cultivate. It is in cultivation of such land that the role of hired field labourers comes "The agriculturists in the hills employ hired field labourers; they receive food and two suits of clothes annually also from Rs. 12 to Rs. 18 per annum in cash. The persons so employed are a distinct class, either Chamars, Kolis or Domna. The percentage such persons bear to the agricultural population is 1/4".

Clearly the agrarian structure reflected the social structure as well. The bulk of the landless agricultural labourers were drawn from what later came to be characterised as the scheduled castes, while the majority of the big land holders belonged to the ruling Kshatriya class.

Yet the agrarian structure differed in a major way from that obtaining in the plains. The class of intermediaries between the state and the tillers of the land, was neither that well entrenched nor did it command the sort of control it did over rural property as in the plains. The hill states never witnessed the agrarian unrest that was a regular feature in the plains. To that extent the work of amelioration of the position of the landless, and abolishment of zamindari system became easier." (Solan/Rizvi/1988)

The same view is expressed by Anil Khachi when he writes about Bilaspur that "the relation between landlord and tenant in Himachal Pradesh have to be understood in the context different from the cowbelt area for one single important reason that in hills the land available to agriculture due to the difficult terrain is very restricted as compared to plain areas. Hence no big landlordism could develop and consequently there was never a strong visible feudalism here. The difference can be understood simply by referring to the word Zamindar. In Uttar Pradesh and Bihar Zamindar means a very big landlord whereas in Himachal every farmer is called a Zamindar even if he is holding just 1 begha of land."

A salient feature of rural life in HP is the absence of both stark, heart- rending poverty as well as conspicuous wealth of the landed rural elite. Owing to vigorous implementation of land reform measures as stated above, it is hard to find a landless family in the rural areas. Similarly landlords holding possession over hundreds of acres of land which are to be easily found in the plains are an almost non-existent breed in H. P. Thus no large-scale disparities exist in the size of plots being cultivated by the peasants in the countryside. In the absence of huge landholdings, there does not arise the need to hire extra labour and hence almost all holdings happen to be self- cultivated. Some of the other reactions to the field situation Division-wise are enumerated below:

KANGRA DIVISION

In the village all the land owners cultivate their lands themselves and there are no tenant or lessees. Land reform measures taken by the State Government have been highly successful and through a number of successive legislations enacted after the independence, land has finally been transferred to the tiller. The landless have been allotted land under different schemes with the result that every family in the village owns land however small it may be. Big landlords did not exist in the village and most of the land owners were cultivating their land themselves even before Tenancy Act came into force. (Una/Aggarwal/1985)

H.P. is one of the few states where land reforms measures have been implemented in the real sense. The revolutionary H.P. Tenant and Land Reform Act, 1972 has conferred ownership rights to all the occupancy and non-occupancy tenants on payment of a meagre compensation to the land owner. This act is so drastic that virtually now tenancy has become a thing of past. (Una/Baldi/1985)

Under the H.P. Tenancy and Land Reform Act, 1972, atleast 10 kanal of land has been given to everyone. Under the Act all the occupancy tenants were given ownership rights and non-occupancy tenants were also conferred such rights after giving due chance for the resumption to the owners. There is thus no landlessness in the village. Also absentee landlordism is totally absent. (Kangra/Prabodh/1990)

As holdings in this village and H.P. in general are small there has been no proceedings under the Land Ceilings Act in the village. There is only one landowner with a holding of 6.5 acres in the village. And only 5 families have holdings varying from 5-6 acres. (Kangra/Murti/1989)

About 3 hectares were allotted to 9 persons of which 50 per cent has been developed because of the suitable terrain. Rest of the area is left because the cost of developing such land is very high. The assistance provided would not be sufficient to bring this under cultivation. (Kangra/Murti/1989)

The landowners who had to give up their land due to the Tenancy Act are sore that adequate compensation was not given to them. The relationship though not hostile is strained between the landowner and the tenant. (Kangra/Murti/1989)

Under the H.P.Tenancy and Land Reforms Act all the occupancy tenants were given ownership rights and non-occupancy tenants were also conferred such rights after giving due chance for resumption to the owners. By this 20 odd tenants have been conferred ownership rights and have got irrigated land varying from 1 to 1.5 kanals. Another 10 cases are with the revenue courts where proceedings for resumption of land are going on. (Kangra/ Murti/1989)

H.P. Tenancy and Land Reforms Act was passed in 1974. Under this Act all the occupancy tenants were conferred ownership on the date this Act came into force. Non-occupancy tenants were also conferred such rights after giving due chance for resumption for those owners were left with less lands. Hence by now most of the 60 odd tenants have been conferred ownership." (Kangra/ Dhiman/1988)

MANDI DIVISION

There are no large scale disparities in the village. Every family owns some land and has a house to live in. There is no heart-rending poverty in sight nor can one see huge palatial mansions of big feudal landowners. (Mandi/Rajpal/1990)

The landholdings in the village are very small and there are no big landlords. Each and every family in the village owns some land and all the previous tenants have become landowners after the implementation of Tenancy and Land Reforms Act, 1972. In the absence of any big landholdings, there is hardly any surplus foodgrains available in the village. Some individuals who have been shown to be landless in the survey are actually often the wards of living land-owning parents and hence not strictly landless. (Mandi/Rajpal/1990)

Land reforms has been implemented quite seriously and effectively in Himachal Pradesh. Every household now has at least some land. Even land ceiling cases were quite few. Now no such case exists. Whatever little land the state has, has been distributed to the landless. Tenants have been made owners and the picture appears rosy from outside. But studying the situation in the surveyed village, the small size of the holdings appear to be the biggest hindrance in the path of benefit derivation. (Mandi/Anita/1989)

The remaining 360 landless families were allotted 1932 bighas of land 268 of these 360 landless families were Scheduled Castes, who were given ownership and physical possession of 1423-16 bighas of land. In fact, the ownership and possession of all 350 landless families granted land under the scheme has been recorded in the revenue papers and possession handed over on the spot. (Bilaspur/Khachi/1988)

The condition of scheduled castes is particularly bad. Six out of seven Scheduled Caste families own land less than 0.5 hec and even this land they received by way of allotment from the Government. In spite of these disparities are not as great as in other states of the country. This is because of limited cultivable land available in hilly terrain. (Mandi/Agarwal/1985)

The small size of operational holdings also limits the scope of raising productivity. The Green Revolution, which came with the introduction of high yielding varieties of seeds, chemical fertilizers, pesticides, irrigation etc. left most small and marginal farmers untouched because of its high capital requirement which they could ill-afford in the absence of any institutional support. (Bilaspur/Khachi/1988)

In village Manwa, which has 122 families (out of whom, only 1 owns no land at all), 55 families have land holdings less than or equal to 5 bighas and 36 have holdings between 5 and 10 bighas. Thus 75 per cent of the land owners fall within the category of small and marginal farmers. Only 6 families have holdings exceeding 20 bighas (in most cases, the larger share being that of uncultivable land). 5 families fall within the definition of agricultural labour. (Bilaspur/Khachi/1988)

The status of land reforms in the villages has seen no changes as the land holdings in the villages are much less than the maximum ceiling laid down in the relevant law. So the persons with low land holdings could not secure any benefits from various land reform laws. In cases where there was nil land holding Government distributed Nautor land thereby changed their status vis-à-vis land holdings. (Mandi/Jagdish/1991)

Ironically, an equitable distribution of land holdings and the fact that the proportion of landless people in the village is negligible has acted as a brake on the wheels of development in the region. The area seems to have got caught in a low-equilibrium trap. The absence of riches is responsible for insufficient generation of demand and hence no industrial activity can be started in the region to cater to this non-existent demand. The fact that every family owns a piece of land, however small its size, results in there being no 'army of unemployed' moving about in search of a job. The wage rates therefore remain high and discourage growth of economically viable units in the region. Big families are forced to eke out.a living out of small pieces of land and this results in large degree of underemployment in these families. This is the basic cause of lower level of economic activity in the region and hence explains its relative lack of prosperity and affluence." (Mandi/Rajpal/1990)

There was no big estate to be abolished under the Abolition of Big Landed Estates Act, 1953 in the village itself, though in the district as a whole, there were about 76 such big landed estates. The state of H.P., Bilaspur district had about 36,213 tenants. Most of them have now acquired, on payment of compensation, the right, title and interest of the landowner in the land of the tenancy held by them. In village Manwa, as per the jamabandi of 1985-86, there were only 2 non-occupancy tenants, that too in cases of protected categories *viz.* a widow and an armyman. Under the ceiling laws enacted by the State, land belonging to 10 land owners be measuring 126 acres was declared as surplus area in the entire district. Out of 126 acres, 34 acres has been handed over to the Forest Department because the land was not fit for cultivation and the remaining 92 acres was vested in 255 tenants and 5 landless and eligible persons.

The state of H.P. has a very good track record in the sphere of land reforms and this is true of the district of Bilaspur also. The process of conferring proprietary right to the tenants both occupancy and non occupancy was a smooth one. In fact the tenants in the district have enjoyed a far better status than their counterparts in other parts of the country, especially Eastern India. The relations were not exactly one of the oppressor and the oppressed. Even during the Raja's time, several steps had been initiated to provide security of tenure to the tenants as also fix the maximum rent. Of course, this is not to suggest that people did not try to circumvent the provisions of the Tenancy Act as well as the ceiling laws. (Bilaspur/Khachi/1988)

SHIMLA DIVISION

The overall impact of the above legislations and schemes has been to drastically reduce number of big zamindaries, confer proprietary rights on the tenants and provide land to the landless and marginal farmers. This fact is also reflected in the survey of the villages. (Solan/Rizvi/1989)

"In 1973 all these four families were provided with five bighas of land each. It is a different question altogether that Rs. 250 given to them as a grant to reclaim the land was extremely insufficient. As a result only one of the four families is now left with more than 2.5 bighas of cultivable land. The owner of this plot, Munna Lal, is still working hard to level the rest of the land. The other three beneficiaries under the Tenancy and Land Reforms Act are still struggling." (Nahan/Sanjeev/1993)

"The Government has allotted land to 7 landless poor in recent years at the rate of 1 acre per such household. The allotted land is being used for cultivation. In fact the allottees have encroached upon adjacent government land also (how enterprising!) which was earlier part of the forest department. The rest of the villagers complained of a reduction of pasture ground for their cattle as a consequence of such encroachment on common land." (Sol/Vivek/1989)

"The total cultivable area is 77 ha. and the number of families is 116. Hence, the average size of holding is 0.59 ha. i.e., approximately 1.5 acres. Another significant feature was that the bottom 45 per cent cultivators owned the same amount of land as the top 10 per cent." (Nahan/Sanjeev/1993)

Observations in the Land Reforms Programme

Although the bulk of the reports are full of praise for the land reform in HP , there are a few stray remarks which give some insight into the programme.

According to H. P. Tenancy and Land Reforms Act, some protected class have been allowed to lease land to the tenant. In this situation the tenant is liable to pay 25% of the crop to the land owner but in actual practice 1/3 of the produce of sometime 1/2 of the produce is taken by the land owner in the contravention of the law due to his commanding position. (Una/Baldi/1985)

Now the land belongs to tiller. However at some places the tenancy is still continuing with the connivance of revenue authorities. (Una/Baldi/1985)

What has been the impact of governments land distribution programme? Although statistics show that there are no landless persons in most of the Districts, yet one gets the impression that most of the land distributed was of poor quality. As holdings in this village specifically and in H.P. generally are small though Ceiling Act was passed but it is difficult to find a single household whose land came under this Act. In Ghaniar village not even a single landholding was affected by Ceiling Act. (Kangra/Dhiman/ 1988)

Although land has been distributed to the landless they are of poor quality both in terms of soil depth and gradient. In some cases the land does not exist on spot as the pattas have been drawn and given by the Revenue Department sitting in the Patwarkhana on order to meet the targets." (Una/Baldi/1985)

Consolidation of land holdings is another area where the land reforms have not penetrated. Part of the reason could be explained by the fact that the farmers in the hills do not have uniform quality of land as seen in the plains of Punjab etc. and also that he requires different types of land in order to minimise the risks, but the fact remains that selective Consolidation of lands can result in better management of agriculture. This is borne out by some of the reports.

The villagers do not exchange land. Most of them have just a single piece of land of 10 kanal received by them after the land reforms. As most of these villagers were accommodated in the government land, they have been allotted land together so there is no need as such for consolidation. Some people of the village who have recently purchased land in the village have not attempted consolidation either on individual bases or through village Panchayat—In any case, such cases are rare. (Kangra/Prabodh/ 1990)

"Although land holdings of the sizeable section of population is quite large their economic condition is not good. This is attributed mainly to the fact that their holdings are fragmented (i.e. land is spread over a large area in small pieces mostly less than one bigha). This makes their land less economical as they have to look after many pieces of land at many places which require too much of efforts and labour. The cropping pattern has not changed towards cash crops mainly because of this reason as logistics become extremely problematic. It is therefore suggested that consolidation of land holdings should be undertaken immediately in this area. Opinion in favour of this was expressed by most of the people who have reasonable size of land holdings. Due to segregated holdings people are unable to grow fruits and off season vegetables." (Mandi/Jagdish/1991)

"The consolidation operations were completed in 1981 and there are 185 khatauni nos. and 339 Bhasara nos. There were two cases in which the land owners had to complain about irregularities during consolidation operations. The consolidation authorities played in the hands of the rich farmers, they alleged. They were ultimately left with inferior quality of land. This was one grievance which was found to be true after going into the land records." (Nahan/Sanjeev/1993)

While land settlement took place in Kehanwal during 1959-65, no government initiated measures at land consolidation have as yet taken place. The fields of landowners are spread out over a radius of about 2 km from the centre of Kehanwal area." (Mandi/Rajpal/1990)

AGRICULTURE AND ALLIED ACTIVITIES

Agriculture in the Himachal, as in all hill states, is of a purely subsistence level. The bulk of the foodgrains produced is of coarse variety and is not sufficient to meet the food requirement of the State. Fortunately the state has an excellent Public Distribution System which takes care of the dietary needs of the population. The State however has taken a lead in Horticulture and has rightly been called the apple state of India.

The Officer Trainees have made copious notes on the agricultural practices of the Himachali farmers. The Region wise comments have been divided into four broad areas *i.e.,* crops grown, fertilizers used, status of irrigation and knowledge of improved agricultural practices. Their comments are as follows:-

Agriculture in Kangra Division

Crops grown

Cropping pattern		
Kharif crops:	Maize	24 hectares
	Paddy	12 hectares
Rabi crops:	Wheat	34 hectares
	Barley	6 hectares

(Kangra/Murti/89)

The average produce of the village is very poor as compared to the district average. While in Padher a farmer gets just 6-7 quintal of maize and paddy, the district average for them is 12.15 quintal per hectare and 12.35 quintal per hectare respectively. As a matter of fact Himachal Pradesh is next only to Karnataka as far as maize yield per hectare is concerned. (Kangra/Prabodh/1990)

One hectare of the land is waterlogged and therefore can be used only for one crop i.e. paddy. Thus we are left with about 15 hectares of land which is capable of returning two crops in a year. In entire 15 hectare wheat (locally called gandam) is sown in November-December and is harvested in May. In May itself about

9 hectare of land is put to Maize cultivation which is ready by mid September. The rest 5 hectare is used for cultivation of Paddy in May and remain occupied by Paddy till October. (Kangra/Prabodh/1990)

"Kharif and Rabi are the two cultivating season. Maize and Paddy is sown in the month of May. Maize is ready for harvest by mid September while Paddy is harvested in the month of October. In the Rabi crop season, wheat is sown in the month of November-December and is harvested in May." (Kangra/Prabodh/1990)

"A very small portion of about 15-20 qts of rice is sold out of the village and the rest is used for the consumption in the village itself. As the quantity of produce sold outside is very small there is no Cooperative Society to handle this. But most of it is sold at the market in Shahpur which is 7 km away." (Kangra/Murti/89)

Fertilizers and Manure

Most of the cattle dung is used as manure in the fields. About 20 per cent of it is used as fuel. About 8 to 10 quintals of cattle dung is applied per hectare of land. The amount of cattle dung is not sufficient to meet the requirements of the village. Cattle urine is used for no purpose in the village. Green manure though not grown is obtained from the forests and woods. These forests also provide fodder and wood for the agricultural implements. (Kangra/Murti/1989)

"Practically all the households have cattles and cowdung is converted into the manures in the compost pits. Chemical fertilizers are also used to supplement the nutritional requirement of soil. Generally, the supply of chemical fertilizers is not a problem." (Kangra/Dhiman/1988)

"The chief manure used in this area is cow-dung, compost manure which is easily available from the livestock reared by the farmer. There is no standard for compost manure and it is used as per the availability with the farmer. As far as chemical fertilizer is concerned, it is generally not used except by few big farmers. These farmers also use very little fertilizer and it varies one to two bag per area which is 1/4 of the standard. When I talked with some advanced farmer for more use of chemical fertilizer, they replied that here, there is no assured source of irrigation and there farming is mainly rainfed. Therefore the use of chemical fertilizer is very risky which they cannot afford." (Una/Baldi/1985)

"The progressive farmer, who uses fertilizer in time, can have a yield of 30 quintals in one hectare. Increasing use of fertilizer by the farmers of this village is hampered by lack of proper irrigation facilities. In the case of those farmers, who cultivate their lands in the interior places, they hardly use any fertilizer." (Chamba/Subramanyam/1986)

The annual yield of the crop depend upon the rains as the agriculture here is rainfed. But it can be said that on an average 1 hectare of land yields about 6-7 quintal of maize. Similarly the production of paddy is also about 6-7 quintal per hectare. The wheat production however is only 7-8 quintal in a hectare of land." (Kangra/Prabodh/1990)

The agriculture in the village is need based and is practised at a very small scale. Generally it is a mean of supplementing the income coming from other sources especially wage employment. On an average a family is able to support just 4 to 5 months of ration from the land available with it. Hence, as the agriculture does not yield money as such and the cultivator lacks other resources, the crop is not exactly cared for more so when it requires investment in fertilizer, quality seed, pesticide, weedicide, etc. However, they do put Nitrogenous fertilizer in maize and wheat but regular use and spray of pesticide is still not very common. The farmers at time do use Vaccine Hexa Chloride." (Kangra/Prabodh/1990)

Improved Agricultural Practices

The farmers in this area are using only some traditional implements like wooden plough and suhaga etc. The modern implements like thresher, seed-storage bin, chaff cutter etc. have not made inroad in their agricultural life. When I talked with B.D.O. Amb regarding this, he told me that agriculture implements like thresher, seed-storage bin, chaff cutter bar, harrow, digging hoe and disc-harrow are available in the block office at the subsidy of $33\frac{1}{3}$% but, he complained that farmers are generally not keen in adopting them, whereas the complaint of the villagers was that, they have to spend Rs. 20 for bus fare to go to Amb and still they do not get the required implement from the block office. Thus in this type of situation I feel that government machinery should be geared in such a way that these agriculture implements can be made available in every village. I think the best way is to make them available is through primary agriculture co-operative society in every village." (Una/Baldi/1985)

"There is another argument for the indifference to scientific farming. For tenants who have become owner under the land reform package of the government, land is more a status symbol rather than the only means of livelihood. The tenant after becoming owner is satisfied with the produce which is in any case more than what he used to get from the same land when he was the tenant. Further there is a weak credit extension system and the farmer on his own is not in a position to adopt mixed farming and the cash crop production. Lack of irrigation facilities in the area has made agriculture in 10 kanal of land only not very much economically viable. As large number of farmers were allotted land out of barren land, common land and cultivable waste, in the absence of scientific treatment of the land, the fertility status of the land has depleted considerably after good initial response. These are some of the factors as a result of which the village is still practising traditional crop system." (Kangra/Prabodh/1990)

"Traditional wooden ploughs are still in use but they are on their way out. Alongwith the wooden plough, the farmer carries a wooden hammer also to break soil lumps. A wooden plank too is required to level the earth. The government is making all out effort for popularisation of soil steering plough, commonly called as S.S. Plough. Almost all the families possess it." (Kangra/Prabodh/1990)

"Farmers have taken to improved variety of seeds in a limited way only as they are very expensive. They prefer S-308 seed for wheat and Ganga Hybrid for maize. There is no seed farm in the village and the seeds are arranged through the co-operative counter only. The farmers regard the Palampur Agricultural University as a wasteful expenditure which has not contributed anything to their agriculture. Some well informed people in the village are enthusiastic about the extension programme likely to be launched in the district by the agricultural department with the financial support of the World Bank." (Kangra/Prabodh/1990)

"There has been no change in agricultural practices like shifting over to commercial crops. Food crops still account for over 90 per cent of the area under cultivation." (Kangra/Murti/1989)

"As the size of holdings is very small and due to the terrain mechanical farming is not possible. Therefore only traditional wooden ploughs are used. A long wooden hammer is used to break lumps in the fields before sowing. After this wooden levellers is pulled over the fields. New agricultural implements like the S.S. plough (soil steering plough) are being used. This is provided by the Block agencies and costs Rs 100. The blade has to be changed every other year. About 3000 kgs, 500 kgs and 1200 kgs of improved seeds for wheat, maize and paddy respectively are used in the village per year. There is no seed farm but these are obtained through the Block Agency which delivers it to the village." (Kangra/Murti/1989)

As the size of holdings is very small and is located along the mild grades, hence mechanical farming is not possible, therefore, only desi wooden ploughs are used. A long wooden hammer is used to break lumps in the fields before sowing. After this wooden plank (levellers) with weights is pulled over the fields and to preserve the moisture content in the soil. For thrashing the harvested crop, thresher and maize sheller are used in this area. In case of maize, HYVs have not made any dent and only local variety is used. And in case of paddy HIM-1 is generally used and has been found very suitable in this area. In case of wheat, sonalika is dominantly used variety. High yielding varieties are being used in the village but in the absence of irrigation yield is not much. Sonalika is the most popular variety of wheat in the village. Normally seed should be replaced after three years but due to ignorance and sometimes due to shortage of cash villagers continue with same seed for longer periods which effects yield." (Kangra/Dhiman/1988)

The land available for agricultural purposes is small and therefore no mechanical farming is in use. As basically the land is used for partial fulfilment of ration need of the family only, there is no change from food crop to cash crop or commercial crop." (Kangra/Prabodh/1990)

Irrigation

"There is no source of irrigation in the village. The entire area is rainfed, but fortunately Kangra district has the advantage of receiving the second highest rainfall in the country. Otherwise, there is absolutely no other mode of irrigation facility in the village either through tanks or pumps. A check dam was constructed by the Irrigation and Public Health Department to provide water for irrigation to the land of the people who were allotted land under the scheme of disbursement of the land to the landless tiller but the scheme failed to take off. There are about 15 bowllies in the village but they are not used for irrigation purposes but are used to supplement the weak supply of drinking water in summer months." (Kangra/Prabodh/1990)

"The villagers are however, very keen to have irrigation facilities. Even 10 kanal of land can be economically viable provided there is assured irrigation. There are farmers elsewhere in the district who are even taking four crops including fodder. During Rabi season they sow wheat in October-November and harvest it in the first week of May. Thereafter they sow fodder maize which is ready by June end. After this á crop of normal maize can be taken till September. Before the start of next Rabi season they have yet another group of peas arke which is a 65 day variety crop." (Kangra/Prabodh/1990)

"The entire cultivated area is rainfed. There is no permanent source of water also. A check dam was constructed to accumulate the water supply in the rainy months. Even pipes were laid till the area where land was allotted to the farmers by the government but this scheme was a failure right from the start because Irrigation is the most important felt need of the villagers and therefore there is a need for repair and restoration of this check dam. As the terrain is rocky, the scope to harness the groundwater for the purposes of irrigation is very remote. A feasible though expensive alternative is to install lift irrigation scheme to lift the water from a rivulet flowing about 500 metres away from the village and about 500 feet below the mean sea level height of Padher. There are 15 bowlies in the village which are used only for drinking of the cattle and also human being when the water supply in the village taps is very scarce in summers." (Kangra/Prabodh/1990)

"The only source of irrigation is through gravity canals locally called kuhls. The water from Khaulikhad which has water throughout the year supplied by rain or melted snow is diverted to the kuhl into the fields for irrigation. The kuhl at the moment is not functional. Rains during the last season caused a landslide which blocked the kuhl. The kuhl is not properly managed leading to a lot of seepage and silting. Hence the present utilisation of its capacity is less and inefficient. Though some work has been done on it, it is still insufficient. To arrest seepage of water through side berms of the canal they may be lind with appropriate material. Silt in the canals have to be removed regularly and is done by the villagers all contributing towards it. Other alternatives could be in creating water ponds were possible which could irrigate more area. Such area should be near the present waste and uneconomical forest areas where orchards is proposed to be planted." (Kangra/Murti/1989)

Agriculture in Mandi Division

Crops Grown

The main crops in the village are wheat, maize and rice. In Rabi season wheat is sown in almost whole of the cultivable land. In Kharif season, about 18 ha is covered by rice and 12 ha by maize. Some other coarse grains like barley, kodra etc. are also grown on the land of inferior quality." (Mandi/Agarwal/1985)

"There does not exist any potential for growing commercial crops in the area. However some forays have been made by some farmers into the field of plum production due to an intensive effort in this direction by the local block authorities. Unfortunately, all the fields of plum trees that I visited were languishing in a state of neglect and decay." (Mandi/Rajpal/1990)

"Trying to convert agricultural inputs and outputs into their monetary terms is a risky venture. It is particularly so for an area where all agriculture is for subsistence purpose and none for surplus or commercial production. Average yield of wheat per acre is about 20 quintals which can fetch an income of Rs. 6000/- in the market. The inputs cost tends to exceed Rs. 6000/- if family labour is given the imputed cost of Rs. 30/- per day but since wheat and maize are grown for family consumption only but often is not enough to feed the family for the entire year, the non-viable nature of agricultural operations cannot be a reason for its discontinuation in the village. As one villages aptly put it before me, 'if we don't produce the meagre crop ourselves, then what are we going to eat?'." (Mandi/Rajpal/1990)

"Some vegetables are also grown for local consumption. There are arbi, brinjal, chillies, ginger, lady's finger, pumpkin and peas. Vegetables can be grown on a large scale for commercial purpose." (Mandi/Anita/1989)

Fertilizers and Manure

As the village is quite rich in livestock, availability of animal manure is quite high, when compared to other areas. The dung is stored in heaps. Its upper layer dries up and the inside remains moist and degeneration continues. Eight to ten quintals of this is used per acre and its dry weight would be nearly half of it. Recommended quantity is 40 quintals per acre. The cattle manure is therefore not sufficient. No green manure is available. The cattle dung is not used for gobar gas plants. This is because the area is very cold and the gobar gas plants installed here have not given good result. Chemical fertilizers such as calcium ammonium nitrate locally known as "CAN' is popular apart from urea and mixed (N:P:K:12:32:16). These are obtained from the Government sale centre at Kataula which is 13 kms away. The input is generally within a range of 30-50 kgs. /acre." (Mandi/Anita/1989)

Improved Agricultural Practices

Slowly, the wooden plough is being replaced by iron plough, but new varieties of seeds are yet to find a place. Tractors, tubewells are obviously not there, more due to the type of topography and size of fields than for any other reason. Tractors are employed on contract basis, mainly for transporting goods. Bullocks are used to plough the field, but not all families own a pair. Some families with small farms hire the bullocks of their neighbour.

"Though on paper much is being done to improve agriculture, very little results are evident on the field. Lack of area under paddy etc. has made availability of green manure very low and fertilizers supplied by co-operative society either does not reach the farms or is a very small amount to satisfy the farms needs. (Bilaspur/Nisha/1987)

Threshers are owned by nine households. They rent it out and charge 10 kgs. per quintal of the grain threshed. This income supplemented by agriculture is sufficient to sustain these families. High yielding varieties of seeds have been introduced in the area and are available at Kataula. According to the people, the yield per hectare has gone up in the case of wheat tremendously." (Mandi/Anita/1989)

A very interesting revelation that came to light during the survey revealed that of the number of tillers owning only one bullock out of a pair, a majority have bullocks who are habitual of being on the leftside while ploughing the land. (One presumed that the tendencies of being a leftist was limited to human beings!) This leads to a problem during the ploughing season as it becomes difficult to get together a workable pair of bullocks." (Mandi/Rajpal/1990)

Most of the farmers are using improved variety of seeds which are made available by the local co-operative society. A few farmers, declined to use this short-stalked variety since it reduces the amount of fodder that is made available after its harvest. This tendency to resist the use of improved varieties was more marked in the farmers owning their own heads of cattle." (Mandi/Rajpal/1990)

"Because of hilly terrain, and absence of irrigation there is a limit to which modern agricultural practices can be used with advantage. Chemical fertilizer does not help much in the absence of assured irrigation. Also in the area where subsistence farming is prevalent there is problem of cash money for buying fertilizer. In this village, farmers use fertilizer only for crops of wheat and maize. Rice crop requires a good monsoon which is unpredictable and hence farmers do not take risk by investing additional money in fertilizer. Consumption of CAN fertilizer, which is most popular is about 120 kg per hec in the village. Wooden ploughs and bullocks are used for preparation of fields. Every family owns at least one pair of bullocks. No mechanical implements are being used for agricultural operations." (Mandi/Agarwal/1985)

"As far as agricultural practices are concerned, it must be noted that traditional implements are still being used by the farmers. The people use the 'desi' plough made of the 'Ban' tree farm and wooden leveller called 'Merha'." (Mandi/Manoj/1988)

In the agricultural field, some improved agricultural implements like threshers, winnowers are being used. (Bilaspur/Nita/1988)

Irrigation

Very little has been done to improve the irrigation facilities which is the main factor that is hindering good crop cultivation. Most of the rainfall is concentrated in the monsoon months of July-September. Rainfall also occurs in the winter months owing to the north-westerly disturbances. The winter rain is much awaited for and is extremely beneficial for the standing wheat crop. The area is quite susceptible to hailstorms which often cause a lot of damage to the crops. (Mandi/Rajpal/1990)

"The only possible source of irrigation is the Suketi Khad (rivulet) that flows past the area hundreds of feet below. The

Irrigation and Public Health Department has constructed a lift drinking water supply scheme which lifts water from the khud in three stages." (Mandi/Rajpal/1990)

"Irrigation in the village agriculture is wholly dependent on the rains." (Mandi/Agarwal/1985)

"In view of the hilly terrain of the village (and indeed the entire district), the possibilities of undertaking major irrigation projects are very remote, if not impracticable. In the absence of any spring/stream in the village 'kuhls' also cannot be constructed. The alternative then is a lift irrigation scheme, given the close proximity of Gobind Sagar Lake." (Bilaspur/Khachi/1988)

"No amount of fertilizer helps if proper irrigation facilities do not exist. In this village there is no irrigated land. Farmers depend upon the vagaries of monsoons." (Bilaspur/Nita/1988)

Agriculture in Shimla Division

"However, land is already a scarce commodity and given the terrain chances of reclamation of much land for agricultural purposes is remote. With time the pressure on land is only going to increase. There is an urgent need therefore to diversify the productive base of the village society." (Solan/Rizvi/1988)

Crops Grown

The main kharif crops are maize, tomatoes, capsicum and cauliflower. In the rabi crop peas is the major crop sown. Some wheat and jowar is also grown. The practice of mixed farming is common.

The cultivation of vegetables and horticulture has gone a long way in ameliorating the condition of the farmers. Off season vegetable is being grown in the area since the 1950s. Ginger and potato were the first to be introduced. This was followed by tomatoes, capsicum and cauliflower. However cultivation on a commercial basis really began in late sixties. Off season tomatoes (SOLAN GOLA) is grown during rainy season when it is not available in the plains. Likewise off season peas appear in the market in April and May. High Yielding varities like LINCON and ARCAL are grown. Besides seed variety cauliflower is also being grown on commercial basis." (Solan/Rizvi/1988)

Fertilizers and Manure

Cattle manure is still the chief source of manuring even though there is a paucity of cattle as they can not be supported by the environment in large numbers. Some of the bigger farmers purchase cattle manure from the milk dairies. Use of green manure is negligible, while the use of chemical manure is increasing." (Sol/Rizvi/1988)

"Cattle dung is used as manure by majority of the farmers, though some have started using urea for their field. There is no dearth of chemical fertilizers which is always available at the nearby Dharampur block." (Sol/Vivek/1989)

Improved Agricultural Practices

"The water table is low at the crest and high at the bottom of the ridge as a result of which lower side is more suitable for agricultural purposes. The cultivation seasons are November-May for wheat and July-November for Maize. All cultivable land is cultivated in the same season. Of late there has been a slight shift in agricultural practices and the valley side has seen the coming up of pea and tomato cultivation. Gadioli flowers are also being cultivated by some of the enterprising farmers. So there has been a switch-over from food crop cultivation to cash crop cultivation but its extent has been limited. The steel ploughs are used in the fields." (Solan/Vivek/1989)

"The most common manure being used is the compost. However, there has been a gradual shift to chemical fertilizers in view of the quick results. The awareness that the chemical fertilizers destroy the humus in the soil is absent. This myopic approach favouring immediate gains is extremely disturbing. As the pulses and other leguminous crops are relatively scarce, urea and other nitrogen yielding fertilizers are very popular. Since there is no distribution centre of the co-operative society, the farmers have to depend upon the traders in Nahan. There is only one bio-gas plant (3 cubic metre capacity) in the village and the manure extracted from it is used by the owner of the plant." (Nahan/Sanjeev/1993)

"Land is still cultivated largely through bullock/cow driven ploughs. The terrain militates against large scale mechanisation. The fields are generally terraced. Hiring out of bullocks/cows or ploughs is rare. Where these inputs are in short supply, village institutions provide for a sharing of resources." (Solan/Rizvi/1988)

"Improved seeds are also available in plenty through the Block office and improved seeds are being used for tomato, pea and maize. The villagers are very receptive to improved methods of cultivation and use of improved seeds, pesticides and fertilizers are becoming increasingly common. Tomato crop is quite vulnerable to a fungal disease called "Tali Tikki" while capsicum and tomato are together susceptible to insects. Spraying of the insecticides on a regular basis has contained these pests to a large extent." (Solan/Vivek/1989)

Irrigation

"According to the latest land revenue records, cultivated land measures only 17.7% of the gross area of the village. Added to it is, the total cultivated area in the village is rainfed and not even an inch of land is being supplied with irrigation water and hence the total cultivated land in the village comes under rainfed area. All these peculiarities tend to reduce agriculture to a bare subsistence level. Many rivulets pass through the village however, without any significant benefit to the villagers." (Nahan/Prasad/1986)

Irrigation is one field in which almost nothing has been done by the government. Whatever little irrigation that exists is through Kuhals or the narrow earth canals which draw water from streams. Tubewells are not possible in the hills. There is however considerable scope for tank irrigation. Soil Conservation Department has a scheme of providing subsidy on the construction of tanks to individual beneficiaries, but very few people have been covered so far. A network of canals and tanks and also pipe irrigation will go a long way in boosting the cultivation of cash crops like off season vegetables." (Shimla/Gupta/1988)

Horticulture

Himachal is known as the Apple State of India, although other fruits like oranges, kinoo, apricots etc. are also grown.

Barring some quantity of apples grown in Kashmir, there was virtually no apple production in the country until 1950. Perhaps a few thousand boxes of apples were grown. In fact, apples were imported. The people in Shimla and Kullu Districts of H.P. where apples are mainly grown, were engaged in subsistence agriculture and they had no cash crops. These people often had difficulty getting two square meals and had to walk miles for a menial job. In just 40 years those thousand odd boxes of apples increased to more than a million tons. Apple production is now the fourth largest crop in the country following mango, banana and citrus fruits. This has led to a rapid economic prosperity in just a couple of decades. The flow of money has empowered the people of these areas in an unprecedented way.

On the other hand, Himachal Pradesh has perhaps suffered ecologically through monoculture (apples), as well as through the use of insecticides, fungicides, and chemical fertilizers. High doses of insecticide and pesticide has caused an increase in environmental pollution. At the same time, unplanned growth has caused pressures on transportation and also led to deforestation. Today, many farmers feel that production has decreased due to too much use of pesticide/fungicide and chemical fertilizers. This in fact is true as there has been a decline in the production of apples in the state of Himachal Pradesh since the last 5/7 years after scab hit the State. Farmers are undecided as to what to do-whether to continue with the sprays and fertilizers as recommended by the extension agencies or to completely stop it. Meanwhile, neither the Horticulture Department nor the Universities have been able to come forth with any solution. The farmers may be using too much of chemicals but to control scab one has to use fungicide. Though insecticides are highly poisonous and require 21 days to 2 months before the ill effects wear off, fungicides have no poison. The causes of low production of late of apples in H.P, could also be due to the bad weather. Snowfall at the blossoming stage or excessive rainfall, which induces scab, could be a reason. Because Kashmir has varieties of apples which self-pollinate, there is little fluctuation in their productivity. If one type fails, the others still succeed. In HP we have primarily the Red and Royal varieties which are highly susceptible to scab. More than the frequency or the amount of spraying, the proper stages and timing of spraying are essential for which the farmers have to be trained. If they skip the exact stage/time it is of no use.

By and large it seems that for the hills horticulture is a better alternative and amongst the fruits available apples seem to be the most practical. Growing almonds is problematic because they require a dry climate. Citrus fruit can only be grown at an altitude 2000 ft. to 2500 ft. which leaves a major portion outside its scope.

In HP there are virtually no large farmers. Disparities between apple growers in H.P. are less than the disparities among other crop farmers. Horticulture, as opposed to traditional field crops, is very important for sustainable development in the hills. There are certain constraints and problems which have to be addressed. But, in spite of all the problems and criticisms no apple grower today will be willing to exchange his orchard for any other crop.

KANGRA DIVISION

The climatic condition of Kangra are most suitable for the growth of various fruits like mangoes, oranges, lemon and galgal. The remarks of the Officer Trainees on horticulture in general are as follows:-

"The effort from government side is miserably lacking to develop this important source of income for the farmers. At present only a few mango trees are existing in the name of horticulture in this village. If Government authorities provide the citrus plants in the village during the right season, then the poor farmers even with their poor holdings could cross the poverty line." (Una/Baldi/1985)

"Regarding crop diseases I feel that failure lies in disseminating plant protection information among the farmers. The Agriculture and Horticulture department should organize plant protection camp at the village level and should provide proper pesticides for various disease." (Una/Baldi/1985)

"Just as we found in the case of marketing of milk, how the middlemen are able to corner all the profits, to the detriment of both the producer and consumer, in a similar fashion, middlemen also operate in buying fruits and vegetables from the producers in the village Jaddera and sell the same at Chamba at profits ranging between 80 per cent and 100 per cent. These middlemen are very rich and know how to tackle the official agencies which are concerned with maintaining reasonable prices. Even in this case, it is generally found, that while vegetables are cheaper at Pathankot and other districts of H.P. despite a good deal of production, prices of vegetables are very high at Chamba. Although District Administration and the District Food and Supplies Controller issue orders frequently to the vendors to sell vegetables at reasonable prices, these instructions are more observed in breach than in practice. Just as in the case of milk suppliers, the vegetable vendors also supply vegetables at cheaper prices to those who matter to them, while all others pay exorbitantly. The middlemen also threaten the producers that if the latter do not sell the vegetables at the price dictated by the former, they can stop purchasing vegetables from them and obtain supplies from Pathankot. The producers thus, find themselves in a predicament, because there are no fixed outlets for marketing their produce, in the main market at Chamba. Thus, they yield to the demands of the middlemen." (Chamba/Subramanyam/1986)

"Horticulture has not picked up in the village. As the land available is limited and is owned by small and marginal farmers who do not opt for long gestation crops like fruits, the horticulture in the area has not picked up. Wastelands and uneconomical forests are the two sources of land for development of horticulture in the village. The area is suitable for fruit crops like mango, litchi, guava and cirtus fruits and is visible in the development of neighbouring areas like Shahpur, Chatru, Kareri have made in this field. So by making available wastelands and uneconomical forests for development, horticulture would increase the income of the village." (Kangra/Murti/1989)

"Dhaula Dhar ranges are frequently subjected to heavy rainfall and hailstorms, which makes it unsuitable for certain variety of fruits like plums, peaches, and apricot, but slopes can be planted with citrus fruits like lemon, kinno, malta and oranges." (Kangra/Dhiman/1988)

MANDI DIVISION

"An area of 4.03 hectare comes under orchards growing plums. But according to the owners, hailstorms in the last few years at the flowering stage of the tree during February have caused great loss to the owners. People have also planted plum trees along the boundaries of their land for growing fruits for their own consumption. Due to the topological peculiarities of this region, there has been a marked increase in the hectrage under horticultural crops. In the State, over 15 per cent of the net sown area has come under fruit crops whereas in the district, this figure comes to 0.415 per cent. In the surveyed area, this comes to 10.2 per cent which is much higher than the district average but lower than the state average." (Mandi/Anita/1989)

"There is no horticulture plantation at any significant scale in the village. People, however, have grown some trees of citrus fruits on their lands. One interesting feature in the village is that almost every family grows some vegetables near its house. As there is no irrigation in the village any large scale cultivation of vegetables is not possible. The villagers, however, grow vegetable for their own consumption by using drinking water which is available in sufficient quantity." (Mandi/Agarwal/1990)

"One of the activities that was started with a lot of hope by some of the villagers is the one of plum cultivation. Even today, about 18 acres of land is still under plum cultivation even as a lot of orchardists have already uprooted their trees after their enterprises failed." (Mandi/Rajpal/1990)

"Nevertheless, much more needs to be done to achieve greater productivity. Maya Singh, 51, a farmer with two acres of land wants a more efficient system for the supply of pesticides and chemicals for orchards. And the first Pradhan of the Panchayat, Narad Ram, 65, says that the Horticulture Department should hold annual camps to educate the villagers on the technicalities of apple growing, especially at the time of planting and pruning of trees." (Mandi/Manoj/1988)

"The area has taken to apple growing in a big way. Introduced way back in the 1960s, every farmer now boasts of atleast some trees in his fields. It seems, the people have learnt much from the success stories in nearby Kulu. During a good season, the area sends about 120 big truckloads of apples to near and far places, even as far as Delhi. There is even a demand for the establishment of a Juice Extraction plant in the area. Says Amar Chand, the Gram Pradhan of the Panchayat—"while our A grade apples have a ready market, the B-grade apples simply rot away, they have no market locally and if we send them to far away places, even the cartage charges are not recovered". There seems to be some substance in the argument and it goes without saying that a juice extraction plant in the Panchayat will go a long way in segmenting the income of the farmers, both big and small, in addition to providing employment to a large number of people, especially the women. In fact, though there has been a tremendous increase in the area and production of fruits in the region, there is scope for still greater expansion. This is possible under a comprehensive and integrated programme, covering all aspects, viz., production, processing, storage, transportation and the marketing of fruits. Such integration is necessary as the fruits ready in the rainy season are sometimes accumulated due to roadblocks by landslides and the absence of timely transportation facilities. At other times, unregulated supplies in the markets in the plains lead to uneconomic prices for the producers." (Mandi/Manoj/1988)

"There is lot of potentiality in this area for the development of horticulture. But no initiative was taken either by the DRDA or

Department of Horticulture. Fruits like guava, mangoes and oranges, galgals (citrus) can be developed." (Bilaspur/Nita/1988)

"At present, no fruits are being grown in the village but in the nearby areas mango, pomegranate, guava, banana, citrus, papaya etc. are cultivated, and one reason why the same cannot be cultivated here too. The people need guidance and motivation, which the government departments can provide, only if there is somebody with vision and initiative manning these departments." (Bilaspur/Khachi/1988)

"Unable to organize the harvesting, packaging and marketing of the output on their own, the small orchardists are forced to engage contractors for their gardens. The contractors who land up in Kehanwal always collude with each other before coming and so force the orchardists to contract their orchards out at a very unremunerative rate. If the orchardists manage picking and packaging on their own, even then the ex-orchard price that the traders are willing to pay them is never more than Rs. 1.25 per kg. This return is totally uneconomic since the cost of a 5 Kg box is Rs. 7 and it takes at least 1 Rs. for getting it packed. Thus the cost comes out to be 1.60 Rupees per kg. No wonder that this activity has failed to take roots in this area." (Mandi/Rajpal/1990)

Shimla

Unfortunately there are no reports from Shimla District which is the layout producers of apples on villages where they are actually grown with the result that we have only the following remarks from Solan District.

"Apart from vegetable, stone fruits are also grown. These include plum, peach and pear." (SOL/Rizvi/1988)

Recommendations for Horticulture

General

- Diversification of horticulture should be encouraged; monocultures create many problems.

- Improve root stock, germplasm, and diversify stock
- Climatic diversity should be taken into account to lengthen duration of fruit harvests.
- A standard grading system for fruits and other products should be adopted. For export quality fruits we need to match international grading standards.
- Any produce which is unsuitable for table value should be processed and converted to marketable products.
- Whatever processing is possible, value additions should be done in the hills to generate incomes and employment. For this purpose, skill and entrepreneurship development as well as adequacy of infrastructure are very important.
- Cold storage should be encouraged in foothill areas for the surplus fruit and vegetable storage so that gluts are avoided and reasonable price levels of products can be maintained.
- Construction of gravity ropeways will aid in transport.
- Himalayan hills have ideal agro-climatic conditions for the cultivation of varieties of flowers which have great market potential in the country and abroad.
- Cultivation of fragrant flowers such as Bulgarian Rose, Wild Rose, Marigold, and Geraniums should be encouraged for supply to cosmetic and pharmaceutical firms.

Marketing of Horticultural Produce

- Communication system to improve farmer's knowledge of product prices should be implemented.
- Marketing institutions in Hill areas should be developed.
- Branding should be adopted for improved marketing of products.
- Attractive and eco-friendly packaging should be used.
- Alternative and reusable packaging systems must be developed. Wood packaging is not sustainable. This will need suitable adjustments in fiscal and taxation policies. This is a high urgency matter.

- Packaging and transportation may be given to private parties rather than depending on the government institutions. This will make these activities economic and competitive. Local entrepreneurship should be encouraged in this context.

Animal Husbandry and Cattle Rearing

KANGRA DIVISION

"An interesting aspect of Animal Husbandry in this village which deserves special study is the marketability of milk and milk products. The present position is that 2 contractors of Chamba town operate as middlemen between the milk producers and consumers. The contractors buy milk @ Rs. 2.75 to Rs. 3.25 from the producers and sell the same @ Rs. 3.50 to Rs. 4.00. The milk is transported by HRTC bus in the morning. It reaches Chamba at 11.00 a.m. Then, the milk is further distributed to various consumers in Chamba through the agents of the contractor. The distance between Jaddera and Chamba is 22 kms. In practice, it so happens that most of the consumers in Chamba do not get good quality of milk. It is invariably adulterated with water. The milk contractors are clever enough to bribe the officials/agencies, which may put an end to their nefarious practices. The milk agents are instructed by their contractors to supply excellent quality of milk (pure milk) to all those officials, who matter to them. These officials, who are required to inspect the quality of milk supplied to the residents of Chamba in general, tend to turn a Nelson's eye on the corrupt practices of milk contractors, since they themselves are not at all affected by the mis-deeds of these contractors." (Chamba/ Subramanyam/1986)

"The dispensary has a veterinary Pharmacist and a class IV employee. Stock of medicines is limited and supply is irregular. A buffalo bull of "Murra" breed is maintained in the dispensary and villagers are charged Rs 10 for getting their buffaloes inseminated. This bull has become very old and this has resulted in less and less villagers visiting the dispensary. Nearest artificial insemination centre is about 10 kms away." (Kangra/Prabodh/1990)

"These dispensaries are manned by Pharmacists. Thus, the villagers of Jaddera, in case of any cattle disease, have to either go to Baror, which is 6 kms. away, or to Sillaghrat, which is equally distant. A Veterinary Hospital manned by a full-fledged Veterinary Doctor is located in a village called Sahu, which is 22 kms. away from Jaddera. One good thing is that both Sahu and Jaddera are telephonically connected and thus, in case of any emergency, Jaddera people can seek help through telephone.

Every year vaccination to cattle against the diseases of Foot and Mouth Disease; Black Quarter and Hemaragic Septicaemia is done. The responsibility for such vaccination of the cattle of Jaddera rests with the Veterinary Dispensary located at Shillaghrat. More often than not, it so happens that because of the dispersal of the cattle population over several hilly areas in Jaddera, the Dispensary Incharge cannot cover all the cattle." (Chamba/Subramanyam/1986)

"The quality of the milch cow is inferior. At best they get 5-6 litres of milk a day. Apart from domestic consumption, the surplus milk is sold in Dharamshala generally to the restaurant owners. The villagers do not use the milk of the goat but they sell them or eat their meat. The villagers care maximum for their oxens." (Kangra/Prabodh/1990)

"Animal Husbandry is one field which requires lot of attention. The cows are generally the upgraded local cows. There is a need to upgrade the quality of the breed. But more important is the provision of the fodder requirements. The only alternative is to go for wasteland development and to plant fodder trees. The initiative must come from the community. If the yield of the milk increases, it will supplement the income of the farmers, as there is a good market for milk and milk products." (Kangra/Prabodh/1990)

MANDI DIVISION

"The average yield of milk of buffaloes (which are more popular than cows) is quite low. Firstly because they are not of very good breed and secondly as good fodder is not available. Something that was leaked by a local boy was quite surprising. All male buffaloes- fed mainly on grass- are gathered and sent to Delhi's slaughter house. This trade has been going on for quite long. Another trade, though harmless, also goes on. Young ones of cattle are brought from plains reared on the grasslands and when they are 'of age' so to speak, they are again sold in the plains." (Bilaspur/Nisha/1987)

Yieldwise, the cattle of Gujjars produce 10 to 14 litres of milk while those reared by others yields 2-3 litre. (Mandi/Anita/1989)

"The farmers kept sufficient heads of cattle with themselves in order to produce a surplus of 600 Kg of milk every day. The milk is of a low fat content and so the efforts at forming a milk procurement society ended in a failure since the price which the society gave to the milk producer was Rs. 2 per Kg. Now the producers freely mix water in their milk and sell it in the town at the rate of Rs. 6 per Kg." (Mandi/Rajpal/1990)

"There is urgent need to improve the breed of milch animal in the village. There is no use of giving Murra breed buffaloes under IRDP because villagers cannot maintain them. Buffalo bull at the veterinary dispensary should immediately be replaced with a healthy one. Apart from this I suggest one or two buffalo bulls should be given to the villagers free of cost. It would be better if all the local bulls are either castrated or removed from the villages. This will ensure that whole of next generation is cross-breed. This would not involve much expenditure as a Murra bull costs only Rs 500 or so. Cross breed buffaloes and cows will give more milk and will be more adopted to local environment." (Mandi/Agarwal/1985)

From the data gathered by us it is evident that livestock holdings in the sample villages is low. This is primarily due to lack of requisite veterinary facilities in the area and appropriate knowhow with regard to the upkeep of the livestock. Potential for development is enormous and the farmers are also interested in going in for rearing these good variety cattle with a view to initiate Dairy Farming in the area. Their main demand is to have better equipped veterinary hospitals and centres. Another shocking information passed on to us was that the entire milk supply to Barot came from areas falling in Kangra district which are similarly placed with no additional facilities except that they had a good veterinary network and knowhow." (Mandi/Jagdish/1991)

"Though number of animals is quite good, most of them are in poor condition. All the milch animals are of local breed and do not give much milk. Milk yield of many animals is as low as 1 kg per day. There is no conscious effort by the villagers to rear the milch animals on scientific lines." (Mandi/Agarwal/1985)

SHIMLA DIVISION

"In this context the tendency of the Administration to continue to supply IRDP beneficiaries with buffaloes is rather incongruous. Probably a shift is necessary towards other activities in the primary and secondary sector particularly those related to horticulture and floriculture. Fodder plantation also need to be encouraged." (Sol/Rizvi/1988)

Only 20 families are able to sell the surplus. Others find this quantity of milk just enough for self consumption. The milk men from Nahan buy it at roughly Rs. 2.50 per kg whereas it is sold at Rs. 4.00 per kg in Nahan town. Such a miserable plight of the starting point sellers is not unexpected in the absence of any co-operative society that can help them in marketing milk at remunerative prices." (Nahan/Sanjeev/1993)

Recommendations on Animal Husbandry

- Quality of livestock should be upgraded by cross breeding. Male scrub cattle needs to be phased off through a castration programme.
- Fodder and feed supply should be improved. This is an area of high priority in the hills.
- Stall feeding should be adopted widely.
- Sustainability of goats in hill areas needs to be carefully evaluated.

- A system by which pasture regeneration can occur should be developed.
- Veterinary services should be provided.

Forests Fuel and Fodder

KANGRA DIVISION

"The people of this village seem to be well aware of the several advantages they derive, if they stop the denotation of the forests in their village. The *Chipko Movement;* popularised by Sunder Lal Bahuguna has also gained some ground in village Jaddera. It is very interesting to learn from the villagers that, as long back as in 1976, when the government earmarked certain area of forest falling in village Jaddera, for the purpose of making charcoal, the people of this village strongly protested against it and the Forest Department could not enforce the writ of the government in this respect. In a similar manner, the people told me, when in 1983, truck loads of wood, illegally felled from their forests, was being transported out, the people have caught those trucks and the culprits were brought to book. It is also interesting to learn that the Chipko leader, Sunder Lal Bahuguna came to Jaddera on 14.3.1983 and gave a clarion call to the people to preserve their forest wealth, since it prevents soil degradation and causes rains for their crops. Although initially some people were against the Chipko Movement, after the Chipko leader galvanised them, these protesters fell in line. It is also very interesting to learn that although drought has gripped the entire Chamba District, in this village, the impact of drought was only limited to 30 per cent. The credit of this goes to the people of Jaddera, who are championing the cause of *Chipko Movement.*" (Chamba/Subramanyam/1986)

"Villagers have a right in the nearby forest to collect a headload of fuel and fodder. They also have a very important traditional right over trees in the forest once in five year if the same is required for domestic purposes. As this area is Chil area, the villagers can get the tree after a requirement certificate is given by the Patwari and forwarded by the Forest Guard. As the houses have roofs of slates, they require large amount of wood and all the wood is consumed therein. The villagers have no major complain about the enforcement of their rights in the forests." (Kangra/Prabodh/1990)

"Almost all families use firewood as fuel for domestic purposes. The villagers use their rights in the forest to collect the wood. Sometime they do purchase wood and coal from the Gaggal market. Two families in the entire village have gas connections. They have to lift cylinders on their own from the Dharamshala depot and have to do without it in case of scarcity." (Kangra/Prabodh/1990)

"The people are greatly dependent on the forests for fuel-wood and other minor forest products. Kikar, Khiar and Tuni are used as timber. Kainth and Khair branches are used as fuel. Leaves of Plah are used as fodder and also for making plates for eating on social occasions (The names of trees are the local ones). On all uncultivable lands, fuel and fodder trees should be planted so that pressure on forest for fuel wood is reduced. At the same time a third crop (after paddy harvest) of fodder grass like Berseim, oats etc. can be introduced. Also the plantation of Ban Oak, Chir, Bamboo etc. is to be undertaken on waste/degraded lands. Introduction of high yielding fodder grasses such as seteria, white clover and napier etc. is must for improving pastures/grasslands in this area." (Kangra/Dhiman/1988)

"Forest and whole of the area comes under forest land as defined in the Forest Conservation Act, 1980. Leaving the few patches where slate mining is continuing, it is dense forest, which faces imminent threat of being destroyed. A distant view of the hills gives very clear picture of the extent to which forests have been depleted in this area. The village Pradhan says there are at least 25,000 persons getting employment in the slate mining—directly or indirectly, but safely put, this figure shall not be less than 15,000-20,000. Thus he says it is impossible to close the mines as rehabilitation of this huge number is not easy. Though slate mining has been continuing here for centuries, but with the passage of Forest Conservation Act, 1980, H.P. Mines and Minerals

Act, 1982, it is only the lack of political will which is coming in the way in the closure of the mines and quarries. A number of local politicians including Pradhan and MLA (former Pradhan) are actively engaged in the slate mining industry as contractors or transporters. Hence immediate steps are needed to stop the destruction of green forests and to preserve the ecological balance in the area. As far as alternative to slates as roofing material is concerned G.I. sheets or Asbestos cement sheets are available in the market in abundance and at comparable prices." (Kangra/Dhiman/1998)

"As a matter of fact fodder is one of the biggest problems in the village. Its availability in the winter months is very acute. They cut grass in the summer, dry it and then store it but ultimately huge amount of fodder is purchased which is imported from Punjab. The wasteland in the village can be put to use by the community for fuel and fodder needs." (Kangra/Prabodh/1990)

"On all uncultivable lands, fuel and fodder trees should be planted so that pressure on forest for fuelwood is reduced. At the same time a third crop (after paddy harvest) of fodder grass like Berseim, oats etc. can be introduced. Also the plantation of Ban Oak, Chir, Bamboo etc. is to be undertaken on waste/degraded lands. Introduction of high yielding fodder grasses such as seteria, white clover and napier etc. is essential for improving pastures/grasslands in this area." (Kangra/Dhiman/1988)

Mandi Division

"The forests are rich in wild life also. Barking deer and Gural are common alongwith a few leopards. Amongst the birds Munal and Phulgar are the varieties of pheasants present. Munal is often hunted by villager for its beautiful feather. The feather is sold at good price and is pinned to the Himachali cap by the people on special occasions." (Mandi/Anita/1989)

"Lumbering is limited in Jhandutta. The altitude and temperature make fine variety of wood trees- deodars, pine etc. non-existent. On an experimental basis some sagwan trees were planted which has been quite successful. Thus, plantation of this tree could be taken up in a bigger way. This would prove to be very profitable also. At present, though the village is covered under a Chir plantation project of the forest department, there are no dense clusters of trees to be found. The only thick clusters may be found that of the bamboos, used for many domestic and commercial purposes. Moreover, the consciousness for ecosystem preservation is little. The overriding need of fuel wood has made the evil practice quite common- of cutting off branches from the trees. Devoid of leans and source of their life, the trees soon wither away. This is done, surprisingly by a government official of PWD department in his area too. Thus, there is a callous approach towards growth of trees." (Bilaspur/Nisha/1987)

"While surveying the area we were informed of instances of wood being smuggled out of this area and route chosen for transportation of this timber is the pedestrian track which leads to Jogindernagar. The public also indulges in illegal tree felling for constructing their houses." (Mandi/Jagdish/1991)

"Grazing in the forests is common. The fodder scarcity becomes more acute during the winter months when the entire area is covered under snow. In fact, the poor conditions for the survival of the cattle in the area is one of the important causes of the rather moderate success of the IRDP in the Panchayat." (Mandi/Manoj/1988)

"The villagers had customary rights to utilise wood from the forest for the purpose of building houses. Now the hills have become barren due to unrestricted felling and villagers face great difficulty in procuring wood for repair and construction of their houses. Till now there is no problem of fuel wood as requirement of the village is met by lopping the trees standing on private land." (Mandi/Agarwal/1985)

"Most common fuel used is wood. Branches and twigs are available in plenty from the neighbouring forest areas. Gobar gas plants have also been introduced. However, out of the 15 installed, only 2-3 are working efficiently and the rest are in a state of disrepair. Most of them are suffering from basic design fault. Also, the plants do well only in summer since in winters, due to low temperatures enough gas is not produced by the plant. Often, enough cow dung is not available since at least 2-3 cattle head are required to run a single gobar gas plant." (Mandi/Rajpal/1990)

"The Block Authorities have done commendable work in the field of propagation of cheaper and safer way to cook food by building smokeless chullhas and distributing pressure cookers etc." (Bilaspur/Nisha/1987)

Shimla Division

"Wood for building purposes is sufficiently available as the villagers have recorded TD rights in the nearby forest lands. However, the villagers do feel a shortage of firewood for which women and children have to often trek for quite some distance. All the three villages have electricity reflecting the general trend as 100% of the villages are recorded in the 1981 census to have electric supply. However there is no arrangement for street lighting." (Sol/Rizvi/1988)

"Kerosene stove and cooking gas are commonly in vogue. Wood is obtained from private land for fuel and construction purposes. The village is totally electrified and there is no scarcity of power." (Sol/Vivek/1989)

"The forest cover is barely 4 to 5 per cent against the stipulated average of 60 per cent by the department of Environment for the hilly areas. Most of the forests have been denuded in the last 5-6 years more as a consequence of human avarice than due to any side effect of development. The unscrupulous felling of the trees has been on account of quarrying of lime-stone which is the feed stock for various cement factories coming up in the industrial vicinity of Kala Amb. (Nahan/Sanjeev/1993)

Recommendations for Rural Energy

- Alternative fuel resources should be encouraged (solar, photovoltaic, hydro, wind, biogas, LPG).
- Non conventional energy systems must be introduced on a wider basis.

- Energy options must be made affordable in price, in fact, definitely cheap if people are to shift away from fuel wood for domestic energy use to other forms of energy.
- Energy conservation methods must be encouraged (smokeless chullha, pressure cooking).

Co-operatives and Rural Credit

"A co-operative society called Barot Co-operative and Marketing Society does not cater to the demands of the area. The village extension officers of Agriculture and Horticulture Departments are stationed at Barot. These officers hardly visit the area under their jurisdiction and provide necessary guidance to the needy. As far as credit facilities are concerned there are branches of H.P. State Co-operative Bank and Himachal Gramin Bank stationed at Barot. A branch of Lead Bank of Mandi District i.e. Punjab National Bank is in Multhan which lies in the area of Kangra district just 500 mtrs. away from Barot. The two Banks have not provided any loan for horticultural purposes to the farmers of the sample villages. The crop insurance scheme is also not operative in the area. This came to our knowledge when we were told by the villagers of Rooland that last year when their crop was destroyed completely due to severe hailstorm, no compensation was defrayed to them under this scheme. The banks in Barot mostly cater to the demands of the employees of PSEB (Punjab State Electricity Board) and HPSEB (Himachal Pradesh State Electricity Board) and businessmen." (Mandi/Jagdish/1991)

"Credit requirements of the villagers are very limited. They need money for marriage of children, or some other such social celebration. An average villager has to spend about Rs. 8,000 to Rs. 10,000 on the marriage of his son or daughter. There is no particular community or family involved in money lending business as such. Loans are generally arranged from relatives or friends which are mostly interest free. Sometimes interest at the rate of 12 to 15% is also paid. There is no other source of consumption loans as primary credit society of Dharampur panchayat is defunct for last few years. This society was running well till 1969. In 1970

Chand Lal of Bardana (village under study) became its Chairman. Money has allegedly been misappropriated by him with the connivance of co-operative inspector. The society is now under liquidation." (Mandi/Anita/1989)

"Since 23.2.1953 Primary Agriculture Cooperative Society is working effectively in the village of Una. It has truly brought cooperation and interaction among the various communities of the village. The total membership of this society is 552, which itself speaks a lot of good about its working. This society is run in its own building which constructed in 1976. Apart from consumer goods, fertilizers and agriculture implements are also sold by this society. The annual turn over of this society ranges from 1.6 lakhs. It has also distributed loan to the tune of 23 thousand to the scheduled castes members. The most impressive thing is that, it is earning a handsome profit regularly, which is distributed among the members." (Una/Baldi/1985)

"There is a co-operative society called the Anji Matla Cooperative Society which essentially does money lending business. Taking loans from the co-operative society has become a very lucrative proposition as loan waiver has become the order of the day. No body is interested in repaying loans anywhere as everyone is confident that it would be waived off after sometime." (Sol/Vivek/1989)

"Since most of the farmers of this village are small and marginal farmers, in 90% of the cases, the produce is meant for domestic consumption. In a few other cases, where marketable surplus exists, they sell their produce at Chamba. The Government of H.P. through the Co-operative Societies and the Department of Agriculture, supplies the farmers with improved quality of seeds; fertilizer; pesticides and weedicides at a subsidised price and thus helps the small and marginal farmers. This village also receives such benefits." (Chamba/Subramanyam/1986)

"Although most of the people, who are below the poverty line in this village, are eligible to receive loans from the government under various anti-poverty programmes, yet; some of them prefer to approach the local Sahukar for loans, mainly because they can secure loans very easily without going through the rigmarole of multifarious bureaucratic channels. Moreover, the rate of interest, the Sahukars charge is 20 per cent only, which is not exorbitantly high. It is understood that there are four Sahukars operating in this village. Loans are secured by farmers against mortgage of their land/house. There are12 families, who are indebted not only to Sahukars but also to Co-operative Societies. It is very interesting to note that there is no practice of bonded labour in this village. For that matter, in the whole of H.P. such cases can be counted on fingers." (Chamba/Subramanyam/1986)

"The marketing arrangements are dismal in these two panchayats. The Barot Co-Operative and Marketing Society is almost defunct to the extent that it does not provide marketing assistance to the needy farmers at all. Its only function that came to our notice was to transport PDS goods to some of its sub depots in the area. It would seem that in the villages of the higher hills, group based activities would have better chances of success than the competitive individual based activities. Unfortunately this is not borne out in the field." (Mandi/Jagdish/1991)

Recommendations in Agriculture and Allied Sector

The people need not bring more land under agriculture as it would lead to bringing very fragile areas under the plough and lead to soil degradation. The emphasis should be on strengthening PDS and providing cash to people through horticulture. The steep slopes, unterraced agriculture should be phased out. Efforts are necessary for diversification of horticulture, apiculture, and floriculture in a multi-varietal context. High value low volume approach should be taken for agricultural, horticultural and similar other crops. Off season vegetables should be grown and marketed in plain areas for income generation.

The extension agencies should make special efforts to reach out to women as most of the work including tending of cattle is done by them. Yet whenever training camps or the T and V personnel visit the villages they only contact the menfolk. The training of the agriculture inspectors must include their gender sensitisation.

Consolidation of fragmented holdings in the hills must also be an important priority. In the hills consolidation has its own limitations as the land is not of uniform quality as in Punjab, Western UP and Haryana. Here the farmer tries to minimise his risk and often would like to have lands of different quality. The farmers to some extent do exchange the lands at their own level keeping in mind the quality and value.

There is need for proper information dissemination. The farmers are utterly confused whether to use organic or inorganic manure. The Krishi Vigyan Kendras and other extension agencies have not been able to fulfil this role in Himachal.

Land use and Crops

- Information related to new farming techniques should be available at the village level through block agencies.
- Land/lab relationship must be based on proven demonstrations in actual field conditions.
- Existing Krishi Vigyan Kendra and other organizations should make information more easily available to farmers for extension and training at district level with sub-centers in production areas.
- Women should be encouraged to take up extension jobs in the hill region.
- Efficient and swift seed certification system should be developed in the hills and seeds and plant material used in the hills should be grown in the hills.
- Mechanism to test high yielding seeds and distribute quickly should be employed.
- Biotechnology should be used for producing disease free seed and plant material.
- A decentralised agrometeorological information system should be developed to reduce risks and protect the profits of the growers.
- Integrated Pest Management system should be adopted with priority given to biological control.

- Total available land in hill areas should be mapped out accounting for macro and micro climates to determine what can be optimally grown.
- Detailed land capability profile should be generated to indicate the land's potential micro-watershed wise.
- On the basis of these profiles the people can be convinced what is in the best interest of their families and village.
- A widespread demonstration approach should be used, allowing the people to choose what they can grow successfully.
- In converting sloping lands to tree or grass cover, suitable compensation must be given.
- Efforts should be made to preserve varieties of traditional cereal crops.
- Animal and human population has to be related to the resource base. This will require suitable and dynamic demographic planning in ways acceptable to the people.
- Watershed should be taken as the primary area of planning.
- Viable size of mountain watershed should be determined.
- Sprinkler and drip irrigation systems should be implemented.
- Hydrams lift irrigation systems should be used in suitable slopey, riverside locations.
- If soils are protected water regimes will improve.
- Spring water resources should be preserved. This will require establishment of spring water sanctuaries.
- Water harvesting should be adopted.
- Moisture conserving agronomic techniques should be adopted.
- Stream and flow data should be generated for use of water in power generation.
- Co-ordination among various watershed departments and multi-disciplinary teams should be ensured
- Role of NGOs is very important as communicators, facilitators, and model builders; but they cannot replace local institutions, they can supplement development and provide the impulse for eco-friendly development based on people's full involvement.

Women's issues in Agriculture

- Women are the backbone of the hill economy.
- Women must be educated so that they can teach their families and villages. Women can play a vital role in extension work in the hills.
- Health/family welfare programs with orientation towards family planning must be implemented.
- Agricultural implements suitable for use by women should be developed.

RURAL INDUSTRY AND LIVELIHOODS

Himachal is predominantly an agricultural economy and the other sectors play a small role. Cottage industries or other forms of self-employment are restricted to a few districts. Unemployment is a major problem amongst the educated. Himachal is a fairly literate state and hence there is a desire for white collar jobs. The extent of able bodied employment can be measured from the fact that each household would have atleast one such unemployed youth. Employment in the villages is generally partial depending upon the season. Apart from agriculture the other sources of livelihood are derived from employment in the Army and government service and therefore some of the districts of Himachal like Kangra and Hamirpur thrive on a money order economy.

The remarks of the Officer Trainees are fairly insightful. The region-wise remarks are reproduced below:-

Kangra Division

"There are few families in the village doing the traditional job of ironsmith and pottery respectively. Two ex-servicemen have started their pottery workshop catering basically to the five villages of the Panchayat. They seldom sell their produce in the market of Dharamshala but primarily rely on the barter system within the Panchayat. There is a strong solidarity for economic and social relations within the unit of Panchayat. The villagers consider a thread of commonality to be running across the Panchayat." (Kangra/Prabodh/1990)

"Another subsidiary occupation of the villagers is to work as casual labour for the construction and developmental work carried out by PWD. and the block agencies especially during the lean season between the months of December to March. The rate paid for a day of casual labour is Rs. 22." (Kangra/Prabodh/1990)

"Kangra district has the proud distinction of contributing handsomely to the recruitment of armed forces and recently to paramilitary forces as well. Padher is no exception to the rule. This year two village lads were selected by CRPF in their regular recruitment camp in the district. There are atleast 30 persons from this village in different government departments generally in class 4 and 3 categories. Selling of milk in the town also fetch some money. Many families in the village have received pack animals under the IRDP and Antodaya programme which are used by them on hire basis for transporting mainly construction material both within and without the village." (Kangra/Prabodh/1990)

"Villagers still insist on government employment more so as they are educated and white collar jobs carry a great deal of social status. But otherwise they would prefer to ply their own taxis due to tourist inflow in the region. Not many want vocational training as they do not foresee much scope in it. As the population is scarce and scattered there is also not much interest in adding to the already existing shops of provisions. At best they suggest a plant to manufacture paper out of the trees from the leaves of Chil tree. But such a plant near Baijnath is running in great losses.

The economy of village depends heavily on agriculture and allied activities and there is very little scope for any industry or business. There is one flour mill with a rice sheller attached to it which is run by a brahmin family. As this is the only flour mill and rice sheller in the village, owner is having good income from it. It runs on electricity. Apart from this there is one water-mill which is operative for only six months in a year. This is owned by a scheduled caste family. One cobbler makes shoes to cater for the local requirement. Market for his product is limited to 40 families of the village, out of which many prefer to buy shoes in the city only. Another factor which has affected his business is preference of villagers for plastic shoes over leather shoes as later one costlier. There are two blacksmiths in the village who make farm equipments and also repair them. Age old system of paying the artisans in kind still continues and a blacksmith is given 20 kg of rice and 10 kg of wheat by every family in a year for the repair of agricultural implements. There is no carpenter or weaver in the village. For these works villagers depend on artisans of adjoining villages.

There is no cash crop in the village. Villagers get cash money mostly by wage employment. Two or three families sell small quantity of milk to Dharampur which has some demand because of being block headquarters. The villagers buy things of daily consumption like toilet items, clothes etc. from Dharampur or Sarkaghat. Recently a provisional store has been opened in the village by an IRDP beneficiary. This shop is running well.

"The farmers are usually unemployed during the months of December to March. This is the period when most of the development works through the Block are done. By this the agricultural labours earn Rs. 20-25 per day by working as casual labour in any construction works of the village." (Kangra/Murti/1989)

"Jajmani relationships have weaken over the years, as the payments made in kind are found to be insufficient as compared to labour rendered. This has led to monetization of the economy. Blacksmiths, Chamars, Barbers etc. leaving their home-base workshops have opened shops on road side in the same village and they accept the payments in cash only, hence traditional system of division of labour has shown decline." (Kangra/Dhiman/1988)

"The women and men also work as labourers in the nearby tea gardens. Though only three women are regularly employed on the rolls of the tea gardens, about 20-30 of them are gainfully employed on the tea gardens round the year. During the plucking time the employment percentage goes up." (Kangra/Prabodh/1990)

"In the name of village industry, there is just one *"atta chakki"* in the entire village which is owned by one of the

Upadhya. The Chakki caters to the requirement of the Panchayat villages and the adjoining area. It employs one local boy." (Kangra/Prabodh/1990)

Mandi Division

"Unemployment is not there in the village in the true sense of the term. Instead underemployment is rampant. Pressure on land is quite high and also because the yield is low. But the hills demand more input of labour for the same yield as in plains. Nearly the entire family barring small kids, is engaged in the agricultural operation. The gain from agriculture is not enough to support the families. So people supplement their income from different sources viz. cattle rearing, forest labourers, tailoring, etc. Only one person from the surveyed village cluster has gone into government job. He has studied upto B.Sc. from Mandi College and is a school teacher at Karsog." (Mandi/Anita/1989)

"Animal husbandry is only subsidiary occupation of villagers and there is no family which depends solely on animal husbandry for its livelihood. Main reason of this is absence of market for milk. Nearest road is 5 kms away. Most of the people own two-three milch animals only and hence it is not economical for them to take the milk to the cities. There is no co-operative society which may help in marketing of milk.

The village has alongwith traditional industry, developed some other enterprising works too. These include furniture industry and a small shop that assembles a sewing machine. The industries include a leather shop, tin smelters four furniture industries, a saw mill and some flour mill. The leather shop is small and makes rough leather shoes for common use. Unlike Chamba, the area does not specialise in design in leather shoes and slippers. The furniture industry in the village number two (not including the traditional carpenters who make household goods at a very small scale). One Naib Subedar, a Rajput by Caste, after retirement from the army has set up a small furniture shop. Incidentally, he is also one of the most prosperous persons in the village. The other industry 'Durga Furniture Industry' is the most interesting study.

The proprietor Mr. Devi Chand is an IRD beneficiary, who has, since he took loan, has prospered manifold." (Chamba/ Subramanyam/1986)

"A sewing machine assembling shop has come to the forefront in the village. The sewing machine is named 'Tohfa'. The parts are brought from Ludhiana and assembled in Jhandutta. It is sold at the rate of Rupees five hundred and fifty. Most of the machines are sold at the time of marriage." (Bilaspur/Nisha/1987)

"Animal husbandry is the only subsidiary occupation of villagers and there is no family which depends solely on animal husbandry for its livelihood. Main reason of this is absence of market for milk. Nearest road is 5 km away. Most of the people own two-three milch animals only and hence it is not economical for them to take the milk to the cities. There is no co-operative society which may help in marketing of milk." (Mandi/Agarwal/ 1985)

"Barot has a trout breeding farm which sells eggs outside instead of developing fisheries in the area despite the fact that necessary infrastructure is available with the District Fisheries Officer posted there. The extent of public involvement in the fisheries project is only to locals employed in the farm. Since the river Uhal and its tributaries provide great opportunities for making fisheries a viable project for the public, their involvement should necessarily be ensured in order to make their already pathetic conditions better. It is ironical to note that every year one or other dignitary visits the area for Angling.

No bee keeping activities came to our notice in the entire area whereas potential for the same is great. Poultry is not absolutely absent from the area but is confined to very few households. Whichever household has hens they are only for personal use. There is only one Government hatchery functioning in the district at Sundernagar which has not taken this programme to remote areas like this, though there is enough potential to develop this economic activity under NREP." (Mandi/Jagdish/ 1991)

"The government opens relief works to provide wage employment to the people. Some of the orchards in the region, however, give employment to some of the agriculturists during the plucking season. Others find employment on private works, road construction and other employment guaranteeing schemes of the government. Some go as far as Kulu and Lahaul-Spiti to work there during apple and potato season. (Mandi/Manoj/1988)

Second major occupation in the area is cattle rearing. All the Muslims in the Chohar valley belong to the Gujjar tribe. Their main occupation is rearing buffaloes. They generally keep herds of buffaloes. Earlier they used to be nomads but now they are undergoing a transition to the settled agriculturist stage of social evolution.

"Sale of milk and milk products is done by the Gujjars. But whereas earlier the Gujjars nearly monopolised the entire dairy business, now with increasing number of milch cattle, this monopoly has ended. The people complained of low returns from milk in recent years in general. This can be attributed to the increasing number of cattle in the area due to conscious encouragement by government. The milk supply has gone up in this area with no outlets leading to areas with higher demand. As a result, prices have gone down. A Chilling plant in the area could improve the economic condition of the people." (Mandi/Anita/1989)

"Apart from these, there are five families of black-smiths who are also agriculturists. Three families of Scheduled Caste are also engaged in house construction activities." (Mandi/Anita/1989)

"The villagers also made slippers out of straw called poolas which is useful for walking on snow also." (Mandi/Anita/1989)

"Six households have also taken up tailoring as a profession. Five of these have been trained under TRYSEM. One person has taken training for watch repair but there is no scope for income through this work in the village. Another person who learned typing, sits at the sub-tehsil office and types applications." (Mandi/Anita/1989)

"They would be willing to work in hotels and factories of far-away places but are constrained from obtaining a job in Punjab, Haryana and Delhi owing to a number of reasons. Firstly, there is an absence of network of their fellow Himachalis who are working in those areas so as to enable them to secure a job through their recommendations and connections. Secondly, the social structure still retains very strong filial ties making the presence of sound at various family functions nearly mandatory. The men can not fulfil these obligations if they are working in distant lands. Thirdly, the army had been a major employer in this area until very recently when it adopted a system of recruitment based on quotas for every state. This has led to a steep fall in the intake of Himachalis by the army thus drying up this major source of employment for the residents of Kehanwal. This realization is slowly setting in now and it would take them some time to make a switchboard to the process of going to distant lands in search of jobs (army recruitment used to be done at their doorsteps) and to settle for lowly paid private sector jobs." (Mandi/Rajpal/1990)

"Gopal, a Harijan, was one of the more enterprising individuals in the village. He had not only set up a flour mill, a small poultry unit and a cattle farm but also had his own piece of land to till. He had only two children and had got himself sterilised after the second. Both his children are studying in the village primary school and he is full of hopes and dreams about the future." (Mandi/Rajpal/1990)

"Similarly, poultry activity in the area too has failed to take off. This activity has proved to be unviable not because of its cost economics but because of a high mortality rate among the chicks due to diseases and frequent failure of electricity." (Mandi/Rajpal/1990)

Shimla Division

"Promotion of agro-based industries is one area that needs a lot of attention. It will ensure greater returns for the cultivators, as well as generate employment in the vicinity of the villages." (Sol/Rizvi/1988)

"It was very disheartening for me to see that not a single village or cottage industry was functioning in this village. The villagers told that the hilly terrain and the apathy of government to develop industries in this area is responsible for this. This contention of the villagers is somewhat right, however, I feel that the lack of entrepreneurship among the inhabitants of this village is also one of the main reason behind the no-development of the cottage industries. There are many small and cottage industries like Ban-making and Bamboo work, Candle making, papad making etc. which could be developed in this area. But this requires an enterprising person and a responsive and helpful bureaucracy which could assist a person by providing information and adequate loan." (Una/Baldi/1985)

No village industries exists. (Sol/Rizvi/1988)

"The art of weaving creates carpets, sweaters and the famous Himachali caps. Weaving is a common hobby among the families which can create a surplus from agriculture. But it is seldom marketed and, therefore, it will be futile to discuss their earnings at large though there are two isolated cases to be discussed later. On the whole about 40 families are engaged in weaving. As far as raw material is concerned, they avail cotton locally and buy wool from the market. There are no marketing facilities available and the middlemen are completely absent. Any indebtedness, whatsoever, is confined to loans taken from the co-operative societies.

The otherwise bleak picture on this front has two glaring exceptions. Smt. Vimla Devi and Smt. Sajno are the harbingers in the secondary sector. They supplement their respective husband's income by earning roughly Rs. 300 per month and they have to really struggle hard for this pittance." (Nahan/Sanjeev/1988)

Heavy Dependence on Government

In Himachal due to its geographical constraints as well as poor agricultural and industrial base, there is a heavy dependency on Government for employment. Being a small State and easy accessibility to the administration and peoples' representatives there is tremendous pressure to employ more and more into Government services. Himachal is probably one of the most overstuffed and best paymaster of its employees in the country. Due to this much of the government funds are exhausted in disbursing salaries and meeting administrative costs only thereby contributing minimally to the programme as such.

"Unemployment is one problem which will explode very soon in the State. There are not many avenues and everybody expects it to be the duty of the government to provide them with employment. Unfortunately, this is the impression which is given to them by the politicians also and therefore there is a strong resentment against the policy of the present government to freeze the employment level." (Kangra/Prabodh/1990)

"This reliance on government for employment has adversely affected the growth of enterprise not only here but even in rich areas of apple belt in Upper Himachal." (Kangra/Prabodh/1990)

"I noticed that villagers were very receptive to the government scheme of giving subsidy for building of individual latrines. They are still waiting for the subsidy of Rs. 1200 though they could've constructed the latrine much before at a lower cost. Even under the liberal scheme of the government if they receive the subsidy now, they would end up spending more money from their pocket but these days subsidy culture has penetrated deep as subsidy has become a great motivating factor." (Kangra/Prabodh/1990)

"With mere agriculture and its allied operations unable to sustain the families depending on it, the families have to per force look towards other sources of income to see them through the entire year. This necessitates a high dependence on government jobs and sundry income-generating labour activities in the towns to provide the family with additional sources of income. With state government jobs difficult to come by, a trend towards increased reliance on service in the armed forces is also discernible. However, due to hitherto low levels of literacy and awareness in the state, most of the recruitment in the district has been in the ranks rather than in the officer cadre of the armed forces." (Mandi/Rajpal/1990)

"My study of the area showed that the high literacy level of the region has resulted in the youth not taking an active interest in the cinema generating activities within the village. They have become aimless wanderers in the village who are constantly on the look out for a Government job. The people are not imbued with any degree of entrepreneurial spirit which might enable them to set up income generating production units within the village." (Mandi/Rajpal/1990)

Recently higher levels of literacy have also resulted in an aversion to manual work. It is impossible to find local labour in the village which would be willing to work at the minimum wage rate of Rs. 22/- per day. Hence, labour has either to be imported from outside the region or has to be procured from within the region at an exorbitant rate of Rs. 35-40 per day. This makes the construction of projects and undertaking of any economic activity in the region economically unviable and hence the region continues to suffer the pangs of underdevelopment." (Mandi/Rajpal/1990)

"Most of the families have one or more of their members engaged in some job or the other. About 225 people are employees with the government. (Mandi/Rajpal/1990)

"Since most of the people are underemployed, about 100-200 people seek employment as daily wage labourers as well. They work as construction labour or work on the roads for the PWD in various parts of Mandi district." (Mandi/Rajpal/1990)

"The State Government distributes subsidy for setting up fish ponds to Scheduled Castes in the form of net, boats, tent etc. But there is no such fish pond in our village and people prefer to walk 3-4 kms down the road and try their luck in the lake. Fishing is banned by district administration from mid July to mid August to facilitate the breeding of young ones.

In all, one can't really say that the economic structure of the village is diversified and the stress to the day is on primary activities. The money generation in the village is from those serving either in armed forces or in the plains. The village itself offers very little prospect for the young men to take up any secondary or tertiary occupation. Thus, much needs, to be done to promote agro-industries." (Bilaspur/Nisha/1987)

Income, Minimum Wages and Bonded Labour

The business of minimum wages is a serious affair in the State and the government sincerely acts as a model employer in this regard. In most of the areas the rates for manual labour and semi-skilled trades is normally more than the minimum wages fixed by the government and therefore the state does not have serious problems in this regard. Many of the developmental works undertaken in rural areas employ labour from outside. One can often see Nepali or Bihari labour working throughout the state.

Bonded labour is not completely unknown in the State. A milder form of it exists in some parts of district Sirmaur. Under this system, known as Bethu system, the labourer works at the house/fields of the employer in return of wages, food, shelter and money during social occasions. The origins of this system lie in the fact that this region of the State is one of the most backward, where there are very few jobs or economic opportunities. The OTs have recorded their findings in the following manner:-

"Minimum wages in Solan is Rs. 20 per day but no labourer charges less than Rs. 25 per day. The demand of labour exceeds its supply and Bihari labourers are employed for most of the works as they provide cheap labour. The local labourer charges Rs. 35 per day while the migrant labourer does work for Rs. 25-30 per day." (Sol/Vivek/1989)

It is very interesting to note that there is no incidence of bonded labour in this village. But some residents who are Nepalies are being subjected to this practice of bonded labour. (Bilaspur/Nita/1988)

The prescribed minimum wage for agriculture and other labour is Rs. 20. But it is usually difficult to engage labour for less than Rs. 25 in the area. This was verified by me when I asked some of the labourers working in the construction of a building in the village.

"The labourers did not have to organize themselves in order to get these wages. This developed when the government agencies were paying these rates for works undertaken by them which in turn increased the awareness of the people and has become a part and parcel of payment of regular minimum wage." (Kangra/Murti/1989)

"Majority of the labour force is local, and it becomes a sort of specialised labour, which is quite organized and can dictate its terms to contractors and as such the wage rate recorded is

Rs. 26 for unskilled and Rs. 40 for skilled categories. In addition to this, large number of labourers are engaged in the transportation of slates to the roadheads, and loading and unloading of the slates on trucks. And 1200 migratory mule owners are also dependent for their livelihood on the slate mining industry." (Kangra/Dhiman/1988)

"The minimum wages fixed by the Government is Rs 15/- per day, the family employing them customarily provides meals and tea, twice a day also. However, there is not much work for these labourers in the village itself, since less than 10 families were employing labour in their agricultural operations and at other times they must go out to other villages to find work, or must work on daily wages in the PWD or I and PH departments." (Bilaspur/Khachi/1988)

The following table 2.8 depicts the income levels of the population surveyed :

Table 2.8 : Income level of population

Sl.No.	*Income range*	*No. of households*	*%age*
1.	<200	3	10
2.	200 to 300	3	10
3.	300 to 500	10	33.3
4.	500 to 1000	4	13.3
5.	1000 to 1500	4	13.3
6.	> 1500	5	16.6

The table depicts that 33.3 per cent earned between 300 to 500 rupees per month and 20 per cent just manage around 300 rupees, half of which earning below Rs. 200. 16.6 per cent earning more than Rs. 1500 does not mean that they are well off because size of family is large and most of them indulge in drinking regularly. Some of the households in the last group has atleast one member permanently employed. (Mandi/Jagdish/1991)

The income of the people of the area was crudely estimated for households and per capita income was calculated in the following manner:

Table 2.9 : Per capita income of household

S.No	*Item*	*Household income (Rs.)*	*Per capita*
1.	Agriculture:		
	a) Rabi	2500.00	412.51
	b) Kharif	3000.00	495.01
	c) Fruits and minor forest produce	50.00	8.25
2.	Animal Husbandry	1500.00	247.50
3.	Wages (mainly forest and PWD labourers)	1000.00	165.00
4.	Household industry (Threshing machine, flour milling machine etc.	700.00	115.50
	Total	8750.00	1443.77

"The per capita income from various sources worked out to be 1443.77 which is very low compared to the states per capita income of Rs. 3614.00. Though the estimate is very crude and may be higher if properly calculated, it gives a broad idea of the economic condition of the area. Even if the estimate goes upto Rs. 2000.00 it is nowhere close to the State's figure." (Mandi/Anita/1989)

"Since income is quite low in the area, high indebtedness was expected. But the level of indebtedness was not as high as expected. The needs of the people are very limited and hence requirement of large sum of money as loan is rare. The existence of moneylenders in true sense of the term is not there. Money required by villagers is generally borrowed from the relatively prosperous households. Indebtedness due to IRDP loans is quite extensive since people have gone in for milch cattle purpose. Some families have brought threshers." (Mandi/Anita/1989)

"The village look as if in an idyllic situation. It is nestled amidst the low ranges of Lower Sivaliks. If there is not great richness, there is no obvious, darkening poverty. There are no extreme differences in level of living and tending of farms." (Bilaspur/Nisha/1987)

"A look at the estimates of income of the surveyed families reveals that those families which do not have any member employed in the services on the government are barely being able to eke a living out of their meagre land holdings. The better off families in the village have their source of relative prosperity in non-agricultural activities like government services and petty shopkeeping." (Mandi/Rajpal/1990)

Small Savings

The hill people are a frugal lot and therefore save as much as possible. The bulk of savings take place in the district of Kangra, Hamirpur, Una and Mandi districts of the state. The State actively promotes small savings and the district administration is put under substantial pressure to mobilise small savings from the public. In fact Small Savings constitute an important source of revenue mobilisation for the State. The comments recorded by the OTs for Kangra would be useful.

"The district has been doing very good in augmenting small saving and every year good amount of prize money is coming for overshooting the targets. This tendency is more in the families who receive money order from the member of family working in government service outside. Majority of the saving is done in the branch post office in the village itself. Almost every household has an account though majority of them are of small amounts generally about Rupees hundred or so." (Kangra/Prabodh/1990)

"The saving is result of activities other than agriculture and villagers are not very keen on investing it in agriculture as they are not much convinced about the viability of the land with them. They do purchase jewellery especially for marriageable daughters but they buy silver ornaments. The increasing price of gold has rendered it as unavailable material for them. There is no family in the village which is in the business of money lending though the shopkeeper does give goods on credit on personal relations." (Kangra/Prabodh/1990)

HEALTH AND FAMILY WELFARE

Demographic Trends

The population of the State registered a growth of 20.79 per cent as against 23.56 per cent at all India level during the decade 1981-91, thus recording a decline of 2.92 per cent as compared to the preceding decade 1971-81. This has been possible through a three-pronged strategy of intensive health cover, improvement in literacy rates specially among the women and making family planning a people's movement alongwith a positive thrust of incentives. The important comparative indicators are presented in the following Table 2.10:

Table 2.10 : Health and family welfare

	Item	*Unit*	*1971 Census*	*1981 Census*	*1991 Census*
1.	Population				
	(a) Total	Lakh Persons	34.60	42.80	51.70
	(b) Male	Lakh Persons	17.67	21.70	26.17
	(c) Female	Lakh Persons	16.93	21.10	25.53
2.	Scheduled Castes	-do-	7.70	10.54	13.10
3.	Scheduled Tribes	-do-	1.42	1.77	2.18
4.	Density of Population	Persons	62	77	93
5.	Decennial Growth	%	23.04	23.71	20.79
6.	Literacy Percentage				
	(a) Total	%	31.96	42.48	63.86
	(b) Male	%	43.20	53.19	75.36
	(c) Female	%	20.20	31.46	52.13
7.	Percentage composition				
	(a) Rural Population	%	93.00	92.40	91.31
	(b) Urban Population	%	7.00	7.60	8.69
8.	Percentage of total Population				
	(a) Scheduled Castes	%	22.30	24.62	25.34
	(b) Scheduled Tribes	%	4.00	4.61	4.22
9.	Sex Ratio : Females per 100 Males	958	973	976	

Coverage of Health Services in HP

The growth and **coverage of health services in HP** has seen a phenomenal change since Independence and more so in the 1980s. The table 2.11 would throw some light on the situation:

Table 2.11 : Coverage of Health Services in Himachal Pradesh

Year	*Hospitals**	*Primary Health Centres including CHC*	*Allopathic Dispensaries including PHC*	*Ayurvedic Dispensaries*	*Health Sub-Centres*	*Total***
1980	58	77	196	404	651	1386
1985	73	161	214	430	1299	2170
1989	73	200	199	539	1614	2625
1990	73	225	197	539	1851	2885
1991	73	225	197	539	1851	2885
1992	74	227	197	539	1851	2888
1993	69	245	178	527	1852	2871**

* Includes Ayurvedic Hospitals.
** Less due to upgradations.

It would be seen that the growth of medical institutions in the Pradesh has resulted in better medical care to the people. This is reflected in considerable lowering of crude birth and death rattes and significant improvement in the infant mortality rate. The comparative data on vital statistics for Himachal Pradesh and all-India for 1991-92 is as under:

Parameter	*All India*	*Himachal Pradesh*
1 Birth / thousand (1991)	29.3	28.4
2 Death / thousand (1991)	9.8	8.9
3 Infant Mortality / thousand (1991)	80	75
4 Couple Protection Rate as on 31-3-92	43.5%	54.1%

Decadal Variation in the Population

The decadal variation in the population since 1901 has been reported as under in respect of Himachal Pradesh :

Year	*Persons*	*%age Decadal Variation*
1901	1,920,294	..
1911	1,896,944	- 1.22
1921	1,928,206	+ 1.65
1931	2,029,113	+ 5.23
1941	2,263,245	+ 11.54
1951	2,385,981	+ 5.42
1961	2,812,463	+ 17.87
1971	3,460,434	+ 23.04
1981	4,280,818	+ 23.71
1991	5,170,877	+ 20.79

Notings on Family Welfare and Health Services

Although the State has not done very badly in the sphere of family planning, the reactions noted in the reports are mixed. The approach to family welfare is largely target oriented. No mention is made about long term measures like, literacy or strengthening of the health-care system. The comments are typical of the District Administration led model of controlling population.

"It shows that impact of the family planning in this village is not much. The village, though on the state highway and only 6 kms away from the district headquarters, with well connected mettled road going through the village also. Unlike other places of Una , it has very few people in army and other civil services. Only six persons are serving in army. One Colonel who is now retired and is settled down in Chandigarh. There is only one M.B.B.S. doctor from here earlier it used to be the part of Punjab and it was a tehsil of Hoshiarpur district in Punjab. Mostly benefits have helped the male population more than females on proportionate basis because the disadvantages of all shortcomings are still shared more by weaker sex." (Una/Negi/1985)

The target achievement was not even 35 per cent. This year, however, the district authorities seem to have learnt the lesson the hard way. Sirmour was running a close fourth in the state as on November 20, 1986. The response in the family planning camps which I attended was more than lukewarm. The main hurdle, I felt, was the lackadaisical attitude of the grass-root motivators. Lack of fixation of some realistic targets per functionary had led to diffusion of responsibility among various agencies such as Patvaris, Gram Sewaks, Village Health Worker and Panchayat Secretaries. There were a far more cases of tubectomy than vasectomy. Another effort in the direction of a family planning was the linkage of the performance of a particular Panchayat with the sanctioning of various relief schemes (such as drought relief) for that Panchayat. A good rapport seemed to emerge between the Deputy Commissioner and the Chief Medical Officer and a small part of Red Cross funds was being mooted to be diverted to provide additional incentives to the cases and their motivators. Nevertheless, a healthy competition existed among 4-5 Panchayats only that were vying for the top spot." (Nahan/Sanjeev/1993)

"A hurried conclusion may be drawn that higher castes are more aware and hence have restricted size of their families, but this is not true in the case of this village. Brahmins and Rajputs have divided their joint families into small families." (Nahan/Sanjeev/1993)

"However, family planning programmes has got some impetuous in last few years and people are voluntarily going for this. The success of family planning can be contributed to this concentrated effort of health department and district administration. Only in last one year three family planning camps have been organized in this very village, which were a grand success. However, tubectomy is more acceptable compared to vasectomy. Now a days villagers are aware of the benefit of the family planning and accept this without any hitch." (Una/Negi/1985)

"There has been a rise in population. The female health worker maintains a register of eligible couples and guides them about family planning. But the feeling of having a son is very great among the families and poses a problem. The average number of children in the families is three to four and the average number of members in each household is six to seven." (Kangra/Murati/1989)

"The reasons for high growth rate seems to be the lack of proper implementation of family planning programmes, illiteracy and practically no emigration from these areas. One more reason that can be assigned here is that population in these areas survives on agriculture and allied activities which according to them needs more hands. Lack of awareness among people could be one of the main causes." (Mandi/Jagdish/1991)

"A hurried conclusion may be drawn that higher castes are more aware and hence have restricted size of their families, but this is not true in the case of this village. Brahmins and Rajputs have divided their joint families into small families. As higher caste people own comparatively large land desire among the brothers to separate their shares is more. Some families were divided to gain double benefits from the Integrated Rural Development Programme. The scheduled caste people do not own much of land and depend on manual work for their livelihood. As they do not have much to divide, they have preferred to maintain joint families. This proposition is supported by the fact that adult-children ratio of people belonging to Scheduled Castes is 2.2 as against 1.6 of higher castes." (Mandi/Agarwal/1985)

"Though 82 per cent of the families fall in the range 2-10 members, the number of single member families is also not very insignificant. The reason for this is that many of them got themselves so recorded so as to be eligible for various Government developmental and other programmes like IRDP. During my survey, I discovered that only 3 genuine single member families existed—the rest were all fictitious. My criteria for judging a separate, single unit family was whether it had its own separate house and kitchen or not?" (Bilaspur/Khachi/1988)

On the aspect of the quality of health services and facilities provided by the Government health care system the notings are as follows:-

"At the height of the gastroentitis epidemic, some people did have loose motions but because of the panic they rushed the patients to the Zonal Hospital at Dharamshala. Water borne diseases are common and even snake bite deaths are not unreported. There are allegations that people want a certificate regarding snake bite even in case of natural deaths, as relief is admissible for snake bite deaths." (Kangra/Prabodh/1990)

Contrary to the high death rates, the infant (children of less than 5 years in age) mortality is not very high. It varies between 90 per thousand to 101 per thousand. A quick look at the birth and death register suggested that there is no tangible difference between the male and female mortality rate. (Nahan/Sanjeev/1993)

"The people generally had more faith in allopathic though even Ayurvedic medicine was resorted to. There has been no cases of epidemics or malaria in the village nor were there any cases of T.B. About once a month mobile immunisation camps are held here where vaccines are administered for polio, measles, tetanus, DPT etc. Yearly camps are held in the schools where it is administered for children upto 5 years of age and tetanus 10 tetanus 16 for the age groups of 10 and 16 years children respectively." (Kangra/Murty/1989)

"There is one civil dispensary located in the village, manned by one doctor and other staff. The building for this has been provided rent free by Gram Panchayat. Nearest P.H.C. is at Tiara, about 25 km from here. But, District and Zonal Hospitals are located at Dharamsala, 10 km from this village.

Due to high awareness level of the masses, general health standards in the village is very good. All routine cases, are treated in the civil dispensary and those involving major operations are referred to the District Hospital. There is no endemic disease in this area, but as the doctor says a few cases of T.B. are reported among the migrant labourers employed in slatemining industry. G.P. having sufficient resources, contributes a lot to the medical health care, by giving financial assistance and medicines on the recommendation of Doctor. For those cases referred to the places like P.G.I. Chandigarh, it provides the travelling expenses to the local residents." (Kangra/Dhiman/1988)

"Gram Panchayat having sufficient resources, contributes a lot to the medical health care by giving financial assistance and medicines. Rs. 7 lakhs have been spent by Gram Panchayat for construction of building of a 10-bed hospital. This hospital when completed will be a milestone of Panchayat's efforts in health care of the villagers." (Kangra/Dhiman/1988)

"The village has a civil dispensary, one private Ayurvedic clinic. The nearest PHC is at Shahpur which is 7 km away. For any major treatment the district zonal hospital is situated at Dharamsala which is 40 km away. About once a month immunisation camps are held here. Yearly camps are held in the schools." (Kangra/Murthy/1988)

"There is no general tendency of the villagers to pick up any diseases. Water borne diseases are common and even snake bite deaths are not unreported." (Padher/Saxena/1990)

"This village has recently been sanctioned one sub health centre and it is yet to begin functioning. Presently there are no facilities for treatment of patients in Jaddera. Lack of hospital facilities in this village speaks volumes as to why the death rate is so high." (Chamba/Subrahmaniyam/1986)

"One sub centre is existing in this village which is also having shelter in one unhygienic room of primary agriculture co-operative society of the village. This is manned by one trained nurse but she always prefers touring than sitting in the sub centre. Patient generally avoid going to this sub centre because instead of providing medicines generally a list of medicines to be bought from the market is given to the patient

The nearest primary health centre is located 4 km away. No maternity or child welfare centre is working in this village. The nearest maternity centre is 18 km away." (Una/Baldi/1985)

"Large number of people suffer from chronic gastro-intestinal problems caused by water borne organics. There is no P.H.C. or dispensary in the village but Registered Medical Practitioners (RMP) are existing in this village who exploit these people and also give proper medical care. Health Centre is at Una. It is very surprising to see that there is no maternity home at whole of this district.

"Cholera, Malaria, T.B. are by and large people suffer from, and typhoid and highfever also come up. The nutritional status of the population changes ,in fact older generation seem to have better health and new ones are addicted to so many problems like alcoholism, drugs." (Una/Negi/1985)

"Jhandutta is benefited by the presence of a PHC. It is an impressive building and stocked well with medicines. The most common disease prevalent in the village is of gastroentritis and Cholera. Polio etc. is not common but stomach diseases are due to lack of clean drinking water. The deficiency of protein and vitamin rich diet leads to disfiguring of joints and "plegra" is common. Average health of children is not very good, though infant mortality rate is very low." (Bilaspur /Nisha/1987)

"The village civil dispensary has been now in existence for the past 9 years. The dispensary essentially provides OPD and maternal-child health care facilities. The average outturn of patients varies between 15-20 and most of them suffer from either respiratory ailment or gastro-intestinal disorder. The source of these medical problem can be traced to the living conditions of the people in the village. The houses are poorly ventilated and have inadequate accommodation. Malnutrition coupled with contaminated drinking water also contribute towards ill-health." (Bilaspur/Khachi/1986)

"There is a civil dispensary in this village, established 10 years ago. It essentially provides OPD and maternal child health care facilities. The average outturn of the patients ranges between 10 to 15 and most of the cases are of gastro-intestinal disorders and malaria fever. But people generally prefer the district hospital." (Bilaspur/Nitta Krishna/1988)

"The primary health sub-centre was established in the Panchayat in 1980. The male health worker is implementing the national project on immunisation of children and expectant mothers besides also overseeing the family planning programme and the OPD in minor cases of fever, dysentery etc. Birth in the panchayat during 1986, 1987, 1988 and 1989 were 14, 38, 27 and 43 respectively. In 1989 there were 16 deaths including that of 4 children in the age group 0-6 years.

"If the health of the people is reasonably good, it is more due to the salubrious climate and the hard life than due to any conscious effort on the part of anyone. T.B. in fact, is present, due to the insanitary habits." (Mandi /Manoj/1988)

"Nearest health facility available to the villagers is PHC at Dharampur. This PHC is equipped with reasonably good facilities like vaccines, X-Ray machine, pathology etc. Main problem is that of staff. Because of lack of communication facilities this block is considered as a bad block. DPT and Polio vaccines are available in the PHC. Due to ignorance, villagers could not availed these facilities." (Mandi/Agarwal/1985)

Sanitation

The overall condition of sanitation in the villages is not very flattering. Some of the comments are :

"Health and sanitationwise the area presents worst picture. Most of the villages have pathetic sanitation and are without any medicare except Barot where an ill-equipped PHC is functioning. Roolang village projects worst picture of sanitation. Due to this occurrence of infectious diseases like T.B. and Gestroentrities is more. Since the distance to be covered to reach so called PHC at Barot is to be travelled on foot, most of the serious patients succumb to their desease on the way." (Mandi/Jagdish/1991)

"The houses don't have latrines. Nearby pine forests are used for this purpose. The village has a good hygiene and is yet to see any epidemic. There is one balwadi run under ICDS. It is doing satisfactory work according to the villagers. Sanitary conditions of the village doesn't need much improvement at the moment." (Sol/Vivek/1989)

"The road is free from filth and garbage because people do not throw their garbage on the street but dump it in the vacant space around there houses. This practice has lead to emergence of insanitary conditions around some of the houses since the dumped garbage starts rotting in the vicinity of the house itself. Another major reason for the prevalence of unhygienic conditions in the village is the absence of septic tanks or soak-pits near the houses.

The water from the kitchen and the toilets is allowed to flow out of the house into the open and very often because of some natural obstruction it does not flow down but collects itself in a pool near the house. It is a perpetual nuisance for the villagers which can be easily tackled by constructing a low cost soak-pit near their houses." (Mandi/Rajpal/1990)

"Sanitary habits-both personal and community- are underdeveloped owing to lack of water. People defecate near the bowlies as well as wash their soiled hands from the same source as the one they draw their drinking water from." (Mandi/Rajpal/ 1990)

"There are no public drains and usually waste is dumped at one side of the valley. The meat and fish snacks shop, like other village shops have numerous flies over the products. Otherwise, the dust is mostly burnt. (Bilaspur/Nisha/1987)

"There are about ten community taps in the village for the purpose of supply of drinking water. Generally the ladies and children collect the drinking water from these taps. Ladies wash the clothes on these taps. Gents take their bath in open at the tap only in summer months. Women and girls prefer to take bath inside the kitchen." (Kangra/Prabodh/1990)

Drinking Water Supply

According to 1981 census there are 16907 inhabited villages in the Pradesh out of which 11887 villages are Problem Villages and 4920 villages are easy villages. Till 31st March, 1993, drinking water facilities were provided to 16733 villages consisting of 11887 Problem Villages and 4846 Easy Villages. During the Annual Plan 1993-94, remaining 196 partially covered Problem Villages, 74 easy villages were provided safe drinking water thus achieving 100 per cent Census villages coverage in providing drinking water. This is another commendable achievement by the Government says the Irrigation and Public Health Department. However the reports have something else to say. The villagers have mainly three sources of drinking water. Firstly, the tap water which is provided by IPH department and water from which comes a water storage tank which is chlorinated manually. Secondly, water from the 'Baoris' a structure made of bricks, uncovered which has either an underground spring as the source of water or water is stored. Thirdly, water from small rivulets and nullahs which is, in mansoons, muddy and hence, not preferred.

"In Jhandutta otherwise water is not a problem as tap water reaches nearly every hamlet of habitation. These taps are for community purposes and private taps are not preferred. Misuse of private taps for use in farming of Onions and garlic has led to hue and cry and is quite a bone of contention. The Gram Pradhan alleges that the JE has partisan attitude in installation of the taps and works in collusion with the haves of the region. The water of taps is also not very clean and if filtered shows presence of fine dust-thus leading to amoebic diseases." (Bilaspur/Nisha/1987)

"The water of the Bouri are more dangerous as people wash clothes or have their bath there (when occasionally machines of IPH department fail) and that is completely unfit for human consumption. The IPH department officials say that they are lacking in funds to set up proper water works and it is left to the imagination and persuasion powers of the rural development authorities to ask people to adopt the simplified filter which consists of two pitchers kept one above the other.

But during summer there is scarcity of water and the tap water may not be sufficient. In such cases they rely on the village bowlies for drinking water, bathing and washing. These bowlies are very unhygienic and is considered as the major factor for the worst ever epidemic of gastroentitis killing over 500 persons in the adjoining district of Mandi and Hamirpur in this summer and rainy season." (Kangra/Prabodh/1990)

"The IPH department has constructed a lift drinking water scheme in the area. Since more taps have been connected to the scheme than is allowed by the capacity of the source, a number of taps, especially the ones towards the end of the line, run dry most of the time. Hence, some traditional natural sources of water (called bowlies) are still in use." (Mandi/Rajpal/1990)

EDUCATION

Literacy Rate in HP

The literacy percentage in Himachal Pradesh increased from 31.96 per cent in 1971 to 42.48 per cent in 1981 and 63.86 per cent in 1991. This literacy rate is higher than the national average. The march of education continued ahead through concerted efforts of expanding the infrastructure of education, providing incentives for retention and enlarged enrolment, the data of which is given below:

Age Group	*Percentage of enrolment to total Population*			
	1985-86	*1989-90*	*1991-92*	*1992-93*
1. 6-11 years				
(a) Boys	111	110	109	107
(b) Girls	91	100	95	97
(c) Total	100	103	102	102
2. 11-14 Years				
(a) Boys	90	101	109	106
(b) Girls	60	77	89	84
(c) Total	75	89	99	93

Educational Institutions

The comparative position of educational institutions is depicted in the following Table 2.12:

Table 2.12 : Comparative position of Educational Institution

As on 31st March

	Institutions	*1989-90*	*1990-91*	*1991-92*	*1992-93*
1.	Primary School Units	7450	7547	7548	7691
2.	Middle School Units	1987	2005	2019	2019
3.	High / Higher Secondary School Units	987	1006	1012	962*
4.	Senior Secondary Units	150	150	150	180
5.	Colleges	25	25	25	25

* Less due to upgradations.

In the field of Technical Education, the Pradesh has made significant strides. As of today there are 31 ITIs and 5 Polytechnics.

Notings on Rural Schools

The findings in the report are useful as they throw interesting light on the functioning of the schools in the villages.

Kangra Division

"When asked to give specific reason for not sending girls to schools, they say "It is the tradition we are following." (Chamba/ Subramanyam/1986)

"Though literacy rate is impressive, higher education is in a poor shape. The result is that Himachal students are poorly placed in open national competitions. If they start doing well outside, the pressure may reduce." (Kangra/Prabodh/1990)

"As compared to national literacy rate 36 per cent (1981), Himachal is above national average having 43 per cent rate, and distt. Kangra 49.12 per cent (Census).This village recorded 1083 literates out of a total population of 2258 (48%). There are two Primary Schools and one High School located in the village. (Kangra/Dhiman/1988)

"As part of the curriculum shramdan forms a part. But some villagers had complained against the headmaster that he was exploiting the children. In the shramdan the children were levelling a certain area to be used as a playground. Funds for constructing the boundary support walls was still being awaited by the school. The children are generally clean and healthy. The dropout rate in the high school for the scheduled castes is 6 in a strength of 80 which is around 8 per cent and for the general category it was around 6 per cent." (Kangra/Murthy/1989)

One primary and one middle school is functioning in the village. There is no separate school for the harijans and boys of harijan families also study in these schools without any distinction.

"In a small village with a population of 1,200 nearly 218 students are studying in the schools, which shows that all the school going age children are attending schools. However, if one compares the strength of boys and girls in primary and middle school, one can reasonably presume that most of the boys continue, their study upto middle as boys strength in primary school and middle school is 53 and 54 respectively whereas in case of girls the dropout rate looks to be high as 73 girls are studying in primary school whereas only 38 girls are studying in middle school." (Una/Baldi/1985)

The village has one high school and one primary school with 323 and 190 students respectively. There are no adult night school or handicrafts school in the village. There is no separate school for the Harijan children who are enrolled in the same school as the others. Children from the villages of three panchayats come to the High school in the village. The children from the other villages would have to commute about 5 km to come to the high school.

The children are generally clean and healthy. The dropout rate in the high school for the scheduled castes is 6 in a strength of 80 which is around 8 per cent and for the general category it was around 6 per cent.

Few students have proceeded to more advanced schools and higher education in polytechnics and agricultural college. Higher education is available nearby in Dharamsala which has:

1. Post-graduate college with hostel facilities
2. Industrial Training Institute
3. B.Ed. college

No student who has received good education has settled down in the village. Most of them have obtained good jobs in the cities and have hence migrated to those places. (Kangra/Murti/1989)

There are two primary school and one high school located in the village. Also the place is nearer to Dharamshala which is having following institutions for higher education:

1. Post Graduate College with Hostel Facilities
2. Iindustrial Training Institute

3. B.Ed.College
4. Centre
5. Sr.Sec. School for boys and girls.

In the period of ten years i.e. 1971-81 literacy rate in the village improved by 33 per cent as shown below:

Item	*1971*	*1981*
Total Population	*764*	*2258*
male	396	1157
female	368	1084
Total Literates	*281*	*1083*
male	189	696
female	92	387
Total Literacy Rate *48%*		*36%*
male	48%	60%
female	25%	35%

"One of the reason for increase in literacy rate over this period is the opening of one more primary school in the village. As compared to national literacy rate 36 per cent (1981), Himachal is above national average having 43 per cent rate and district Kangra 49.12 per cent. This village recorded 1083 literates out of a total population of 2258 (48%). (Kangra/Dhiman/1988)

This village has in total three schools, two primary and one middle. Out of the two primary schools, one is that of government and the other is run by panchayat. On the basis of data collected from the registers of the middle school, the following statistical inferences can be drawn about the students of the school:

1. The no. of students admitted in this school is fluctuating during the period under review.
2. Although the intake of girls in the primary school stage is more, there is no corresponding admission of girls in the middle school, which shows that most of the girls end up their educational careers with the primary schools.

3. The no. of dropouts in the boys is more than that of girls, which may be because the no. of boys studying in the school is more.

The reasons for the drop-out which were elicited from the parents as well as teachers are as follows:

- All the parents of these students of both primary and the middle schools are illiterate. They do not realise the importance of education for their children.
- Out of 98 households are having an yearly income ranging between 500 to 4000. This shows 95% of these families are below the poverty line.

Nearly half of the population of this village consists of Gujjars, a scheduled tribe who migrate during the winter months to the plains of Punjab, Haryana and UP form the hills of Himachal Pradesh. This kind of a migratory habit of these people also acts as a stumbling block in the process of education of their children.

- Moreover, most of these Gujjars of this village being muslims do not like to send their children to the schools meant for all." (Chamba/Subrahmaniyam/1986)

"The village has a primary school and a middle school the both are housed in adjoining semi pucca temporary types of structure. The maximum distance that any student is required to travel is not more than 1.5 kms. The primary school has a total strength of 229 students. The break-up is 103 girls and 126 boys. The headmistress claimed that there is no dropout and in any case the lesser number of students in any year is explained by migration of the families. The middle school has a combined strength of 137 students. Hence again the head master claims that there is no dropout.

For higher education the nearest place is Dharamshala. In the town there is a post graduate college with separate hostel facilities for boys and girls. There is also a women's polytechnic as well as a B.Ed. college." (Kangra/Prabodh/1990)

Mandi Division

"There is a wide awakening regarding education in the people of the area. It is particularly so with regards the education of the children since the illiterate parents have realised the disadvantages they had to face as a result of their being illiterate. I did not meet even a single family, including those of the Harijans, which was not sending its children to schools. The survey has revealed that parents consider basic educational qualification to be the essential prerequisite for getting a government job and hence this race for getting one's wards educated." (Mandi/Rajpal/1990)

"Literacy rate is as low as 10% among males. Peculiarity is that 100% females of the area are illiterate. Now, few have started sending their female wards to schools. Discrimination against the female population is due to they being put to use for domestic and agricultural activities. It is traditionally also believed that female wards are not to be sent to school." (Mandi/Jagdish/1991)

The villages under survey have one primary school. It has 21 students enrolled. Out of the 21 presently enrolled, two are from the SC and one is a Gujjar. Four of them are girls while seventeen are boys. Apart from this school at Batheri (named Seri) another school at Khalboot enrols 39 students 26 boys and 13 girls. Attendance in the school is quite irregular. A rainfall can cause the drop in attendance to two. Dropout rates are quite high. The teacher said that it was true more in the case of girls. They generally dropped out a few months after enrolment for middle or high school education, one has to go to the tehsil hqrs at Paddhar (60 kms away) or to Mandi town (33 kms).

To date only one Rajput boy has gone to college at Mandi and after doing B.Sc. he works as a school teacher at Karsog. One matriculate person has learnt typing under TRYSEM and types at sub tehsil office. Another person who has gone matriculation is also a Rajput.

Amongst the older lot illiteracy is rampant. Most of the people could not read or write. According to the Patwari very few people could write their names. Most of the children who studied in the school could not retain their reading and writing capacity.

The district literacy rate is 40.21 per cent (52.96 per cent males and 21.45 per cent females). Comparing with this figure, it is obvious that the area is educationally quite backward. Amongst the muslims, level of education is negligible. Only one Muslim boy goes to the school. The Muslim children are mostly engaged in cattle grazing activity. (Mandi/Anita/1989)

There is no school in Bardana village. Children go to primary school Banwar Kalan which is only .5 km away from the village. There is one secondary school at Dharampur i.e. 5 km from the village. This school has very good facilities, like pucca building and play ground. Nearest college is at Sarkaghat which is about 60 km away.

"Villagers are aware of need to educate their children and sending them to school. There is no boy above 6 years and below 15 years who is not going to school. There are only 6 girls of school going age who are not going to school. Two of them belong to SC and rest belong to other castes. There are very few children above VIII standard. Almost all the children are sent to primary school but number of children going to senior secondary school reduces appreciably. Very few girls study beyond primary level. People are still not convinced that education is necessary for girls also." (Mandi/Agarwal/1985)

Gram panchayat has a high school and a primary school. The Kathayari middle school was upgraded to high school only last year after the villagers constructed a building through shramdaan. There are about 225 children in the primary school and 200 students in the other classes. The ratio of the boys to the girls is 55:45.

"Another interesting observation that can be made about the village is that while most of the older people have studied upto the primary level and while all the families, both of the Rajputs as well as the SCs send their children to primary school, nobody is much optimistic about the efficacy of education in their lives." (Mandi/MANOJ/1988)

In Jhandutta high school there is, the primary section of which primarily caters to the children of this village and Bairan panchayat. Though according to school authorities attendance is regular the reality is different. The approach of teachers is lackadaisical to say the least. They themselves are irregular in taking classes and for most children school is a place where they can play without being under the surveillance of their parents. The result for middle and high school is below the Board level, e.g. in 1988 while 43 per cent students passed in board examination only 42 per cent school students passed. Similarly while Board result for middle examination was 48.3 per cent for the school it was a mere 35 per cent. There is no vocational training whatsoever." (Bilaspur/Nisha Singh/1987)

"There is a wide awakening regarding education in the people of the area. It is particularly so with regards the education of the children since the illiterate parents have realised the disadvantages they had to face as a result of their being illiterate. I did not meet even a single family, including those of the harijans, which was not sending its children to schools. The survey has revealed that parents consider basic educational qualification to be the essential prerequisite for getting a government job and hence this race for getting one's wards educated." (Mandi/Rajpal/1990)

Shimla Division

"There is one primary school in the village which has 40 students. High school is situated at a distance of 2 kms and has 15 students of the village. Of the 40 students of the village in the primary school, 30 are harijans while of the 15 high school students, 10 belong to the scheduled caste. This is a very strange phenomena and it could be attributed to the growing awareness about education amongst the depressed classes and the lack of enthusiasm for education in the landowning class and the incidence off more well of people staying in places like Dharampur, Solan and Parwanoo. Not a single person in the village however has studied in a college. The dropout rate is low in school but after high school, there does not seem to be much incentive for studies. The average literacy rate is quite below that of the country and much below than that of the state." (Solan/Vivek/1989)

"Primary, middle and high school facilities are available in all three villages within 2 to 3 kms. Out of a total child population of 264 only 12 children in the school going bracket were not attending or had not attended any school. No discrimination seems to exist in sending boys and girls to school. Nor is there a noticeable trend of Harijan families not sending their children for education. Progress on the education front is quite encouraging. In all the three villages combined only about 18 per cent of the males were illiterates. The corresponding figure for the women is 43 per cent. The cumulative illiteracy works out to be around 29 per cent which compares very well with the national average and state averages.

Only a handful of families with sufficient financial resources at their command are able to send their children for higher/ technical education." (Solan/Rizvi/1988)

ROADS AND RURAL INFRASTRUCTURE

Roads

Roads have been the **life-line of the state** of Himachal Pradesh. The credit goes to the first Chief Minister of the State **Dr.Y.S Parmar**, who gave top priority to this sector. For the first few Plans he emphasised predominantly on the roads sometimes even at the cost of other sectors. Any person who has travelled by air over the State would understand the comport of the statement .The entire range of rugged mountains seem to have been thrown into a network of roads and pathways zigzagging the entire state and linking even the remotest of the villages.

The position of roads in the State in Himachal Pradesh (upto 31st March, 1993) is as follows:

Type of Road	*As on 31st March*				
	1985	*1990*	*1991*	*1992*	*1993*
(a) Motorable double lane	1994	1994	1994	1994	2000
(b) Motorable single lane	12669	14889	15296	15701	16160
(c) Jeepable	409	835	826	835	865
(d) Less than Jeepable	4641	4280	4329	4250	4328
(Track)					
Total	19713	21998	22445	22780	23353

(All in Kms)

Apart from the road length aspect, achievements under allied activities as on 31st March, 1993 were as under:

Description	*Unit*	*Position as on 31st March*				
		1985	*1990*	*1991*	*1992*	*1993*
1. Motorable Road	Kms	14663	16883	17290	17695	18160
2. Roads Provided with cross drainage	Kms	6245	7493	7643	7769	8031
3. Metalled and tarred length	Kms	5300	6392	6542	6717	6922
4. Bridges	No.	608	752	782	817	847
5. Villages connected with Roads						
(a) Above 1500 Pop.	No.	165	175	178	179	179
(b) 1000-1500 Pop.	No.	198	214	214	215	216
(c) 500-1000 Pop.	No.	756	809	815	816	817
(d) 200-500 Pop.	No.	2324	2413	2421	2438	2446
(e) Less than 200 Pop	No.	3640	3805	3828	3848	3863
Total (5)		*7083*	*7416*	*7456*	*7496*	*7521*

Observations about Roads in the Villages

In the backdrop of above scenario, the observation made by the Officer Trainees at the micro level are enlightening and interesting.

"The livelihood of most of the people of Jaddera, who have a marketable surplus of milk and vegetables, is directly dependent on the daily transport of H.P.S.R.T.C. inasmuch as, these commodities, which are very much needed by the residents of Chamba, are transported every day from Jaddera to Chamba." (Chamba/Subramanyam/1986)

"The village has better transport facilities than the other villages for the reason that in the previous government the Transport Minister belonged to this area and the Sarah Panchayat happened to be a part of his constituency. Ever since the change of the government, the villagers allege that the bus service is not very regular and at times the drivers do not stop at all. In rainy season even if the road is slightly cut off, they prefer to take the convenient route. They remember that when the local MLA was the Transport Minister the bus driver used to go make all out attempt to negotiate the cut off road. (Kangra/Prabodh/1990)

The distance of bus stop from the village is beyond 13 kms. distance. This distance is from Batheri. From there a fair weather jeepable road comes upto the village. (Mandi/Anita/1989)

Rural Electrification

According to 1981 census, there are 16807 inhabited villages in the Pradesh and in the year 1988-89 all were electrified. Since then the area of concentration is strengthening of distribution system and electrification of left out hamlets. This is no mean achievement for any state especially a mountainous one where apart from laying the lines, maintenance is a major task in view of the terrain and weather.

"Himachal has the distinction of cent per cent rural electrification and Padher is no exception. Almost the entire electricity is used for domestic purposes. However there are no streetlights in the villages. No electricity is consumed for agricultural purposes as there are no tubewells or lift pumps in the village." (Kangra/Prabodh/1990)

Communication

"One Sub-Post Office has been functioning for the last few years in village Jaddera. However, it was only recently in June, 1987, one Telephone Public Call Office was opened, facilitating telephonic communication facilities, which is a sign of development. The entire village has only 2 telephones. One is the Public Call Office and the other is a telephone installed in the residence of Pradhan." (Chamba/Subramanyam/1986)

The village doesn't have any road. It is connected to the highway by abridge path. The village also does not have any post and telegraph office. The nearest PandT office is situated at a distance of 3 kms from the village. The village is in dire need of a road as everything has to be carried in the village by head loads. This not only escalates the cost of any construction work but also creates problems in marketing of the produce, especially cash crops. Road is a necessity if the village has to develop." (Sol/ Vivek/1989)

PANCHAYATI RAJ AND DECENTRALISED PLANNING

Panchayat Pradhan

In the villages, the institution the Gram Panchayat has taken firm roots. The Lambardars of yester-years have been long forgotten . Now in each village one finds a person who is more educated than the others, seems to control and own the ration depot, is the main contractor of all Government works, the MLAs and District officers consult him and he generally thrives on VIP visits. He is the village Pradhan, the up and coming icon of power in rural India. We will begin with the impressions on this gentleman.

"The Panchayat Pradhan Sagar Singh appeared to be the most prosperous person of the village as also the ex-Pradhan. Sagar Singh owns a general store in Batheri which stores everything from utensils and clothes to biscuits and other eatables. Sagar Singh's son Inder Singh runs a shop of licenced country liquor. (Mandi/Anita/1989)

The Pradhan of the Village Panchayat is a staunch believer in communism. I wish to study how a young energetic, and enterprising Pradhan of a village, with all communist leavings, especially, when the party in power at the Panchayat Samitti and state level is a different one, can give direction to the process of development in his village.

The Pradhan of the village, who is young; energetic and enterprising, has earlier tried to break the back of these middlemen, inasmuch as, according to him, neither the producer, who works hard to keep the cattle in a good condition and maximise the yield, nor the consumer, who pays a handsome amount is the beneficiary in the existing state of affairs, but it is the middlemen, who corner all the benefit. Under this initiative the Pradhan convinced all those milk producers in his village not to sell their milk to the middlemen. He engaged a private truck on a monthly basis and a few unemployed youth who can go to Chamba town and distribute milk further to various points. The milk contractors were hit hard and it is natural, they retaliate. These contractors began to create lot of hurdles to this new venture of the Pradhan. The vehicle carrying milk was stopped several times on the way so that milk supply does not reach Chamba in time. Moreover, they tried to pocket the agents who come from Jaddera. Ultimately, they became successful and it so happened that those unemployed youth, who were supposed to safeguard the interests of the milk producers, themselves turned into middlemen and joined hands with the Contractors. This is how, the initiative of the Pradhan to safeguard the interests of the milk producers and eliminate the unscrupulous middlemen was stifled. The Pradhan, however, claims that if these middlemen are eliminated, he can certainly provide good quality of milk and milk-products to the residents of Chamba at a much cheaper price." (Chamba/Subramanyam/1986)

"The factions at the moment are basically on party basis. The present Pradhan who is an ex-serviceman is supposed to be a Janta Dal supporter. The candidate he defeated was supposed to belong to the Cong.(I). He won the election by a narrow margin of only 3 votes. The panchayat forms a part of the Shaghpur legislative constituency whose MLA is from the Janta Dal and is also ex-serviceman. Hence the indication that the factions are mostly on party-cum-personal lines." (Kangra/Murti/1989)

Panchayat and their Working

The types of work done by the Panchayats could be well understood by the following notes in the Reports:

The achievements of the Jaddera Panchayat are more in the realm of creating infrastructure for the villagers. The following works were completed by the Panchayats:

- School buildings, alongwith play ground
- Mule roads of 4 to 5 kms. each
- Water supply schemes including construction of source tanks; storage tanks
- Rural Sanitary Latrines

- One Reading Room, one store room and one community hall.
- One TRYSEM shop.

"The Panchayat is being given lot of construction works, under the Model Village Scheme another notable achievement of this Panchayat is that it has acquired a land of 2 hectares and developed it in such a way, that the land, which has been barren for the last 20 years has been put into use and thus, they have produced this year, matter (vegetable) worth Rs. 4000/-. (Chamba/ Subramanyam/1986)

"Out of 19 hectare which is classified as the area under cultivation, about 2.5 hectare is occupied by the community garden having trees of fruits and grass for fodder. It is maintained by the Panchayat which auctions the right to collect fruits and grass and fuelwood. In the current year it was auctioned for Rs. 2500/- and was very ill-maintained." (Kangra/Prabodh/1990)

The resources of the Panchayat are limited and it relies on government funds. They collect around two thousand rupees from the house tax. The major activity relates to implementation of the schemes under 80 per cent share of JRY." (Kangra/Prabodh/ 1990)

The major schemes of development relate to Antodaya and IRDP. One two room tenement has also been built. JRY is another very important sector of development. This year so far 4 latrines have been sanctioned. With the new scheme coming up there is possibility of more such sanctions." (Kangra/Prabodh/1990)

"The performance of the Panchayat was not stated to be outstanding by the people. People in general felt that the construction of school room was started this year purposely by the Pradhan since the elections were due. This is not true since sanctions for school buildings have come recently and are time barred. But this speaks volumes about the peoplesperception of the politicians' behaviour." (Mandi/Anita/1989)

"The main source of revenue for the panchayat is Government grant of Rs. 1,20,000. The panchayat also levies taxes, house tax and on weddings, fairs etc. Other than that the panchayat also owns some shops whose monthly rent goes to supplement its income. The main contribution of the panchayat to the development of the village includes building of water storage tanks and link roads. Under its jurisdiction 12 Bighas 4 biswas of land had been made into a nursery, a road from Balghad to Jhandutta has been built. Some temple repairing work is also taken alongwith help to the needy locals in marriage etc. But one can not help observing that most of the funds are misutilised and the panchayt has a very poor record in sponsoring training works and starting commercial works or some concrete educational programmes. With the funds at its disposal, it could have easily started adult education centres, or small co-operative poultry farms. Other similar projects could have also been taken up. The panchayat is more of a political and less of a working body. (Bilaspur/Nisha/1987)

Before 1975, there was not even a road leading to the higher villages of the Panchayat. The present road was built, in phases, as drought work, in the late 70s and the early 80s and was completed only in 1989. In fact, during the entire period, it was inaugurated thrice by the Ministers! In 1975, the village school was also Primary. It's now a High School. The Patwarkhana was also built after 1975. Similarly, a water pipeline was laid after 1975. Before that, the villagers had to trek long distances to small streams and rivulets. Small ponds have also been dug at many places. That they could not be used due to inadequate rainfall is a different matter, though." (Mandi/Manoj/1988)

Sources of Funds for G.Ps

Regarding the sources of funds for G.Ps Dhiman in 1988 has made a fairly good analyses of it in his village in Kangra district. He states that the Gram Panchayat has following sources of Income:

House Tax : It is levied at the rate of Rs 3, 5, 7 from lower, middle and upper classes households respectively. Total income during this year was Rs 6,750.

Community Orchard : This Gram Panchayt owns an orchard having area of 150 kanals (around 6 hect.) at Sidhpur, which was started around 4-5 years back. Following fruit trees have been planted (Litchi, Mango, Amla, Lemon, Sour Orange [Galgal], oranges, Guavas, Almonds, Peaches, Jackfruit etc., a total of 600 plants out of which only a few yield fruits at present. Total income of panchayt from this is around Rs. 2,000- p.a. which will increase over the years.

Royalty on Slate Quarrying: Slate mining industry is owned by Gram Panchayat which actually is given to contractors for quarrying and royalty at rates (mentioned in the chapter on slate mining) is charged by panchayat, from which total income is Rs. 3,64,000 during 1988-89 and Rs. 4,00,000 during this year (upto Dec.1989).

Grants of Land Revenue: 20 per cent of the total land revenue collected in panchayat area is given to Gram Panchayat. During 1989-90 it was Rs. 234.50.

Income from Khads: Gair-Mumkin areas covered by khads are also vested in Gram Panchayat. Local people and contractors extract sands and bajari (pebbles and gravels) from these two khads Manjhi and Manooni from which total income during 1989-90 was Rs. 20,000.

Rents from Buildings: Panchayat also owns buildings which are rented out for various purpose like Canteen, Telephone Exchange etc. from which Rs. 3,000 p.a. is received as rent.

Funds received under JRY: A total or Rs. 1,04,000 was received under JRY which is being spent on construction of Janj Ghar and metalling of footpath.

On the funds spent : In addition to these minor sources of revenue, royalty from slate mining industry received by this panchayat over the period of 11 years (from 1.4.79 to 31.12.89) is Rs. 31,59,104 which is enormous as compared to the other panchayats and Gram Panchayat has meticulously been utilising these funds for the developmental activities. Among other following works were executed by Gram Panchayat over these years:

Government High school building
Primary school building at Ghaniara
Additions in Gram Panchayat rest house
Beds hospital building (under construction)

Crematorium (Shamshan Ghat)
Sidhpur Orchard measuring 150 kanals with irrigation facilities
Government primary school building at Chakban
Metalling of all the katcha footpath
Construction of 15 small culverts
Construction of 8 Bowlis (shallow perennial wells)
Purchse of 150 chairs in Janj Ghar
Pay the land revenue of all estates in Ghaniara Panchayat every year. (Kangra/Dhiman/1988)

Common Property Resource

The Panchayat garden and the wasteland of the village is used for defecation by the residents. (Kangra/Prabodh/1990)

"There is no perceptible change in the CPRs over the last 5-10 years period, excepting that potable water has been provided to almost every village. CPRs available are (a) Forests (b) Government land (c) Infrastructure (d) Community facilities (e) Water resources (natural). The villagers have easy access to the CPRs excepting restrictions on Timber drawing rights which become due after every 5 years per family. The population is free to draw benefits from Government land i.e. grazing cattle, wood collection etc. The infrastructure here means road only. The maintenance of CPRs is with the Government. There is a social restriction on use of water resources for SCs imposed by the villagers. But their access to other CPRs is free." (Mandi/Jagdish/1991)

IMPACT OF GOVERNMENT SCHEMES

General Remarks

The Officer Trainees have made detailed observations about what they found in the field concerning the functioning of the various schemes of the Government. It is one thing to get an idea of the scheme through brochures and papers and quite another seeing them implemented in the field wherein inter-personal relationships, social and political standing etc. have an overreaching impact in all the outcomes. The Government seems to be spending crores of rupees for welfare and other rural based schemes primarily in the name of the poor but the real impact on them seems to be debatable. In fact the actual gainers are the set of people who are already well-off or are in-charge of these schemes. Some of the comments are as follows:-

An overwhelming majority of the people were of the opinion that the government is not sensitive to the needs of the rural poor. They accepted that government has provided them assistance but felt that the quantum of the assistance should go up. They felt that facilities like those of health and education should be augmented. Setting up of a primary school and a primary health centre in each village (none of the three villages surveyed had one of their own) was a recurrent demand. Another common refrain was that whatever the government does, only a small per centage filters down to the people.

"I noticed that the area was struggling to express its urge for development but it was getting continually stifled owing to various factors beyond the control of the village. This striving towards development places the village in a state of flux where all kinds of experiments and innovations are being tried out with a majority of them ending in a failure." (Mandi/Rajpal/1990)

Talking to people, one tended to get the impression that they have become too dependent on the government. Would like it to do everything for them. Consequently they are unable to think of taking initiatives on their own. For instance we can take the production of stone fruits. Most villagers want that the government should fix a procurement price like in the case of apple and buy all their produce. As to what happen to the produce does not seem to bother them. There are problems in the marketing of the fruits. However, the only way to counter the same is probably through the cultivators organising themselves. Yet they seem to be quite reluctant to do so. It is such tendencies that we must guard against.

Development must generate self-reliance and not dependence. (Sol/Rizvi/1988)

"The systematic wooing of their electorates by successive governments in HP has blunted the spirit of self-help and of community's own responsibility towards itself to such an extent that no philanthropic or community activity has got generated even from the local temple. This trend of overdependence on the government needs to be reserved." (Mandi/Rajpal/1990)

Scheme-wise remarks are as follows:

IRDP

So much so good. But the main problem is with respect to the selection procedure. The beneficiaries were to be selected by the Gram Sabha in the open general body meeting and here enters the politics. The Panchayats are constituted on party lines. As the number of persons to be selected in the first phase was restricted, it gave the local politicians the scope and the lever to manipulate, not just to ignore the eligible person but also to include the ineligible person. This procedure was further compounded by the fact that at many places the Pradhan and the MLA belonged to different political parties. Panchayat elections were held about six years back when Congress was in power but now the ruling party is BJP. The local administration only has the power to delete a name subsequent to enquiry but it has no power to include a name. A deserving person has no alternative but to wait for the second phase and there also the procedure will be same. Lot of deletions were made by SDMs and BDOs. In Padher so far 12 names have been deleted. Any large scale exercise of this nature is not preferred as it is construed as an attempt to subvert the local participatory democracy by the back door. To cut a long story short, antodya selection is considered to be a politically motivated identification. To be frank I think that not a single family in this village qualified on the income criteria strictly. There is not a single family which is homeless, landless or is otherwise starving. Here it is essentially a relative phenomenon more with a political angle. How can any village be denied the scheme must have been the dilemma for extending the village to every block. It does not require any investigation to find out the extent of unfair selection." (Kangra/Prabodh/1990)

One Basanti Devi, a widow and Harijan by caste got the loan in 1986 and her animal gives about 4-5 kg. per day. After paying off most of the loan, she has now hopes that the animal could be helpful in enhancing her income. (Hopeful!)

Another case of Narayan Singh Chandel by caste who had brought a buffalo in 1984 on 1/3rd subsidy under the IRD programme. He has not repaid the loan, rather laments that the buffalo is a faulty animal, that it does not give milk rather is a burden because of the cost of the fodder. The animal has been under the examination of the local veterinary doctor, in vain.(Not that hopeless!)

What I could perceive was a map of corruption in which one of the workers of block, perhaps the doctor and traders were involved in sale of bad/not too healthy animals at quite high prices. Good animals at same or even lower price could be bought from the Punjab plains. Clearly, something is wrong in the way the programme is run. (Hopeless!)

"The most successful case of IRD loan is Mr. Devi Singh who is a Luhar by caste. With a subsidy of Rs. 4800/- he started a small wood workshop in a tin shed in 1984. Since then, he has made amazing progress. The small tin shed has expanded into a small scale industry called 'Jai Durga Industry'. His income has increased manifold as have his assets- both domestic and commercial. When I met him, he was busy building a medium sized fishing boat at a rate of 70 per day labour. Apart from this, he worked on simple furniture articles in his spare time. He attributes his success to sheer hard work and sincerity and believes that IRD plan can only be a success if the beneficiaries themselves are of enterprising and hard working nature. In P-12 he is seen with his two helpers, employed on a monthly wage of Rs. 500 and 700 and two trainees under the TRYSEM programme." (Bilaspur/Nisha/1987)

"In four cases minor benefits has been given which could never bring the families above poverty line. These benefits were given just to complete the targets." (Mandi/Agarwal/1985)

An example of plight of artisans is best provided by a resident of Roolang village who had taken a loan of Rs. 3000 for purchasing implements to carry on his profession of Carpentry. But due to non-availability of work he has not been able to improve his position. So much so he is unable to repay the loan. Even making both ends meet has become difficult for him.

It may also be mentioned here, that, the experiment of giving Jersey cows under the IRDP has not proved very successful in this Panchayat. This is due to the hostile climate not suited to the delicate structure of the Jersey cow. In addition, there is an acute shortage of fodder in the region, especially during the winter months. The cows, therefore, remain undernourished and the calves are, in most cases, unable to survive. This point was repeatedly stressed by most of the IRDP beneficiaries.

"Moreover, as the P.O. DRDA pointed out—"In the higher regions, if the cows give more milk, it remains unutilized. It cannot be consumed locally as there is no demand for the extra milk; and it cannot be sold off as the villages in these regions are not on the `milk route'." (Mandi/Jagdish/1991)

Under the I.R.D.P. out of the 20 beneficiaries, 16 had been provided with milch-cattle as the first or second dose. Out of these 9 got a goat unit, 4 got Jersey cows and 5 got buffaloes. A physical verification showed that all of these beneficiaries possessed the asset given to them, but in four cases the IRDP tag was missing giving rise to suspicion. Seven out of the nine goats were running dry, thus becoming a liability rather than asset. The reason forwarded by the villagers for this state of affairs was that they were fleeced by the veterinary doctor who acting in collusion with the seller under-estimated the age of the animal. In case of five buffaloes, one was suffering from Haemorrhagic Septicemia and was also moribund. The other four buffaloes were yielding 4.5, 2.5, 1.5, 2.0 kgs. of milk respectively.

The beneficiaries claimed that they were duped by the seller who before bringing the animal to the Mandi had not milked the animal for more than two times, thus increasing the apparent milk yield dramatically. However, I felt that the lack of proper feed was also one reason for the poor yield.

"The choice of beneficiaries was shocking to say the least. The four families which were landless before 1973 were denied any help under this scheme, though they had repeatedly approached the Gram Sewak. On the other hand, people like Mr. Amar Singh who owned approximately 5 acres of land had been liberally assisted." (Nahan/Sanjeev/1993)

"Moreover, the people of this village have also obtained milk cattle under the I.R.D.P. Since Himachal does not have its own local breed of cattle, the cattle come from Punjab and they are sold in Cattle Fairs to the IRDP Beneficiaries. These cattle cannot so easily acclimatise themselves to the weather conditions in Himachal. That is how, generally the cattle in this village die. However, it is interesting to learn that there have been no epidemic outbreaks in this village so far." (Chamba/Subramanyam/1986)

"H.P. Government implemented Antodaya programme under which foodgrains are provided to the beneficiaries at very low prices. This programme also provides for social security insurance cover and extends loan on easy terms. This programme has been implemented in this area. Under IRDP, loans were extended on easy terms for asset generation like purchase of livestock and equipments to farmers and artisans respectively. These half hearted assistance did not actually change the economic status of these beneficiaries for, the livestocks so acquired perished for want of proper medical care." (Mandi/Jagdish/1991)

"At present three groups are functioning in this village; these groups, in addition to the IRDP, loans are given revolving fund of Rs. 15,000 per group for working capital. At present, with active participation of women, all the three groups are making good profits and helping in raising the awareness level among women. With the demonstration effect of these groups, now other women are also tempting to go for such productive activities. As I found that most of the women were feeling envious of DWCRA members and demanded that they should also be given such assets." (Kangra/Dhiman/1988)

"Similarly-under IRD programmes instead of giving the usual milch cattle, which is of dubious benefit, fish ponds could be encouraged. The co-operative movement is at present, non-existent in the village, the same could be encouraged to set up medium sized, if not large, poultry farms or fish farms. Fifthly, there is a great need to promote industry." (Bilaspur/NISHA/1987)

All of them were unanimous in their view that IRDP in general has benefited them. But, not all of them reaped the equal benefit. Some were benefited more and thus crossed the poverty line and some are in the process of receiving the second benefit, to cross the poverty line.

In general, all of them expressed one difficulty about the quality of animals given to them. Lot of cattle-politics seems to be involved in the buying of cattle for the IRDP beneficiaries. Cattle fairs are held every month in Chamba Town. The purchasing committee, which includes a Veterinary Doctor as well as the beneficiary decides the animal to be purchased. It is understood that these cattle come from the plains of Punjab. The cattle owners, in order to create an impression that their cattle give huge quantity of milk, resort to various devilous practices such as giving milk and water to the cattle for 2 or 3 days before they are brought to the cattle fair; giving some injections to induce the cattle for more milk. It is interesting to note that even the Veterinary Doctors, who are professionally competent to determine the quality of breed are beguiled by such cattle owners, as a result the IRDP beneficiaries purchase those animals, under the impression that they are good milk-givers, but, to their surprise find that those cattle are worth much less than what they paid." (Chamba/Subramanyam/1986)

Rural Sanitation Scheme

"The rural sanitation schemes have made no impact in the village. Firstly no one was allotted under the scheme in the village. Very few houses have latrines in them. On talking about this with the Pradhan he was saying that the villages in and around Dharamsala because of this proximity to the D.C.'s office get all the allotments." (Kangra/Murti/1989)

Van Lagao Roji Kamao

"Lapas village has been covered under Van Lagao Roji Kamao programme of HP Government under social forestry. This envisages to provide job opportunity to people along with increasing forest cover. The idea is noble but results are still awaited as it has been implemented fairly recently. No biogas plant is operating in the area, mainly because it is a low temperature zone. The forest deptt. indulges in tree plantation once in a while but public participation in this is never sought." (Mandi/Jagdish/1991)

Intensive Agriculture District Programme

"As Narottam Ram, 60, an illiterate farmer, who owns three acres of land in the area, says—the government advises us to go to the Agriculture Service Sale Centre at Nagwain (a distance of 14 kms). But there the standard reply given is "out of stock." Theoretically speaking, under the Intensive Agriculture District Programme at the Block level, two agricultural Inspectors have been posted. They are supposed to visit the villages regularly and advise the farmers on the appropriate use of agricultural inputs such as fertilizers and pesticides. But most of the farmers said—we have heard that there is an agriculture Inspector somewhere and that he draws his salary. But we have never seen him." (Mandi/Manoj/1988)

The government programmes have had positive effect on the life of the people. Agricultural yield has gone up due to the HYV package. Schools exist in villages for education, Panchayat ghar and community centres are also built, relief money for drought is helpful to people so on, so forth. But one striking thing that emerges on the scene is that every attempt has been half hearted. Multiplicity of programmes has led to superficial effect on the peoples' life. The amount spent is enormous but the effect is little and shortlived." (Mandi/Anita/1989)

SEEUY

Ishwar Das, a young I.T.I. Shamshi (Kulu) trained mechanic is, at present, unemployed. His name is registered at the Employment Exchange, Mandi. I asked him why did not he start something on his own, instead of waiting for that elusive letter from the Employment Exchange (which in any case, comes just days before the interview date, making it impossible for him to make it on time). he said that the loan ceiling of Rs. 35,000 for opening a workshop, on the loan given by the Block, under the scheme for providing self-employment to Educated Unemployed Youth (SEEUY) is unrealistic. According to him, atleast Rs. 1,00,000 are needed to start a workshop on his own and to purchase machinery and tools. He, thus stays unemployed.

More importantly, many ongoing programmes for Rural Development do not conform to the ground realities at the village level in the remote areas. For example, the SC Development Corporation, which started in 1985-86, imparts TRYSEM- type training to the people on IRDP pattern. However, most of the activities sanctioned under it have no place in the village life- e.g. motor mechanic, shoe making, watch repair, tailoring, radio repair and so on. (Mandi/Manoj/1988)

Smokeless Chullha

"Most of the households are having new Dhauladhar Smokeless Chullha; it has gone a long way in improving the women's health and saving of fuel wood. LVDC gives training to the local women in construction of these chullhas with the help of trained workers. This helps women to come together and discuss common problems." (Mandi/Manoj/1988)

"Recently, 14 improved version of smokeless chullhas were installed in the houses of 14 people. When I approached the people, they told me that except one or two, all others have stopped using the same. It is interesting that their reply, that they are not using it, because, unlike the conventional chullha, this improved version of smokeless chullha, is not providing them with sufficient heat, which is essential in winter in Himachal, seems to be logical." (Chamba/Subramanyam/1986)

Special Projects

"Jaddera, in Chamba Block, has been selected and included in the Project SPARK (Simultaneous Participation of All for Rural Kendra) which on an innovative and pilot basis, has been introduced and being implemented in Chamba district under the initiative of the Deputy Commissioner, in order to concentrate efforts of all development departments through the District Rural Development Agency in a particular village in an integrated manner." (Chamba/Subramanyam/1986)

Apni Mandis

"In order to safeguard the interests of both the producer and consumer as under the provisions of H.P. Agricultural Produce Markets Act, 1969, by regulating market prices, the Government of Himachal Pradesh in each district is starting, *Apni Mandis* where the marketing activities are regulated. In Chamba also, site has been selected and efforts are on to start such a Mandi, where all the fruits and vegetable growers bring their produce and the same is auctioned in public. It is also understood that these contractors also gratify the officials concerned, who once start accepting such illegal gratification other than the legal remuneration, are bound under a perpetual obligation to protect and shield the former. This is a nexus between the bureaucracy and the middlemen. The milk contractors, it is understood, also keep the political executive under their influence, by several ways, which are anybody's guess." (Chamba/Subramanyam/1986)

TRYSEM

"All the four of the above mentioned youth who got trained in the trades mentioned against their names, are now earning a monthly income ranging from Rs.400 to Rs.800 and have become self-reliant. The fifth one is still under training." (Chamba/Subramanyam/1986)

Public Distribution System

One Fair Price shop is existing in this village. It is operated through the Agricultural Co-operative Society. There are 98 Ration Card holders in this village. It is understood that almost all these card holders take the commodities supplies by the Fair Price Shop. For the supply of the ration to the villagers, the co-operative acts as the fair price shop. Here again there is a problem of regularity of supply as the co-operative because of economic reasons only want to lift the rest of the ration after first lifting the sugar quota. If there is delay in supply of sugar which happens quite frequently especially in the rainy months then the rest of the supply for the village is automatically withheld. In case of shortage, the preference is given to antodaya family which is again a cause of heartburning which will be analysed later on. The co-operative is for the total Panchayat. 320 ration cards are enrolled with it in addition to 32 antodaya families." (Kangra/ Prabodh/1990)

"One fair price shop is existing in this village. It is being run by the co-operative society. There are 120 ration card holders in this village. They take commodities like sugar, wheat, rice supplied by the FPS." (Bilaspur/Nita/1989)

NGO

There is no voluntary organisation working in the area. The village has no incidence of bonded labour. Even child labour is almost absent. The reason is not far to seek because the government agencies have nothing to benefit from child labour." (Kangra/ Prabodh/1990)

Antodaya Programme

The introduction of new schemes under Antodaya programme is also viewed with scepticism by the people. Antodaya families referred to the meagre gain from the programme. However, certain new facilities have been announced for the Antodaya families, the impact of a reaction to which is yet to be assessed." (Mandi/Anita/1989)

ICDS

"Anganwadi was opened in the area two years back. On visit to the Anganwadi, it was obvious that whatever infrastructure was provided in the form of books, slates, etc. are not in good condition. The children are provided roasted gram with sugar. On inspecting the papers related to child immunisation programme, it was observed that vitamin A solution was not in stock for the past eleven months. This had deprived 56 children from their due dose of vitamin A." (Mandi/Anita/1989)

3

PUNJAB

Brij Pal Singh

Punjab—The Wonder of India

Punjab, literally meaning the land of five-rivers, has been the cradle of Indian civilisation since ancient times. Vedas were written on its riverbanks and modern civilisation of India owes its origin in the soils of Punjab. Punjab suffered the brunt of invasions by Greeks, Duranis, Abdalis, Pathans and Mughals on India's western frontier. It was rightly called the Sword of India.

Today Punjab is one of the richest States of India and has maintained highest per capita income (among all states of India) since 1966. Its mechanised agriculture (5 lakh working tractors in Punjab are one third of the total in the country), with highest yields (4040 kgms per hectare for wheat and 3493 kgms per hectare in rice in 1993-94) is the pride of India. The contribution of wheat and rice to Central Pool at 65 per cent and 50 per cent respectively in 1993-94 is the highest by any state. It is rightly called the "granary of India". Punjab enjoys very high standards of consumption. Per capita availability of eggs is 90 and that of milk 968 gms per day and both are highest in the country. As per the estimates of "Expert Group on Estimation of Proportion and Number of Poor" of the Planning Commission, Government of India, (1993), Punjab has the lowest percentage of poor (in 1987-88 at 12.7%) among all the states and union territories in the country. Punjab's industrial growth is based on small industry and is the envy of the country. Punjabis are known all over the world for their enterprise, straightforward culture and wit. Punjab has also seen the worst of extremism and terrorism in the last decade and has come out of it. Even during this difficult decade Punjab continued to lead the country.

Historical and Geographical Setting

Historically Punjab meant the land-block through which five rivers (Sutlej, Beas, Ravi, Chenab and Jhelum) flowed. Punjab has faced many separations and divisions in the twentieth century although the Kingdom of Punjab was annexed to India after the Anglo-Sikh Wars on 31st March, 1849. In 1901, the North-Western Frontier Province was separated from it. In 1947 the state was partitioned as a consequence of division of British India into India and Pakistan. The rich canal colonies and other developed areas went to Pakistan and relatively backward eastern part became part of India. Punjab and East Punjab States Union areas were merged with Punjab in 1956 as a consequence of reorganisation of class B states in India. Haryana state and some areas now in Himachal were carved out of Punjab in 1966. The present state of Punjab came into being through linguistic reorganisation on November 1, 1966.

Geographically, the state extends from 29° 30' N to 32° 32' N latitude and 73° 55' E to 76° 50' E longitude. It covers an area of 50,362 sq. kms. More than ninety per cent of it are alluvial plains. Punjab has three perennial rivers that flow through it namely Ravi, Beas and Sutlej, although Ravi just touches Punjab. Renowned Bhakra-Nangal Project is on the river Sutlej. Punjab has a continental semi-arid to sub-humid climate.

The range of temperature is very mild and average rainfall is 50 cm, major part being concentrated during the monsoon months. Of the 15 agro-climatic zones identified by Planning Commission, Punjab is serial number 6 known as the Trans-Gangetic Plain. It is subdivided into Northern Sub-Division comprising Jallandhar, Kapurthala, Amritsar, Gurdaspur, Ropar and Hoshiarpur districts and Southern—Central Sub Division comprising Ferozepur, Ludhiana, Patiala, Sangrur, Bhatinda and Faridkot districts.

Very recently new administrative districts of Mansa, Fatehgarh, Moga, Mukatsar and Nawansahar have been carved out of some of the older districts. We shall be referring to the Punjab of old 12 districts and three Divisions of Jallandhar, Patiala and Ferozepur. This is because the period of socio-economic reports pertains to the 12 districts of Punjab.

Demography and Politics

Total population of Punjab was 16.79 million in 1981 and 20.19 million in 1991. Growth rate over the decades of 1961-71, 1971-81 and 1981-91 have been 21.70, 23.89 and 20.26 per cent respectively. Fall in growth rate in 1991 has been probably due to much lower immigration and flight of industry from the disturbed areas. It could also be attributed to the fact that Punjab has reached the high development stage with mature stable population and the success in population control programmes. Couple protection rate of 63.73 per cent achieved in Punjab in recent years it is much higher than the national target of 60 per cent (envisaged) to be achieved by 2000 A.D. The density of population has increased substantially. So the pressure of population on land is more but Punjab's income as highest in the country has shown that enterprise and administration can continue to produce good results.

Punjab is basically a rural economy and its impact on Punjab's growth strategy, its consumption pattern and its politics is an important aspect for researchers to study. Rural population constituted 76.9 per cent in 1961, 76.3 per cent in 1971 and 72.3 per cent of total in 1981.

There are very special demographic-economic features to be noted which have a bearing on the recent economic-political situation in Punjab. About 60 per cent of the population of Punjab are Sikhs and virtually dominate rural areas. Hindus constitute about 40% of the population and mainly concentrated in the urban areas. Agriculture is predominantly a Sikh enterprise and industries and business are predominantly in the hands of Hindus. Shiromani Akali Dal is a religio-political party of the Sikhs and has been a powerful force in Punjab politics reflecting the Sikh discontent. Its major demands have been based on emphasising religious identity of Sikhs and protecting the agricultural-rural interests.

Terrorism was easily nurtured by disgruntled elements when legitimate economic demands of Punjabis were not met in 1981. Then the old Naxalite elements and the new fundamentalists of Khalsa joined hands. Support and stimulus from Pakistan was readily available. Unemployment among educated Sikh rural youth in the wake of developed mechanised agriculture and green revolution added a new dimension to religio-political scenario.

Punjab passed through a worst decade from early eighties to early nineties. Akali Dal passed into the hands of religious fundamentalists. Hindus were not averse to rural economic demands put forth by Akali Dal but their religious political and economic base was not the Akali Dal. Unfortunate handling of rising terrorism through Operation Blue Star and Operation Woodrose and widespread Communal Riots of 1984 against the Sikhs in the wake of Mrs. Indira Gandhi's assassination and incapability and unwillingness of administration to control them, made Punjab a hotbed of terrorist crime, robbery and murders for about a decade.

Fortunately Punjab has come out of the difficult decade because of efficient police handling and also because of the perennial Hindu-Sikh communal harmonious traditions in Punjab imbibed through historical religious traditions of so many centuries and the enlightened Sikh masses who are the backbone of Punjab model of development.

Agricultural Growth and Green Revolution in Punjab

Pre-independence agricultural growth has been ably studied by George Blyn who found for Punjab a positive growth rate in output, area under cultivation and to some extent even in yield for all crops from 1891-92 to 1945-1946. Raj Krishna's study over 1913-14 to 1945-46 has shown stagnation in yields of 11 crops but output grew positively because of extension of irrigated areas. A.K. Dasgupta studied separatcly East Punjab (India) and West Punjab (Pakistan) from 1906-07 to 1941-42 and found that agricultural growth was visible only in West Punjab. We can therefore take it that Indian Punjab was agriculturally a stagnant area at the time of independence. In fact present Punjab was a deficit area in food production.

Quick recovery and growth of agricultural output was visible in Punjab between 1952-53 to 1965-66 in the pre green revolution period.

Table 3.1 : Agricultural Index Numbers (All Commodities) in Punjab and India Base 1950-51 = 100

	1955-56		*1960-61*		*1965-66*	
Crop	*Punjab*	*India*	*Punjab*	*India*	*Punjab*	*India*
Rice	100	134	214	168	273	149
Wheat	111	136	170	170	187	161
Maize	103	150	261	236	453	279
Total Cereals	109	131	171	163	210	147
Total Foodgrains	114	131	160	161	170	142
Oil Seeds	104	111	220	135	402	124

Punjab surpassed Indian figures even before the Mexican dwarf varieties ushered in green revolution. Economic revolution in agriculture was already on its way before the agro-biological revolution took over Indian agriculture. It was not only extension of agriculture to new areas due to irrigation but growth in yields was also visible. While national figures shown stagnation or very slow growth, Punjab figures show growth and surpass national figures even where they started from lower base.

Table 3.2 : Crop Yields in Punjab and India

(Quintals per Hectare)

	1950-51		*1955-56*		*1960-61*		*1965-66*	
Crops	*Punjab*	*India*	*Punjab*	*India*	*Punjab*	*India*	*Punjab*	*India*
Rice	8.92	6.70	7.18	8.17	10.09	10.10	11.36	9.33
Wheat	9.01	6.60	8.79	7.10	12.44	8.50	14.24	8.73
Bajra	3.82	2.90	3.84	3.00	4.72	2.90	5.81	3.57
Groundnut	5.78	7.80	6.42	7.50	9.25	7.50	1.83	6.63

Why has it been so, is the million rupee question? One is the timely completion of Bhakra-Nangal Project and actual realisation of its benefits by Punjab farmers. Millions of Punjab farmers, who had migrated from Pakistan already knew the value of irrigation, electricity and good healthy seeds to crops. They quickly reaped the benefits and made others, (*i.e.* the original East Punjab farmers) learnt quickly by demonstration effect. Incidentally many of the migrants from West Punjab were really the progressive migrants from East Punjab who had gone there just two generations ago. They were quick to learn the methods of cultivation of irrigated agriculture. Government of Punjab, also saw to it that major planning effort went to agriculture. Sectoral allocation of actual Plan expenditures in Punjab amply bear it out, as shown by the following Table 3.3:

Table 3.3 : Percentage Sectoral Allocation of Total Expenditure in Five Year Plans of Punjab

Head of Department	*First Plan*	*Second Plan*	*Third Plan*	*Fourth Plan*
Agriculture and Community Development	18.10	16.70	17.21	12.0
Irrigation and Power	58.60	51.70	52.79	55.43
Industries and Mining	0.90	3.40	4.06	3.24
Transport and Communication	5.80	7.0	5.62	14.85
Social Services	8.50	16.40	18.75	13.25
Miscellaneous	8.10	4.8	1.57	1.23
Total	100	100	100	100

We can see that more than half of the plan expenditure went into Irrigation and Power and together with that on agriculture and community development it meant more than 2/3 of total plan expenditure. Punjab, thus realised much earlier the importance of providing basic infrastructure to agriculture. It is further borne by a glance at the generation and consumption of electric power in Punjab and India.

Table 3.4 : Generation and Consumption of Electric Power

Year	*Total Generation Million KWH*		*Per Capita Consumption KWH*		*Percent Share of Electricity Consumed by Agriculture*	
	Punjab	*India*	*Punjab*	*India*	*Punjab*	*India*
1951	207.18	5,640	5.89	17.80	6.90	8.62
1956	440.82	9,276	11.07	26.40	13.73	7.95
1960-61	1,003.64	16,215	28.12	38.20	14.47	9.10
1965-66	1,818.79	31.343	98.35	61.40	19.24	9.42

While Punjab started from a very low level of 5.89 KWH per capita consumption in 1951 compared to 17.80 for India, that is about 1/3 of Indian figure, it reached 1.5 times the Indian figure in 1965-66. Not only in total consumption but in the percentage of total electricity consumed in Agriculture, Punjab started at 6.90 compared to 8.62 for India as a whole. However, in 1965-66, Punjab figure of 19.24 compared to 9.42 for India is more than the double.

It appears while India was making efforts for grand designs of industrialisation, Punjab was quietly, steadily and certainly increasing its attention to the backbone of its economy and people that is the agriculture.

Capital Structure in Punjab agriculture shows that these investments and availability of power were actually changing the technology.

Number of power-operated cane crushers increased almost to 7 times between 1951 and 1966; net sown area per tubewell came to 83 hectares in 1961 from 2222 hectares in 1951. Total number of tractors increased to more than 9 times in 1966 compared to 1951 and net sown area per tractor came down to 356 hectares in 1966 compared to 3125 hectares in 1951. Punjab farmers were actually moving to the new technology that is the mechanised, irrigated and power operated agriculture. It was not merely the extension of irrigation to more areas or more land reclamation but active adoption of new technology with the availability of new facilities. Punjab farmers were only waiting for some new revolutionary development to bring new revolution in Agriculture.

Table 3.5 : Capital Structure in Punjab Agriculture

Item	*1951*	*1956*	*1961*	*1966*
Bullocks				
(a) Total No. (00')	13,78 (1.00)	14,148 (1.03)	14554 (1.06)	15335 (1.12)
(b) Net Sown Area Per Bullock (Hectares)	2.6	2.6	2.6	2.5
No.of Ploughs				
(a) Iron	1,53,000 (1.00)	2,66,000 (1.74)	4,11,815 (2.70)	6,34,144 4.15)
(b) Wooden	6,67,130 (1.00)	8,25,435 (1.24)	6,73,835 (1.01)	6,99,157 (1.05)
No. of Cane Crushers				
(a) Power Operated	476 (1.00)	547 (1.15)	1,566 (3.29)	3,223 (6.78)
(b) Bullock Operated	61,308 (1.00)	71,568 (1.17)	73,961 (1.21)	83,768 (1.45)
Tube-wells				
(a) Diesel Engines (No)	1,285 (1.00)	3,972 (3.10)	6,983 (5.44)	25,670 (19.98)
(b) Electric Motors (No.)	300 (1.00)	6,355 (21.19)	6,565 (21.89)	20,233 (67.45)
(c) Net Sown Area Per Tube-well (Hectares)	2,222	356	277	83
Tractors				
(a) Total (No)	1,418 (1.00)	2,909 2.54)	4,935 (4.30)	10,636 (9.27)
(b) Net Sown Area Per Tractor (Hectare)	3,125	1,235	758	356

Note: Figures in parentheses are index numbers with Base year 1951 = 100.

New technology in terms of high yielding varieties of seeds came from International Centre for Wheat and Maize Improvement, Mexico for wheat and from the International Rice Research Institute Philippines for rice. The high yielding varieties mature earlier (shorter duration); are of dwarf size and very responsive to fertilizer. They can absorb 2.5—3 times more nutrients per acre for grain yields which do not add to stalks; being photo insensitive they are less dependent on duration of day light.

Punjab farmers took to high yielding varieties and the associated technology in a dramatic manner and by 1989-90 almost the entire area under rice, wheat, maize and bajra was that of high-yielding varieties.

Table 3.6: Area under High Yielding Varieties

(Percent of Total)

Items	*1971-72*	*1980-81*	*1989-90*
Rice	68.1	92.6	100.00
Wheat	72.6	98.0	100.00
Maize	7.3	33.2	98.56
Bajra	47.6	49.3	100.00

Same way the use of chemical fertilizers in terms of nutrients increased.

Mechanisation also dramatically increased as more production could not have resulted due to shortage and problems of labour. Punjab agriculture became commercial in the real sense. Following Table 3.7 shows the pace of mechanisation:

Table 3.7: Peace of Mechanisation

Items	*1971-72*	*1980-81*	*1989-90*
Tractors ('000)	41	119	269
Threshers ('000)	134	250	367
Harvest Combines (Number)			
Self-propelled	-	190	1400
Tractor-driven	-	1000	3600

While net area sown to total area has stayed constant (almost the maximum having been achieved), irrigation mainly through diesel and electricity-operated tubewells, have increased the area sown more than once and its impact on cropped area has been obviously positive.

	1971-72	*1980-81*	*1989-90*
Area Sown more than once (lakh hect)	16.48	25.72	32.0
Percent of Area Sown more than once to total sown area	40.43	61.37	76.35
Total Cropped Area (lakh hect)	57.24	67.63	73.91
Cropping Intensity Percent	140	161	176

It may be noted that the cultivable area is 43 lakh hectares and net area sown was 41.91 lakh hectares in 1989-90.

Increase in cropping intensity and increase in the area sown more than once has obviously been because of increase in the irrigated area. Net area sown was 41.91 lakh hectares and net area irrigated was 39.29 lakh hectares. Gross area irrigated was 69.27 lakh hectares giving irrigation intensity equal to 176 per cent. Of course favourable rainfall has been a national phenomenon and Punjab has also reaped well its luck, as given by figures below:

Irrigation

	1971-72	*1980-81*	*1988-89*	*1989-90*
Net Area Irrigated (Lakh hect)	29.55	33.82	37.76	39.29
Net area irrigated to net area sown (per cent)	72	81	90	94
Gross area irrigated (Lakh hect)	43.77	57.81	68.37	69.27
Irrigation Intensity (Per cent)	148	171	181	176
Tubewells (Lakh)	--	6.0	7.42	7.65
Average Rainfall (Cms)	67.97	73.91	112.27	52.58

Seeds, water, machines have been combined with increased use of fertilizers. Consumption of fertilizers was 2.90 lakh nutrients tonnes in 1971-72. The figure in 1989-90 at 11.45 and in 1993-94 at 11.99 shows an increase to a fourfold level.

Punjab farmers produced the results which have won them admiration all over the world. Production of rice was 9.20 lakh tons in 1971-72 and in 1989-90 it reached the level of 66.80 lakh tons and in 1993-94 the level reached is 76.35. Wheat production was 56.18 lakh tons in 1971-72 and in 1989-90, it was 115.48 lakh tons and for 1993-94 the figure is 133.4. Cotton production in 1971-72 was 10.30 lakh bales and in 1989-90 it was 24.57 lakh bales. Pulses and oilseeds showed decline, however, as technology and necessary concomitant government services in extension, supply of inputs and price support were not available with the same efficiency and enthusiasm as in the case of wheat and rice. Cotton and sugarcane have followed a bit late while other crops lagged behind. Recently sunflower has been introduced. During 1990-91 it was grown on nearly 14000 hectares, giving a production of only 22000 tons. In 1993-94, area under sunflowers was 1.01 lakh hectares, giving a production of 1.65 lakh tons.

It is interesting to have a look at the figures of index numbers of agricultural production in Punjab.

Table 3.8 : Agricultural Production in Punjab
Index Numbers (1967-68 to 1969-70 = 100)

Items	*19771-72*	*1980-81*	*1989-90*
Cereals	137.16	239.71	407.13
Foodgrains	124.21	196.74	321.08
Non-Foodgrains	109.43	126.31	205.47
All Commodities	118.92	171.52	279.70

Thus Green Revolution in Punjab has meant increase to four times in cereals, three and a quarter times to foodgrains, two times to non-foodgrains and to two and three quarter increase in all commodities in agriculture during two decades. Let it not be thought that increase in wheat, rice, cotton production by bringing in more land under cultivation alone. The significant increase in yields per hectare prove that revolution has been really a revolution in technology, enterprise and government support and services.

Table 3.9 : Yield Per Hectare

Items	*1971-72*	*1980-81*	*1988-89*	*1993-94*
Wheat (Kgms)	2406	2730	3667	4040
Rice (Kgms)	2045	2733	2770	3493
Cotton (Cleaned) (Kgms)	369	308	475	444* (570 in 1992-93)

*Unprecedented damage was caused due to Helio disease and floods in this year.

Of course production increase has been not only due to increase in yields but also because of increase in cropped area, as cropping intensity increased due to extended tubewell irrigation which number is 8.5 lakhs now.

Increase in production has meant more market arrivals, which created problems and in response led to creation of more regulated markets, infrastructure in these markets, strain on village link roads, problems of godowns, procurement and payments, transportation by rail and trucks — sort of problems not thought of in most other states. Punjab farmer is a true commercial producer now.

Table 3.10 : Market Arrivals

(Lakh Metric Tonnes)

Year	*Wheat*	*Paddy*
1970-71	27.22	8.46
1980-81	43.92	44.32
1990-91	70-76	78.94
1993-94	68.19	90.00

Indices of Net State Domestic Product at factor cost show that from 1960-61 to 1967-68, it grew by 46.6 per cent at constant (1960-61) prices. This is in line with the growth in the primary sector whose major component is agriculture (others being livestock, forestry and logging, fishing and mining and quarrying). Primary sector grew by 45.3 per cent during the same period. Average annual growth rate of State Income at constant (1970-71 prices) from 1970-71 to 1973-74 was 3.2 per cent and that of primary sector was 1.8 per cent. The comparative figures for India are 1.6 per cent for total national income and 0.03 per cent for primary sector in the same period. Thus while state income was growing double the rate of national income, Punjab's primary sector was growing 6 times that of India's primary sector. This means Green Revolution technology and impact was hardly visible in India while Punjab was making big strides.

If we take a longer period from 1970-71 to 1983-84 then the picture is as under:

Table 3.11 : Annual Growth Rate of State Income of Punjab and National Income of India (at 1970-71 prices) from 1970-71 to 1983-84

Sectors	*Punjab*	*India*
Primary Sector	3.5	2.0
Secondary Sector	5.7	3.9
Tertiary Sector	6.5	5.6
Total State/National Income	4.7	3.6

Punjab was positively ahead of India as a whole in terms of rates of growth of sectoral and total income. It is way ahead in primary sector but not so in other sectors. Agricultural growth was taking Punjab ahead, it appears.

If we take the yearly rates of growth of the first four years of Seventh Plan Period, for which data is available, the story is identical.

Table 3.12 : Average Annual Compound Growth Rate of Gross State / National Income (at 1980-81 prices) Percent per annum

	1985-86	*1986-87*	*1987-88*	*1988-89*
PUNJAB				
Primary	8.18	(-)0.3	4.38	3.59
Secondary	11.97	9.69	7.44	10.31
Tertiary	3.28	7.72	7.13	5.39
Total State Income	7.52	4.09	5.00	5.67
INDIA				
Primary	0.54	(-)1.58	0.56	16.87
Secondary	8.54	8.24	3.35	7.67
Tertiary	7.32	6.22	7.04	6.94
Total National Income	5.07	3.96	3.82	10.41

The point to be noted is that while primary and secondary sectoral rates of growth in Punjab are way ahead compared to Indian sectoral rates, Punjab lagged behind India in the growth rates of tertiary sector all these years except the heavy drought year of 1986-87. The inference is that while Punjab's agricultural growth did make manufacturing, construction and electricity, gas and water supply follow, the tertiary sector (transport, storage, communication, trade, hotels, banking, real estate etc.) did not get the initial stimulus from agricultural growth in Punjab.

Primary sector's contribution in percentage terms to net output at factor cost (at 1960-61 prices) of Punjab was 52.9, 55.3 and 54.7 for the years 1966-67, 1967-68 and 1968-69 respectively. That of secondary sector hovered around 20 per cent and that of tertiary sector around 25 per cent for these years.

After giving the initial success the primary sector's percentage contribution began to decline. As a percentage in Net State Domestic Product at Factor Cost at constant (1970-71) prices, it was 58 per cent in 1970-71 and came to 51 per cent in 1984-85. Taking the series of constant prices of 1980-81, it came down from 51 per cent in 1985-86 to 48 per cent in 1988-89. After agriculture, the other major component in primary sector is animal husbandry. Agriculture came down from 35.17 per cent in 1985-86 to 32.96 per cent in 1989-90. Livestock's contribution at 15-16 per cent remained constant throughout.

Per Capita State Income

But agricultural growth did bring prosperity to Punjabis in general. Per capita Net State Domestic Product at current prices was Rs.1070 in 1970-71 and rose to Rs.4,416 in 1985-86. At constant

Table 3.13 : Per Capita Income in Selected States in India at Constant (1980-81) Prices

(Rupees)

State	*1980-81*	*1985-86*	*1988-89*
Andhra Pradesh	1,380	1,552	1,689
Gujarat	1,951	2,049	2,631
Haryana	2,370	2,778	3,160
Karnataka	1,612	1,723	2,041
Maharashtra	2,427	2,710	2,026
Tamil Nadu	1,498	1,823	2,030
Punjab	2,675	3,167	3,421
All India	1,630	1,852	2,078

prices of 1970-71, it was Rs.1,621 in 1985-86. Figures of per capita income for late eighties are available at constant 1980-81 prices and we can compare Punjab figures in these years with other industrially developed states as well as that of All India.

Thus Punjab model of growth of emphasis on agriculture, modern inputs and modern technology enterprise of the people in willing to learn and practice modern technology has brought prosperity. It has been pointed out that Punjab farming is a commercial enterprise and most of the increased output has found its way to market which, through efficient procurement system, has meant increasing contribution of Punjab to Central Pool for public distribution in India thus helping solve India's food problem as well.

Table 3.14 : Percent Contribution from Punjab to the Central Pool

Year	*Rice*	*Wheat*
1970-71	16	74
1980-81	45	76
1990-91	41	61
1993-94	50	70

Landholding Pattern

Punjab model of modern inputs, technology, irrigation and state support was workable in Punjab for one big reason. This is the landholding pattern and peasant proprietorship. Historically British rule in Punjab was less exploitative in the Punjab than elsewhere. For one thing the British annexed Punjab to the Empire only in 1849. The Sikh wars had shown them that unless they won sturdy, militant, Sikh peasants to their loyalty, British rule would never be stable in Punjab. The British had, in fact, won the Anglo-Sikh wars by treachery of Sikh ruling class actively propped by and encouraged by the British. Sikh masses would not easily forget and forgive. Hence, the historical "healing touch" was deliberately planned. It was put to practice by John Lawrence and Henry Lawrence who were the Governors in the formative period.

The pernicious system of permanent settlement was never imposed in Punjab. Land institutions and revenue system were reformed. An extensive system of canal irrigation was developed and progressive farmers from Eastern districts in Punjab were encouraged to settle in the new canal colonies of Sargodha, Shahpur and Lyalpur. The outstanding step forward was that of encouraging consolidation of holdings through cooperation and later introducing a "compulsion clause" for others if the "Majority" agreed to consolidation.

While partition came as a rude and shocking massacre to Indian Punjab and meant compulsive migration for millions of Punjabis from West Punjab to East, it had two positive impacts in East Punjab in independent India. First it meant that progressive, enterprising, rich farming population was joining India to restart their economic life from scratch. The "refugees", as they were called, never begged or sat idle in the streets. They demanded Muslim evacuee land in place of fertile lands they left. They had left 67 lakh acres of fertile land in Pakistan (of which 43 lakh acres were irrigated). Muslims evacuee land was only 47 lakh acres of which only 13 lakh acres were irrigated. Responsive and sympathetic Government of India and Punjab did a miraculously efficient task by allotting and handing over these lands by 1951. Cuts have to be there; same amount of land could not be given. At top cuts were to the extent of 95 per cent. And these lands were infertile and needed efforts of "reclamation". The refugee farmers sat to this task earnestly.

It was around this time that compulsory consolidation of holdings was introduced in Punjab and actively administered by the visionary Chief Minister of Punjab, Sardar Partap Singh Kairon. The entire task of consolidation of holdings was completed by 1965-66; while it is still under way in mid-nineties in many states of India. Consolidated land was 89.37 lakh hectares in Punjab. Bhakra Nangal Project provided canal irrigation. The refugees knew the value of utilisation of irrigation facilities through "Water Bandi" (rotation of turns) system and learning quick from them everyone adopted it.

The other very beneficial impact of consolidation was that investment in tubewells was not only a possibility but a very big attraction with electricity being available from Bhakra Nangal at cheap rates. Owner cultivators were encouraged to self-cultivate the land and reduce the leased out area.

"Gentleman farmers" in Punjab were receptive and ready for new technology. They are the retired military personnel. It may be noted that largest percentage of recruits to Indian army is provided by Punjab.

Land Reforms

A word on land reforms in Punjab must complete our story of Punjab land situation. Land relations in Punjab before independence were less retrogressive than in other states. Punjab tenurial system was such that 57 per cent of cultivated area was under tenant cultivation. Security of tenure to tenants in Punjab came rather later than elsewhere. In Punjab it came in 1953 and in Patiala and East Punjab State Union (PEPSU) in 1955. The Act commenced its operations in 1964 and by that time the "recorded tenants" had almost vanished, although reported figure in 1955 was 5.8 lakh tenants. So the proprietary rights were given only to 13,353 tenants by 1964 in Punjab and in PEPSU areas to 5,989 tenants only. They together held 1,27,794 acres out of total area of 188 lakh acres in 1963-64.

Concerning land ceiling laws, a Planning Commission report stated that 3.92 lakh standard acres were the estimated surplus. But after giving exemptions and exceptions, the area actually estimated as surplus was 2.56 lakh standard acres. Till 1966, 63,520 tenants were resettled on 1.22 lakh standard acres. Punjab Land Reforms Act, 1972 was more radical and changed the ceiling from 30 standard acres to 7 hectares of irrigated land worthy of two crops.

The report of the Revenue Department of Government of Punjab for the period ending 30th September, 1994, the total estimated surplus under 1953 and 1972 Acts together was 3.06

lakh acres but actual net area declared surplus was only 1.32 lakh acres. Area actually taken possession is 1.05 lakh acres. Only 27,290 acres are yet to be taken possession of. This is the area under litigation. Total area distributed is 1.02 lakh acres and total number of beneficiaries are 26,647 out of which 10,074 are scheduled castes.

The major flaw of ceiling laws and their actual operation has been the difference between estimated surplus and declared surplus. The discrepancy involves 1,73,495 acres of land. It is almost 1.5 times the declared surplus.

Thus clearly Punjab ceiling and tenancy laws and their operation have been pro-owners of land. Punjab ruling elite both in legislature and bureaucracy has been land-owning class. In fact it is quite surprising for an insider of Punjab to believe that one lakh acres of land have actually been distributed.

One could, of course, say that Punjab land reform legislation and its operation has been pro-production and not pro-distribution. As the political situation now stands there is hardly a scope for brighter prospects. Even as general incomes have risen, consumption standards have soared and education-health expenditures and liabilities have grown, a "legal" 7 hectare farm is not a high income earning asset.

Actually people in Punjab are now more concerned about productive opportunities of raising non-farm incomes through diversified agriculture rather than reopening the question of land relations and land reforms. A landless labourer gets wages and employment that affords him much better living in Punjab than elsewhere in the country. Most of the landless workers are immigrant seasonal workers from Bihar, U.P. and Rajasthan and they are obvious mirrors of the situation elsewhere and they keep the Punjabi landless worker "disciplined" and restrained both because of economic logic as because of social reality. Otherwise also agriculture holdings in Punjab are much more diffused over different classes and there is much less skewness and sharp differences of the type elsewhere is rare. We compare the situation in Punjab with Bihar on the basis of figures provided by Agricultural Census of 1985-86.

Table 3.15 : Percentage of Number of Operational Holdings and Percentage of Area Operated by Major Size Groups

	No. of Operational Holdings		*Area Operated*	
	Punjab	*Bihar*	*Punjab*	*Bihar*
Marginal	23.5	76.9	3.4	27.8
Small	19.1	11.2	7.6	17.1
Semi-medium	26.7	8.0	20.4	24.9
Medium	23.9	3.4	38.7	22.0
Large	6.8	.44	29.8	8.0
All	100	100	100	100

Source: Based on Agricultural Statistics, At a Glance by GOI, 1990.

Thus land based social tensions are almost absent; both are reconciled to the present social set-up as long as prosperity in agriculture continues and gets passed on to rural labour as well.

There are doubts, however, whether this prosperity can continue to grow. Punjab agriculture, in terms of irrigation and sown area is already at its peak. New HYV are not forthcoming as quickly as earlier. The difference in yield between previous and new varieties as earlier is not significant. Problems of overuse of water and fertilizers are also cropping up. Hence the recent policy change to diversification in agriculture and focussing on horticulture and processing industries is very welcome. These changes of shifting to oilseeds, sugarcane, horticulture, floriculture, bee-keeping, mushroom cultivation, fisheries, and agro-processing small and medium industries might be the new areas that take Punjab farmers to continuing prosperity. Otherwise, a disenchantment with agriculture is widely discernible in rural areas among landowners in recent years. The future of Punjab farmers shall be decided by them outside the usual wheat-rice crop syndrome.

Rural Development

As on 31st March 1970, community development programme was actively covering 12,889 villages in 166 blocks. IRDP was launched in April, 1978. By 1980-81, Punjab had already benefited 1,02,700 families by making a total expenditure of Rs.731 lakhs. Under NREP, by 1980-81 cumulative employment of 56.5 lakh mandays was created and 46000 metric tonnes of foodgrains had been utilised.

TRYSEM programme was launched in August, 1979. In two years 1980-81 and 1981-82, Punjab had trained 1,880 persons and 1,960 persons respectively and made 891 and 2471 persons self-employed. Similar figures are available for later years as well. Activities of Rural Development Agency were actually covering 12,337 villages, 118 blocks and total expenditure in the year 1990-91 reported was Rs.1050 lakhs. It means, of course, that all the villages and blocks were completely covered. Of the total of 35,944 beneficiaries, 18,198 were scheduled castes.

These figures do not tell the real story of poverty in Punjab. Poverty in Punjab does not mean finding impossible to make both ends meet in terms of requisite food and necessary calories. Poverty is a comparative concept in Punjab, rather than the absolute concept elsewhere. Do these relatively poor people of Punjab really need the subsidy, loan asset or wage programmes tailored for the absolute poor elsewhere? We have our doubts. But since funds from Government of India are available only under these tailored programmes and Government of Punjab does not want to deprive itself and its people of these funds. Thus, the programmes, agencies and personnel under them continue to live. TRYSEM has some meaning in Punjab, but IRDP hardly any. It would be better to allow Punjab to make its own poverty-alleviation programmes with these funds and generate skills and create employment for skilled and unskilled people.

Industries

Punjab is known more for its agriculture but its industrial development, especially in small and medium sectors, can not be ignored.

Theoretically agricultural growth must give way, ultimately, to industrial growth if rise in growth rates of income is to continue. Per labour productivity in agriculture has always lagged behind that of industry because of reasons of technology, market, long term consumption-profile and value addition in production.

In 1969, there were 4,141 registered working factories in Punjab and all (except 5) were working with power employing on an average 1.05 lakh workers, nodal location being in Amritsar and Ludhiana districts. There was 715 joint stock companies. Number of registered factories was 6,624 in 1979. Registration of factories really picked up in early eighties and by 1984, the number stood 9,184. Addition to registered number of factories in late eighties is as under:

Table 3.16 : Registered number of factories

Years	*No. of Registered Working Factories*	*Addition over Previous Year*
1970	4501	360
1979	6624	NA
1983	8,535	NA
1984	9,184	649
1985	9,271	87
1986	9,754	483
1987	10,255	50
1988	10,419	164
1989	10,734	315

Terrorism had its impact by slowing down the increase in number of registered factories. Newspapers did report of industries trying to shift to safer havens. Situation has stabilised in recent years and industrial activity has picked up markedly, though annual data of post-nineties is not available with us.

Punjab's position may be compared to other states by looking at the following Table 3.17 :

Table 3.17 : Registered Working Factories in India by Selected States

States	*1981-82*	*1982-83*	*1983-84*	*1985-86*	*1986-87*
Andhra Pradesh	12,001	10,904	11,837	12,746	12,328
Bihar	4,988	3,759	3,904	4,988	3,747
Gujarat	12,984	10,073	10,494	10,305	10,697
Haryana	2,664	2,648	2,745	3,026	2,877
Karnataka	5,694	5,146	5,602	5,456	5,655
Madhya Pradesh	3,472	3,069	3,235	4,009	3,214
Maharashtra	16,699	14,983	14,546	14,970	15,148
Punjab	5,946	5,036	5,380	5,710	5,325
Tamil Nadu	10, 932	11,303	11,918	12,429	12,616
Uttar Pradesh	7,949	7,697	7,539	7,550	7,842
West Bengal	7,281	5,836	5,635	5,619	5,224
Delhi	3,159	2,874	3,240	3,186	2,843

Punjab's position comes after Maharastra, Tamilnadu, Andhra Pradesh, Gujarat and Karnataka which have the advantages of industrial centres of Bombay, Pune, Madras, Hyderabad, Surat, Baroda and Bangalore. Punjab is the Western border state and in spite of terrorism, it maintained its industrial position. Punjab would certainly have outpaced Karnataka atleast but for the terrorist troubles, in the past decade.

Index of industrial production, taking 1975-76 = 100, shows growth as under:

Table 3.18 : Index of Industrial Production

1975-76	100
1976-77	110.11
1980-81	177.6
1982-83	200.24
1984-85	215.73
1985-86	228.86
1986-87	246.32
1987-88	275.34
1988-89	303.65

In terms of gross value of production, important industries are woollen textiles, cotton textiles, rice milling, fertilizers, cycle and cycle parts industries in that ranking order. Other industries of note in Punjab are sugar, sports goods and hand tools.

Workers employed in registered working factories were 1.19 lakh in 1971-72, 2.02 lakh in 1980-81 and 3.45 lakh in 1989-90. Workers in industries per lakh of population were 862 in 1971-72, 1,206 in 1980-81 and 1,699 in 1989-90.

General Services

Punjab is foremost in most social services provided. In 1989-90, with 5,063 motor vehicles per lakh of population (more than 10 and 9 thousand in Jallandhar and Ludhiana, respectively), with a road length of 200 kms. per lakh of population, with 100% villages linked to roads and provided with electricity, with 24 km. area being served per scheduled commercial bank branch, and with highest per capita egg availability (90 in Punjab and 22 in India) and with highest per capita availability of milk (698 gms) and the only State in India having a Mahila Swasthya Sangh in every village and urban slum area, Punjab is the wonder state of India which has shown the path of overall development to others in India and abroad.

—But what is the situation in her "poor" villages as seen in the micro-studies of IAS officers under training?

—That is our main concern in the back-ground of this overall introductory glance and a macro view.

AGRICULTURE AND AGRARIAN RELATIONS

Agriculture—The Social and Economic Base

Agriculture is not only the main activity of the majority of the people but is also the hub of all activities in a village. Politics, social relations and most of the Government programmes also centre around agriculture and farmers. Most of the studies really start with the description of the changing pattern of agriculture especially the cropping pattern, emerging problems of sustaining or changing this pattern and its impact on general economic conditions of the people. A brief description is on agrarian relations.

There are some important inter-district differences but let us take the common factors first as reported by the Officer Trainees of IAS from 1984-1995.

Most of the holdings are owner-operated and are of small to medium size. Small holdings are the nodal class. Holdings of 10 to 50 acres are few and beyond 50 acres, almost rare. Almost all probationers, reporting from different districts and different years have reported it by citing the ownership holding pattern of the village studied.

Few examples are given below:

Village Randhawa Masanda (District Jallandhar 1991) **Agriculture Ownership Holdings**		Village Bela (District Ropar, 1989) **Agriculture Holdings**	
Upto 5 acres	138	< 1 acre	397
5-10	83	1-5 acres	322
10-50	9	5-10 acres	161
		10-50 acres	112
		> 50 Acres	5

Village Pona (District Ludhiana, 1991)		Village Massinghan (District Patiala, 1989)		
Agriculture Holdings		**Agriculture Holdings**		
< 1 acres	6	< 5 acres	931	
1-5	130	5-10	83	
5-10	28	10-50	41	
10-50	7			
> 50	Nil			
Village Kot Umra (District Ludhiana, 1988)		**Village Dada (District Hoshiarpur, 1990)**		
Agriculture Ownership Holdings		**Agriculture Holdings**		
< 1 acres	2	<2.5 acres	423	
1-5	46	2.5 - 5	45	
5-10	10	> 5	34	
10-50	2>			
50	Nil			
Village Ajitpura (District Bhatinda, 1984)		**Village Jahangir (District Amritsar, 1986)**		
Agriculture Holdings		**Agriculture Holdings Land in Acres**		
1-5	76	< 1 acres	15	13
6-10	31	< 5 acres	20	35
11-20	36	<10 acres	25	650
21 and above	6	<20 acres	11	210

When B. Vikram (1994) took a random sample of 25 households within his randomly chosen village Chorewahi in his selected district Jallandhar, of the 12 households owning land, 6 had land between 1-5 acres and 4 had land between 5-10 acres. Only 2 persons were in the "big farmer" category owning land more than 10 acres. Of these two one had 15 acres of land, the biggest farm.

This land holding pattern ensures inter-class harmony among different people. The sort of tensions reported in the Bihar studies are almost absent here at least in the given studies in the given villages. The influence of CPM in Punjab villages have not been insubstantial but since the green revolution and after the 1972 land reforms law, the interclass tensions have been not the economic-political issue in Punjab villages. CPM has raised the demands and interests of small and marginal farmers. Religio-economic demands of Akali Party in Punjab have also tried to represent the interests of farmers (all classes, though) ... like higher procurement prices, more water for Punjab in Ravi-Beas, inter-state water distribution question and more funds and industries for Punjab.

Landless labourers in Punjab have turned to seek higher wages and stable employment. Thus, while keeping alive the village links, they have found placement in the rising small scale industrial and trading sectors. Migrant labour from U.P., Bihar and Rajasthan have tried to fill the gap in villages at least in sowing and harvesting operations. In fact Punjab farmers have taken now some of these migrant workers as their permanent farm helpers.

Consolidation of holdings has been a land mark achievement although tenants and landless workers suffered injury to their interest. Almost all probationers have reported and lauded consolidation of holdings in Punjab. In fact some have rather suggested another round of consolidation as, after three decades, holdings have been fragmented again. (Vijai Kumar, 1990 reporting from Naushera—Nalbandha in district Gurdaspur and also Vijoy Kumar Singh, 1991, village Pona, district Ludhiana).

Although most of the cultivation in Punjab is owner cultivation yet tenant cultivation has also been reported. These are not recorded tenants, however, Karan Bir Singh Sidhu (1985, village Kakyala, District Patiala) aptly remarks:

"It is surprising that the entire 835 hectares owned by the peasants is shown as 'Khud-Kasht' (self-cultivated) in the 'Jamabandi'." This would imply that there are no tenants at all, which may be justified by the argument that where the holdings are very small, there is no question of tenants being encouraged. However, the fact is that although tenants do exist, they are not reflected in the 'Jamabandi' because then the eviction becomes very difficult on account of the provisions of the PEPSU Tenancy and Agricultural Lands Act, 1955. Informal inquiry reveals that about 10% of the area is under tenants, paying rents.....".

Again Karan Bir Singh writes candidly:

"Generally no written agreement is executed between the landlord and the tenant. However, it is implicit that the tenant shall not insist on his name being recorded in the "Khasra Girdawari" as the cultivator. Where land is a very scarce commodity, the tenant is generally compelled into acquiescing in this condition of the landlord. The tenants are generally not completely landless and they take additional cultivation as tenants to supplement their income."

Shri KAP Sinha (1993) reports almost the same way about concealed tenancy in his village Gobindgarh Jejian in Sangrur district Sarvjit Singh (1993), village Jallahkheri (Patiala) also reports 11 cases of concealed tenancy (ranging 2 to 7 acres rented by small farmers) although girdawary register did not show a single tenant.

Mostly, tenants cultivate lands of those who have gone to settle in cities or are army personnel unable to cultivate in person.

Land distribution under Land Reforms Act, wherever has taken place, has been commended by the probationers. Land has actually been transferred and irrigation and input facilities etc. have also been provided. Cases of five such families were reported by Jaspal Singh in 1993, in village Mehal Singhwala of District Ferozepur. Ravneet Kaur reported one case from village Massinghan in Patiala.

But most interesting cases have been reported by Sh. K.A.P. Sinha in his studied village Gobindgarh—Jejian in 1993. Mr. Jaswant Singh's descendants had large chunk of land which was declared surplus but ownership has not yet changed legally in records. The land's possession has now been taken up by different persons who, without any apprehension from any quarter, feel very happy over this possession of land and its cultivation. The author has, unfortunately, not revealed if possession is held by persons who were entitled to distribution under the Land Reform Acts or is held by others.

In the same village, Mr. Sinha reports, Hazoora Singh's land was declared surplus but he got the land transferred to some other fake names or persons reportedly living elsewhere. This man cannot be legally prosecuted for this nor does his own share get affected in any way. (In Haryana under an amendment of the Ceiling Act, the sale after the declaration of surplus land is tantamount to sale out of the share of the seller himself).

In this village 11 acres of land were declared surplus which were undisputed and land was to be distributed among beneficiaries. It had not been effected. Now the possession of land has been given to the beneficiaries but the legal ownership has not yet been transferred to them, because they had yet to deposit some money for that purpose. But the poor were very happy to posses and cultivate the land. No body disputes their right.

This reported situation in Punjab is in contrast with the one in Bihar where thousands of ownership pattas have existed for decades but the new "owners" have not been allowed to possess, cultivate or come near that land in actual practice by the erstwhile "owners" or real encroachers. Mr. Sarvjit Singh (1993) village Jallahkheri (Patiala) in his study of Land Reforms did report where a landlord's migrant labourers "legally" held the land but, for a handsome happy consideration of monthly income, allowed the land possession, cultivation and income to the landlord whose heirs after the legal expiry of the stipulated period got his land "legally" back by "buying" it from the legal owners now. In Punjab, a lot of attempts have successfully been made to "avoid" the application of provisions of ceiling law under the loopholes of the language of the law (which may, possibly have been deliberately planned by vested interests). But once the law prevails then possession and benefits do flow to the poor.

Unfortunately, advantage of the legal loopholes or an unclear situation has always been reaped by the strong-muscled or moneyed persons in Indian society. There is the interesting case of the land called Jumla Malkhan / Mushtaraqa Malkhan in the village. Certain cut in the lands of the owners were effected under consolidation of holdings to provide for exigencies and village commons. When the work of consolidation was completed and a portion of that land was still available, it was not given back to owners but entered in the revenue records as Jumla Malkhan/ Mushtaraqa Malkhan. Normally these lands in Punjab are operated by Gram Panchayats who rent out these lands to increase their incomes and thereby lay claim on matching grants under District Planning and Development Board. But in quite a few cases, these lands have been, mostly in collusion with influential and powerful people, encroached upon. The "legal ownership" of these lands is not in the Panchayats probably and they can not fight to take them back through courts. Any party who gets a "temporary" court decree in its favour, virtually becomes legal owner, until the Courts (Appeal Courts and so on) finally decide the case. The cases linger on and the possessor becomes virtually the owner.

No law and no language can be perfect, it is true. But one suspects mischief. Some flaws and vague provisions are deliberately made by vested interests to help themselves. Interesting part is even while some cases are decided the law and its language is not made completely transparent. Poor have never benefited by any such vagueness in law and its language. Poor, ignorant and illiterate people always suffer on these counts. Can't something be done ?

Agriculture

This is the most important activity of rural Punjab and whole socio-economic scenario as also the political developments in Punjab centre round it.

The most striking feature is the change in the cropping pattern in Punjab noted by every officer trainee. We have already taken an overall glance of the changing agricultural situation in the introductory chapter. It is proper and interesting to have a micro outlook now.

First important step is to understand the micro division of Punjab into smaller regions. Punjab can culturally as also geographically be divided into three distinct regions:

Majha
Doaba
Malwa

Majha really means middle or central region. Majha comprises the border districts of Amritsar, Gurdaspur and

Ferozepur. It really was once the economic, cultural, educational and locational centre of Punjab especially before Partition of 1947. The standard Punjabi is really the language as spoken and written in Majha or more precisely in Lahore and surrounding areas—much the same way as standard Hindi (Kharhi Bhasha) was as written and spoken in Allahabad. Majha has been commercially more developed, characterised by more urbane influences, its people area of better physique, bigger height than usual and agricultural holdings are of bigger size than elsewhere. Of course, Majha suffered the onslaught and massacre of partition the most and hence suffered on all counts. While Ludhiana and Jallandhar have developed as the two other big industrial commercial centres of Punjab, Amritsar is still one of the biggest and vies and excels Ludhiana in some respects. In the recent administrative reorganisation of districts, the three districts of Majha have been kept intact.

Malwa, apart from Ludhiana, comprises really the old Punjab and East Punjab States Union (PEPSU) which in fact were Sikh princely states in British India. It now comprises Ropar, Patiala, Sangrur, Bhatinda, Faridkot and Ludhiana. Recently, four new districts have been carved out: Mansa, mainly from Bhatinda and Fatehgarh mainly from Patiala (both in 1993) and Moga and Muktsar mainly from Faridkot (in 1995). With these new districts, Malwa is the biggest region in Punjab comprising nine districts. Malwa traditionally had more native and rustic glamour in culture compared to others. Culturally and economically, except for Patiala, it has been the backward region. Land has been less fertile. Crime has been of higher order here, especially in Bhatinda. Liquor and Tobacco consumption was also more here. But we are really talking of the past. Today it is as developed as the rest of Punjab. Sandy areas of Bhatinda have been converted into fertile lands with the waters of Bhakra irrigating them and the region has responded very well to new technology. Patiala now is probably the cultural centre and capital of Punjab; Ludhiana is the industrial centre and Bhatinda, with the Thermal Plants, as the energy centre of Punjab.

Doaba, literally means the area between the two rivers and really it meant area between Beas and Sutlej. The three important districts are Jallandhar, Kapurthala and Hoshiarpur. In Doaba land is very fertile and water is available in abundance. Holdings area much smaller in size, compared to other regions.

Over the recent years, due to widespread irrigation through Bhakra Canal system and tubewells and through rapid spread of education and most of all through communication revolution, the differences between different regions have been blurred. This three-region division is slowly becoming a matter of past.

In fact geographers used to divide Punjab traditionally, on the basis of areas between different rivers. Thus *(Upper) Bari Doaba* was area, between Beas and Ravi; the *Bist Doaba,* the area between the rivers Beas and Sutlej and *Malwa* as the area between the rivers Sutlej and Ghaggar. After the British annexation of Punjab, the princely states comprised Malwa and a small part of Bist Doaba and probably because of the princely rule, this area remained less developed.

G.S. Ghosal and Gopal Krishan in their study, *Regional Disparities in Levels of Socio-Economic Development in Punjab,* divided Punjab geographically into the following regions based on tehsils as units:

1. *Siwalik Hills and the Foothill Zone*: Pathankot (District Gurdaspur); Dasuya, Hoshiarpur, Garhshanker, Balachaur (District Hoshiarpur) and Anandpur Sahib, Ropar and Kharar (District Ropar).
2. *Upper Bari Doaba* : Gurdaspur, Batala, (District Gurdaspur); Ajnala, Amritsar, Taran Taran and Patti (District Amritsar).
3. *Bist Doab*: Kapurthala, Sultanpur Lodhi (District Kapurthala); Jallandhar; Phagwara, Nakodar, Phillaur, Nawanshahar (District Jallandhar).
4. *Northern Malwa*: Ferozepur, Zira (District Ferozepur), Moga (District Faridkot); Jagraon, Ludhiana, Samrala (District Ludhiana).
5. *Southern Malwa*: Fazilka (District Ferozepur); Mukatsar, Faridkot (District Faridkot); Bhatinda, Rampura Phul,

Mansa (District Bhatinda); Barnala, Malerkotla, Sangrur, Sunam (District Sangrur); Fatehgarh, Nahha, Rajpura, Patiala, Samana (District Patiala).

Inder Sain in his *Transformation of Punjab Agriculture,* (B.R. Publishing Corporation, Delhi, 1987) divided Punjab into three zones, taking Tehsils as units:

***Zone:I* (Paddy—Maize-Wheat Zone)**

Amritsar, Ajnala, Taran Taran, Patti, Sultanpur, Zira, Ferozepur, Samana, Patiala, Dasuya, Pathankot, Gurdaspur, Batala, Sirhind, Rajpura, Anandpur Sahib, Balachaur, Garhshankar, Hoshiarpur, Phagwara, Nawanshahar and Kharar.

***Zone:II* (Maize-Groundnuts-Wheat Zone)**

Kapurthala, Phillaur, Ludhiana, Jagraon, Samrala, Ropar, Malerkotla, Nabha, Nakodar, Jallandhar and Moga.

***Zone:III* (Cotton-Bajra-Wheat Zone)**

Mansa, Rampura Phul, Sunam, Sangrur, Barnala, Faridkot, Mukatsar, Fazilka and Bhatinda.

Punjab Agricultural University has divided Punjab into six Agro-climatic Zones, subdividing each of the first five zones into two A and B sub-zones on the basis of soil. A symbolising medium to heavy textured soils and B symbolising light to medium textured soil Regions are as below:

I. Sub-Mountain Undulating Region
   (a) Sub-Mountain Undulating Region North and South
   (b) Sub-Mountain Undulating Region Central

II. Undulating Plain Region
   (a) Undulating Plain Region North and South
   (b) Undulating Plain Region Central

III. Central Plain Region
   (a) Central Plain Region North
   (b) Central Plain Region South
IV. Western Plain Region
   (a) Western Plain Region North
   (b) Western Plain Region South
V. Western Region
   (a) Western Region North
   (b) Western Region South
VI. Flood Plain Region (Bet)

Since there has ceased to be a standard universally acceptable cultural-geographic regional division of Punjab, we fall back to the administrative division. And we take the administrative division into twelve districts as until early nineties. Officer trainees have done their surveys and studies when Punjab comprised these twelve districts only. Other regional divisions whenever mentioned may be taken specially to the context and purpose stated therein.

We shall have a general view of the districts on agricultural situation in Punjab and then put the micro-studies of the probationers in this context and examine the issues that emerge.

The Census data of 1971 and 1981 are our basic reference. Let us take agricultural workers as per cent of total workers and cultivable area per agricultural worker, as our starting point of information and description.

We can see that Ferozepur, Faridkot, Bhatinda, Sangrur and Patiala on the basis of % workers in agriculture may be termed as more agriculture-based districts than others and this position was maintained from 1971 to 1981 although Ludhiana, Jallandhar, Ropar and Patiala reduced their dependence on agriculture markedly over the decade. Interestingly, all these districts show bigger area per agricultural worker compared to all other districts (except Kapurthala), which has more area per agricultural worker that of Sangrur and Patiala. Unfortunately we do not have figures for 1991 census to compare.

Table 3.19 : Agricultural Workers as % of Total Workers and Cultivable Area per Agricultural Worker

	%age Agricultural Workers		*Cultivable Area Per Agricultural Worker (Hect.)*	
Districts	*1971*	*1981*	*1971*	*1981*
Gurdaspur	58.85	55.95	1.49	1.15
Amritsar	55.85	53.70	1.45	1.23
Kapurthala	61.47	53.46	1.84	1.78
Jallandhar	50.69	46.70	1.48	1.31
Hoshiarpur	61.51	57.39	1.53	1.38
Ropar	62.65	51.33	1.35	1.32
Ludhiana	50.80	43.84	1.55	1.36
Ferozepur	73.48	69.52	2.35	1.93
Faridkot	74.57	68.97	2.02	1.76
Bhatinda	76.42	68.94	2.11	1,81
Sangrur	71.48	70.98	1.82	1.47
Patiala	63.23	57.56	1.90	1.47

In terms of area also these are comparatively the bigger districts and they have shown higher percentage of net area sown to State net sown area. Same way it is true for irrigation too.

Amritsar is the only northern district which compares well with these Southern districts. Taking Amritsar along, this may be termed as the agricultural concentration area, though whole of Punjab in a way is the agricultural state. If we take combined contribution of Amritsar, Ferozepur, Faridkot, Bhatinda, Sangrur and Patiala, they comprise 63.44 per cent of total area, 66.39 per cent of State net area sown and 69 per cent of State net irrigated area. They also provide 68.9 per cent of total wheat and 64 per cent of rice production in the state.

Table 3.20 : District-wise Concentration of Agriculture

Districts	*%age of Distt. Area to Total State Area*	*%age of Distt. Net Area sown to State Net Area Sown*	*%age of Distt. Net Area Irrigated to State Net Irrigated Area*
Gurdaspur	6.95	7.09	6.14
Amritsar	10.05	10.36	11.03
Kapurthala	3.32	3.34	3.60
Jallandhar	6.78	6.95	7.38
Hoshiarpur	7.77	5.86	3.81
Ropar	4.23	2.66	1.80
Ludhiana	7.51	7.71	8.27
Ferozepur	11.58	12.00	12.66
Faridkot	11.45	12.26	12.69
Bhatinda	11.01	11.64	11.54
Sangrur	10.15	10.88	11.69
Patiala	9.20	9.25	9.39

In rice, however, Faridkot and Bhatinda with 7.74 per cent and 2.66 per cent respective contribution to state total are less important being sandy areas of Punjab. Ludhiana with 12.69 per cent contribution to state total is much more important. Faridkot and Bhatinda are more important Bajra (18.4% and 24.8% contribution respectively to total state production) and Barley (32.8% and 20.5% respectively contribution to total state production) producing areas in Punjab.

Another important combination is of Ferozepur, Faridkot and Bhatinda for cotton production in Punjab. They respectively provided 18.36 per cent, 34.31 per cent and 40.40 per cent of total cotton production in the state, together accounting to 93.07 per cent of state total in 1990-91.

In terms of size of holdings Ferozepur and Faridkot and Sangrur show the concentration of big holdings. In 1985-86 holdings of size of 50 hectares and above were 226, 134 and 142 in Ferozepur, Faridkot and Sangrur respectively while all other districts had only two-digit figures for this size and total such holdings for the state being only 733 in that year.

Having had an overview of inter-district agricultural

comparisons, we can now see how the IAS Probationers in their micro-studies reveal the actual situation.

From district Ferozepur, we have only one report that of Village Mehal Singh Wala by Mr. Jaspal Singh and pertains to the situation in 1993-94. It is a rather sketchy report and covers some 6-7 aspects and on agriculture, it has a half page note.

Mr. Jaspal has noted that average field is just 4-5 acre big only. Main crops are rice and wheat. Interestingly he has given the yields per hectare of rice and wheat since 1965-66 presumably in kilograms.

Years	*Rice*	*Wheat*
1965-66	1159	1134
1989-90	3337	3750
1991-92	3350	3800

Source of the figures is "Lal Kitab" maintained by Patwari.

This small village on Abohar-Ferozepur road (18 kms from district headquarters) inhabited predominantly by scheduled castes, lacking in infrastructure of health and education with people mostly living in katcha houses and high rate of illiteracy yet remarkably represents the district of Ferozepur in agricultural yields. The district average yield for 1991-92 was 3816 kgm for wheat and 3261 for rice. The state average yield in wheat and rice respectively for this year were 3803 and 3257 kgms respectively as per *Statistical Abstract of Punjab 1992*. Comparatively underdeveloped village in Punjab by standards of general economic conditions and infrastructure, the village has adopted the modern technology of water, fertilizer and high yielding varieties and successfully shown the way to progress. Since in Punjab, as elsewhere, the infrastructure and provision of services are entirely provided and supported by Government, if they have not reached here it may be due to caste and political reasons that this agriculturally prosperous village is still poor. Or is it that the figures of yield are not correct ?

Amritsar is also agriculturally prosperous district of the Majha region. We have socio-economic studies of two villages pertaining to it. These are for *village Dhaul Kalan by Mr. Kripa Shankar Saroj* and for *village Jahangir by Shri T.R. Saranghal*. Mr. Saranghal's reporting year is 1986-87 and Mr. Kripa Shankar's is 1990-91.

Village Jehangir is 17 kms away from Amritsar on road to Batala and is habitated by scheduled castes, backward classes and Jat Sikhs. Tenancy on shared crop or rent basis is reported here. Although, fixed share of tenant as per law is 1/3 of produce, actual prevalent rate is 50% of produce. But there is no absentee landlordism. Wheat, Paddy, Sugarcane, Toria and Barseem are the crops grown. Shifting trend from food crops to commercial crops at slow pace has been reported. Modern machines—harvester combines, tractors and drills are in use. Farm yard manures and chemical fertilizers, high yielding seeds and pesticides are commonly used. Irrigation is by canal and tubewells. Animal husbandry is very popular. Some 700 Milch cattle with the total number of 270 families gives an average of 2.6 units per family and some 2000 litres of milk per day were being produced. This gives the farmers supplementary nutrition and income both the hotly pursued things in Punjab. Animal husbandry is also modern and outward looking and cross-bred cows are common possession. Veterinary hospital at Mudhal, 4 kms away, is available. About 50% milk produced is marketed and given to local vendors who collect door to door and give regular payments in contrast with Verka Milk Plant practices.

Mr. Kripa Shankar's village Dhaul Kalan is just 10 kms away from Amritsar city with 310 houses and 613 families and a total population of 1760, half of them being scheduled castes. But land owning classes are Jats. Of the total 829 acres of land, one scheduled caste family own 9 acres only. Wage rates for unskilled agricultural workers at Rs.35 per day plus food are reported to be three times that in UP, Bihar and Orissa on the personal knowledge of the author who belongs to that region.

Agriculture has given prosperity: 40% owned television in the village; there were 3 Maruti cars and 17 scooters and motor vehicles. Liquor consumption was common. Farmers sold produce in regulated markets and Mr. Kripa Shankar suggests setting up agro-based industries in this area.

Selected Amritsar villages show signs of prosperity more than that of the village in Ferozepur. Reason could be proximity of selected village to Amritsar city and better attention by government to general services making people care more for private consumption.

In district Gurdaspur, village Naushera Nalabandha's socio-economic study has been prepared by Shri Vijai Kumar in 1990-91. Of the cultivable land 294 hectares are irrigated predominantly by tubewells (254 hectares and 40 hectares by private canals) and unirrigated land is 192 hectares. Holdings are small and no non-cultivating owners exist. There are 30 tenants but they are cultivating Panchayat lands. But informal private-land tenancies do exist.

In this village people combine agricultural cultivation with their service at Air Force Station nearby or MES. In cultivation people have shifted from course grains and pulses to paddy and wheat. Modern machines, tubewells and modern agricultural practices are common.

Net income per year from an acre of land is only Rs.3000 (Rs.2000 from paddy and Rs.1000 from wheat). Marketed surplus is 3000 quintals of wheat and 4000 quintals of paddy. Most of the labour is from other states and local labour prefers other professions.

Dairying is very common with 60 cows and 300 buffaloes in the village. Fodder is grown as no grazing facilities exist. Artificial insemination facility is available within the village.

Compared to the poor village of Mr. Jaspal Singh and prosperous villages of Mr. Kirpa Shankar and Mr. T.R. Sarangal, this is a medium type of village. It might have been poorer in production than the one in Ferozepur but for the supplementary salary incomes obtained from working in the nearly cantonment. There are 125 unemployed persons but they do not depress agricultural wages; they live on family income and search "better" or white collar jobs in preference to working in the fields.

The three districts of Ferozepur, Amritsar and Gurdaspur complete the Majha belt of Punjab. Agriculture has prospered and so have the people but animal husbandry has played an important role in supplementing the incomes of the people. Efficiency of Government services in supplementing extension, high yielding varieties and fertilizers, co-operatives as suppliers of credit for machinery, a network of regulated markets have all played a part in changing the rural face of Punjab.

We now turn to the two districts of Doaba for which socio-economic studies are available. These are Hoshiarpur and Jallandhar districts and give us three and six reports respectively. Kapurthala district of Doaba does not have any report.

The three villages and authors of reports district *Hoshiarpur* with years of study are:

Sl. No.	*Name of the Villages*	*Name of the Officer Trainee and Year*
1.	Pur Hiran	Mr. Dharamvir (1985-86)
2.	Bajwara	Mr. Venkat Ratnam (1991-92)
3.	Dada	A. Venu Prasad (1992-93)

Pur Hiran with 8456 population in 1981 has 1000 Hindu families and 750 Sikh families. There are 2500 Eastern UP labourers who live on the outskirts of the village, adding to its economy. Some irrigation was provided by 497 tubewells. The village was surrounded by hilly torrents called "choes", known for flash floods. 85 per cent of cultivable was unirrigated. People have learnt that food crops get destroyed by floods but fruit trees survive, so the trend is to fruit cultivation. Nearness to Hoshiarpur industrial areas is the helping factor. This traditional village had only one tractor. Wooden ploughs and oxen were still in use in 1985-86. But chemical fertilizers were being used. Some 2611 landowners were cultivating a total of 1727 acres of land only. In addition 115 tenants were cultivating 177 acres. Only 19 persons had holdings of more than 10 acres.

There were only 105 cows and 472 buffaloes giving 2000 litres of milk a day in Pur Hiran which is not sufficient for a population 8.5 thousands. So milk is actually brought into the village from outside. Floods, lack of irrigation and hence lack of fodder are inhibiting factors to discourage animal husbandry. Veterinary services are available only at Hoshiarpur.

This was the story of an underdeveloped village in 1985-86.

Mr. Venkat Ratnam studied his village Bajwara in 1991-92—an ancient village going back in history to 6th century. The village population declined from 1971 to 1981 when it was 4428.

Bajwara has 1323 acres of irrigated land against 351 which are rainfed. Here also 90 per cent holdings are reportedly marginal. Maize is the major kharif crop accounting for 312 acres, rice taking only 69 acres. Wheat, vegetables and fruit are rabi crops. Yield figures per acre reported are:

Maize	1300 kgm.
Rice	2000 kgm.
Wheat	1700 kgm.

Converted into yields per hectare, the figures seem to be much higher than the state and district figures.

The author bemoans the declining profitability of farming because of escalation of costs compared to slow growth in yields and procurement prices. Here farmers complain lack of availability of hybrid seeds as only 50 per cent of demand is met. Acute shortage of seeds of newer varieties and of sunflower is reported. Similarly fertilizers and pesticides are not available in the village co-operative outlet. Credit needs are met by Co-operative Bank but 20 per cent recourse to money lenders does exist. Fruit and vegetable cultivation has taken place but lack of marketing has meant very low profitability to growers.

This is an interesting story of a village where farmers are progressive but Government and institutional infrastructure and service facilities have lagged behind making the village much less developed than its potential. Is it a strong case of inefficient officials and administration supervision or something more is at the base? The question is unanswered.

The study of Mr. R.Venu Prasad is more recent one. His village "Dada" is dominated by scheduled castes, while total population of the village was 1203 in 1981 and 1465 in 1991. This village in Kandi (Submountaneous) area has problems of shortage of water, soil erosion and floods. Uncanalised and unrestrained hill torrents called choes are the other big problem. Land holding pattern follows the usual story of dominance of small holdings. Only 34 owners have holdings more than 5 acres. Quality of soil being loamy sandy to sandy clay loam also poses problems. With 40 per cent rainfed area and very low level of water table, even tubewells are of less help. Yet 50 per cent area is under wheat, 21 per cent under paddy (in kharif) and 32 per cent area is under maize.

Supply of inputs is a major problem reported here too, especially of hybrid seeds and sunflower seeds where subsidy by Government per acre is available. Fertilizer consumption, on this count, as also due to scarcity of water is very low at 70 kgm. per hectare. Even then fertilizers and pesticides are not available from official outlets. Marketing of fruit and vegetables within the local market at throw away prices makes farmers poor and frustrated.

All the three village studies from Hoshiarpur show the Government efficiency and planning at a low level while people are struggling against natural difficulties of loamy/sandy soil, hill torrents bringing floods, lack of water and very small holdings. It is strange that the acute shortage of modern inputs at official outlets is persisting while elsewhere in Punjab agriculture is prospering . Where people have tried to go in for vegetable and fruit cultivation they have to sell at throw away prices these perishable commodities, presumably because cold storage facilities, chilling plants and official market support is not available.

Jallandhar District, the premier district of Doaba to be precise Beas-Satluj Doaba or Bist Doaba is characterised by modern industry and a centre of political activity and vernacular press.

We have four village studies from *Jallandhar* as under:

Sl. No.	*Name of the Village*	*Name of the Author and Year of Study*
1.	Kadiana	Ms. Vini Mahajan (1988-89)
2.	Lesariwala, Arjanwali and Chhuhharwal	Ms. Anjali Gupta (1989-90)
3.	Ghorewahi	Mr. B. Vikram (1992-93)
4.	Kuhar Khurd	Ms. Raji P. Srivastava (1994-94)

Village Kadiana with 56% pucca houses and with electricity in 58 per cent houses is among better than average villages. It is a small village with 1877 population in 1981. Of the total 2031 cultivated area, only 32 acres are un-irrigated. But entire irrigation is by tubewells. Modern machines like harvester combines and tractors are commonly used. Village has 42 tractors. Main crops were wheat and Paddy. There were 800 cows and buffaloes and milk is bought by traders from Ludhiana.

The cluster of three villages Lesariwala, Arjanwali and Chhuhharwal are located within 6 miles radius of each other and are 12 kms away from Jallandhar on Adampur road with a total population of 4297 in 1981. Lessariwala and Arjanwali have canal irrigation in addition to tubewells while Chhuhharwal is wholly dependent on tubewells. All tubewells are privately owned, even though small holdings predominate (only 67 holdings out of 502 holdings are of more than 10 acres in the three villages). Yields per hectare are as under:

Rice	3199 kgms.
Maize	2000 kgms.
Wheat	1700 kgms.

State average yields in 1989-90 were 3510 for rice, 1902 for maize and 3593 for wheat. The villages show reasonably good yield for wheat but behind the state average in the other two crops.

Like other prosperous villages animal husbandry for milk is a regular activity, probably more so in this cluster where a total of 1515 buffaloes and 485 cows and 200 goats supply milk for consumption and sale.

Village Ghorewahi is also predominantly agricultural. Mr. B. Vikram the author of the socio-economic survey of this village took a random sample of 25 households for study yielding him 23 households directly dependent on agriculture as land-owners or as wage-labourers. Fertile land, assured irrigation and modern agricultural technology has given to the entrepreneurial Punjabi agriculturists a prosperous standard of living. But limits of holdings and limits of technology do not afford them very high standards over more than one generation.

Village Kuhar Khurd is the same story of prosperity through commercial agriculture, though Kuhar Khurd has only 75 cattle.

The overall situation in the Jallandhar district is much better than that of Hoshiarpur. The contrast of the two districts of Doaba is very sharply brought out by the village studies in terms of overall prosperity and production and productivity results. Normally, one would have attributed the differences to the peculiar difficulties of Kandi areas of Hoshiarpur, its soil and problems of hilly choes. But our micro-studies also reveal that where people are trying to overcome these difficulties by diversifying into fruit/vegetable cultivation and turning towards higher cash-promise crops like sunflowers, Government agencies in Hoshiarpur district, atleast in the studied villages have failed. They have not responded with marketing and infrastructural facilities nor even with normal services of providing inputs and credit etc. Government in Hoshiarpur is at much lower level compared with Punjab's own standards of efficiency.

On the other hand agricultural prosperity of the villages studied has certainly revealed the undertones of concern to a keen-eyed observer. We would like to quote Mr. B. Vikram from his excellent analytical study of the village Ghorewahi. His words have a much wider applicability for whole of Doaba, perhaps of the Punjab agriculture itself:

"The infrastructure support to agriculture is well developed enabling farmers to get maximum returns on investment. Institutional credit is well channelled allowing farmers to make judicious investments and to increase their profits. New technology in the form of improved seeds, fertilizers and mechanised tools is easily available and even the smallest farmer has access to information." But limited land gives limited prosperity and with each generation holdings go smaller and with limited growth in agricultural technology people are found still struggling for prosperity. "Marginal farmer will continue to exist at the margin, unless some stroke of misfortune wipes him out and reduces him to landless labourer." Upward mobility and job opportunities in the secondary and tertiary sectors are limited. Educational ambitions of an average agriculturist's child are not very high nor has he high hopes of a bright—distant future.

Ludhiana is probably the best-known district of Punjab for its extraordinary progress in industry and agriculture. It is within Malwa and its industrial uniqueness marks from other districts. It leads to the State in high yields. In 1991-92, the average yield of rice in Ludhiana was the second highest at 3579 kgm per hectare after Faridkot (3775 kgms). In wheat also it showed second highest average yield at 4252 kgms. after Sangrur (4258 kgms).

We have following socio-economic reports of probationers from Ludhiana:

Sl. No.	*Village*	*Author*	*Year of Study*
1.	Hambram	Mr. N.J.S. Kalsi	1985-86
2.	Sanghol	Mr. A.S. Chhatwal	1987-88
3.	Kot-Umra	Mr. Sunil Kumar (Now in U.P.)	1988-89
4.	Sahnewal	Mr. Sanjay Kumar	1989-90
5.	Pona	Mr. Vijoy Kumar Singh	1991-92
6.	Budewal	Mr. S.R. Ladhar	1992-93

Hambram is a small village of 1712 people and 293 households just 17 kms away from Ludhiana city on Ferozepur road. 48 per cent families directly cultivate land or engaged in poultry/ dairy. With 266 tubewells, 97 per cent area is irrigated. Panchayat leases its land for cultivation, so do about 12 service class or business class people who go to work in the city. But number of tenants is 4-6 only and they have 10-15 acres each only. Operational holdings are small; only 10 households had more than 12 hectares. It is also a village using all the modern practices of farming and 1254 milch animals supply milk. Veterinary services are available within the village.

Sanghol or Ucha Pind is 15 kms from Samrala, the sub-divisional town of Ludhiana and has population of 3425 people with 27 per cent scheduled caste population. Of 362 families, only 40 own land more than 15 acres, but smaller holdings are held by low-caste or scheduled castes. One of the interesting findings reported is that relatively prosperous farmers with bigger holdings want their sons to adopt different occupation while smaller farmers want the sons to continue with agriculture but want more land. Education is sought by all.

Kot-Umra is a Sidhwan Bet Block and is 18 kms away from main Ludhiana-Firozepur Road and is 3 kms away from Bhundra, a small town-like village. With 452 population and 75 households, it is a small village with 80 persons immigrating from Rajasthan. But modern agriculture has penetrated here. It has 20 tractors, 50 diesel engines, 16 electric motors and 17 tubewells. Paddy and wheat are main crops and "chara" or fodder is cultivated on 20 acres. One person has ventured into fruit cultivation on four acres. Holding pattern is also similar to other villages as also the animal husbandry with 187 buffaloes, 67 cows and 19 goats. Poultry did not succeed.

Sahnewal Kalan in District Ludhiana has been studied by Sanjay Kumar in 1989-90. The village comprising 1035 households and a population of 4934 is located on main G.T. Road and main railway track. Agriculture is tilted towards paddy and wheat. Tractors and improved tools are in use. Farmers in Sahnewal take seeds directly from Punjab Agriculture University, Ludhiana. But Sahnewal is really a town and only 187 are land-owning families, of which 119 have small holdings between 1-5 acres only and 58 have 6-10 acres, 7 families have 11-15 acres and only two have 16-25 acres. No family has more than 25 acres. Farmers are mostly Jat Sikhs and labourers are scheduled caste and backward castes, 60 per cent being migrant labourers. Rest of the story is the similar one of prosperous modern agriculture supplemented by dairying at home.

Pona with population of 1789 in 1991 (it has 728 persons below 12 years age) is 7 kms away from Ludhiana on Ferozepur Road and 7 kms from Jagraon. It is classified as underdeveloped area of Sidhwan Bet—the low lying flood prone areas. But it has progressed well in the last 10 years. It has one combine-harvester, 45 tractors and 167 tubewells and 100 per cent irrigation and of course is electrified. Adequate flood protection and soil treatment has made the land fertile. People with no tubewells purchase water from others at Rs.25 per hour. Tractors are available on hire from other farmers. Wheat, paddy and fodder are main crops. Potato is also grown here. Dairy is an important activity for landlords and landless. Unrecorded tenants for yearly rent of Rs.4000/- an acre do exist. Milk co-operative works well and villagers own 600 buffaloes and 200 cows.

Budewal, 22 kms from Ludhiana city and 4 kms away from Ludhiana Chandigarh road is again a developed village. It has 132 households. People used to have houses within farming land for closer, supervision but they built houses in the village after terrorism for collective safety. Of 801 population, 250 are scheduled castes. Water table is 7 ft. from the surface and lift irrigation is popular. Of 606 ha. net cropped area, 560 is irrigated. Paddy, wheat and sugarcane are main crops. A sugar mill has popularised sugarcane cultivation. No forest land or waste land exists. Modern machines, fertilizers and high yielding seeds and pesticides complete the agricultural scene here too. Of 132 families, 111 have holdings less than 10 acres. Concealed tenancy rates are Rs.2000-4000 per acre. 40 per cent labour is migrant from U.P. and Bihar. Milch cattle for dairy and self consumption is popular and total of 348 buffaloes, 120 cows and 41 goats supply milk. There is a milk collection centre of Milkfed Punjab and animal semen centre is 22 kms away.

Ludhiana District has shown important common factors through these micro-studies—high irrigation percentage, high crop intensity, fertile land, small holdings, modern practices of agriculture, supplementation of peasant income by animal husbandry operations, readiness to diversified agriculture if given opportunity (availability of sugar mill nearby) and a desire to achieve higher social status and standards along with efficient government service and supply—this is really the confirmation of our Punjab model of development through these field studies.

Village Bokhra is in District Bhatinda is 10 kms away from Bhatinda on the road to Goniana-Faridkot. The village had 396 households and a population of 2636 in 1981. Of the 240 land-owning households only 38 land between 10-20 acres. About 40 non-land-owning households cultivate land (200 acres) as tenants. 70% land is irrigated in the village. Paddy, wheat and fodder are main crops. There are 70 tractors in the village and owners give on hire too at the rate of Rs.35 per acre. Modern practices of agriculture are common. Livestock rearing is popular with 840 buffaloes, 278 cows and 232 goats. Daily production of milk is 2500 quintals and about 25 per cent is sold out of the village. Milk producers co-operative is there but Secretary committed irregularities and was closed at the time of reporting. Veterinary dispensary is within the village.

Village Maneli (District Ropar) was surveyed and studied by Shri M.S. Sandhu in 1985-86 and village *Bela* (District Ropar) was studied by Dr. Roshan Sunkaria in 1989-90. *Maneli* has 128 households with population of 869. Bela had population of 1464 in 1981. Both the villages are well irrigated by tubewells. Wheat, sugarcane and paddy and fodder are common crops. Holdings are much smaller in Maneli with 240 holdings being in 0-5 acres range and only 23 in the range of 10-15 acres. In Bela, of 999 farming households 719 have holdings less than 5 acres; 5 have holdings of 5-10 acres, 112 have 10-50 acres and 7 have more than 50 acres. Of the 16 harijans who own land 3 have 75 acres.

Bela has 10 unrecorded tenants. Share-crop arrangement gives them 50 per cent produce while fixed rent charges are Rs.1800-2200 per acre. Landlords prefer fixed rent system. Mr. M.S. Sandhu has reported from Maneli that landless workers prefer to work with landlords rather than in the public works. In general both villages are adopting technology in agriculture and livestock supplements the incomes.

The premier Malwa and princely district has given us the following surveys:

Sl. No.	*Villages*	*Authors*	*Year of Study*
1.	Darola	Mr. Suresh Kumar	1984-85
2.	Kakrala	Mr. Karan Bir Singh Sidhu	1985-86
3.	Bhunesheri	Mr. Viswajeet Khanna	1988-89
4.	Massinghan	Ms. Ravneet Kaur	1989-90
5.	Jallah Kheri	Mr. Sarvjit Singh	1993-94

Mr. Suresh Kumar in Darola took 60 per cent families for

survey through random sampling and results are very interesting. This was a small village with 606 population in 1981 but showed 273 per cent growth over 1971. Of 54 family households surveyed, 33 were land-owning ones and only 6 of them owned land of 10 acres or above but all had irrigation. All used fertilizer and owned livestock this is also true for scheduled castes. Of the 16 scheduled castes, 11 had of enough employment within the village. Mr. Suresh Kumar reports, otherwise, all the traits of a modern developed agriculture in the village.

The village Kakrala is big with 320 families and a total population of 2857. 87 per cent of the land had irrigation, 72 per cent by tubewells and 15 per cent by canal giving 80 per cent double cropped area. The Jamabandi records showed 86 per cent operational and 76 per cent ownership holdings as less than 5 acres. Only two operational holdings were more than 10 acres. Ten per cent of total cultivated land is under unrecorded tenancy. Farmers have adopted modern practices in agriculture.

Village Bhunerheri is on main road of Patiala-Delhi via Kaithal and is bisected by this highway. It is a big village of 2000 population with 150 shops. Arnoli Minor from Bhakra main line provides irrigation besides tubewells. Modern technology and rich loamy soil ensures it prosperity in agriculture which is further supplemented by careful rearing of Milch cattle. *Land ceiling laws have been a complete failure, however, as revenue machinery helped farmers to retain land in fictitious names.* But Nazul land was distributed to scheduled castes. Prosperity of the village is evident in the 7 diesel engine repair shops, four welders and electric repair shops, four radio repair shops.

Massinghan village with 2402 population in 1981, is situated some 31 kms away from Patiala. The number of persons owning less than 5 acres of land is 931 while those owning 5-10 acres are 83 and these 10-50 acres are 41. Farmers build field huts and live in them. Main crops are wheat and paddy and yield are 1976 kgms for wheat and 3550 kgms for paddy. State average for the yields of wheat and paddy were 3593 kgms. and 3510 kgms respectively. Reported yields are rather low. There might have been some mistake in reporting of Ms. Ravneet that there are advanced agricultural practices and general prosperity. Most households retained 2 quintals of rice and 10 quintals of wheat; rest is sold out. Some 500-600 buffaloes and 80-100 cows provide dairying activity to villagers.

Mr. Sarvjit Singh studied Jallahkheri Village recently in 1993-94. This entire village was really "declared surplus" land of one owner who had his own land elsewhere. The tenants became the allottees of land. The village is in the flood plain of Ghaggar river. Sub soil water is rather close to surface. Ghuram Distributory of Narwana Branch of Bhakra provides irrigation to the village. But there are enough supplementing tubewells. Land is productive giving 18 quintals of wheat and 22 quintals of rice per acre. Open market sale is about preferred for its reliability. The net workable profit from wheat-paddy combination per acre is Rs.8000/-. Sunflower can give double the profit. But people prefer time-tested assured crop cultivation. Poultry and dairying supplement their income.

Agriculture and Agrarian Relations- An Overview

The common strand in the studies reveals:

- Holdings, as per revenue records, are mostly small or marginal. Very few owners have holdings more than 10-15 acres. In general high caste Jat Sikhs and Saini Sikhs have bigger holdings and low caste people have smaller holdings.
- Land reform laws are quite stringent but surplus land distribution cases after ceiling laws have been very few. People, on record, have very small and always less than ceiling, holdings to the allottee and is being cultivated by him. However Panchayat Land or Nazul Land wherever available, has been distributed to the scheduled castes who have titled possession with them and cultivate those lands like all other farmers.
- Unrecorded tenancy cases of about 5-10 in a village are positively there but the land in question is not more than 5-10 acres. The tenants are marginal farmers or landless

labourers and the persons who lease out these lands are service class people or business people who were earlier farmers and do not want to sell the lands or stop farming.

- Tenancy terms are either share-cropping or *batai* system ranging mostly at 1/2 basis but sometimes 1/3 also as per law. Landlords prefer *"Chukta"* or lumpsum rent which ranges Rs.2000 to Rs.4000 per acre leaving very meagre real income to the tenants. It is, however true that the tenants at will are seeking and demanding law to supplement their income.
- Forests and village commons for grazing of cattle are extinct in Punjab. Some trees eucalyptus and poplar varieties may be seen in some villages on borders of cultivable land or on Panchayat lands but common grazing grounds are not available at all. Hence, all cattle are fed at stalls and all farmers grow fodder for their animals.
- Land is fertile; mostly irrigated and double cropped. Water is sold by those who have extra to others who have not.
- Modern implements like tractors, drills, diesel engines, harvester combines are widely used. Relatively big farmers own them and small/marginal farmers take on hire.
- All farmers, big and small, use high yielding varieties, chemical fertilizers and insecticides.
- Labourers get decent high wages compared to government—fixed minimum. Demand for labour at sowing and harvest time is more than that can be supplied from natives of the village. About 50-60 per cent labour supply is from migrant U.P., Bihar, M.P. and Rajasthan labour. Some of the migrant labourers are working on regular monthly/yearly basis and some have settled in the villages. No bonded labour or exploitation of labour cases are reported.
- Landlords and their sons do not perform manual work and prefer higher education and high status jobs.
- Cropping pattern follows almost a textual path of wheat in rabi and paddy in kharif with fodder for animals in both

seasons. Wherever sugar mills are around, sugarcane is also a popular crop. Return-wise among the three, sugarcane is best, next is rice and at lowest scale is wheat.

- An acre of farm land gives a crop income range of Rs.4000 to Rs.8000 per year for two crops under assured irrigation and with best of modern agricultural practices and machines and with best of government services available.
- Crop income with assured Government price and procurement support is generally preferred to diversification into vegetables and fruits cultivation where government support and marketing is not yet available.
- The desire to go in for new crops (*like oilseeds especially Sunflower) vegetables and fruit is very strong when people realise the "possible" benefits.
- Crop income alone does not ensure a reasonable prosperous standard of living. Every farming and non-farming household has milch cattle of high quality, mostly cross-bred by artificial insemination at the conveniently available government veterinary dispensary. Good milk yield provides the rural folk supplementary income and nutrition.

A network of efficient government services and government supported co-operative credit and other services helps the farmers to have:

(i) modern input supply-seeds, fertilizers and insecticides.
(ii) credit from co-operatives for inputs, marketing and for cattle.
(iii) adequate milk-marketing facilities either commercially if near the cities or through co-operatives.
(iv) a network of regulated markets giving support price and lifting of entire marketed surplus.
(v) a network of extension facilities and information on new seeds, new technology, soil testing and other new developments and supply of these services.

(vi) research and extension work of Punjab Agricultural University, Ludhiana is most commendable.

It means by all round efforts of the Government, institutions and ready, receptive and forward-looking farmers and best of land and climate and scientific agricultural techniques farmers continue to have reached the possible peak in incomes and farming has reached its limits. The next step forward has to be a steady change over from farming to agro-processing and other industrial activity.

Issues

Punjab agriculture throws unique issues and challenges.

Let us be clear about a starting point on land reforms and especially the land ceiling part of it. All the probationers have gone only by the Jamanbandi records, looking at the figures of ownership and operational holdings. These are given as number of Khewats (proprietary land holdings) and number of Khataunis (operational land holdings) in revenue records. It is unthinkable that these would not be as per ceiling laws. That, however, is not the real ownership. Most of the landlords who own and operate land more than the ceiling have these lands in the name of relatives who physically are living hundreds and thousands of miles away but readily lend their names and signatures to "save" the lands of their kith and kin. All these lands are shown as "Khud-Kasht" or self-cultivated. In some cases these lands arc under fictitious names of animals and so on. Mr. Viswajit Khanna has referred to it in his village report on Bhunerheri in Patiala but could not unearth these cases. No other probationer brings this issue on surface. Mr. Viswajit has rightly pointed out that in Punjab all revenue officials really "helped" the farmers in "saving" their lands by giving prior information of laws, procedures/ regulations and suggesting loopholes, of course, for a small price.

But on the other hand we do find that big exploitative and high-handed criminal landlords "owning" hundreds and thousands of acres did not exist and certainly do not exist now. Glaring cases of above-ceiling ownership have been taken care of and lands thus found surplus have been allotted and given possession to allottees as per the law. On the whole people who own excess of land are part of the village common folk and of course are better off than others. The few exceptions are known political heavy weights in Ferozepur and Faridkot districts. Even these, who are anyway no match to rich industrialists, have cultivated the village folk as friends and as part of them rather than being above them or their exploiters. Being champions of small farmers' cause, they are taken as persons of respect and admired by all unlike the situation in Bihar.

And then even with best of conditions and support given the declining level of the growth rate of prosperity in farming, is it worthwhile to open the question of ceiling laws in Punjab? Farmers have worked hard and enriched Punjab. An average Punjabi, including the revenue official does not mind farmers having more than prescribed ceiling by a few acres. In any case fragmentation of holdings is taking place and new generation of farmers may be owning land mostly within the prescribed limits now.

On the question of quality of land, again the revenue records hardly tell the truth. In order to "save" land from ceiling clause, most of the land shown is "barren" or unirrigated, as the ceiling limits are higher for such lands while as we found from the micro-studies and from our general records actually, more than 90% land is irrigated. It would be interesting to research to compare the total irrigated land as per revenue records and the same as per records of irrigation department. But our comment of previous paragraph applies here too.

Probationers have truthfully brought the real situation of unrecorded tenancy. No owner of a 10-15 acres of land would like to engage a tenant if it would ultimately deprive him of the ownership rights. He would sell or self cultivate if tenancy provisions were strictly imposed. But then the "tenant" who is seeking land to supplement his income would lose this opportunity. As the cases are few (Karan Bir Singh Sidhu estimated them at 10% of total in his village) and are certainly not of exploitative nature, it is again worth ignoring them.

However, more important issues are the contribution of agriculture to general prosperity in Punjab and its future prospects.

Incomes have risen in Punjab but they have not remained only with big landlords or only with farmers. Technology and supply of services has reached even the small farmers. Nowhere has it been mentioned that small farmers or marginal farmers are impoverished or are languishing. Commercial sale of water and tractor services within the village from big to small farmers show the technology reach to the latter and their ability to afford this service. It is of course true that big farmers would gain big and small farmers gain small. Important issue of interest and investigation was, have the marginal farmers been forced to sell land. Have they become landless labourers and thus worse off in this process? Unfortunately, these aspect again has not been explored by the probationers.

However, prosperity of farming has brought relief to labour and more employment in various agricultural operations. If we take the model reporting that 60 per cent migrant labour and 40 per cent internal labour make the total, then, keeping the willingness to work at old constant level, the labour demand and supply (in ex-post statistical sense) must have increased to that much. But as probationers have reported that unskilled manual labour is socially shunned by medium and big farmers, we should give less credence to increase of employment opportunities, matching and contrasting it by increased unemployment among educated and less-educated youth in the rural areas. Some probationers have reported labour preferring to work for the landlords to government work schemes showing that agricultural labourers are treated better by the landlords than as casual labour treated by the bosses in Government. But the question of overall impact on employment is not clear. Probationers have reported positively on unemployment in the villages during the lean seasons.

Farming in Punjab is certainly not the crop cultivational one. Each and every study reports that each and every farmer (and even the landless labourer) has Milch cattle to supplement nutrition and income. In fact Rs.4000-6000 per acre yearly income from crops alone, would have depicted a very different story of Punjab villages. A network of credit and veterinary dispensaries and fodder crops of agriculture department combine to give farmers increase in real income. This fact, unfortunately, has mostly been ignored in most studies on green revolution. Important area of study is the measurement of actual contribution of dairying to real income of farmers in Punjab. Probationers have not gone farther than reporting the number of Milch cattle and the average milk yield. Next step should not be difficult for the researchers.

On crop cultivation and need for diversification and agro-processing industries and natural limits to agrarian prosperity, we have already quoted the study of Mr. B. Vikram in village Ghorewahi of District Jallandhar. We need not repeat it here.

Last issue is of theoretical interest but worth mentioning. Punjab agriculture is based on peasant proprietorship in capitalist mode of production but very actively supported by the government machinery which itself is heavily pro-peasants. It is a moot point if the modes of production and government's patronage had not matched, how would Punjab have fared—better or worse? Commercialisation within villages (sale of water, sale of tractor services, high rates of tenancy rents etc.) has given rise probably to the new social relationship in villages. Is it better or worse off than before? Answer depends on the framework of our own ideology perhaps.

One last point is that in most cases Government services and operations have been reported in positive way, may be because government officers as probationers are reporting it, one might say. We believe that farmers do feel, inwardly, grateful to Government for these services. They take them so much a part of their everyday life that, in spite of commercialisation of their own intra-village relations, they take Governments free or subsidized services as their right. But shall the Government go on giving these concealed subsidies? What then is the real market income of farming operation, if Government subsidy is taken off? Who would like to stay as a farmer if value addition in industry is taken as an alternative? Is the Punjab model of farming growth worth emulation by others? This must be answered from its fundamental roots.

GOVERNMENT PROGRAMMES

Poverty Alleviation Programmes

Special attention to the rural poor has been a cardinal policy of rural development. It is true that all the programmes in the agriculture and allied sectors, in rural and village industries, transport, communication and power sectors and in the social sectors ultimately lead to allround rural development. Yet there are certain sections of the people, generally those at the lowest rung of the ladder, who get not direct or indirect immediate benefits. In the late seventies, it was thought that these sections need special help and special programmes to lift them from below the poverty line. Major programme in this line is Integrated Rural Development Project (IRDP) which seeks to give earning assets to the needy and wage-employment programmes which seek to give or generate specific mandays of employment to the rural poor at fair wage-rates. Wage-employment programmes have now been integrated into Jawahar Rozgar Yojana or JRY.

Micro Studies

Mr. Suresh Kumar (1984-85) reports that a state level survey was conducted for identification of poor families defined as having annual gross income of Rs.3600 or below. All these persons have been given *"Yellow Cards"* called *"Vikas Patrika"* of yellow cover page which is an identity-cum-monitoring card of the people below poverty line. The objective was that identifying the poor would not remain the task for local development staff to do each year.

Taking an overall review of the year 1981-82, there was more than 100 per cent achievement of the targets in terms of number of beneficiaries disbursement of the amount of subsidy. An amount of Rs.60 lakhs in subsidy was distributed among 7504 beneficiaries, the majority of them got benefit under dairying. In 1982-83 also dairying was the top activity—as 4544 out of 8502 total number of beneficiaries got benefit under it.

From a sample study of 64 beneficiaries 90 per cent beneficiaries had their assets intact. All those who lost or sold their assets belonged to scheduled castes.

Out of these only 30 per cent were able to cross the poverty line (for scheduled castes, percentage is 23 per cent only). Tradewise, of dairy cases only 26 per cent crossed poverty line while in other trades—animal carts or small trade, success rate was 100 per cent. Most of the defaults in payments were also from dairying.

This scheme's failure rested on the following reasons:

(a) Animals bought were invariably of poor quality—some going dry within a week of the purchase.
(b) Beneficiaries sold milk to local vendors in the villages—no organized marketing arrangement was made.
(c) Paucity of cattle feed.
(d) No training on animal breeding or up-keep.
(e) All failure cases were of those who purchased one buffalo only. When the lactation period was over, income came to end.
(f) No actual monitoring of the cases is done in DRDA.
(g) Information gap among various three agencies exist *i.e.* DRDA, Banks and Block Development Officials.
(h) Meetings of the Review Committees at Sub-Division level do not take place.

In Sheron village in Sangrur district and has found the same story of major chunk of beneficiaries, 67 out of 105, got the loans for dairy farming.

Mr. Jagpal Singh noted that money got for an asset is used to pay off old debts. His important observation is:

> "While issuing yellow cards, economic backwardness was not the consideration but the person's influence counted. In the village there are yellow card holders who own land and pucca houses and availing benefits".

Mr. Jagpal believes as far as programme for needy persons is concerned it has failed. The needy are not selected, if selected they are shunted between DRDA and the Banks and end up frustrated. But the programme of creating assets for rural masses or community asset programmes is very successful.

Mr. Navreet Singh Kang's study of Bhatinda, however, shows that selection of profession dairying accounted less than 37% (except in 1983-84 when it was 49%) for all years from 80-81 to 84-85 but it was still the nodal choice. Camel carts, rural industry and small business were other important activities getting subsidies.

Most of the difficulties/defects in the programme are similar. But Mr. Navreet has highlighted the lack of political interest in the schemes as the local MLA does not attend the monitoring and advisory committees. He also notes that most bank officials ask for "cuts" before they sanction the loan.

Mr. Navreet also notes many undeserving people having been issued yellow cards among the total of 70,000 in District Bhatinda on political or social-affiliation basis or simply because of corruption.

Mr. Karan A. Singh studied IRDP for Sangrur in 1985-86. He noted that benchmark survey carried out in 1981-82 surveyed 87,511 households out of the total of 1,61,690 and identified 66,500 households below the poverty line. Later another round was taken "to cover the left-out families" and issue of yellow cards rose to 90,000. Another survey was in progress to weed out the bogus yellow cardholders now.

In the first 3 years of DRDA, 90 per cent of loans were for dairy purpose. The low income yield and the high rate of default and misuse of loans in this case has slowly led to a diversification of loans. He has a very interesting point to make that really questions the "individual approach" underlying the programme:

> "The individual approach to beneficiaries leaves to them entirely the function of assessing which avenues would yield better returns to them. Planning on a group basis for a village or a cluster of villages (the cluster being linked to a bank

branch or a focal point), would have allowed for a match between the infrastructure and market demands of the area on the one hand and activities of the beneficiaries on the other hand".

The real issue is of linking "needs of beneficiaries" and "potentialities" of the area. Unfortunately, programme as implemented and monitored examines it in terms of physical and financial target achievement. But "potentialities" of the person to be assisted are also important such as assessing "skills" and "assets" already with him along with the demand and supply infrastructure available. TRYSEM can better be linked to it to give training to a group of such promising persons in an area of promise. The administration has realised the limitation of reliance on dairying. In the targets for next year it is listed to have 100 cases in the total of 2140 cases.

A state level review was taken for the years 1981-82 and 1982-83 by taking a sample of 1431 beneficiaries.

It showed that out of 1431 cases:

Dairy Schemes cases	1116 cases (other cases 315)
Defaulters	250 cases
Misutilisation	253 cases
Crossed poverty line	523 cases.

For the district Sangrur, a review in 1984 revealed that in five years 33,200 cases out of 90,000 yellow cardholders were covered and 50 per cent beneficiaries had crossed the poverty line. This is roughly the same percentage as that of state level.

Mr. Karan Bir Singh Sidhu (1985-86) reports that in Patiala district 72,895 persons (35685 scheduled castes) the yellow cardholders forming 35 per cent of total households in 1981 (NSS estimate is 10 per cent poverty) and from 1980-81 to 1984-85, a total of 36003 beneficiaries were covered under IRDP.

Pointing out the defects of yellow cards survey he reports the inclusion of many undeserving cases and exclusion of deserving ones. Mr. Karan Bir asserts, "possessing a yellow card issued on the basis of a hasty survey conducted some six years ago is, in my opinion neither a necessary nor a sufficient condition for being regarded below the poverty line". Another important observation is that to identify the prospective beneficiaries, all yellow cardholders are taken as one group. No income quartiles are made or studied to take up the poorest among the poor—as stipulated in the actual scheme. Banks of course prefer persons with higher incomes.

Government of India's instructions (circular letter No. 5.11011/26/82-IRD-I dated 2-3-82) are that final selection of the beneficiary has to be made at a General Body meeting of the Gram Sabha. But Mr. Karan Bir points out:

"This practice has virtually not been adopted in the district". He suggests an annual survey after giving full publicity of the scheme and impending dates of survey in the village.

A very interesting suggestion made is to have a village Master Register, kept at Panchayat Ghar and open to be seen by all. This should contain information and particulars of all persons assisted by various agencies including RDA and updated regularly in the presence of village Panchayat and checked by all visiting senior officers.

Mr. Karan Bir Singh randomly selected 10 villages in Bhunerheri Block of Patiala district and collected complete information of all beneficiaries and compared it with Bank records—9 cases were fictitious entries must have been made. Of the 74 beneficiaries actually contacted, he found 44 *had crossed* or were above poverty line. Dairy accounted 65 per cent of beneficiary schemes but success rate was least at 44 per cent while workshops and mule-carts showed very high success rate of 100 per cent and 88 per cent respectively. But 26 per cent of total beneficiaries were default cases. Again dairying showing the highest default rate at 36 per cent and 42 per cent of them had lost the asset. In non-dairy cases 92 per cent beneficiaries still have the asset.

Mr. Nirmal Jit Singh Kalsi (1985-86)—reported that 55,117 families in Ludhiana were identified as below poverty line and by the end of 1982-83 while a total of 22489 beneficiaries had been assisted, 16,483 were in the primary sector and 11,526 in dairy only. The same story is repeated in this district as in Patiala, Sangrur and Bhatinda.

Mr. M.S. Sandhu (1985-86) reports that Punjab State Institute of Public Administration conducted a random sample survey in Ropar district in two blocks Nurpur Bedi and Majri. It revealed that:

—35 per cent beneficiaries did not purchase the asset at all.
—On an average a sample beneficiary had to make four visits to get his case processed—it meant an expenditure of Rs.82.
—40 per cent of old beneficiaries had over dues in payment and 45 per cent had lost the asset or sold it out or the asset perished.

Mr. M.S. Sandhu made a personal survey and found the official survey was faulty and well-off persons had been issued yellow cards. His conclusion is "The whole process is fraught with misutilisation, leakages, undue influences etc."

Mr. D.P. Reddy (1986-87) reported from Hoshiarpur that identification of viable schemes is not done by DIC, agricultural department etc. He also suggests functional cluster approach or a family approach. Administrative efficiency and more staff is recommended. In his district of Hoshiarpur a total of 24,594 beneficiaries have been taken up from 1980-81 to 1983-84.

Ms. Kalpana Mittal (1986-87) from Ludhiana spells out required administrative efficiency in proper planning, supervision, implementation, monitoring and evaluation. But her own judgement on implementation is:

> *a close study of the programme in district Ludhiana reveals that its impact on the rural poor has not been as good as was expected by planners.*

Since 1981-82, 64700 families have been assisted but only 28.7 per cent families have managed to cross the poverty line.

Mr. Satish Chandra (1986-87) from Bhatinda reports that DRDA has prepared the cost-benefit analysis of 40 schemes in primary, secondary and tertiary sectors and these displayed on a notice board. The most popular scheme is dairying.

In three years, 1984-85 to 1986-87 beneficiaries assisted were 20,539 and financial achievement was Rs.2.55 crores. He feels satisfied that some real poor have been assisted. But he suggests proper publicity so that instead of DRDA trying to find cases, the people should be chasing DRDA.

Mr. T.R. Sarangal (1986-87) from Amritsar interviewed all concerned (officials and people) to assess the schemes. His conclusion is that "people are not getting proper benefits from the special programmes". He found that genuine people without yellow cards and undeserving had received them. Local Sarpanchs and rich farmers exert influence to get those schemes selected which serve their purpose.

Mr. Sarangal made a sample study of 91 households in 5 randomly selected villages out of 83 villages in Taran Taran block of Amritsar. All the 91 households had been identified as belonging to weaker sections. Of these 74 per cent were engaged in agricultural labour a work for the downtrodden. Interestingly, he found 26 per cent of these owned some land ——in fact 20 per cent owned more than 5 acres and yet they were taken as below-poverty line. He found that 33 families had radios, 5 had T.V. sets and 3 scheduled caste families possessed tape-recorders. His own conclusion is that 71 per cent of total houscholds were having income above Rs. 3600 per year. He asserts:

> It may be concluded from the findings of the survey that the special programmes launched by the government for the weaker sections could not uplift the down-trodden households. Whatever benefits were provided by the different agencies are reaped by the upper strata of the society and the richer among the poor.
>
> Last but not the least, it may be suggested that special programmes will be successful only when the rural poor are organized for justice.

Micro Studies as part of Socio-economic Studies

In District Sangrur, Mr. Anirudh Tewari (1991-92) commended the help to 34 people under IRDP in his village *Channo* but finds JRY not very helpful as it gives only seasonal employment.

In District Jallandhar, Mr. M.P. Singh in village "*Allewali*" commends different programmes like animal husbandry, balwadis, schools, Mahila samiti, craft training centre etc. in the village.

Ms. Anjali Gupta (1989-90) reports unwillingness of labourers to work under government programmes as they get higher wages elsewhere. People support programmes that uplift the village like pavement of roads and disposal of sewage water. Many yellow cards holders are still waiting for IRDP loans. People demand a craft centre for girls.

Ms. Raji P. Srivastava (1991-92) reviewing the general situation in the district and village *Kuharh Khurd* of her study remarks:

The schemes like Employment Guarantee Scheme, TRYSEM, Nehru Rozgar Yojana and so on, have not really influenced the lives of the villagers substantially. In the village we are studying, none of the unemployed or partially employed had heard of these schemes.

Assets creation and Minimum Needs Programme, as introduced by the central and state governments from time to time, are in operation, but again, none in the village could tell me if he had benefited from them.

However, under the DWACRA scheme training is being provided to village women in economic activities.

Mr. B. Vikram (1992-93) has reported that development schemes are too tailor-made. He bemoans that they give little freedom or initiative at the local level. In the last five years, his village Ghorewahi received funds for repair of school building, paving of village drains and build pucca village outfall drain. Funds are not sufficient, hence "the poorest sections of the village, the Harijan Basti have remained untouched. These parts of the village have neither proper streets nor drains and they invariably get water-logged and slushy during each monsoon." But it is interesting and surprising that the village has a Harijan majority and Sarpanch is also a Harijan.

Same way for Indira Awas Yojana, standardised and specific 25 grants over 3 years have been given. Of 50 beneficiaries under IRDP, 47 had taken Milch cattle but his 10 per cent check revealed that they had genuinely benefited, though 2 had defaulted in payment.

Since "matching grant" system has been abandoned to help poorest villages, the element of personal interest and monitoring by villages has vanished. They just want more and more funds and the spirit of self help is no more there.

In district Ludhiana Mr. A.S. Chhatwal (1987-88) reviewing IRDP in village *Sanghol* has noted the fact of yellow cards having been issued to people not deserving it. He had 21 IRDP cases in his village and found only 4 dairy cases, rest being in small shops and trades. Regular income has been enhanced because of IRDP help. But "quite a number of beneficiaries conceded not using the whole amount of advance for buying the asset." His comments are important:

> My finding has been that none of the beneficiaries belonged to the poorest of the poor category. Most of them were no doubt poor but many more poorer than them (were) left out.

Mr. Sunil Kumar (1988-89) found in his village Kotumra "very few families living below the poverty line". "As a matter of fact hardly anyone would be truly eligible for loan under IRDP". Exactly same comments are given by Mr. Sanjay Kumar (1989-90) about his village Sahnewal. He commends group insurance scheme under IRDP. Since most people getting benefit under IRDP are not genuinely poor, "they just want to take money and enjoy it".

"In my personal opinion not more than 5% to 10% beneficiaries really utilise the loan for meaningful purpose and those who have done are doing quite well".

Same comments are about village *Pona* from Mr. Vijoy Kumar Singh that no family lives below poverty line. But he commended the system in the village whereby Harijan beneficiaries under Indira Awas Yojana transfer money received to Panchayat with affidavit and Panchayat very efficiently builds houses for them. Mr. S.R. Ladhar (1992-93) reports about village *Budewal* in the same tone that very few families would be below poverty line, although there were 65 yellow cardholders (52 harijans). Out of 15 assisted, 5 are defaulters.

In district Patiala Mr. Viswajeet Khanna (1988-89) reporting from *Bhunerheri* village has commended that 29 beneficiaries under IRDP have been successfully helped as also six under TRYSEM. "The BDO's office has also taken up construction of drains and streets, latrines and planting of trees in the village with good results as also helping out in the creation of other assets."

Ms. Ravneet Kaur (1989-90) found in 1987-88 115 Harijans and 84 others as holders of yellow cards in village *Massinghan*. Since 1983, about 27 people got loans under IRDP, 17 of them for dairying, six persons were trained under TRYSEM but no work is reported under NREP and RLEGP. A street was paved in Harijan area under JRY.

Mr. Sarvjeet Singh's (1992-93) village *Jallahkheri* had only 2 beneficiaries under IRDP who had consumed the loan and gave the usual explanation that the buffalo died after some time. Mr. Sarvjeet finds lack of interest by officials in the development organisation as the cause for spoiling the package for self-employment programme degenerating into an easy-loan activity.

In district Amritsar Mr. Kripa Shankar (1990-91) found that in his village *Dhaul Kalan,* all the 17 persons he surveyed had misutilised the loan amount taken under IRDP. JRY is better as Panchayats use it for paving the streets and making a drainage system. In general he reports frustration of people with the individual beneficiary programmes.

In district Gurdaspur Mr. Vijay Kumar has shown satisfaction that majority of the people assisted under IRDP have benefited and are better off. Of the 249 yellow card holders, 127 had been given some aid. Under community assets programme or under development grants from government good work has been done by the Panchayats.

In district Ropar Dr. Roshan Lal reported that in his village *Bela* of 112 families below poverty line, 55 families (including 15 Harijan families) had been assisted. But his inquiries showed that assets were intact in only 30% cases. "Most of the families have not got benefited from it and have remained below the poverty line".

Overview

Special studies of IRDP and comments on IRDP in Socio-economic studies reveal certain common points about Government programmes of poverty alleviation. Almost all probationers have found that survey campaign of identification of the poor was a farce. Persons with five acres of land or having running shops and pucca houses have been listed as below poverty while quite a few real deserving cases have not been included. Some reports allege that the real needy have not been selected at all. It is not to say that these poor were at all places deliberately left out but certainly a careful proper survey with widespread publicity was not done. The idea of one-time survey and listing and then taking away cases only from this list has many logical defects. It permanently shuts those poor families off who, out of their own ignorance or inefficiency or political/caste bias of the surveyors could not get listed in the first instance. In some districts, a resurvey was done to include the "left-out" cases but that was to include the "favoured" cases only. It is a strange administrative efficiency that takes all-important things as a one-time campaign—including the counting of poor.

Most of the probationers in their reports have described the administrative inefficiency and lack of real feelings for the poor. This is a widespread feeling as far as the case of real needy are concerned and applies to almost all the stages of the programme—like giving due publicity to the scheme with requirements and benefits; choosing the cases from the yellow card holders; choosing the schemes and doing the homework in looking to the viability of schemes; dairying as the first and easiest and most common scheme chosen; sanctioning of loan and subsidy; long red tape, deliberate or otherwise, involved in making the actual payment or procuring the asset; corruption and cuts at different stages even upto the purchase of assets; lack of co-ordination among various agencies involved; lack of monitoring once the assets have been purchased; whole process and approach smacks of fulfilling the targets and sending cosmetic statistical returns. These have been pointed out again and again in contrast with the efficiency of administration in other spheres like agriculture, flood control, hospitality and so on.

Our own opinion, based on frequent visits to villages all over the country, is that situation elsewhere is much worse than in Punjab. Here Punjabis are atleast alert and sharp-tongued by nature and able to point out the open. But that could not be an excuse for the inefficiency and lack of interest by the officials here.

Recommendations

Mr. K.B.S. Sidhu has given a very workable suggestion of maintaining a village Master Register for a proper information system as an inherent incentive to tone up efficiency. One of the interesting points raised is that of individual beneficiary approach versus group of beneficiaries and cluster of villages approach. Most probationers have preferred the latter. They report commendable results in building community assets through development assets and it is rare that Panchayats or individuals have misutilised or misused the funds. Bias to caste clusters, however, has been reported. But the real question is do the officials do their homework at all in looking to the ultimate viability of an asset in the demand and supply setting of the village? That is rarely done. More fundamental question is, do the officials concerned have the competence and capability to do it? And do they have the desire to do it? And do we have any system of reward and punishment for the officials and officers concerned?

The unfortunate "no" to all these questions raises many fundamental issues to which we shall come later.

Another critical point is the lack of interest among the political representatives. They confine themselves only to getting particular persons selected as beneficiaries. They rarely attend the co-ordinating meetings or monitoring meetings. Question again is, why?

Quite a few probationers have recommended more "powers" to the higher officers and more staff. This is a typical bureaucratic solution to most of administrative ailments. It has not worked elsewhere unless where it was the only problem in the system. We believe inherent problems of the programme and the administrative system need to be looked into.

Probationers have not complained of problems and defects only. Some positive aspects have been brought to the fore. Most of them agree that some important help has actually gone to the selected beneficiaries. The success rate is different at different villages in different districts—range being 20 per cent to 70 per cent. This is natural because we are taking selective cases and at different time periods. The extreme have been reported some saying that schemes have done very good to the beneficiaries and other asserting that all went waste.

Overall, Punjab picture that emerges is that since the inception of the programme some 50% yellow cardholders have been covered and the programme, with some modifications, has been recommended to be continued.

Issues

There are certain important issues that emerge in the context of poverty alleviation programmes in Punjab.

Most of the probationers, in their micro studies have reported that *very few* real poor or those below the poverty line as per the criterion of Government of India exist in Punjab. In most cases identifying and helping the people below the poverty line is a farce in which political and administrative wings of the government willingly join. The reason is simple. No state government would want to lose the central government grants by saying, "we do not have people below the poverty line". The flaw is in the Central programme itself where a fixed all India criterion of people below the poverty line has been imposed across the board for all the lakhs of villages in the country. Rs. 3600 per month in Manipur, Kerala or Punjab do not mean the same thing. State level criteria could be devised in consultation with the techno-economic experts in that state.

It also brings us to the question of the very concept of poverty. Even if absolute poverty of the type in Bihar, U.P., or M.P. villages does not exist in Punjab, the relative poverty within a village is a hard fact. A person in Punjab who is not able to afford milk for daily consumption, who does not have his own Katcha hut or house to live in the village or is unable to send his children even for free schooling because of high alternative earning help lost, is as deprived socially and mentally in the village as a person below poverty line in a Bihar village.

This is so in spite of the fact that he may be able to afford his two meals without getting into any family debt trap. These poor cannot be deprived of the benefits under special poverty alleviation programmes. Hence the administrative and political willingness to accept the central funds. If the central criterion of poverty can be made more realistic, this farce can end.

This brings us to the other structural flaws in the scheme which makes it too difficult to be administered efficiently. The whole scheme envisages an entrepreneurial investigation into the economically viable projects which can be handled by the unskilled poor. Both these are too tall claims from persons completely ill-equipped in this respect. If the beneficiaries were equipped with entrepreneurial ability and finance was the only difficulty; it should have been OK. But that hardly is so. On the other hand if the officials concerned were really of entrepreneurial ability, they would not have been on these petty office jobs. Wherever we do have glimpses of such abilities, success rate is high. In fact, if the successful case studies were investigated further, one would find some good and able officer who worked behind. If the success rate is higher in Punjab than elsewhere even at this low level, it is because of the inherent enterprise ability of Punjabis.

Wherever the beneficiaries concerned were persons already doing some such work (owning a shop, a cart etc.) and were helped (in spite of not being below the poverty line), success rate has been the highest.

That brings us to the crux of the problem. How then to help the real poor under poverty alleviation programmes? The best is to provide services under minimum needs programme, build community assets and infrastructure which is of immediate relevance to the poor and then offer the finance and training services only to those who come forward with some contribution, may be 10 per cent only, from their own resources. This looks like being harsh to the poor, but otherwise they remain on State crutches forever. If starvation stalks some people, it is better to have free community kitchens ("Langar") from socio-religious institutions rather than create a whole big log of government structures that spends Rs.80/- on itself to give Rs.20 to the poor and then makes the poor permanently dependent on government.

Interestingly almost all probationers and other studies have conceded that we have reached a point where people have become completely dependent on government to do every thing. Government has been doling more and more funds in the name of more development, of course by taxing the same people indirectly, and crippling their own initiative, enterprise, innovation and self-help community institutions. It is time to halt the introduction of more programmes and tax less and let government confine itself to build infrastructure and provide minimum social needs only.

We give below a table that tells how people's contribution in Rural Development Programmes in Punjab has been dwindling in absolute as well as percentage terms while as we know per capita State Income and prosperity has been rising:

Table 3.21 : Peoples' Contribution in Rural Development Programmes in Punjab

(Rs. Lakhs)

Year	*Agri. and Animal Husbandry*	*Health and Rural Sanitation*	*Education*	*Communication*	*Village and Small Industries*	*Other works*	*Total*	*People's Contribution as %age of Total Government Expenditure on Rural Devpt.*
1970-71	0.34	3.01	-	-	-	12.68	16.03	11.54
1975-76	0.67	4.65	-	-	0.01	9.90	15.23	4.70
1980-81		9.81	2.16	10.15	-	5.51	27.63	1.83
1985-86		1.56	0.05	14.87	-	0.27	16.75	0.55
1990-91		0.10	0.51	6.65	-	0.65	7.91	0.10

The real question and issue is, shall we try to revitalise the programmes and make more and more expenditures and employ more people with more facilities under government service to give a bit more to the poor or shall we not now revitalise the very people who need help so that slowly they are able to live well without help and shun help altogether?

ECONOMIC AND SOCIAL CONDITIONS

Prosperous Punjab

We have already noted in chapter 1 that macro-data reveals high level of development especially in agriculture and dairying in rural Punjab. The indices of growth of production and infrastructure in rural Punjab are at much higher level as compared to any other state in India.

We have also seen that cases of absolute poverty in Punjab are rare especially among native population while 40-60 per cent of labour in peak agricultural season is from other states. Higher than minimum wages do prevail in general. Population Below

Poverty Line is only on official record to avail loans and subsidies. These facts have been noted and commended upon by probationers in general.

Sunil Kumar reports from village Kot Umra in Ludhiana (1988-89) "There are very few families which can be said to be living below poverty line". Vijai Kumar (1990) reported from village Naushera—Nalbandha in Gurdaspur that majority of the yellow cardholders had already got IRDP assistance and benefits. Similarly other officer trainees have reported about their case studies.

Economic Conditions

But absence of absolute poverty does not mean that general economic conditions are uniformly good for all sections. We do not have macro-statistical information on inequalities of income or inadequacy of services to lower rungs in the social structure. It is therefore good to have a look into the micro-studies to see the reality.

A word about the economic condition of tenants, who are really the concealed tenants as already reported in earlier chapters. Tenancy can be on "Batai" system which generally is on the basis of 50% share in produce. Dr. Roshan Sunkaria from village Bela in Ropar reported that the damage to crops, if any, means heavy loss to them. Even then tenants prefer this system to that of fixed rents because rents in the range of Rs.1800-2000 are very high for tenants who have to bear all costs and inputs. Landlords prefer the system of fixed rents. Tenants eke out a meagre income out of tenanted land but still they want it as this is the most convenient supplementation to their income from small-owned holdings. Marginal farmers are therefore living just a minimal standard of living.

Vijai Kumar reported the sad case of tenants in village Naushera Nalbandha in Gurdaspur. Out of the 1969 acres of total area of the village, 572 acres were acquired by defence authorities and a decent compensation of Rs.50000—Rs.75000 per acre was paid. But the compensation went to the landlords. Not a paisa was paid to the tenants who got deprived of their permanent livelihood. The result is aptly reported: "The acquisition of land has brought prosperity for the landowners and misery for the tenants". Land Acquisition Act does not mention that compensation has to be paid only to the owners of land. Yet who will fight for the underprivileged?

Landless labourers have bigger problems compared to tenants. There is no assured employment for all throughout the year. Vijai Kumar had reported 125 unemployed people in his village in 1990. There are no village industries or crafts that could employ or sustain them. Although sericulture and beekeeping is common but these only supplement the meagre earnings of small farmers. Similarly Jaspal Singh reported from Mahasingh Wala village in Firozepur that rural industries hardly existed except for the traditional skill-based occupations like shoe-making and pot-making. People were ready to work for Rs.40 per day for any number of days. High unemployment in lean season has been reported by Anurag Agarwal also in the village Randhawa Masanda in Jallandhar district. He estimated 200 educated unemployed within the village.

Within the class of landless unemployed people, scheduled castes with no traditional skills have the bigger problems of sustenance. Unfortunately, IRDP assistance is not offered to them as a top priority class. Rather caste-based favouritism in favour of higher costs in poverty alleviation programmes has been generally reported by all officer trainees. There are no rules or clear instructions that the cases of the poorest or/and scheduled castes must be taken first. They find their turn rather at the end of the line.

Illiteracy among the lowest castes and the poorest in the villages has also widely noted. The three obvious reasons can be advanced. The poor do not have means to provide for the uniforms, books and other wherewithal that go with education even in low-attendance uncared government schools in the village. Secondly the alternative cost of education to the poor families is very high in terms of percentage of total family income foregone if the children do not work to supplement family income. Thirdly, the poor have seen that educated unemployment among the upper-class income groups is high. Hence, the attraction of education and schooling for better prospects in economic terms does not exist. The result of this poverty and lack of education is that inter-class and inter-caste vertical mobility is completely absent. Social tension in the long run is bound to arise as and when the gap between the poorest and the upper classes increase even though the poor may not be starving for want of food. .

Condition and provision of general services is clearly biased against the poor. Katcha houses, invariably, belong to the scheduled castes. Their localities have no drainage and no paved paths or roads making them look like slums especially during rains. Health and education access is denied to them as poor condition of these services is reported by most of the officer trainees. Rich farmers are able to have access to privately offered higher priced better quality services which are now available in many Punjab villages. Poor are the usual sufferers.

Common Property Resources

This brings us to the important question of common property resources which were, in older times, equally shared by all classes of people. These are common grazing lands for the cattle, playgrounds, village Panchayat lands etc.

Although, by customary law, village Panchayat lands called "shamlat" in Punjab, are managed by the Panchayats, there is no clear legal title in revenue records that these lands are "owned" by them. Hence, wherever a clever encroacher is able to have a legal injunction in his favour, the long arduous legal process involved in dispossessing him makes him a virtual owner. It is time that Panchayat Department of Government of Punjab did something about it. At present these lands are widely encroached by big landlords and it is legally very difficult to get them out. In most cases the encroachers are big landlords or politically weighty persons. The sufferer is the village community, which includes the poor.

In Punjab most of the Panchayat lands are given on rent to cultivators and this rental income is added to the Gaon Sabha Fund which is used to ask for matching grants from government for village development schemes. According to Section 5 of The Punjab Village Common Land Regulation Act, 1961 "if shamlat is more than 25% of village area then after keeping 25% area, 1/4 of the remaining area is to be used for settlement of landless tenants and rest for distribution among small landowners." The stipulation is that the poor shall get some land for settlement and 25% of village area would remain as Shamlat Deh. Actually Shamlat Deh is very much smaller in area and the poor therefore have hardly benefited out of these common property resources. This land is auctioned each year for cultivation and the rent goes to Panchayat funds.

Suresh Kumar noted in village Darolo in Patiala district that Panchayat leased out the land to the poor at a nominal annual rent of Rs.50 per acre. But he writes, it has not helped the poor as the land is barren and they have to spend a lot to make it cultivable.

But it is not that poor are universally uncared for. There are some good examples. Anirudh Tewari (1991) reports from village Channo in Sangrur district, "Basic amenities in the Harijan basti are also available, although the streets need to be paved". A Dharamshala for Harijans was built in the village and ***all*** the villagers participated in its construction. In Panchayat meetings scheduled caste panch is "able to put forward the problems of the weaker sections of the society". T.R. Sarangal (1985) noted that in village Jahangir (Amritsar) landless poor were given four marla plots for Indira Awas Yojana.

On the other hand Dr. Roshan Sunkaria (1989) reports that Panchayat is not happy to have government grants as they allege corrupt officials take away "half the money". In this village all the streets were pucca except half of one street and therein is located the Sarpanch house.

One point is surely and universally reported that there are no common grazing lands and the non-land-owning poor people cannot easily have milch cattle that would give them decent income. Cattle rearing has to be stall-fed and the poor do not find it cost-effective.

Social Conditions

Most of the officer trainees have reported inter-caste harmony and interclass amity among the village folk of Punjab. This is remarkable because we are referring to the deadly decade of terrorism in Punjab. Most of the outside world had discounted this completely and some elements were sometimes predicting a civil-war-like situation in Punjab. This happily never happened and the deep shadow of that decade is over. That Hindus and Sikhs were able to live through this decade as one community, is the biggest credit to the people of Punjab.

Some of the trainee officers did note an undercurrent of tension, caution and apprehension and they reported that people in general avoided talking about the news and views on Punjab terrorist activity. For one thing, most of them were convinced that this was a passing affair and ultimately peace and sense would return to Punjab. Secondly, they feared that open talks might reach the ears of terrorists or "the boys" as they were called, and people would not like taking risk on any argument or quarrel with them. "Missing persons" or "misguided youth" was the maximum mention that they came to.

While the village folk would not talk about the "methods" of and "approach" of the "boys", they did not oppose the "cause" espoused by them — discrimination to Punjab in political, social and economic matters and police excesses and false cases of encounters. Even on these matters, the trainee officers reported, that villagers would not like discussion, analysis or argumentation.

In private talk the damage to life and economic condition because of "unfortunate happenings", and the "police excesses" were the matters referred to, especially when no names or incidents were mentioned. Many of these matters were not recorded in writing by the officer trainees and the author is writing these words on the basis of oral reports to the author as Counsellor for Punjab Cadre.

Inter-caste discrimination as it exists in a mildler form in Punjab. Lower caste people move freely among the upper castes. They invite them for marriage functions etc. and also offer food. But in all these cases, the Harijans keep a respectful distance and eat separately. Their houses are in separate clusters but are not too far away from the main centre. In some villages even this group segregation is getting blurred as some Harijans with land join the prosperous people. Almost all Harijans have their own houses, but mostly katcha houses unlike the pucca houses of the upper castes.

Lower caste people and upper caste people in Punjab have learnt to live together in peace in a sort of social balance. Lower castes do not exert and shout for complete equality and keep a socially respectful distance from the upper castes. The latter, on their part, extend co-operation and consideration to the lower castes and treat them as part of the total village community and take pride in being socially friendly to them. This harmonious balance has given great social amity to Punjab villages. By and large slow social and economic vertical mobility of the lower castes is tolerated and sometimes encouraged but complete equality is absent.

Inter-caste marriages are strictly forbidden and any such love-affair-marriage would upset this harmonious balance. In most villages Harijans have their separate clusters and separate religious places. Their customs and festivals are not always identical with those of the upper castes. But all castes do visit and participate in these functions.

Vini Mahajan reporting from village Kadian (1989) in Jallandhar has analysed this inter-caste balance and harmony. One of the important reason mentioned is the influence of Sikh religion which preaches and emphasises caste equality and professes to forge a casteless community. Not that this has actually been achieved in practice but it does act as a strong helping factor to reach the commonly found balance. When you profess Sikh religion out of voluntary inner sincerity, you cannot but try to live upto some socially workable standards even if not strictly as per the prescribed tenets. Secondly absence of absolute poverty and a discernible movement to higher standards of living by all sections blunts the sharpness of the edge of the razor-like differences and tensions found elsewhere.

CONCLUSION

Analysis and Conclusion

We have tried to faithfully reflect the reality as seen and reported by the IAS Officer Trainees of Punjab Cadre from 1983-85 to 1992-94 batches. The reports emanate from official study assignments and do not always give indepth analysis of the current reality. In some cases they represent a very brief descriptive reality as seen at that time. In some other cases real issues are side-tracked. But we have found, in general, the reports as intelligent and sincere work of the officers of Punjab. The officers are faithful and unbiased reporters and are neither pro-administration nor anti-administration.

As the majority of the reporting Officer Trainees come from states other than Punjab and involuntarily compare the situation in Punjab with that found and experienced elsewhere, they are visibly impressed the smooth economic and social reality and remarkable achievements of Punjab rural folk and administration. However, we feel that the day-to-day economic problems of the lower class and lower caste people have not been penetrated enough to be reported and analysed in detail.

While the general prosperity and absence of absolute poverty have been well highlighted, the officer trainees have also tried to look towards the factors behind it. The enterprise of the Punjabis, the good base of natural resources and infrastructure and the helpful positive role of administration have been rightly pointed out and lauded. Wherever administration or some sections of the people have failed, the keen observing Officer Trainees have not failed in noting and pointing out.

But the social realities, inter-caste relationships, inter-class income/wealth differentials have not been properly noted and commented upon. In many cases Officer Trainees have not tried to underline the socio-economic basis of the Punjab's crisis situation nor did they bring out in the forefront its economic and social implications. The crisis and turmoil was at peak and the situation was that of complete confusion for the people as well as the observers. Fear psychosis was also widely prevalent. One could quietly discuss the matters among intimate friends but could not write about them.

Even on the economic front while the officer trainees have duly reported the facts they have not been able to view village socio-economic reality as one pattern or one structure. Village economy in its entirety and the overall comprehension of the model of development do not emerge out of these studies.

The undercurrents and implications and impending predicaments and contradictions of the Punjab model of development have rarely been brought out. Except for one or two studies, the penetrating analysis is missing.

But the vibrating and living is Punjab is vividly reflected through these studies. The unbiased intelligent look into a real situation and its faithful reporting certainly make them valuable micro-study documents to understand and comprehend the Punjab Rural life.

SELECT BIBLIOGRAPHY

Adiraju, Venkateswar Rao. *Sikhs and India : Identity Crisis, 1991.*

Agricultural Development in Punjab : Issues in resources use and sustainability by Chopra, Kanchan 1990.

Alagh, Y.K. *India: Development Planing and Policy.* New Delhi : Vikas Publishing House, 1991.

Aryan, K.C. *The Cultural Heritage of Punjab : 3000 B.C. to 1947 A.D.* New Delhi : Rekha Prakashan, 1993.

Bal, S.S. *British administration in the Punjab and its aftermath,* Amritsar : Guru Nanak Dev University, 1986.

Chand, Atar. *Jawaharlal Nehru and Politics in Punjab.* New Delhi : H.K. Publishers, 1989.

Chaudhri, D.P. *Agriculture and the Development Process : A study of Punjab,* D.P. Chaudhri and Ajit K. Dasgupta. London : Croom Helm, 1985.

Chaudhri, D.P. *Agriculture and the Development Process : A study of Punjab,* D.P. Chaudhri and Ajit K. Dasgupta. London : Croom Helm, 1985.

Chopra, V.D. *Agony of Punjab*/V.D. Chopra, R.K. Mishra, Nirmal Singh. New Delhi : Patriot Pub., 1984.

Dal, Surjit Singh. *A brief history of the modern Punjab* Ludhiana: Lyall Book Depot., 1974.

Dalip Singh *Dynamics of Punjab Politics.* New Delhi : Macmillan, 1986.

Dang, Satyapal. *Genesis of terrorism : An analytical study of Punjab terrorists.* New Delhi : patriot Publishers, 1988.

Deb, P.C. *Bazigars of Punjab (A socio-economic study).* Delhi : Mittal, 1987.

Deol, J.S. *State Politics in India (with special reference to Punjab)* 2nd ed.— Jallandhar : New Academic, 1986.

Gajrani, S. *Peasants and Princes : Agrarian unrest in the East Punjab States,* 1920-48. Delhi : Anmol, 1987.

Gill, Manohar Singh. *Agriculture co-operatives : A case study of Punjab.* New Delhi : Vikas Publishing House, 1983.

Gobinder Singh *Religion and politics in the Punjab.* New Delhi : Deep and Deep Publishers, 1986.

Gopal Krishan *Special dimensions of unemployment and underemployment (a case study of rural Punjab).* New Delhi : Concept Published, 1986.

Gosal. C.S. *Regional disparities in level of socio-economic development in Punjab* by G.S. Gosal and Gopal Krishan. Krukshetra : Vishal Publications, 1984.

Gupta, A.K. *Sociological implications of rural to rural migration. (a case study of rural immigrants in Punjab).* Allahabad : Vohra : 1988.

Gupta, A.K. Sociological implications of rural to rural migration. (a case study of rural immigrants in Punjab). Allahabad : Bohra, 1988.

Hari Singh *Punjab Peasant in freedom struggle,* New Delhi : People's Publishing House, 1984.

Hari Singh *Agrarian Scene in British Punjab.* New Delhi : People's Publishing House, 1983.

India. *White Paper on the Punjab Agitation.* New Delhi : Government of India, 1984.

Iqbal Singh. *Emerging Patterns of Tenancy and Labour Contracts in India,* in G.K. Chadha (ed) Sectoral Issues in Indian Economy. New Delhi : Har-Anand Publications, 1994.

Jagjit Singh. *Status of Social forestry in Punjab.*

Juergensmeyer, Mark *Religious rebels in the Punjab : The social vision of untouchables.* Delhi : Ajanta Publications, 1988.

Kahlon, A.S. *Modernisation of Punjab Agriculture.* New Delhi : Allied Publishers, 1984.

Kurien, C.T. *The Economy.* New Delhi : Sage Publication, 1992.

Mahajan, V.S. *Economic Development of Border States of India.* New Delhi : Deep and Deep Publications, 1988.

Malhotra, S.L. *Gandhi, Punjab and the partition.* Chandigarh : Punjab University, 1983.

Matto, Anita *Reform movements and social transformation in India,* New Delhi : Reliance, 1991.

Mohan Lal *Disintegration of Punjab.* Chandigarh : Sameer Prakashan, 1984.

Nagpal, C.S. and Mahajan, R.K. *Economic Policies.* Delhi : Anmol Publications, 1992.

Nirbhai Singh *Philosophy of Sikhism : Reality and its manifestations.* New Delhi : Atlantic Publishers, 1990.

Oberai, A.S. *Causes and consequences of internal migration : A study in the Indian Punjab* by A.S. Oberai and H.K. Manmohan Singh, Delhi : Oxford University Press, 1983.

Package of practices in agricultural engineering, edited by Gill, G.S. Mangat I.S., 1993.

Pandit, M.L. *Industrial development in the Punjab and Haryana (domination of Footloose industries)* Delhi : B.R. Publishers, 1985.

Paul, R.R. Rural—*Urban migration in Punjab : An economic analysis* Bombay : Himalaya, 1989.

Performance of afforestation schemes in Punjab. Chandigarh : Economic Adviser to Government of Punjab, 1987.

Political dynamics and crisis in Punjab edited by Paul Walloce and Surendra Chopra, Amritsar : Guru Nanak Dev University, 1988.

Pritam Singh. *Emerging Pattern of Punjab economy.* New Delhi : Sterling Pub., 1983.

Punjab Agricultural Handbook 1993 : edited by Gill, R.S., 1992.

Punjab Department of industries. Facilities for non resident Indians, 1989.

Punjab Economic Adviser to Government Economic Survey of Punjab 1992-93, 1993.

Punjab Economic Adviser to Government. Equipping and modernisation of industrial development centres in Punjab, 1991.

Punjab Economic Advisor to Government. Integrated Child development series scheme in Punjab, 1989.

Punjab, Integrated Rural Development Programme (an evaluation) Chandigarh : The economic adviser to Government of Punjab, 1987.

Punjab. The fatal miscalculation/edited by Patwant Singh and Harji Malik. New Delhi : Patwant Singh, 1985.

Punjab. Crisis : Context and trends/ Pramod Kumar . (et. al). Chandigarh : Centre for Research in Rural and Industrial Development, 1984.

Punjab. Department Science Technology and Environment. Status of the environment in Punjab : A first status report. Chandigarh : Department of Science, Technology and Environment, 1984.

Punjab. Economic and Statistical Organisation : Statistical Abstract of Punjab (annual).

Punjab. Facts About Punjab, 1991.

Punjab. Integrated Rural Development Programme (an evaluation). Chandigarh : The Economic Adviser to the Government, Punjab, 1987.

Puri, Nina, *Political elite and society in the Punjab.* New Delhi : Vikas Publishing House, 1985.

Sain, Inder. *Transformation of Punjab agriculture.* Delhi : B.R. Publishing, 1987.

Sharma, Inderjit. *Land Revenue Administration in the Punjab* (1849-1901). New Delhi : Atlantics, 1985.

Sharma, Satish Kumar. *Social movements and social change* (a study of Arya Smaj and Untouchables in Punjab). Delhi : B.R. Publishing, 1985.

Sher Singh. *Philosophy of Sikhism.* Amritsar : Shiromany Prabandhak Committee, 1986.

Shiva, Vandana. *The violence of the green revolution : Ecological degradation and political conflict in Punjab.* Dehradun : Research Foundation for Science and Ecology, 1989.

Sims, Holly Political Regimes, Public Policy, and Economic Development : Agricultural performance and rural change in two Punjabs, 1988.

Singh, Brij Pal. *Educational Progress and Economic Development in Punjab.* Patiala : Punjabi University, 1974.

Singh, Inder Pal. *Rural Income Distribution (an analytical study of Punjab).* Delhi : B.R. Publishing, 1986.

Singh, Inderjit *Nutrition Health and Hygiene for women,* Bajaj Satinder Edited by Bhambi Ahooja, 1989.

Tewari, V.N. *Punjab : A cultural profile.* New Delhi : Vikas Publishing House, 1984.

The women of Punjab edited by Yash Kohli. Bombay : Chic Publishers, 1983.

Upinder Jit Kaur. *Sikh religion and economic development.* New Delhi : National Book Organisation, 1990.

Urbanisation and urban development in Punjab, edited by Mishra S.N., 1985.

4

HARYANA

PADAMVIR SINGH

Administrative Units

On November 1, 1966, plains of former Punjab state were bifurcated to form the states of Haryana and the present Punjab.

Administratively Haryana is made up of 4 divisions and 16 districts. The districts are further subdivided into 43 sub-divisions, 57 tehsils and 109 blocks. The state has 6759 villages and 94 towns. The administrative units were reorganized in 1989 when four new districts, Panipat, Rewari, Yamunanagar and Kaithal were carved out of the existing 12 districts.

Physical features

Haryana has an area of 44,222 sq. kms. and after Delhi, Nagaland and Kerala, is the smallest state in the Indian Union. Situated in the northern region of the Indian Union, the state is bounded by the plains of Punjab in the north-west, sharply rising hills in the north-east, Uttar Pradesh separated by the river Yamuna and the state of Delhi in the east and the sandy tract of Rajasthan in the south and the south-west. The state is bounded by river Ghaggar in the west.Topographically, the state possesses large tracts of land well suited to arable farming and the use of farm machinery. The average height of topography ranges from 700 to 900 feet above sea level. Physically, Haryana falls into two broad natural divisions, the sub-Himalayan and the Indo-Gangetic Plain which run into a south-eastern direction, almost parallel to each other.

A major part of the soil in Haryana is alluvial loam (central Haryana), the rest being silty loam, coarse loam, sandy loam or sandy. The soils are largely fertile and responsive to irrigation. Rocky and 'pahari' areas are almost insignificant.

Climate

The climate is very hot in summer and markedly cold in winter. The maximum temperature recorded during May and June is 49 degrees Celsius and 2 to 3 degrees Celsius in January.

Except in a few areas the rainfall in the region is low and erratic. The maximum rainfall is about 216 cm occuring mainly in the foothills. The minimum rainfall is 25 to 38 cm in the southern part of the state. About 80 per cent of the overall rainfall occurs between July and September, often resulting in local floods.

Agro-climatic zones

North Eastern Zone

(Karnal—Kurukshetra—Ambala)
The zone has very hot summers with temperatures going as high as 45^0C in May, June and July and cold winters with temperatures as low as 2^0 C in December and January. The average total rainfall during thc ycar is about 110 cms and is received mainly in July-September. The rivers Yamuna, Ghaggar, Markanda, Tangra, Saraswati carry heavy discharge during the monsoon and often cause floods. The soil is mainly loamy.

Central Zone

(Rohtak—Sonepat—Jind)
Very similar to the above zone with respect to climate, this zone has sandy loam soil and an average annual rainfall of about 71 cms. This region is also frequented by floods during the monsoon.

South Western Semi-arid Zone

(Hissar—Bhiwani—Sirsa)
Bordering the Rajasthan desert the area is arid. The average annual rainfall is only 48 cms. Hot and dry winds and duststorms are common during the summer.

(Gurgaon—Faridabad—Mahendragarh)

This zone is also arid and dry. The rainfall is scanty and unevenly distributed averaging about 59 cms annually. The soil texture of Mahendragarh bordering Rajasthan is sandy and hard calcareous whereas that of Gurgaon and Faridabad is sandy-to-sandy loam.

Demography

The total population of Haryana is 16.46 million (1991 census) constituting 1.95 per cent of the total population of India with a proportionate area of 1.3 per cent. The density of population is 372 per sq. km. as against 267 per sq. km. for India as a whole.

The increase in population during 1981-1991 was 27.4% as against 28 per cent for the period 1971-81 and 32 per cent for 1961-1971. The corresponding figures for the Indian Union are 23.5 per cent (1981-1991), 25 per cent (1971-1981) and 24.8 per cent (1961-71). The achievements of population control in the state during the period 1971-1981 could not be sustained during the subsequent decade. The rural population as a percentage of the total population declined from 82.3 per cent in 1971 to 78.1 per cent in 1981 and then to 75.4 per cent in 1991. The corresponding figures for the Indian Union are 80.1 per cent (1971), 76.7 per cent (1981) and 74.3 per cent (1991). Cultivators as percentage of total workers in Haryana are 38.77 per cent (1991) as against 38.75 per cent (1991) for the Indian Union. However agricultural labourers as percentage of total workers for Haryana is only 19 per cent (1991) compared to 26.15 per cent for India as a whole. This indicates the predominance of the owner-cultivator in Haryana. The Scheduled Caste population as percentage of total population in Haryana is 19.75 per cent as compared to 15.8 per cent for the Indian Union. However, in general demographic terms, Haryana appears to be a good representative sample of the Indian Union. (see Table 4.1)

Table 4.1 : Demographic Indicators of Haryana

	Haryana	*All India*
Population	16,463,648	846,302,688
Population of Haryana as % of total population of India	1.95	
Rural population as % of total population	75.37	74.29
Scheduled Caste population as % of total population	19.75	15.80
Density	372 per sq. km	257 per sq. km
Decennial Growth rate of Population	27.40	23.51
Sex ratio	865	929
Cultivators	1,829,530	110,588,822
Cultivators as % of total workers	38.77	38.75
Agricultural labourers	896,782	74,649,217
Agricultural labourers as % of total workers	19.00	26.15
Household industry workers	72,195	10,373,099
Household industry workers as % of total workers	1.53	3.63
Other categories of workers	1,920,219	89,811,775
Other category workers as % of total workers	40.70	31.47

Source: Derived from Statistical Abstract of Haryana (1991-92), Government of Haryana.

The sex ratio of Haryana is however much lower than the Indian union: 865 (1991) compared to 929 (1991) for the Indian Union. The Literacy rate in Haryana was 55.33 per cent (1991) as compared to 52.11 per cent (1991) for the Indian Union.

Agriculture and Land Utilisation

The total area of Haryana is only 1.3 per cent of the total area of India. However the net area sown is 2.5 per cent of the net sown area of India; and the total cropped area is 3.3 per cent of the total cropped area of India, around double that of India as a whole. (see Table 4.2 and Table 4.3)

The area under rice in Haryana is only 1.5 per cent of the area under rice in India. However, the production is 2.5 per cent of the total rice production in India. The area under bajra is 6.4 per cent with a corresponding production of 7.6 per cent of the total production in India. The area under wheat in Haryana is 7.7

per cent of the total area under wheat in India; the corresponding production figure is 13 per cent. The total area under cereals in Haryana is 3.3 per cent of the total area under cereals in India; the corresponding production figure is 5.6 per cent. The area under gram is 10.1 per cent with production at 9 per cent. The area under pulses is 3.0 per cent with Haryana producing 3.8 per cent of the total production of pulses in India. The total area under foodgrains is 3.3 per cent of the total area under foodgrains in India. Area under sugarcane is 4.3 per cent and under cotton 6.7 per cent.

Table 4.2 : Land Use and Area under Major Crops (1990-91)

(In hectares)

	Haryana	All India
Total area	4,378,000	328,726,300
Culturable area	3,792,000	
Net area sown	3,575,000	1,41,700,000
Area sown more than once	2,344,000	.
Total cropped area	5,919,000	1,80,100,000
Area under Rice	661,200	42,600,000
Area under Rice as % of total cropped area	11.16	23.60
Area under Bajra	608,600	10,500,000
Area under Bajra as % of total cropped area	10.30	5.80
Area under Wheat	1,850,100	24,000,000
Area under Wheat as % of total cropped area	31.00	13.30
Area under other cereals	217,000	26,000,000
Area under other cereals as % of total cropped area	3.70	13.60
Area under cereals	3,337,300	103,100,000
Area under cereals as % of total cropped area	56.40	57.20
Area under Gram	649,300	7,400,000
Area under Gram as % of total cropped area	11.00	4.10
Area under other pulses	92,700	13,400,000
Area under other pulses as % of total cropped area	1.60	7.40
Area under pulses	742,000	24,400,000
Area under pulses as % of total cropped area	12.50	13.50
Area under foodgrains	4,079,300	127,500,000
Area under foodgrains as % of total cropped area	68.90	70.80
Area under oilseeds	488,500	24,000,000
Area under oilseeds as % of total cropped area	8.25	13.30
Area under Sugarcane	147,800	3,682,000
Area under Sugarcane as % of total cropped area	2.50	2.00
Area under Cotton	490,600	7,780,000
Area under Cotton as % of total cropped area	8.30	4.30

Source: Derived from Statistical Abstract of Haryana (1991-92), Government of Haryana and Statistical Pocket Book of India (1992), Government of India.

Table 4.3 : Area, Agricultural Production and Yields

	Proportionate area in Haryana compared to the Indian Union	*Proportionate production in Haryana compared to the Indian Union*	*Total Production Haryana 1990-91 (in '000 tonnes)*	*Total Production India 1990-91 (in '000 tonnes)*	*Yield Haryana (in kg. per hectare) 1990-91*	*Yield India (in kg. per hectare) 1990-91*
Rice	1.5	2.5	1834	74600	2775	1751
Bajra	6.4	7.6	526	6900	864	661
Wheat	7.7	13.0	7083	54500	3479	2274
Cereals	3.3	5.6	9017	162200		
Gram	10.1	9.0	469	5200	722	701
Other pulses	0.7	1.1	73	6400		
Pulses	3.0	3.8	542	14100		
Oilseeds	2.0	3.4	638	18500		
Cotton	6.3	12.0	1155*	9579*		

* In '000 bales of 170 kg. each.

Source: Derived from Statistical Abstract of Haryana (1991-92), Government of Haryana and Statistical Pocket Book of India (1992), Government of India.

The above data clearly demonstrates the increases in agricultural productivity which Haryana has been able to achieve, especially in foodgrains production. On the basis of 1990-91 agricultural data, the yield of rice per hectare in Haryana was 2775 kg. compared to 1751 kg. for India. In the case of wheat, the yield per hectare in Haryana was 3479 kg. compared to 2274 kg. for India. Similarly, in the case of bajra, the yield per hectare in Haryana was 864 kg. compared to 661 kg. for India.

The average consumption of fertilizers per hectare rose from 3 kg. in 1966-67 to 115.15 kg. in 1994-95. Similarly the consumption of certified seeds rose from 17,000 tonnes in 1966-67 to 2,89,000 tonnes in 1993-94. The number of tractors in Haryana during the same period rose from 4,800 to 1,65,000. In 1989-90 the per hectare consumption of plant nutrients for Haryana was 90 kg compared to 62.4 kg. for India.[1]

Land Distribution

The peasant cultivator mode of production prevalent in Haryana has led to a distribution of agricultural holdings which are far more progressive than the national average. Whereas 75 per cent of agricultural land holdings at the all India level are small or marginal *i.e.* having less than 2 hectares of land, only 57 per cent of the holdings in Haryana are small or marginal. On the other hand, whereas only 23 per cent of the all India holdings are semi-medium/medium *i.e.* having 2-10 hectares of land, in Haryana, 38.5 per cent of the holdings belong to this category. The average size of operational holdings in Haryana is also considerably higher than the national average. In 1985-86, whereas the average size of operational holdings in Haryana was 2.76 hectares, the all India average was only 1.69 hectares. The distribution pattern of operational holdings in Haryana seems to have had a positive impact on productivity levels in agriculture. However, it is a matter of concern that the average size of holdings in Haryana has been decreasing at a very rapid rate. Between 1980-81 and 1985, the average size of holdings in Haryana dropped from 3.52 hectares to 2.76 hectares, recording a 21.6 per cent decline, the highest in the country. Comparatively Punjab, registered a decline of only 1.3 per cent, from 3.82 hectares to 3.77 hectares. At the all India level the holding size became smaller by 9.1 per cent during this period.[2] (Table 4.4 and Table 4.5)

Table 4.4 : Operational Holdings—Haryana (1985-86)

	Haryana
% of Operational holdings of size 0 - 0.5 ha.	22.18
% of Operational holdings of size 0.5 -1.0 ha.	15.09
% of Operational holdings of size 1- 2 ha.	19.65
% of Operational holdings of size 2 - 3 ha.	12.37
% of Operational holdings of size 3 - 4 ha.	8.51
% of Operational holdings of size 4 - 5 ha.	6.08
% of Operational holdings of size 5 - 10 ha.	11.66
% of Operational holdings of size 10 - 20 ha.	3.81
% of Operational holdings of size 20 ha. and above	0.65

Source: Statistical Abstract of Haryana (1991-92), Government of Haryana.

Table 4.5 : Operational Holdings—Haryana and India (1985-86)

		Haryana	*All India*
% of Operational holdings of size 0 - 1.0 ha.	Marginal	37.27	57
% of Operational holdings of size 1- 2 ha.	Small	19.65	18
% of Operational holdings of size 2 - 4 ha.	Semi-medium	20.89	14
% of Operational holdings of size 4 - 10 ha.	Medium	17.74	9
% of Operational holdings of size 10 ha. and above	Large	4.46	2

Source: Derived from Statistical Abstracts of Haryana, Government of Haryana and Agricultural Census 1985-86, Government of India.

Animal Husbandry

Haryana is rich in productive livestock. In numbers too, Haryana has a relatively greater proportion of cattle and buffalo population in relation to the area of the state. The state has only 1.3 per cent of the area but possesses about 2.2 per cent of the cattle and buffalo population.[3] It has the second highest population of buffaloes per household in the country. Whereas Punjab had 226 buffaloes per '00 rural households in 1982, Haryana had 204 buffaloes. Haryana is well known for its famous breeds of Haryana cows and Murrah buffaloes. The average milk yield for cows and buffaloes in the state has been estimated at 550 and 1300 kg. per lactation period. This is much higher than the all India average of 173 and 491 kg. respectively.[4]

Per capita income and Poverty

The overall progress that Haryana has been able to achieve is reflected in the rise in per capita income and the reduction in poverty especially in rural areas. Planning Commission statistics of 1987-88 show only 11.7 per cent of the rural population in Haryana living below the poverty line, compared to 33.4 per cent for India as a whole. Even with respect to the urban population, in Haryana the population living below the poverty line was 11.7 per cent compared to 20.1 per cent for India as a whole. Similarly the per capita Net State Domestic Product during 1990-91(at current prices) for Haryana was Rs.6936 whereas the per capita national income for the country for the same period was only Rs. 4974.[5]

Table 4.6 further demonstrates the accelerating growth rate of the Haryana's economy. In 1991-92, the growth rate of the Net State Domestic Product (NSDP) and the per capita NSDP had overtaken that of Punjab. Whereas during this period, the NSDP of Punjab grew by 6.17 per cent, that of Haryaña grew by 7.38 per cent. Similarly the growth in the per capita NSDP registered an increase of 4.9 per cent compared to 4.3 per cent for Punjab. The table also demonstrates the dramatic increase in the share of the Tertiary and the Secondary sectors in the NSDP. The share of the Secondary sector rose from 11.7 per cent in 1971-72 to 21.5 per cent in 1991-92 and that of the Tertiary Sector from 9.8 per cent to 31.9 per cent. Thus, whereas the share of the Primary sector fell by only 13 per cent in Punjab during the period 1971-72 to 1991-92, Haryana registered a 32 per cent decline in the share of the Primary sector during this period. These changes can partly be explained by the proximity of Haryana to Delhi, but the fact remains that the pace of change in Haryana appears to be outstripping that in the most prosperous state of Punjab. Although in agricultural productivity Haryana is still lagging behind Punjab as may be seen from Table 4.7, the increasing role of the tertiary and secondary sectors may well compensate for this.

Table 4.6 : Net State Domestic Product (NSDP), growth rate, per capita (at 1970-71 prices) and sectoral contribution (per cent share) in Punjab and Haryana

Period	*NSDP (Rs. crores)*		*Per capita NSDP (Rs.)*		*Primary Sector*		*Secondary Sector*		*Tertiary Sector*	
	Punjab	*Haryana*	*Punjab*	*Haryana*	*Punjab*	*Haryana*	*Punjab*	*Haryana*	*Punjab*	*Haryana*
1971-72	1399.4	893.6	1022.7	878.8	59.6	78.5	13.6	11.7	26.8	9.8
1981-82	1843.8 [3.34]	1211.6 [3.11]	1084.6 [0.6]	924.6 [0.5]	44.1	53.5	21.3	20.7	34.6	25.8
1991-92	3356.6 [6.17]	2469.8 [7.38]	1649.7 [4.3]	1486.6 [4.9]	46.6	46.6	21.4	21.5	32.0	31.9

Source: 1. Statistical Abstract of Punjab (for various years), Government of India.
2. Statistical Abstract of Haryana (for various years), Government of Haryana.

Note: Figures in brackets show the compound growth rates in the respective years.

Table 4.7 : Yield of Major Crops in Punjab and Haryana

(kgs. per hectare)

Period	*Rice*			*Wheat*			*American Cotton*		
	Punjab	*Haryana*	*All India*	*Punjab*	*Haryana*	*All India*	*Punjab*	*Haryana*	*All India*
1971-72	2045	1843	1141	2406	2041	1380	407	354	151
1981-82	2955	2475	1308	2932	2357	1691	334	387	166
1991-92(P)	3257	2831	1751	3803	3597	2394	636	464	216

Sources: 1. Statistical Abstract of Punjab (for various years), Government of India.
2. Statistical Abstract of Haryana (for various years), Government of Haryana.
3. Area and Production of Principal Crops in India 1986-88, Ministry of Agriculture, Government of India.
4. Agricultural Statistics at a Glance, Ministry of Agriculture, Government of India.

Infrastructure

The development of infrastructure has also kept pace with the overall economic growth. 100 per cent of the villages in Haryana have been electrified compared to 79 per cent for the country as a whole. The length of surfaced and unsurfaced roads per 100 sq. km. for Haryana in 1988 was 58.7 k.m. compared to 56.1 k.m. for the country as a whole. The percentage of net area irrigated to net area sown for Haryana is 72.7 per cent (1990-91) compared to 31.9 per cent for India.

In social sectors the performance of Haryana has not kept pace with its economic development. The literacy percentage is only a little higher than the all India figure. Haryana's literacy rate is 55.3 per cent compared to 52.1 per cent for India. Haryana is 15th among the 25 states of India. The number of beds in hospitals is 64 per lakh population compared to 92 per lakh population for India as a whole. The position of the state is third from the bottom, with only Uttar Pradesh and Orissa faring worse.

Table 4.8 : Tractors, Tubewells, Electrification, Literacy, Roads, Hospital Beds, Population below poverty line and per capita NSDP in Haryana and India

	Haryana	*All India*
Tractors	1,65,648	
Tubewells	5,11,059	
Villages Electrified (Central Electricity Authority, M/o Energy, GOI, 1990)	100%	79%
Literacy	55.85	52.11
Length of Surfaced and Unsurfaced roads (per 100 sq. km.) (m/o Surface Transport, GOI, 1988)	58.7	56.1
No. of Beds in Hospitals (per lakh population) (DGHS, m/o of Health and Family Welfare GOI, 1991)	64	92
Population below poverty line, Rural India (as % of total rural population) (Planning Commission, GOI, 87-88)	11.7	33.4
Population below poverty line, Urban India	11.7	20.1
Per capita Net State Domestic Product (at current prices, 1989-90) (Directorate of Economics and Statistics)	6248	4252 per capita national income

Source: Statistical Handbook of Haryana (1991-92), Government of Haryana and Statistical Pocket Book of India (1992), Government of India along with the sources mentioned in parenthesis against each item.

DEMOGRAPHIC PROFILE OF THE DISTRICTS

Haryana has been carved into 17 districts (Panchkula has been made a district in 1995). The state has 6988 villages of which 6759 are inhabited. Against an average number of 437 villages to a district, Ambala, Gurgaon, Yamunanagar, Hisar, Rohtak, Bhiwani and Faridabad have more than the average number for the state, with Ambala having the largest number of 738 villages. Panipat has the lowest number with only 232 villages. The state has 94 towns. The largest number of towns are in Gurgaon district with 11 towns, and the smallest number of towns are in Rewari, Panipat and Sonepat, with 3 towns in each of the districts. (refer Table 4.9)

Table 4.9 : Number of Villages and Towns in Haryana

District	*Total number of villages*	*Number of inhabited villages*	*Number of towns*
Ambala	738	711	9
Gurgaon	730	688	11
Yamunanagar	654	627	10
Hisar	510	504	9
Rohtak	492	473	8
Bhiwani	439	433	6
Faridabad	439	414	5
Rewari	417	402	3
Kurukshetra	396	389	4
Karnal	394	377	6
Mahendragarh	371	366	4
Sirsa	323	319	4
Jind	305	301	5
Kaithal	288	287	4
Sonepat	260	248	3
Panipat	232	220	3
Total	*6988*	*6759*	*94*
Average	*437*	*422*	*6*

Source: Statistical Handbook of Haryana (1991-92), Government of Haryana.

Kurukshetra has the smallest area of 1217 sqkm. Hisar has the largest area of 6279 sqkm. In terms of population, Rewari has the smallest population of 6.23 lakhs. Hisar has the largest population of 18.4 lakhs. In terms of density of population, Sirsa has the lowest density of 211 per sq. km. On the other hand Faridabad has the highest density of 702 per sqkm. In fact all the districts around Delhi, especially those located on the Grand Trunk Road to Chandigarh, have a relatively higher density of population. After Faridabad, the next most densely populated districts of Haryana are Sonepat, Kurukshetra, Panipat and Ambala,

Table 4.10 : District wise Area, Population, Density of Population, Decadel Variation in Population, Sex Ratio, Rural Population and Scheduled Caste Population as Percentage of Total Population

District	*Area in sq. km.*	*Population (1991 census)*	*Density of Population per sq. km.*	*% decadel variation in population 1981-91*	*Sex Ratio*	*Rural population as % of total population*	*Scheduled castes as % of total population*
Sirsa	6279	903536	211	27.90	883	78.84	26.65
Yamunanagar	5140	821880	468	27.27	841	66.31	24.96
Hisar	4411	1844634	294	23.83	861	78.88	23.21
Ambala	4276	1116878	468	30.42	885	64.46	22.99
Kaithal	2799	820685	293	20.78	852	85.30	21.44
Karnal	2760	885797	450	26.54	865	72.54	20.02
Kurukshetra	2736	641943	527	23.41	879	75.99	19.77
Jind	2385	963104	352	23.10	838	82.81	19.56
Rewari	2105	623301	400	25.45	927	84.73	19.30
Bhiwani	1967	1139718	222	22.90	880	82.75	18.97
Rohtak	1756	1808606	410	19.28	851	78.69	18.40
Panipat	1754	833501	475	33.49	854	72.84	17.89
Sonepat	1683	754866	545	27.15	865	76.42	17.84
Faridabad	1559	1477240	702	49.80	828	51.43	16.06
Mahendragarh	1385	681869	405	27.91	910	87.59	15.46
Gurgaon	1217	1146090	415	32.66	871	79.70	13.59
Haryana		**16463648**	**372**	**27.40**	**865**	**75.37**	**19.75**
India		**846302688**	**257**	**23.51**	**929**	**74.29**	

Source: Statistical Handbook of Haryana (1991-92), Government of Haryana.

all located between Delhi and Chandigarh. The low density districts are mainly those located in the western semi-arid zone and include Sirsa, Bhiwani, Kaithal, Hisar, Jind, Rewari and Mahendragarh. The decadel growth in population between 1981 and 1991 has been highest in Faridabad (49.80%), followed by Panipat (33.49%) and Gurgaon (32.66%). Again this increase corresponds with the proximity of these districts to Delhi (the explosion of population in and around Delhi). The districts registering the lowest decadel growth rate have been Rohtak,

Kaithal, Bhiwani and Jind in that order, with Rohtak registering a decadel growth rate of 19.28 per cent and Jind of 23.10 per cent. We thus notice that districts around Delhi have been growing almost twice as fast as some of the other districts. Regional variations in even a small state like Haryana are prominent. The sex ratio measured in terms of females per 1000 population is highest in Rewari (927) and Mahendragarh (910); and lowest in Faridabad (828) and Jind (838). It is significant that even Rewari with the most favourable ratio of 927 is lower than the national average of 929. Rural population as percentage of total population is lowest in Faridabad (51.43%), Ambala (64.46%) and Yamunanagar (66.31%) and highest in Mahendragarh (87.59%), Kaithal (85.30%) and Rewari (84.73%). Scheduled castes population as percentage of total population is highest in Sirsa (26.65%), Yamunanagar (24.96%) and Hisar (23.21%); and lowest in Gurgaon (13.59%), Mahendragarh (15.46%) and Faridabad (16.06%).[refer Table 4.10]

The Working Population

The percentage of cultivators to total workers is highest in Bhiwani (54.79%), Jind (50.01%) and Mahendragarh (49.10%) and lowest in Ambala (21.44%), Yamunanagar (25.60%) and Faridabad (26.32%). The percentage of agricultural labourers is highest in Karnal (28.68%), Yamunanagar (28.32%) and Sirsa (27.69%); and lowest in Mahendragarh (10.36%), Faridabad (11.63%) and Rewari (12.40%). The percentage of other categories of workers to total workers is highest in Faridabad (61.15%), Ambala (60.28%) and Sonepat (48.94%); and lowest in Kaithal (25.94%), Jind (28.17%) and Sirsa (28.49%). The data shows how the western districts of Bhiwani, Jind, Mahendragarh, Kaithal and Sirsa continue to remain predominantly agriculture based, whereas Ambala, Yamunanagar, Faridabad and Sonepat have gradually shifted from the primary to the secondary and tertiary sectors. In fact, Haryana as a whole has made a definite shift from the primary to the secondary and tertiary sectors. Of the Net State Domestic Product by Broad sectors (at current prices) in 1980-81,

54 per cent of the NSDP came from the Primary sector, 19 per cent from the Secondary sector and 26.4 per cent from the Tertiary sector. A decade later in 1990-91, the share of the Primary sector had dropped from 54.6 per cent to 44.5 per cent, the share of the Secondary sector had gone up from 19 per cent to 24 per cent and that of the Tertiary sector from 26.4% to 31.5%. (refer Table 4.11)

Table 4.11 : Percentage of Cultivators, Agricultural Labourers and Other Categories of Workers to Total Workers (1991)

District	*Population (1991 census)*	*% of cultivators to total workers*	*% of agricultural labourers to total workers*	*% of other categories to total workers*
Bhiwani	1139718	54.79	12.92	30.73
Jind	963104	50.01	20.15	28.17
Mahendragarh	681869	49.10	10.36	38.98
Kaithal	820685	47.61	24.95	25.94
Hisar	1844634	46.25	22.84	29.70
Sirsa	903536	42.64	27.69	28.49
Rohtak	1808606	42.54	15.95	40.53
Rewari	623301	42.26	12.40	43.18
Gurgaon	1146090	40.15	13.72	44.73
Panipat	833501	32.92	21.29	43.10
Kurukshetra	641943	32.66	27.68	38.54
Sonepat	754866	31.63	17.97	48.94
Karnal	885797	28.81	28.68	40.49
Faridabad	1477240	26.32	11.63	61.15
Yamunanagar	821880	25.60	28.32	43.59
Ambala	1116878	21.44	16.10	60.28

Source: Census of India 1991.

AGRICULTURE

Infrastructural development which began in the 1950s took positive shape with the agricultural policies of the 1960s and brought about the Green Revolution in Haryana. The Bhakra system provided water and electricity; roads provided access to the emerging markets for agricultural produce, finance and inputs. An effective agricultural extension system was put in place to transfer technology from the agricultural universities to the farmers. Consolidation of holdings made application of the high return technology feasible. And Haryana began to witness the spectacular yields and returns which were to put the state along with Punjab among the most affluent of the Indian states. Political and administrative will, the convergence of the efforts of the scientist and the administrator and the entrepeneurship and diligence of the farmer brought about a sustainable pattern of agricultural development.

With the availability of water and markets, cropping patterns began to change. Wheat and rice gradually began to replace the coarse grains. Hisar and Sirsa began to emerge as important cotton belts of the country. Because of the availability of water, the north east zone along with Hisar, Sirsa and Rohtak developed into the large cereal producing basket of the state. The semi-arid districts of Mahendragarh, Gurgaon, Rewari and Bhiwani have however lagged behind. But on the whole, rural Haryana has forged ahead in terms of material prosperity.

Village Garhpur Khalsa, District Karnal

...Indri block is also basically an agricultural block where intensive agricultural development has taken place during the last few years...now this area has emerged as a major wheat, rice and sugar growing area. In Garhpur Khalsa village too these crops are grown as major crops. In addition to these, garlic, onion, coriander, snuff potato and ajwain are other commercial crops which yield good dividends as they are quite profitable commodities.

The area under commercial crops is increasing day by day. After keeping the stocks for self consumption, the remaining stocks are disposed of in the market. Since commercial crops are grown in a large area, the economic condition of the people is reasonably good.

The farmers of this village are progressive and practise scientific farming. The rotation of crops is undertaken without fail. The average size of holding is around six killas (acres) per family. This village has a total area of 808 acres out of which area under cultivation is 655 acres and non-cultivable area is 153 acres. The cultivable area is under assured irrigation, either by means of electric tubewells or pumpsets which is the main reason for the prosperity of this village. Apart from this, this village has got ten tractors. A unique feature of this village is that Harijans too have land for agriculture and are quite prosperous and progressive in their outlook. ...[Chander 1984: (Karnal)]

Village Barana, District Karnal

There has been a change in the cropping pattern over the years in Barana. People have changed over to cash crops like potato, sunflower, pulses etc. The main reason is the presence of a number of mandies around the village. The cash crops give better returns but due to the high costs of cultivation only rich farmers are able to takc up their cultivation.

The major source of supply of seeds is the Agriculture Department at Nilokheri and the arhtiyas in the mandies. The supply of sunflower seeds is through the agents of big seed companies. The farmers invariably rely upon the advice of the agriculture workers at the field level to purchase these seeds. Quality sugarcane seeds are provided by the Karnal Cooperative Sugar Mill to its member shareholders. The mill is located some 30 kms. from the village. The Government is also supplying metallic bins at 50 per cent subsidy to marginal farmers to store seeds for the next season.

Mechanisation in agriculture has increased. Even marginal farmers owning less than 5 acres of land use tractors. Wheat in almost half of the area in the village is harvested using Combine Harvestors. The use of manures is however, uneven in favour of urea, due to its low pricing. The farm incomes have increased due to mechanisation. There was no paddy cultivation in this area some fifty years ago but today the entire village grows paddy utilizing the underground water resources for irrigation.

There is lack of knowledge regarding crop diseases in the village. The Department of Agriculture continually educate the farmers on crop protection against insects, pests and deseases. People use weedicides to help control weeds in the crop. Pesticides are also used for potato crops. One reason for the low use of pesticides is their high prices and frequent supply of inferior quality by private traders. Unfortunately, trade in pesticides is not regulated in the state and shopkeepers in the state can be seen keeping a store of pesticides for sale.

The crops are marketed in the mandies through the arhtiyas or comission agents. There is no cooperative marketing in the state as prevalent in parts of Maharashtra. The Government procures wheat and paddy through the various procurement agencies namely Food Corporation of India, Department of Food and Civil Supplies, HAFED and Haryana Agro Industries Corporation. There are four mandies near the village Amin in Kurukshetra, Taraori, Samana Bahu and Nilokheri in Karnal. All mandies are within a radius of 15 kms. from the village. There is no need to buy foodgrains from outside the village. Even the landless families belonging to Scheduled Castes get their annual requirements of foodgrains from the landowners in lieu of the labour done at their fields. [Khemka 1992: (Karnal)]

Village Kheri Dabdalan, District Kurukshetra

...During rabi, the crops sown include wheat, gram, pulses, rape, mustard, potato, fodder crop like barseem and certain vegetables. In kharif, the principal crops grown are paddy, maize, cotton, sugarcane, pulses, oilseeds, potato, vegetables and fodder crops like chari, Makchri etc. The major rabi crop is wheat, paddy is the kharif crop and sugarcane is the annual crop.

...In wheat the commonly sown varieties are RR-21, 1553 and 2009 and the average yield per acre of wheat comes to 16-20 quintals. In paddy the main varieties sown are Jaya, Sella and Basmati. The paddy yield per acre is 15-20 quintals whereas the Basmati (superior fine rice) yields 8-10 quintals per acre. For sugarcane the main varieties sown are 48, Jai-64 and SC-58. The average yield is 250-300 quintals per acre and the recovery percentage for sugar is 8-10 per cent.

The entire land is under assured irrigation by way of tubewells which are 168 in number. There are two government tubewells also installed by the Minor Irrigation and Tubewell Corporation which sells water to the farmers. Sweet water is available at a depth of 80-100 feet. The farmers are aware of the use of improved high yielding varieties being recommended by the agricultural universities of Hisar and Ludhiana.

The soil is of *Domat* (loamy) variety and is very good for cultivation. There are 30 tractors in the village used for cultivation. These tractors are also given on hire to other villagers at the rate of Rs.100 per acre of land. The levelling charges for hiring a tractor are Rs.40-45 per hour. Besides tractors, bullocks are also used for cultivation. There are iron as well as wooden ploughs used with the bullocks. These ploughs are manufactured within the village itself by the village carpenter and the blacksmith.

The farmers use both chemical fertilizers as well as farm yard manure. However, the extent of farmyard manure used is far less than the amount of cattle dung produced in the village. A major portion of dung is used for fuel purposes. ...Although there is neither any fertilizer sale depot nor cooperative society in the village, the requirement is made good by purchase from Ladwa town.

The agricultural produce is taken to the mandi in Ladwa town by means of tractor trolleys, bullock carts etc. and sold to the commission agents (*arhtiyas*). The role of the arhtiya is very important for a farmer. He extends loans to farmers for any purpose including marriage but charges at the rate of 2 per cent per month. (Kumar 1985)

Cropping Pattern, District Sirsa

The period between 1930-31 and 1980-81 witnessed changes in the cropping pattern. The area under rice, wheat, gram, oilseeds and cotton increased manifold. Increase was more in Sirsa significant for cotton and oilseeds—two main cash crops of the district. The increase in area under rice and wheat was also significant but increase in area under gram was not much significant. On the other hand area under jowar, bajra and barley decreased considerably.

These changes in cropping pattern have given a direction to the economy of the district. The tract where earlier mainly bajra and gram were grown is now known as cotton belt of Haryana. Bajra, the most important crop of the district in the beginning of the present century has now been relegated to sixth place whereas cotton is now second most important crop of the district, next only to gram. Tremendous increase in cotton production has given rise to the opening of many cotton ginning factories.

The changes in cropping pattern more or less static. Most of these changes were apparently due to additional facilities made available under various Five Year Plans in the form of irrigation, chemical fertilizers, better seeds, credit and marketing and better agricultural extension services. Cropping pattern in the district responded favourably to these changes in the infrastructure. [Rajasekhar 91: Village Kheri (Sirsa)]

Cropping Pattern in Village Nahla, District Hisar

Important kharif crops are cotton, bajra, guar and jowar, whereas rabi crops mainly include gram, wheat and oilseeds. Among fodder crops, jowar, guar and barseem are the main crops. Other crops grown in a limited area are rice, urd, moong, chilles in kharif, and barley, barseem, masoor and methi during rabi. Gram covers more than one fifth of the gross cropped area and is the dominant crop. Cotton and bajra occupy nearly one fifth each. Wheat occupies one seventh of the gross cropped area. The above four crops together share as much as 76 per cent of the gross cropped area in this village. [Khandelwal 1986: Nahla (Hisar)]

Changing Cropping Pattern in Village Nasibpur, District Mahendragarh

The area under wheat has increased substantially over the last few years. This has been possible due to electrified/mechanised tubewells and canal irrigation.

The area under gram decreased drastically over the last two decades. This is due to shift from gram to wheat. Productivity and thus profitability of wheat being higher, HYV of wheat have made a big difference. Also prices of wheat are more remunerative.

Barley has been steady.

Area under oilseeds has constantly declined. This is also true for pulses.

Area under bajra has also shown a decline.

The commercial crops sugarcane and cotton have become almost extinct. *'Chari'* cultivation is on a decrease, while jowar is increasing correspondingly. [Jowel 1987: Nasibpur (Mahendragarh)]

Wheat and Mustard in Village Dhauj, District Faridabad

There has been a noticeable change in the cropping pattern in the last 10 years. Earlier barley and gram (pulses) were the principal rabi crops with 90 per cent of the cultivated area covered by them. Wheat and mustard were grown in only 10 per cent of the area. There has been a reversal now with wheat and mustard dominating and barley and gram reduced to less than 10 per cent of the cultivated area. This shift in the cropping pattern has occurred because of:

Better irrigation facilities which make it remunerative to grow crops like wheat rather than rain-fed crops like gram. The increased fertilizers use has also influenced the shift.

Higher prices for wheat and oilseeds have also influenced farmers to switch to these crops.[Mishra 1991: Dhauj (Faridabad)]

Main Crops

Wheat and Vegetables in Village Palwali, District Faridabad

The main crops in rabi are wheat, mustard, charichara and vegetables. Vegetables include tomato, cauliflower, brinjal, radish and cucumber. Rice, arhar, bajra, vegetable are the kharif crops. There is a gradual shift towards growing of vegetables. Charichara has been showing a gradual dip. Now roughly 85 per cent of the land is under vegetables during kharif. However in rabi, wheat continues to be the single main crop. [Walgad 1992: Palwali (Faridabad)]

LAND HOLDINGS AND LAND RELATIONS PRACTICE

Sharecropping in Village Silakhari, District Faridabad

In village Silakhari there is no traditional tenancy. In certain cases, where the land has been divided between various members of the family, one member may look after the whole land. Thus the average size of the cultivation is much higher than shown by the ownership size. This also speaks of the tradition where the family may divide the *chulhas* i.e. stay separately but they do their cultivation jointly.

The above agricultural practice shows that the tenancy in a varied form continues till today. It is a kind of hidden tenancy where the name of the labourer/cultivator does not figure in any official records. Thus the landlords who are not able to look after their land themselves have devised ingenious ways of getting their land cultivated and at the same time to remain within the purview of the law. [Gupta 1993: Silakhari (Faridabad)]

'Naukars' and Tenancy in Village Rajpur, District Gurgaon

In the village most people self cultivate their land. Bigger land owners keep labour, generally Harijans, to whom a fifth share of the produce is given as wage. There is also the system of engaging *Naukars* (servants) for assisting the land owner in cultivation. These naukars are generally Scheduled Caste persons of the village who do not have any land and work in the fields of others as agricultural labourers. There is perfect mutual understanding between landowner and the servant with respect to salary, leave, loans and advances, etc. Some of the land owners like old people having no son or government employees give their land on lease for one year. This lease is on mutual understanding and there is no written *Patta* (lease document). There is no entry of lessee as cultivator in the revenue records. *Girdawari* still exists in the name of the landowner. On the part of the lessee also there is no attempt to get his name entered in the revenue records. [Ankur Gupta 1991: Rajpur (Gurgaon)]

Consolidation of Holdings in Village Mehrana, District Rohtak

The consolidation of the village took place in 1963-64. With this, the lands of cultivators have been brought into continuity. The consolidation department established by the government in 1949 had done this work, without which no systematic and large scale agricultural development could have been possible. The land is now in a compact and standard shape. The regular size of fields enable the use of new agricultural techniques. Circular and approach roads have increased the mobility between houses and villages. The fragmentation of holdings is largely due to increase in population and breaking-up of the traditional joint family system. [Joshi 1990: Mehrana (Rohtak)]

Agricultural Finance in Village Theh Bahri, District Jind

Finance is needed by the farmers for purchasing tools, seeds, fertilizers, bullocks etc., defraying water rates for canal irrigation, for sinking wells/tubewells, payment of wages to agricultural labourers and meeting cost of transportation of agricultural produce to the town for marketing. Besides personal savings, the chief sources of agricultural finance are loans taken from the Cooperative Credit and Service Society (Durana), Oriental Bank of Commerce (Rajaund), Central Cooperative Bank (Jind), Land Mortgage Bank (Jind), arhtiyas of Kaithal and private money lenders. Cooperative societies and banks charge 11-12 per cent interest per year on the loans advanced by them. The arhtiyas advance loans at a high rate of interest *viz.* 2.5-3 per cent per month. The interest charged by the private money lenders on the loans is very exorbitant *i.e.* 5 per cent per month. [Sharan 1991: Theh Bahri (Jind)]

MARKETING OF AGRICULTURAL PRODUCE

Village Mangali Jhara, Singhram, District Hisar

The state government has developed marketing centres to attract the farmers from rural areas to meet the growing needs of producers and purchasers. There are 15 principal market yards and 12 sub-yards in the district and all the markets are regulated. Despite all this, the entire marketable surpluses of the farmers do not reach the market and some local intermediaries collect them at comparatively lower prices and earn a good margin in the market. Thus establishment of some purchasing centres at important points would eliminate this practice and help the producers with small surpluses to get better share of the consumer's prices. The nearest market for the villagers at present is Hisar. Storage facilities for foodgrains are inadequate in the district and cold storage facilities are needed to be established for storing grains and promoting horticultural and vegetable crops and dairy and poultry products. Pricing policy and its enforcement needs a lot to be desired. The farmers last year could get only about Rs. 300 per quintal for wheat after a bumper crop. But towards the beginning of this calendar year the wheat was selling at the rate of anything around Rs. 400 per quintal. Just imagine that the farmer who has toiled hard throughout the winter, who has taken all the risks of cultivation who has taken all the beating at the hands of officials from the agricultural department, irrigation department and banks etc., gets much less remuneration for his crop than the middleman who perfects himself in hoarding and price manipulation by creating artificial shortages in the market. [Rastogi 1991: Mangali Jhara, Singhram (Hisar)]

Role of the Agricultural Department

The Agricultural Department guides the farmers in the latest technological advances in agricultural production. These include intensive methods of cultivation for higher production per unit area through new cropping pattern suited to their conditions. These also comprise preparation of crop plans, control of various pests and diseases affecting agricultural crops and gardens, use of fertilizers and good seeds, and laying out of demonstration plots to show to the cultivators the superiority of new strains and agronomic practices recommended for the district. The Agricultural inspectors impart training and education to the farmers in their respective areas on matters relating to improved techniques resulting in better management for getting more production use of improved seeds, manures and fertilizers, improved agricultural implements, plan production horticulture and other agricultural practices.

The Agricultural Extension Agency gives a great push to scientific agriculture through the package field demonstration on a large scale. The demonstration are laid on the fields by the farmers themselves with the scientific knowledge provided by the Government experts. When the results of field demonstration are found to be of marked improvement, Kisan Melas are held on such fields where all the package operations are explained to the farmers. Seminars are also held in these melas and discussions amongst the farmers on various improved agricultural practices are held where the extension specialists and the extension officers remove such doubts as the farmers may have with the evolution of high yielding varieties the results have been convincing and widespread.

The administrative machinery not only provides knowledge and practical demonstration but also administers financial and other help under various heads as provided by the state. [Gulati 87: Khanna Majra (Ambala)]

MAIN CROPS

Rice

The North-eastern zone comprising the districts of Kaithal, Karnal, Kurukshetra, Panipat, Ambala and Yamunanagar are the principal rice producing districts of the state. The districts of the Central Zone comprising Rohtak, Sonepat and Jind are also produce rice. However, in the South Western Semi Arid Zone, it is only in limited areas of Hisar, Sirsa and Faridabad that rice is produced.

The districts of Rewari, Mahendragarh and Bhiwani produce no rice. Kaithal district is the largest rice producing district of the state, in terms of area under rice and the total production of rice. However, in terms of yield, the performance of Kaithal is lower than Karnal, Kurukshetra, Yamunanagar, Hisar, Sirsa, Jind, Faridabad and Gurgaon. It is interesting to note that Hisar has the highest yields per hectare of 3679 kgs., way above the yield of 2622 kgs. per hectare in Kaithal. Hisar, Yamunanagar, Sirsa, Kurukshetra and Gurgaon have yields higher than the average yield for the state in 1990-91 of 2768 kgs. per hectare. Rohtak, Ambala, Sonepat and Panipat have the lowest yields.

Table 4.12 : Area under Rice, Rice production and Yields (1990-91)

District	*Population (1991 census)*	*Area under Rice (000 hectares)*	*Rice produc-ction in '000 tonnes*	*Yield (Kg. per hectares)*
Kaithal	820685	119.4	312	2622
Karnal	885797	115.2	309	2690
Kurukshetra	641943	101.6	299	2959
Panipat	833501	76.8	196	2539
Ambala	1116878	58.8	149	2531
Yamunanagar	821880	43.9	137	3123
Hisar	1844634	37.1	136	3679
Jind	963104	43.2	119	2758
Sirsa	903536	26.3	78	3006
Sonepat	754866	19.9	51	2563
Faridabad	1477240	7.7	21	2673
Rohtak	1808606	9.7	21	2070
Gurgaon	1146090	1.6	6	2778
Rewari	623301	—	0	—
Mahendragarh	681869	—	0	—
Bhiwani	1139718	—	0	—
Average		*50.86*	*114.63*	*2768*
Total		*661.2*	*1834*	

Source: Statistical Handbook of Haryana (1991-92), Government of Haryana.

Karnal district as a whole is known as the Rice Bowl of Northern India. During the late sixties, the maximum impact of the Green Revolution was felt in this area on account of assured irrigation, higher fertility of the soil, responsiveness of the farmers to the modern technology of agricultural production and also the economic condition of the farmers which favoured modern and mechanical forms of agricultural production. Because of the emphasis on high yielding varieties, fertilizer and insecticides, by a well knit and integrated structure of agricultural extension through lab to land programme of the Krishi Gian Kendras, the agricultural production of this area has grown manifolds.

A crop like rice which was alien to this area has been fully adopted by the farmers and in fact they are competing with the traditional rice growing areas in a big way.[Singh 90: Village Dabri (Karnal)]

Wheat

Hisar, Kaithal, Sirsa, Rohtak, Jind, Karnal and Panipat, in that order, produce the highest quantities of wheat in Haryana. Hisar with a production of 9,78,000 tonnes produces more than double the average of the districts of Haryana. Significantly the area under wheat in Hisar is not double of the average area under wheat in the districts of Haryana. The semi-arid districts of Mahendragarh, Rewari, Bhiwani and Gurgaon, alongwith Yamunanagar have the lowest production of wheat. Kaithal, Karnal, Hisar, Kurukshetra, Panipat, Mahendragarh, Rewari and Sirsa have an average yield of wheat which is higher than the average yield for the state as a whole. Thus the semi-arid districts of Mahendragarh, Rewari, Sirsa and Hisar are fairly productive areas, so far as yields are concerned. Kaithal and Karnal top the yields with productivity of 3907 and 3870 kgs. per hectare. The lowest yields are in Gurgaon, Ambala, Faridabad, Rohtak and Yamunanagar, in that order. Districts with the smallest area under wheat are Mahendragarh, Rewari and Yamunanagar.

Table 4.13 : Area under Wheat, Wheat Production and Yields (1990-91)

District	*Area under wheat (000 hectares)*	*Wheat production in '000 tonnes*	*Yield (Kg. per hectare)*
Hisar	256.2	978	3820
Kaithal	176.5	688	3907
Sirsa	165.9	612	3685
Rohtak	185.5	573	3078
Jind	150.5	508	3364
Karnal	129.0	499	3870
Panipat	112.8	426	3774
Kurukshetra	105.2	400	3808
Faridabad	111.9	327	2922
Ambala	92.9	271	2909
Sonepat	80.5	266	3330
Gurgaon	98.1	258	2637
Bhiwani	59.3	197	3339
Yamunanagar	57.7	181	3120
Rewari	39.3	144	3701
Mahendragarh	28.8	108	3707
Average	*115*	*402.25*	*3436*
Total	*1965.1*	*6436*	

Source: Statistical Handbook of Haryana (1991-92), Government of Haryana.

In Village Singhpura, District Rohtak, land which is prepared for wheat cultivation is given seven to ten ploughings from the middle of August to the middle of November, when one casual watering is given to the fields and sowing takes place with the final ploughing four days subsequent to watering. This crop is sown during November and December. Wheat is largely irrigated and is grown on a fairly large scale. There are lines of 'Sarson' in between the wheat fields. [Kundu 1987: Singhpura (Rohtak)]

In Village Kachhwa, District Karnal, wheat in rabi and paddy in kharif is the major crop. The average yield for both the crops is 16 quintals and 20 quintals per acre respectively. The prevalent sale price which the farmer gets in the peak season is Rs.185 per quintal for wheat and Rs. 165 per quintal for paddy.

During kharif 1988, 109,350 quintals of paddy was produced against which approximately 9,000 quintals was used either for seed or for domestic consumption in the village. During rabi 1988, approximately 87,400 quintals of wheat was produced against which about 18,000 quintals (21%) was used for domestic consumption.

It was also noted that the latest implements are being used by the farmers in the village. The villagers also approach the extension officers/workers according to their requirements and the extension staff of the Agricultural department and Haryana Agricultural University is giving demonstration in the fields of farmers.[Singh 88:, Kachhwa (Karnal)]

Input-Output Relations of Wheat and Cotton in Village Telanwali, District Hisar

Input-output relation is totally dependent on the rains in the unirrigated areas. In irrigated areas also, rains play an important role as the intensity of irrigation is quite low. Consider the case of 1 acre of irrigated land under wheat:

Input cost (in rupees)	
Cost of DAP (50 kg.)	400
Cost of Urea (75 kg.)	120
Cost of pesticides	150
Cost of seeds	200
Harvest charges	250
Marketing charges 100	
Miscellaneous	250
Total	1500

The total input costs excluding the labour done by the farmer comes to around Rs. 1500. If the farmer gets a yield of 16 quintals from the acre, then at a market rate of Rs. 300 per quintal, he gets Rs. 4800. Thus he earns around Rs.3300 per acre for his labour.

For 1 acre of American cotton, input cost per acre are as follows:

Input cost (in rupees)	
Cost of DAP (50 kg.)	400
Cost of Urea (75 kg.)	120
Cost of pesticides	150
Cost of seeds40	
Harvest charges	1500 (at the rate of Rs. 150 per quintal)
Marketing charges	200
Miscellaneous	600
Total	3000

Supposing the farmer gets 10 quintals of cotton, he gets at the rate of Rs. 1200 per quintal, Rs.12,000. Thus he earns Rs.9000 per acre. But this is the best scenario when everything goes right, the crop is normal, pests do not destroy the crop and he gets the quoted market price. [Garg 1992:P Telanwali (Hisar)]

Bajra

The semi-arid districts are by far the largest producers of Bajra. Except for Hisar, the districts which top the list in the production of Bajra are the ones which produce very little wheat or rice. Significantly the least producing districts are those located in the north-east comprising Kurukshetra, Karnal, Yamunanagar and Ambala. In fact Kurukshetra and Karnal do not report any area under Bajra. Bhiwani has the largest area under Bajra of 1,84,300 hectares. The production figure of 1,13,000 tonnes is also the highest. However the yield in Bhiwani of 616 kgs. per hectare is among the lowest. Only Panipat with a yield of 500 kgs. per hectare has a yield lower than that of Bhiwani. Yields in Rewari and Hisar of 1250 kgs. and 1193 kgs. per hectare are almost double that of Bhiwani.

Table 4.14 : Area under Bajra, Bajra production and Yields (1990-91)

District	*Area under Bajra (000 hectares)*	*Bajra production in '000 tonnes*	*Yield (Kg. per hectare)*
Bhiwani	184.3	113	616
Hisar	74.5	89	1193
Rewari	52.6	66	1250
Mahendragarh	95.2	65	687
Gurgaon	54.0	54	997
Rohtak	48.1	47	985
Jind	46.7	41	876
Faridabad	24.6	26	1025
Kaithal	11.8	10	869
Sirsa	8.3	8	938
Sonepat	3.4	4	1090
Panipat	2.4	1	500
Ambala	0.8	1	864
Yamunanagar	1.2	1	864
Karnal	0.5	0	-
Kurukshetra	0.2	0	-
Average	*38.04*	*32.88*	*911*
Total	*608.6*	*526*	

Source: Statistical Handbook of Haryana (1991-92), Government of Haryana.

Cereals

Hisar, Kaithal, Karnal, Sirsa, Kurukshetra and Rohtak in that order are the largest producers of cereals. Hisar and Kaithal lead with 1.22 million tonnes and 1.01 million tonnes respectively. Of the total cereal production in 1990-91 of 9.01 million tonnes, wheat contributed 6.43 million tonnes and rice 1.83 million tonnes. Thus wheat contributed 71.4 per cent to the cereal production in Haryana.The contribution of Bajra was only 0.52 million tonnes.

Table 4.15 : Cereals Production (1990-91)

District	Population (1991 census)	Rice production in '000 tonnes	Wheat production in '000 tonnes	Bajra production in '000 tonnes	Total cereals production in '000 tonnes
Hisar	1844634	136	978	89	1220
Kaithal	820685	312	688	10	1014
Karnal	885797	309	499	0	811
Sirsa	903536	78	612	8	709
Kurukshetra	641943	299	400	0	703
Rohtak	1808606	21	573	47	682
Jind	963104	119	508	41	680
Panipat	833501	196	426	1	625
Ambala	1116878	149	271	1	451
Faridabad	1477240	21	327	26	398
Gurgaon	1146090	6	258	54	342
Yamunanagar	821880	137	181	1	330
Sonepat	754866	51	266	4	327
Bhiwani	1139718	0	197	113	317
Rewari	623301	0	144	66	230
Mahendragarh	681869	0	108	65	178
Average		114.63	402.25	32.88	563.56
Total		1834	6436	526	9017

Source: Statistical Handbook of Haryana (1991-92), Government of Haryana.

The production in Hisar, Kaithal, Karnal, Sirsa, Kurukshetra, Rohtak, Jind and Panipat was higher than the average district production of cereals of 0.56 million tonnes. Hisar and Kaithal produced more than double this average. Mahendragarh with 0.178 million tonnes and Rewari with 0.23 million tonnes produced less than half the average for the disricts of Haryana. The districts of Ambala, Faridabad, Gurgaon, Yamunanagr, Sonepat and Bhiwani fall in between.

Pulses

In 1990-91 Haryana had a total production of pulses of 0.54 million tonnes. Of this 0.469 million tonnes was made up of Gram. Bhiwani, Hisar, Sirsa, Rohtak and Mahendragarh are the pulses producing districts of Haryana and produce more than

Table 4.16 : Production of Gram, total pulses and total foodgrains (1990-91)

District	*Population (1991 census)*	*Gram production in '000 tonnes*	*Total pulses production in '000 tonnes*	*Total Foodgrains production in '000 tonnes*
Bhiwani	1139718	194	197.9	515
Hisar	1844634	98	103.0	1323
Sirsa	903536	59	59.6	769
Rohtak	1808606	26	38.1	720
Mahendragarh	681869	36	36.1	214
Jind	963104	23	31.5	712
Sonepat	754866	1	13.1	340
Rewari	623301	13	13.0	243
Ambala	1116878	3	10.0	461
Kaithal	820685	3	8.4	1022
Gurgaon	1146090	7	7.7	350
Faridabad	1477240	1	7.1	405
Yamunanagar	821880	2	5.1	335
Panipat	833501	1	5.0	630
Karnal	885797	1	3.7	815
Kurukshetra	641943	1	2.4	705
Average		*29.31*	*33.86*	*597.44*
Total		*469*	*541.7*	*9559*

Source: Statistical Handbook of Haryana (1991-92), Government of Haryana.

the average for the districts of Haryana. Bhiwani produces 197,000 tonnes which is about six times the average district production of 33,800 tonnes. Hisar with 103,000 tonnes comes next. Kurukshetra, Karnal, Panipat, Yamunanagar produce about 5,000 tonnes or less, which is less than one sixth the average for the districts. In the total foodgrains production of 9.58 million tonnes in the state, the share of pulses of 0.54 million tonnes is however very low.

In the total foodgrains production, it is again Hisar, Kaithal, Karnal, Sirsa, Rohtak, Jind and Kurukshetra in that order, which top the list. Hisar and Kaithal together contribute almost 25 per cent to the total foodgrains production in the state. Hisar alone contributes about 14 per cent. On the other hand Gurgaon, Sonepat, Yamunanagar, Rewari and Mahendragarh together contribute only 15 per cent to the total foodgrains production of the state. Mahendragarh contributes as little as 2.2 per cent.

Oilseeds

The total oilseeds production in the state in 1990-91 was 6,38,000

Table 4.17 : Oilseeds Production(1990-91)

District	*Total oilseeds production in '000 tonnes*
Hisar	102.4
Rohtak	102.2
Bhiwani	83.2
Rewari	80.1
Mahendragarh	79.0
Gurgaon	73.4
Sirsa	59.1
Faridabad	25.4
Jind	15.2
Kaithal	4.2
Ambala	4.2
Sonepat	4.0
Yamunanagar	2.6
Karnal	1.0
Kurukshetra	1.0
Panipat	1.0
Average	*39.88*
Total	*638*

Source: Statistical Handbook of Haryana (1991-92), Government of Haryana.

tonnes. To this, Hisar and Rohtak being the highest producers, contributed 102,400 tonnes and 102,200 tonnes respectively. Their production was followed by Bhiwani, Rewari, Mahendragarh and Gurgaon. Together these six districts contributed 520,000 tonnes *i.e.* 81.5 per cent of the total oilseeds production of the state. It is the semi-arid belt which contributes to oilseeds production. The north-eastern zone contributes very little. Kaithal, Ambala, Sonepat, Yamunanagar, Karnal, Kurukshetra and Panipat together contribute only 18,000 tonnes, which adds up to only 2.8 per cent of the total oilseeds production in the state.

Sugarcane

Yamunanagar is by far the largest producer of sugarcane in the state. Of the total production of sugarcane (*Gur*) in 1990-91 of

Table 4.18 : Sugar Cane Production and yields (1990-91)

District	*Total Sugar cane (Gur) production in '000 tonnes*	*Yield (Kg. per hectare)*
Yamunanagar	256	5699
Rohtak	126	4845
Kurukshetra	73	6100
Jind	67	5598
Ambala	46	4569
Karnal	44	5451
Panipat	39	4930
Sonepat	39	5509
Faridabad	37	4133
Kaithal	25	5059
Hisar	20	4929
Gurgaon	5	5273
Bhiwani	3	3279
Sirsa	0	-
Mahendragarh	0	-
Rewari	0	-
Average	*48.75*	*5028*
Total	*780*	

Source: Statistical Handbook of Haryana (1991-92), Government of Haryana.

780,000 tonnes, Yamunanagar alone contributed 256,000 tonnes, *i.e.* 32.8 per cent. Yamunanagar and Rohtak together contributed about 50 per cent to the total production of gur in the state. Only four districts, Yamunanagar, Rohtak, Kurukshetra and Jind had production figures higher than the average for the districts of Haryana. The semi-arid areas of Mahendragarh, Rewari and Sirsa do not grow any sugarcane. In terms of productivity, Kurukshetra recorded the highest yields of 6100 kgs. per hectare, substantially higher than that of Yamunanagar with only 5699 kgs. per hectare.

In Village Singhpura, District Rohtak, the land intended for sowing sugarcane is ploughed three to four times from the middle of January to the middle of February. It is watered and ploughed again. The fields are then carefully levelled by several runs of the Sohaga and after the final setting is done, the seed is sown. Sowing is usually over by the middle of March and the harvesting starts from Diwali onwards. It is an age old custom here to pick up five gannas on the Diwali day and it is considered to be sinful to take out even a single piece of sugarcane before Diwali from the field. Singhpura being located at a place which is very near to the sugar-mill, the sugarcane is sold there. Most of the culturable are in Kharif is under sugarcane in normal years. The yield is generally quite good and many people also sell their cane to persons owning private crushers or Kolhus to press the sugarcane and prepare Gur out of it, which is subsequently sold in the mandi.[Kundu 1987: Singhpura (Rohtak)]

Cotton

Hisar and Sirsa with a production of 997,000 bales of cotton lint account for 86.3 per cent of the total cotton production of the state. Hisar leads with 597,000 bales, followed by Sirsa with 400,000 bales. The other cotton producing districts are Bhiwani, Jind, Rohtak and Kaithal. Ambala, Panipat and Sonepat produce 1,000 bales each. The rest of the districts do not produce any cotton. The total production of cotton in the country in 1990-91 was 9,759,000 bales. It is interesting to note that of this total production, 10.21 per cent was contributed by Hisar and Sirsa, with Hisar alone contributing 6.1 per cent of the total cotton production of the country.

Table 4.19 : Cotton Production (1990-91)

District	*Cotton lint production in '000 bales of 170 kg. each*
Hisar	597
Sirsa	400
Bhiwani	64
Jind	63
Rohtak	17
Kaithal	11
Ambala	1
Panipat	1
Sonepat	1
Mahendragarh	0
Rewari	0
Gurgaon	0
Yamunanagar	0
Karnal	0
Kurukshetra	0
Faridabad	0
Average	72.19
Total	*1155*

Source: Statistical Handbook of Haryana (1991-92), Government of Haryana.

In Sirsa, the shift is towards cotton and the area under cotton has increased by about 150 per cent in the last decade. Nearly all the irrigated area has cotton on it now. The increase is because cotton is a cash crop and returns on it are better than the alternatives available to the farmers of the village. The method of growing cotton was brought over by the immigrants from West Punjab after partition and once the Bhakra system was complete the people of the area took to it in a big way, lured undoubtedly, by the huge profits available to the grower. [Singh 1992: Ganga (Sirsa)]

Use of Insecticides

Cotton is an important cash crop of Village Nahla, District Hisar and is grown in almost all the villages of the block. Two types of cotton, namely Desi and American are commonly grown, and the area covered under these varieties is almost equal. G-27 and Ganganagar are the important varieties among Desi cotton, whereas F-320, Bikaneri and H-14 are the common improved varieties. Average yield of Desi cotton in these villages varies from 5 to 6 quintals per hectare, while American cotton gives an average yield of 8 to 10 quintals. Desi cotton is normally grown without spray and without fertilizers. Less number of irrigation are required for Desi cotton as compared to American cotton because the former has less vegetative growth and is also more resistant to drought. However, the yield is quite low because the use of inputs like quality seed, balanced fertilization and proper type and quantity of pesticides is not provided according to the recommended criteria.

Bajra is most important among the coarse grains and is grown extensively in this village. Important varieties of Bajra are Desi and hybrids like HB-3, P-HB-14 and BJ-104. However, only about 24 per cent of the total area under bajra is sown with high yielding varieties. Average yield obtained from Desi bajra varies from 6-8 quintals per hectare, whereas hybrids normally produce as much as 12-14 quintals per hectare. Yield of bajra is generally low because of its susceptibility to diseases like downy mildew, ergot and smut. Also, due to unfavourable market prices, use of fertilizers in this crop is far below the recommended doses.

Gram is the most extensively cultivated crop of this village as well as of the district. Gram varieties include C-214, G-24 and G-130. Average yield of gram in this area is 10-12 quintals per hectare, which is fairly better than the district average of 8.47 q/ha during 1975-76. However, there are wide variations in the yield of this crop from year to year. Normally, this crop is grown without fertilizer, without irrigation (at the most one irrigation) and without plant protection. It is an important crop contributing significantly to the farm economy. About 20-30 per cent of cropped area falls under this crop in this village.

Cotton is the most important crop of this area which requires plant protection measures. Occasionally, oilseed and pulse crops are also treated with pesticides. Important insecticides/pesticides used in this area are Dimecron, Metasystox, Rogor, Anthio, D.D.T., Malathion, Metacid, Folithion and Nuvacron. Distribution of these insecticides/pesticides in this village during 1975-76 and 1976-77 showed an increasing trend. [Khandelwal 86: Nahla (Hisar)]

IRRIGATION

Of the total net area sown in the state, the net area irrigated is 72.7 per cent. Sonepat tops the list at 99.1 per cent, followed by Karnal with 98.7 per cent, Kaithal with 98.6 per cent, Panipat with 97.4 per cent, Kurukshetra with 95.7 per cent and Jind with 95.3 per cent. Hisar, Rewari, Yamunanagar and Sirsa range between 70-80 per cent, with Hisar at 80.4 per cent and Sirsa at 71.3 per cent. Mahendragarh and Bhiwani have less than 50 per cent irrigation of the net sown area. Bhiwani is at the bottom of the list with 39.8 per cent. The agricultural productivity of the state follows this broad pattern of irrigation. However, it is worth noting that Hisar, which, without being at the top of the charts in irrigation, is definitely at the top of the charts in agricultural production in the state.

Of the 2.6 million hectares of net area under irrigation, 1.33 million hectares are irrigated by Government canals and 1.24 million by tubewells. Most of the area in Hisar, Sirsa and Rohtak is irrigated by Government canals. In Sirsa 88 per cent of the irrigation is by Government canals. In Hisar 87 per cent is by Government canals. In contrast, over 80 per cent of the irrigation in Karnal, Kurukshetra, Gurgaon, Rewari, Yamunanagar, Mahendragarh and Ambala is through tubewells, most of which are privately owned. Individual initiative has contributed as much to irrigation in the state as governmental effort. The magnitude of the private initiative can be guaged by the fact that in 1991-92 there were over 2.08 lakh diesel pump sets and over 3.02 lakh electric pump sets operational in Haryana.

Table 4.20 : Net Area Irrigated (1990-91)

District	*Government canals*	*% irrigated by Government canals*	*Tubewells*	*% irrigated by tubewells*	*Other sources*	*Total*	*Percentage of net area irrigated to net area sown*
Hisar	385	87	58	13	-	443	80.4
Sirsa	234	88	32	12	-	266	71.3
Rohtak	184	71	75	29	-	259	69.1
Jind	125	61	80	39	-	205	95.3
Bhiwani	104	66	54	34	-	158	39.8
Kaithal	99	47	103	49	10	212	98.6
Sonepat	53	50	52	50	-	105	99.1
Panipat	46	30	105	70	-	151	97.4
Faridabad	39	49	40	51	-	79	50.3
Karnal	27	18	126	82	-	153	98.7
Kurukshetra	19	14	114	86	-	133	95.7
Gurgaon	12	13	82	87	-	94	51.9
Rewari	3	3	90	97	-	93	72.7
Yamunanagar	3	3	88	97	-	91	72.2
Mahendragarh	3	4	72	96	-	75	48.1
Ambala	1	1	77	93	5	83	56.8
Total	1,337		1,248		15	2,600	72.7

Source: Statistical Handbook of Haryana (1991-92), Government of Haryana.

Tubewell Irrigation in Village Mamupur, District Hisar

In 1960 electricity came to the village which revolutionised the lives of the people. By 1964-65 electric tubewells had started operating. Then came the Bhakra canal system which brought canal water to this village. By the year 1966 about 20 electric tubewells had been installed in the village. The first tractor had been introduced in the village in 1964. This coupled with assured canal irrigation raised the acreage produce to 16-18 quintals per acre for wheat from the earlier 12 quintals per hectare. At this stage the improved seeds had also been introduced. With assured irrigation, now regularly two crops were being raised every year. The second crop was mainly paddy.

There are 57 tubewells all operated on electricity in the village *i.e.* for about 5 hectares of agricultural land there is one tubewell. The Sarpanch who cultivates 30 hectares of land has 5 tubewells.

In the past few years with increased awareness and availability of facilities, farmers have begun to harvest a third crop also *i.e.* between rabi and kharif. The crop usually harvest either potato or watermelons.

In a few villages there are conflicts over the sharing of canal water: Distribution of canal water by means of enforcement is indeed difficult. But in Mamupur most of the farmers rely on tubewell irrigation rather than canal irrigation. This is because the farmers own large chunks of land and are economically very well off and thus can afford tubewells. This apart, the ground water unlike the rest of the district is sweet and suitable for irrigation. Lastly, an assured supply of electricity also goes in favour of tubewells.

The farmers in the village are aware of the number and timings of irrigation to be given to a crop. A self service supply of water is essential which can be provided only by the tubewells and not canals. [Bajaj 1990: Mamupur (Hisar)]

In Village Barana, District Karnal, 100 per cent of the area is tubewell irrigated. The cost per B.H.P. of installed tubewell at flat rate is currently Rs. 39 per month with effect from 5.6.92. The Bhartiya Kisan Union is agitating in the state against this increased rate which was earlier Rs.29 per B.H.P.. The metred rate of electricity supply is Rs. 4 per B.H.P. towards demand charges and 50 paise per unit of electricity against 30 paise per unit earlier.

The Government irrigation projects in the region are the Western Jamuna Canal and the tubewells of the Haryana State

Minor Irrigation and Tubewells Corporation (HSMITC). The rates under canal irrigation area is Rs.20 per acre against which the farmers get water for an average of 1 to 2 hours per week per acre of holding under the '*warabandi*' system operating in these regions.

There is no canal irrigated area or Government tubewell in the village. The private tubewells function well with the installation of a 5 B.H.P. motor because the water table is at a maximum of 50 feet below the ground surface.

Water is also sold from the private tubewells to marginal farmers at the rate of around Rs.10 per hour. The water rate works out to Rs.2.50 per hour under the '*warabandi*' system in the canal irrigated areas. Hence the private water rates are four times the Government rates but note must be taken of the fact that the Government rates are several years old and have not been revised since long.

I can say out of my experience of stay in the village that private irrigation projects of small size is a viable proposition, as installation of tubewells in each of the operational holdings leads to inefficient utilization of resources. A scheme of panchayat operated tubewells with appropriate pricing mechanism would go a long way in improving the agricultural productivity, besides bringing down the cost of cultivation of small holdings. [Khemka 1992 Barana (Karnal)]

In village Hirmathla, District Gurgaon, agriculture used to be totally rainfed till a decade back. But now with the branch of a Gurgaon canal passing by one side of the village, people having fields close to the canal are taking two crops and are growing rice also, which is a commercial crop here. Otherwise by and large still only one crop during rabi is cultivable, that too if the rains do not fail. Agricultural land is being sold here at an average rate of Rs. 30,000 per acre.[Ramsekhar 1989: Hirmathla (Gurgaon)]

In village Bukharaka, District Gurgaon, the main occupation of the people in the village is agriculture. The soil is of a very low productivity and owing to lack of irrigational facilities the farmers barely manage to take one crop per year, that too only when there is rainfall. Those farmers owning tubewells manage to take two crops a year.

The major crops of the area include wheat, bajra, mustard, jowar and fodder crops. Some of the more enterprising farmers have now taken to a crop each of kharif onion which is proving to be very good in terms of the yield and the returns for the farmer.

Most farmers here use the traditional inputs like cattle for ploughing and manual labour is employed for all the other activities except for threshing etc. Very few farmers own tractors and mechanised implements. [Anupama 1992: Bukharaka (Gurgaon)]

The people of Bajina village in district Bhiwani are primarily engaged in agriculture. The village is having a total area of 2306 hectares and has been covered under consolidation. Out of this 2142 hectares is cultivable land, about 80 hectares of land in the north side of the village is black soil while the remaining land is sandy. A large number of undulating sand dunes are generally seen in the fields of the village. These sand dunes change their places quite frequently. According to the revenue record,, 550 hectares of land is irrigated, while the remaining 1593 hectares of land is dependent on rainfall. The only source of irrigation is the canal. The fields of the village are irrigated by 'Kairu" Minor. The canal water is lifted at two places. Pump houses have been set up for this purpose. The underground water could not be utilised for irrigation purposes as it is not fit for the growth of the crops. Only one tubewell was installed in the village but the water contents were found very harmful for all the crops and also it degrades the land.

The area sown and irrigated between 1981-82 and 1983-84 decreased year by year. This is all due to drought in district Bhiwani during the last five years. About 74 per cent of the land depends up rainfall. Due to drought, the barrani land could not be brought under cultivation. The availability of canal water has also decreased year by year. In this area canal water supply is dependent upon the supply of electricity because canal water is lifted by the electric motors fitted in two pump houses. Due to scarcity of electric supply in the entire state and in Bhiwani in particular, adequate canal water supply could not be provided to the village during these years, which has resulted in a decrease in irrigation. [Singh 85: Bajina (Bhiwani)]

Scarcity of water permeates all aspects of livelihood, including agriculture in village Khol, district Rewari. There are no adequate facilities for irrigation. A large portion of the land is rainfed. Gradually, the number of tubewells in the village is increasing, alleviating water scarcity to some extent. Sprinkler sets are commonly used by better-off farmers to conserve water. Seeds and fertilizers are provided through outlets of HSDC, HAFED and IFFCO. [Chandra 1990: Khol (Rewari)]

Since a large cultivable area in the village Bhankari, district Faridabad is rainfed, the effects of the drought conditions in the year 1987 affected the agriculture yield of that year. The Girdawari of the kharif crop in 1987 reveals that of 57 hectares sown, 49 hectares *i.e.* 84 per cent of the sown area did not yield healthy crops and was classified as *"Kharaba"* in the revenue record. Only 16 per cent of the crop could be saved with the help of tubewell irrigation. Almost 100 per cent of the crop sown in the rainfed area was affected by drought. Even in the irrigated area about 50 per cent of the crop was damaged. [Sekhri 1987: Bhankri (Faridabad)]

Fertilizer Consumption

Consumption of fertilizer per hectare of cropped area was highest in Kurukshetra in 1990-91 with a figure of 189 kgs. per hectare. This was followed by Panipat at 180 kgs., Karnal at 171 kgs. and Kaithal at 148 kgs.. Although Hisar consumes the highest quantity of fertilizer in the state, the high figure is partly on account of the very large cropped area in Hisar. Hisar has a total cropped area of 950,000 hectares, much above the average of 370,000 hectares for the districts of Haryana. Bhiwani has the lowest fertilizer consumption of only 19 kgs. per hectare. Faridabad, Rewari, Rohtak, Mahendragarh and Gurgaon have fertilizer less than 100 kgs. per hectare, lower than the average for the state.

Table 4.22 : Fertilizer Consumption (1990-91)

District	*Total fertilizer consumption in tonnes*	*Total cropped area (000 hectares)*	*Consumption of fertilizer per hectare in kgs.*
Kurukshestra	48,299	255	189
Panipat	44,282	246	180
Karnal	50,172	294	171
Kaithal	55,976	379	148
Yamunanagar	26,275	195	135
Sonepat	19,656	160	123
Sirsa	70,819	591	120
Ambala	28,533	240	119
Jind	45,394	417	109
Hisar	97,828	950	103
Faridabad	20,889	254	82
Rewari	12,074	199	61
Rohtak	27,533	523	53
Mahendergarh	13,791	263	52
Gurgoan	12,274	295	42
Bhiwani	12,497	658	19
Total	*586,292*	*5919*	
Average		*370*	*107*

Source: Statistical Handbook of Haryana (1991-92), Government of Haryana.

Agricultural Machinery

The data in Table 2.42 pertains to the 12 districts that existed in 1988. The ownership and use of agricultural machinery shows wide variation within the state. Whereas Kurukshetra has 38 tractors per 1000 population, Gurgaon and Bhiwani have only 4 tractors per 1000 population. The use of tractors is highest in Kurukshetra, Karnal, Sirsa, Sonepat, Jind and Ambala, in that order. Mahendragarh, Faridabad, Bhiwani and Gurgaon have less than 6 tractors per 1000 population. The agricultural prosperity of the north eastern belt is once again reflected in the distribution of agricultural machinery.

Table 4.22 : Tractors (All Types), 1988

District	*Population (1991 census)*	*Tractors all types*	*Tractors per 1000 population*
Kurukshetra	641943	24262	38
Karnal	885797	21348	24
Sirsa	903536	16403	18
Sonepat	754866	13479	18
Jind	963104	13328	14
Ambala	1116878	14671	13
Hisar	1844634	22923	12
Rohtak	1808606	19167	11
Mahendragarh	681869	3893	6
Faridabad	1477240	7550	5
Bhiwani	1139718	4313	4
Gurgaon	1146090	4311	4

Source: Statistical Handbook of Haryana (1991-92), Government of Haryana.

Agricultural Implements used in Village Khanna Majra, District Ambala

Any improvement in agriculture is inconceivable without a corresponding improvement in the implements used. Modern implements are being gradually adopted by the farmers in accordance with their utility and scope for use. These are popularised by the Government through different schemes. The agricultural implements used in the district are given below:

Traditional implements

Baguri	Small Khurpa like implement used for the hoeing of sugarcane at the time of the first and the second hoeing
Balan	Hand ginning mill, also sugar-press
Behli	Bullock cart
Bijoudi	Seed bag

Charsa	Leather bucket
Chhaj	Winnowing basket
Damcha	Watchman's controlling station
Datrali	Used for wat bandi in the irrigation areas
Dhainkli	Appliance for manual water-lifting suitable for small holdings
Dranti	Sickle
Gadi	Cart
Gandasa	Hand fodder cutter
Gandasi	Long handled chopper used for cutting sugarcane, cotton sticks and bushes
Gandola or Khodna	Digging tool
Garhi-ki-machine	Wheat thresher
Gharaunchi	Stand for oiling card
Gopia	Bird scarer
Gori	Leveller
Gulail	Bird scarer
Hal	Plough
Jali	Four pronged fork
Jua	Yoke
Kasola	Large mattock for weeding and hoeing
Kasoli	Smaller mattock for weeding and hoeing
Kassi	Spade
Khurpa	Grass spade
Kohari	Hatchet
Kolhari	Axe
Kolhu	Round cold-crusher
Kuthla	Seed storage
Kutti-ki-machine	Chaff cutter
Maij or Sohaga	Flat cold-crusher
Orna	Seed drilling tube
Phala	Large mattock spade
Rahat	Persian Wheel used where water table is not low

Rath	Chariot
Rehru	Small cart
Santa	Ox goad
Tat	Bird scarer
Thela	Four wheeler bullock cart
Tipaya	Stand for winnowing
Untgadi	Camel cart

Modern Implements

Anaj Nikalney ki machine	Power Thresher
Beej-aur-Khad Boney-ki-machine	Fertilizer cum seed drill
	Cultivator Harrow
Mitti Palatney wala hal	Soil inverting plough
Nalai gudai wala hal	Hoe
Panch datta	Five tined cultivator
Pumping Set	
Sooki-davai-ki-machine	Duster
Tar-davai-ki-machine	Sprayer
Tractor	
Triphali	Three tined tiller
Trolly	
Tubewell	

The Plough

The plough consists of three major parts: the beam (*halas*), wooden body (*hal*) and the coulter (panhiari and kuis). It may be of wood or iron but one in common use is generally of kikar wood, made by the village carpenter. It merely scratches the soil up to 4-5 inches and does not really serve the purpose of a plough. The chief defect in it lies in the fact that it leaves ridges of unploughed land between the V-shaped furrows which it makes. The plough also fails to eradicate the weeds properly. However in the small land-holdings and fragmented and non-contiguous plots, the plough is very much suited and it does not disturb the level of the land. [Gulati 87: Khanna Majra (Ambala)]

COMMON CROP PESTS AND DISEASES

Rice Bug

This is the most destructive pest of the paddy crop. It appears generally in August and does maximum damage during August and September. The insect is essentially diurnal and is active in morning and evening. Both adults and nymphs suck the juice from grains during the milky stage.

Loose Smut of Wheat

This is a serious disease of the wheat crop. It burns the grain ears completely into a black powder. Infection is carried through the seed.

Earcockle of Wheat

In young plants, the disease is characterised by wrinkling, rolling, twisting and distortion of the leaves, all these symptoms tending to make the plants bushy and considerably dwarfed in size. Plants may die in the seedling stage. Earcockle galls being lighter than water can be separated from wheat seed by the floatation method combined with solar treatment.

Downy Mildew

The infected plants remain stunted and unthrifty. Leaves turn yellowish and undersurface of the leaves covered with white powdery mass. The ears transform wholly or partially into leaf like structures which remain green for longer period.

Ergot

Pinkish or light coloured thick gummy fluid starts dropping from spikelets of the infected earhead, later on brown to dark coloured sclerotia appear on these spikelets in place of normal grains due to the invasion of ovary by the fungus.

Stored grain pests

To guard against the damage caused to stored grains by Khapra, Susri and Dhora, the stores are dusted or sprayed with B.H.C. The infested stored grain could be saved by fumigation by making the stores completely air tight. The fumigation is very commonly done by Aluminium Phosphide tablets @ one tablet per metric tonne of grain.

Emerging trends in Agriculture

The Green Revolution has taken place in Haryana, about this, there can be no dispute. Awareness of scientific farming has been on the ascendancy all over the state. Progress may have been faster in the traditionally richer agricultural belt and where irrigation is well developed. There can be no doubt, that the entire state has witnessed dramatic changes in agricultural practices. The role of the state and the agriculture scientists has been central in this process of transformation. Apart from the consolidation of holdings, the critical factor contributing to this change, has been the increase in the availability of surface irrigation and tubewell irrigation. Extension work, whether through the Krishi Gian Kendras, the extension workers or through the media has also been an important factor contributing to the adoption of improved practices. The availability of improved seeds, chemical fertilizers, pesticides and weedicides through cooperatives and private trade made possible the widespread adoption of the techniques taught by the agricultural scientists. Electrification of villages and building of village road networks emerged as the next important landmark in the changes that were to sweep this region. Villages which could not get water from surface irrigation, now, found alternative irrigation in tubewells. Roads brought the tractor and the combine harvester to the village. Improved cultivators, tillers, harrows, seed drills, threshers all became part of the plant and machinery of the emerging modern farmer. Those who could not afford tubewells or tractors could nevertheless, hire these services from those who had them. The road system led to a growing network of "Mandis"—

agricultural markets, where farmers could sell their produce, obtain loans and buy inputs. Also at the village level, in addition to the money lender, institutional finance became available through the Cooperative Societies and Banks, Land Mortgage Bank, Gramin Banks and Commercial Banks. And finally, to assure a good price for the produce to the farmer, the national food policy provided reasonable support prices and a network of purchasing centres through the Food Corporation of India.

So far as the cropping pattern is concerned, wheat and rice have, overtime, replaced the coarse grains in most of the districts. In Hisar and Sirsa, cotton has emerged as an important cash crop. Sugarcane continues to remain important in Yamunanagar and Rohtak. The new set of developments, however, are beginning to focus on commercial crops. Garlic, Onion, Coriander, Potato, Ajwain, Sunflower, Mustard, Vegetables, Chillies, Pulses and fodder crops like Barseem, Guar, Jowar and Chari are already becoming popular. Farm forestry especially of Eucalyptus and Poplar has come to stay. Horticulture is picking up and as global markets open up, floriculture may well define the road to prosperity in the 21st century. As the less developed states catch up with the Green Revolution, the pioneering states are likely to advance into activities with higher returns. And as information technology brings the world to the doorstep of the villager, the gulf between rural and urban India is likely to be bridged in a future that may not be too far away.

ANIMAL HUSBANDRY

Second only to agriculture, animal husbandry is the most important occupation of the villagers in Haryana. Most households possess livestock of some kind. Cows and buffaloes constitue the main livestock in the state. The poorer households rear pigs, sheep and goats. Poultry units varying in size are also becoming popular. Cross-bred varieties in cows, pigs and poultry are fast becoming popular in the state.

Veterinary care facilities are gradually increasing to cover most villages. The Pasudhan Centres (Veterinary care centres) provide veterinary cover to groups of villages. Although all the villages have not been adequately covered by these centres, most villages now have access to veterinary care in some form or the other. Many villages still practice local remedies for the common diseases, however, once the animal is found to be in an incurable state, they seek the assistance of a veterinary doctor or compounder, who visit villages and attend to the animals for a fee.

Cattle breeds are gradually responding to artificial insemination. This facility is available at the Pasudhan Centres and Veterinary Hospitals. Consequently, bovine animals are becoming more productive. Although the average yield of buffaloes is still about 8 litres of milk a day, the maximum yields are going up to 15 litres. Similarly maximum yields of Jersey and Holstein cross-breds are going above 20 litres of milk per day.

Grazing lands which were common property resources are gradually decreasing. Moreover, the cross-bred cows and buffaloes respond much better to stall feeding. This has led to an important focus on fodder cultivation. Barseem, lucerne, chari, jowar and other greens are being grown by farmers as fodder. This is being supplemented by dry fodder in the summer months. Concentrates are also increasingly being resorted to for improving yields.

Much of the milk is still used up in the villages as fluid milk or as ghee, butter, paneer or lassi. However in many villages, especially those near urban centres, surplus milk is being generated for marketing. Milk Cooperative Societies cover a large number of villages. These societies procure the milk on the basis of fat content and S.N.F. (Solids not Fat) content. A reasonable price is thus made available to the farmers. These societies sell their milk to the Cooperative Unions of the districts. For further processing, the Milk Federation procures the milk from these Unions. Along with the cooperatives, private dairies and private vendors also collect milk from the villages.

Poultry farms are also emerging as profitable units. Apart from the small poultry units financed by the District Rural Development Agencies and the local banks, larger and more profitable units are increasing in villages of Haryana, especially in villages located on highways and near urban centres.

Haryana has been doing well in animal husbandry. However,

there is still need to further develop veterinary care facilities closer to the villages. Cooperative societies for marketing of milk also need to be strengthened in terms of coverage. With the white revolution already underway in Haryana, there is now need to focus on piggery, sheep and goat rearing and processing of livestock products in the villages.

In village Nahla, District Hisar, animal Husbandry ranks second to agriculture. For generations, people of this village have taken up this profession as one of the main sources of livelihood. Cattle, buffaloes, sheep, goats, camels, donkeys and pigs are the main species of domestic animals found in this village. Practically, every house maintains milch animals both cows and buffaloes. Normally backward class people keep sheep and goats and a few scheduled castes people rear pigs and poultry.

For draught purposes, bullocks are mostly used. Some farmers also use camels for ploughing and carting. Out of the total livestock population of this village, cattle account for about 32%, buffaloes 41 per cent, sheep about 12 per cent, goats 6 per cent, poultry birds nearly 6 per cent, and camels, donkeys, pigs and horses together constitute only about 4 per cent. The bovine population is thus about 72 per cent of the total livestock population. The importance of livestock in this village is evidenced by the fact that the number of livestock per household, excluding poultry birds comes to about 5. Even a landless household maintains a few heads of domestic animals.

The villagers purchase the animals either from nearby villages or from cattle fairs organized in the district. On an average, a local cow costs around Rs. 2000 and a pair of bullocks about Rs. 6000. A few cross-bred cows of Haryana-Jersey and Haryana-Holstein may be found with progressive farmers. A grown up cross-bred cow normally costs around Rs. 7000. A sheep costs around Rs. 700 and a goat Rs. 600.

The life span of a cow is 10 to 15 years, of a bullock 8 to 12 years, and that of a buffalo 14 to 18 years. Cows and she-buffaloes normally achieve maturity at the age of 2½ to 3 years. [Khandelwal, 87: Village Nahla (Hisar)]

Because of their sentiments, most of the farmers here take good care of their cows, bullocks and buffaloes. Most of them share the accommodation with their animals. Only a few farmers have got separate cattle sheds for domestic animals. Because of ignorance and lack of proper understanding, the accommodation provided to the animals is not properly ventilated and scientific.

A majority of the farmers provide green fodder mixed with dry fodder to their animals except during May and June when there is a dearth of green fodder. Green fodder includes jowar, bajra, barseem, lucerne, guar and sometimes sugarcane tops, maize and oats. Dry fodders constitute wheat straw, bajra karbi, jowar karbi, maize karbi, gram straw and barley straw. Common concentrates which are fed to these animals are guar, gram, bajra, cotton seed, maithie and occasionally, barley, gur and oil are also given. Among the by-products, mustard cake, cotton seed cake, gram bran and wheat porridge are also fed. During winter, particularly in the months of November and December, a few farmers give ghee to their bullocks. [Khandelwal, 87: Village Nahla (Hisar)]

Animal Diseases and Care in Nahla, District Hisar

Common diseases among the cattle are Haemorrhagic Septecaemia (H.S.), Foot and Mouth Disease, Black Quarter (B.Q.), Milk Fever, *Mastitis*, Pneumonia, Protein Deficiency, Theileriasis, Anaplasmosis and Parasitic Infections. Mostly young calves suffer from Ascariasis, Calfsour and Pneumonia. Bullock's common diseases are retention of urine and parasitic diarrhoea. Besides Pneumonia, Milk Fever, Mastitis and H.S., mineral deficiencies and Haemoglobinuria have also been reported among buffaloes. Buffalo calves normally suffer from Ascariasis.

Among sheep and goats, Pneumonia, Mastitis, parasitic infection and Gastro-intestinal Nematodes are found. In camel, Bronco-pneumonia and Pica diseases have been reported. Common diseases of poultry are Rani Khet and Raillietine infection. A few other diseases like Stringhalt and Reticular Hernia have also been found among the animals.

When an animal falls ill or develops a disease, the farmers first resort to local treatment including the administration of native herbs. The services of veterinary doctors and compounders are utilized only when local treatments fail. Normally, doctors are called by the farmers to their places because it is very difficult to take the ailing animal to the veterinary hospital or dispensary. In such cases, the farmer has to pay the travelling charges as well as fees to the doctor. [Khandelwal, 87: Village Nahla (Hisar)]

Pasudhan Centre

In village Khorma, district Mahendragarh there exists a Pasudhan Centre. This centre provides health services and other veterinary cover to the animals. In the last two years 323 cows and 389 buffaloes were artificially inseminated.

According to the veterinary doctor, the supply of frozen semen of Jersey, Murra and Haryana Buffaloe is regular with adequate storage facility. Artificial insemination has 50% success rate. Though the villagers give a different version stating only 20% success rate. At the Pasudhan centre farmers are informed about improving the breed of animals through artificial insemination, improving quality of fodder and various treatments and vaccines that ought to be given to various animals in different seasons.

Haemorrhagic Septicaemia (HS), Goat Tissue Vaccine (GTV) and Foot and Mouth Disease (FM) vaccines are made available in this centre. Deworming of all the animals is done after the rainy season. Apart from this, treatment in case of simple wounds, diarrhoea, infection, respiratory disorders etc. is given in the centre. In case of serious diseases, the animals are sent to the Veterinary Hospital at Narnaul. Medicines are supplied through Pasudhan Centre, free of cost, but according to the villagers, these are rarely made available and mostly they have to purchase them from the market.

According to the veterinary doctor, health of the animals is satisfactory, with average lactation period of 8-9 months in buffaloes and 7 months in cows. The average milk yields are 8 kg. in the case of buffaloe, 5 kg. in cows and 2 kg. in goats. In the case of Haryana cross bred buffaloes the yield is 15-16 kg. No surplus milk is available for marketing. There is no milk society functioning in this village. Animal Husbandry is not the primary economic activity of the villagers. Villagers keep these milch animals to meet their own milk supply. [Kumar 89: Village Khorma (Mahendragarh)]

Mouth and foot disease are common among the cattle in village Ismailpur, district Ambala. The Officer Trainee noted an interesting operation was being performed in the village. The cattle of the whole village had got infected with this disease. For this the villagers had called the *Ojha* (priest) who would perform puja the whole night. Nobody was allowed to go out of the village after 8 p.m. and nobody was allowed into the village before 6 a.m. the next morning. During this period nobody cooked anything. They had prepared the food in advance. The people had faith that this would cure the animals of the disease. Later, I found that this was all a farce and the animals had not been cured. Instead their condition had deteriorated. [Arora, 1989: Village Ismailpur (Ambala)]

The common animal diseases prevalent in village Mangali Jhara and Singhram, district Hisar are cow pox, foot and mouth disease, anthrax fever and Galghotu. The people have adopted various indigenous methods to cure these diseases. For *Sitla* (Cow Pox) the people put the animal in a closed stable and protect it from cold. They sometimes give it balls of pounded Bhang also. For foot and mouth disease the animal is administered half a kilogram of molasses and the mouth of the animal is kept tied for some hours so as to keep it shut. For anthrax fever, locally called Goli-ki-sat, the people have no remedy. For Galghotu, the neck of the sick animal is scorched by applying burning grass. These indigenous treatments are still followed but the people value veterinary assistance from veterinary hospital located at a neighbouring village Aklan also. [Rastogi, 92: Village Mangali Jhara and Singhram (Hisar)]

Dairy Cooperatives, District Ambala

As part of the Government efforts to develop dairy industry on commercial lines, the Dairy Development Corporation established a milk plant at Ambala in 1973-74 with a daily capacity of 20,000 litres of fluid milk. The plant manufactures standard bottled milk, toned bottled milk, sweetened flavoured milk, ice-cream, paneer, butter and ghee. This milk plant is providing assured and standard milk to the consumers and a ready market for the milk produce to farmers.

In the village there is a milk supply cooperative with a total membership of 60 people. It has an executive committee of 9 members including one President, one Vice President and one Secretary. The cooperative collects milk from all the members and it is sold to the milk point at a fixed rate of 50 paise per unit of fat content per litre. The highest fat content can be 10 units and therefore maximum price of milk is Rs. 5 per litre. The members of the cooperative meet once in a month for taking decisions.

The Government on its part assists the cooperatives by providing subsidies and loans at subsidised rates. [Gulati 86: Village Khanna Majra (Ambala)]

The Milk Cooperative Society in village Sullar, district Ambala was set up in 1972 with barely 15 members today has an impressive membership of 169, of which 25 members are from outside the village. Every day about 100 people sell their milk to this society, which adds up to about 5 quintals daily. This milk goes to the Milk Plant at Ambala, twice a day by truck. The yearly income of the Society is nearly Rs. 60,000 and it succeeded in paying Rs. 27,000 and Rs. 18,000 as dividends to its members in August 1984 and April 1985. The Society's income comes from the one paise per kilogram of fat paid by the Milk Plant to it.

The fat content of the buffaloes according to the Secretary of the Society is 10 per cent maximum and 4-5 per cent minimum. The Society has nine executive members who meet on the 18th of every month and three employees, the Secretary, the Testor and the Sweeper, who are paid Rs. 600, Rs. 450 and Rs.35 per month respectively.

The Society provides for veterinary health care. A doctor visits the dairy once a week and first aid is available 24 hours. The Society has also been attempting and encouraging artificial insemination provided by the stockmen centre. However, the success rate of artificial insemination has only been 30 per cent for buffaloes and about 60 per cent for cows.

The villagers claim that the credbility of the society is very good and that is why people from outside the village prefer to send their milk to this society in preference to their own society. Some of the people in the village however give milk to the private vendors who give them the rate of Rs. 2.80 or Rs. 2.75 per kg. . The main reason is that the private vendor not only pays them immediately, but also makes advance payment, whereas the society pays them every ten days. [Nain, 86: Village Sullar (Ambala)]

Cattle

The tables containing livestock statistics are again limited to the 12 districts that existed prior to 1989. The population of cattle per '00 rural households is highest in Kurukshetra with 438 cattle, followed by Ambala with 294 cattle, Karnal with 284 cattle and Jind with 232 cattle. In contrast Sonepat has only 89 cattle per '00 households against an average for the state of 195 cattle per '00 households. Hisar, Sirsa, Bhiwani, Gurgaon, Faridabad, Rohtak and Mahendragarh all have cattle population per '00 rural households lower than the average for the state.

Table 4.23 : Cattle, 1988

District	*Number of rural households (1981)*	*Cattle in '00*	*Cattle per '00 rural households*
Kurukshetra	59733	2618	438
Ambala	88275	2599	294
Karnal	80245	2282	284
Jind	97323	2257	232
Hisar	176938	3253	184
Sirsa	82997	1311	158
Bhiwani	110738	1736	157
Gurgaon	100447	1287	128
Faridabad	83862	1070	128
Rohtak	140407	1787	127
Mahendragarh	70123	872	124
Sonepat	104483	929	89
Average			*195*

Source: Derived from *Statistical Handbook of Haryana* (1991-92), Government of Haryana and Census of India (1981).

Buffaloes

Kurukshetra with 739 buffaloes per '00 rural households has a density of population of buffaloes which is double that of the state average of 344. Karnal follows with 527 buffaloes per '00 households, to be followed by Jind (392), Ambala (363) and Faridabad (348). Bhiwani has the lowest population of buffaloes as also the lowest population per '00 households of 171. The other districts fall in between. It is essentially the Ambala, Karnal, Kurukshetra and Jind belt which is rich in buffaloe rearing.

Table 4.24 : Buffaloes (1988)

District	*Number of rural households (1981)*	*Buffaloes '00*	*Buffaloes per '00 rural households*
Kurukshetra	59733	4417	739
Karnal	80245	4232	527
Jind	97323	3815	392
Ambala	88275	3206	363
Faridabad	83862	2917	348
Mahendragarh	70123	2068	295
Rohtak	140407	3882	276
Gurgaon	100447	2676	266
Sirsa	82997	2135	257
Hisar	176938	4459	252
Sonepat	104483	2572	246
Bhiwani	110738	1906	172
Average			*344*

Source: Derived from *Statistical Handbook of Haryana* (1991-92), Government of Haryana and Census of India (1981).

DRDA's Murrah Breeding Farm at Lakaria, District Rohtak

The DRDA has set up a Murrah Breeding Farm-cum- Frozen Semen Bank and Insemination Centre at Lakaria, from where quality semen is now delivered at various service centres established in several nucleus villages. This scheme, when it becomes popular, can bring about radical improvement in the livestock breed as well as in the milk yield. Incidentally, the breeding farm at Lakaria boasts of the best breed in the country. [Kundu, 1988: Village Singhpura (Rohtak)]

There is an interesting system in the village Mehrana, district Rohtak for rearing cows and buffaloes. The big landlords give their newly born cows and buffaloes to the people of the lower caste on *"Byaaj"* (interest). The whole responsibility of feeding lies with the person who is given the animal. After 4 or 5 years when the grown up animal is sold, the net income from the animal is shared on 50:50 basis between the actual owner of the animal and the person who brought up the animal. [Joshi, 1991: Village Mehrana (Rohtak)]

All those who own land in village Kheri Dabdalan, district Kurukshetra grow green fodder on a part of their land *viz.* Chari, Jowar or Bajra in the Kharif season and Barseem in winter. The wheat straw and paddy straw are used as dry fodder. Besides it, the milking animals are fed concentrates in the form of oil cakes (Khal) of cotton seeds or groundnut or cottonseeds as such (Binola). [Kumar, 86; Village Kheri Dabdalan (Kurukshetra)]

The maximum milk yield per buffalo is 15 litres with a fat content of around 9 per cent and S.N.F. content 8.8 per cent in village Barana, district Karnal. The average milk yield of a buffalo is around 8 litres with a fat content of 8 per cent and S.N.F. content of 8.7 per cent. The average milk yield of a cow is 12 litres with a fat content of 4 per cent and S.N.F. of 8.6 per cent. The milk is marketed through the village milk cooperative society. The milk is procured by the Karnal Kurukshetra District Milk Producers Union for processing at the milk plants of Haryana Dairy Development Cooperative Federation Ltd.. The price is as per the rate chart and depends on the fat and S.N.F. content of milk. However, the average price realisation is around Rs. 4.50 per litre of milk. A private dairy with a capacity to process about one lakh litres of milk per day is coming up some 10 km. from the village. This would help in better realisation of milk prices in the future. [Khemka, 93: Village Barana (Karnal)]

About 42 per cent of the milk is consumed in liquid form by way of drinking and 44 per cent of the milk is converted into

"Ghee" by using local methods and *"Lassi"* is got as a byproduct which is very popular in the village Bajina, district Bhiwani. This is distributed to the weaker sections of the village free of cost by the farmers. In this way about 14 per cent of the milk is marketable surplus. This surplus is also converted into ghee. The ghee thus prepared is sold in Bhiwani which is at a distance of about 20 km. from the village. Most of the villagers sell ghee to "Adhatis" and take cattle feed in exchange and cash in some cases. [Singh, 85: Village Bajina (Bhiwani)]

Sheep

Sheep rearing is mainly in the districts of Sirsa, Bhiwani, Kurukshetra, Mahendragarh and Jind. Sirsa has 168 sheep per '00 rural households, Bhiwani follows with 112 and Kurukshetra with 107. Gurgaon, Faridabad and Sonepat have less than 40 sheep per '00 households against an average for the state of 77 sheep per '00 households.

Table 4.25 : Sheep (1988)

District	*Number of rural households (1981)*	*Sheep in '00*	*Sheep per '00 rural households*
Sirsa	82997	1395	168
Bhiwani	110738	1244	112
Kurukshetra	59733	637	107
Mahendragarh	70123	696	99
Jind	97323	948	97
Hisar	176938	1439	81
Karnal	80245	632	79
Ambala	88275	428	48
Rohtak	140407	602	43
Gurgaon	100447	341	34
Faridabad	83862	256	31
Sonepat	104483	293	28
Average			*77*

Source: Derived from *Statistical Handbook of Haryana* (1991-92), Government of Haryana and Census of India (1981).

Goats

Mahendragarh, Bhiwani, Gurgaon and Sirsa are the main goat rearing districts of Haryana. Mahendragarh with 136 goats per '00 households is way above 8 districts which have 50 or less goats per '00 households. By and large goat rearing in the north eastern belt is not so popular, perhaps because of the swith to stall feeding of buffaloes.

Table 4.26 : Goats (1988)

District	*Number of rural households (1981)*	*Goats in '00*	*Goats per '00 rural households*
Mahendragarh	70123	951	136
Bhiwani	110738	1098	99
Gurgaon	100447	944	94
Sirsa	82997	729	88
Ambala	88275	462	52
Kurukshetra	59733	281	47
Faridabad	83862	387	46
Hisar	176938	700	40
Jind	97323	335	34
Rohtak	140407	457	33
Karnal	80245	202	25
Sonepat	104483	206	20
Average			*59*

Source: Derived from *Statistical Handbook of Haryana* (1991-92), Government of Haryana and Census of India (1981).

Sheep and Goat Rearing

Population of sheep constitutes nearly 12 per cent of the total livestock population of this village Nahla, district Hisar. The agro-climatic conditions in this area are very much favourable for the health and development of sheep. As such, sheep husbandry has considerable scope. Most of the existing sheep belong to local

Hissar and Nali breeds. However, nowadays an exotic cross-bred known as "Hissar Dale" is gaining popularity among the farmers. This is regarded as a good breed for producing more wool and mutton.

Population of goats constitutes nearly 6% of the total livestock population of this village. There are no well defined breeds of goats. Most of them are local and non-descript. Normally, the poor people keep these animals for milk and mutton. In this village, use of mutton is limited to a few communities. However, urban centres provide its market. [Khandelwal, 87: Village Nahla (Hisar)]

Pig Rearing

Pigs are normally kept by the scheduled caste persons in village Nahla, district Hisar. Most of the pigs found in this area are local, however, an exotic Yorkshire strain is becoming popular among the farmers. This breed has a good demand as these animals are prolific converters of roughage into animal fat. There is no local market for these animals, otherwise a good proportion of the lower caste people could adopt this practice. [Khandelwal, 87: Village Nahla (Hisar)]

Poultry

The districts of Ambala, Gurgaon and Mahendragarh are the main poultry producing districts of the state. Ambala led in 1988 with 1661 birds per '00 rural households, followed by Gurgaon (1180) and Mahendragarh (1156). Karnal and Kurukshetra had between 500-600 birds per '00 households, whereas the other districts had less than 250 birds per '00 households. Hisar and Bhiwani had less than 100 birds per '00 households.

Poultry keeping is an occupation that has become popular in the last few years in village Dhauj, district Faridabad. It now has 10 poultry farms and a hatchery which supplies to surrounding areas. On an average one poultry farm has 200 broiler birds. These are sold when they are 40 days old for a minimum of Rs. 30. The poultry farm owners have arrangements with traders or restaurants

Table 4.27 : Poultry (1988)

District	*Number of rural households (1981)*	*Poultry in '00*	*Poultry per '00 rural households*
Ambala	88275	14660	1661
Gurgaon	100447	11852	1180
Mahendragarh	70123	8109	1156
Karnal	80245	4791	597
Kurukshetra	59733	3434	575
Sonepat	104483	2514	241
Jind	97323	2256	232
Sirsa	82997	1280	154
Faridabad	83862	1055	126
Rohtak	140407	1730	123
Hisar	176938	1429	81
Bhiwani	110738	280	25
Average			*512*

Source: Derived from *Statistical Handbook of Haryana* (1991-92), Government of Haryana and Census of India (1981).

in Faridabad and the birds are picked from the village itself. On a rough estimate, each poultry farm generates a net income of at least Rs. 2000 per month indicating its high profitability. [Misra, 1992: Village Dhauj (Faridabad)]

HEALTH AND SANITATION

Health care and family welfare in rural Haryana is largely the responsibility of the Government. Although private doctors, especially Registered Medical Practitioners are gaining popularity on account of the poor functioning of governmental health institutions, the government health centres and hospitals because of their infrastructural strengths, continue to remain the backbone of health care in the state. The facilities in the state are, however, unevenly distributed. Bhiwani, Rohtak, Ambala and Hisar have more than 85 hospital beds per lakh of population, whereas Gurgaon, Panipat, Kaithal and Rewari have less than 37 beds. The skewed nature of health infrastructure is best demonstrated by the fact that, whereas Bhiwani has 124 beds per lakh of population, Rewari has only 32 beds.

Table 4.28 : Hospital Beds Per lakh of Population (1990-91)

District	*Beds per lakh of population*
Bhiwani	124
Rohtak	107
Ambala	86
Hisar	85
Jind	75
Yamunanagar	56
Karnal	49
Faridabad	48
Mahendergarh	44
Sirsa	42
Sonepat	41
Kurukshestra	38
Gurgoan	37
Panipat	35
Kaithal	34
Rewari	32

Source: Statistical Handbook of Haryana (1991-92), Government of Haryana.

At the village level, the Sub-Health Centres and the Primary Health Centres (PHC) are the key health care institutions. Whereas the PHC are staffed with doctors, compounders and nurses, the Sub-Health Centres have the key village level field functionaries in the form of Lady Health Visitor, Auxiliary Nurse, Multi-purpose Workers and Field Workers. They provide health cover for common ailments, immunization against communicable diseases, and also function as the family planning centre for the area.

Although diseases like Tuberculosis (T.B.), Polio, Diabetes, Heart ailments, Tetanus continue to take toll of human life, the common diseases afflicting most villages are Malaria,

Gastroenteritis, Diarrhoea, Dysentery, Cholera, Respiratory Tract Infections, Asthma and Skin infections like Scabies. For the communicable diseases immunization is done by the PHCs, the staff of the sub-centres and most important of all, by the Anganwadis. For treatment, where the governmental institutions are properly managed, people visit them. However, most of the institutions are badly managed. Medicines are often in short supply and people are unable to get medicines from the governmental institutions. Even civil hospitals are unable to provide the attention that patients desire. Private doctors, despite their fees are able to fulfill these needs and are thus being preferred to government health centres. For minor ailments, people still resort to local (desi) home remedies. Only when these cures fail they visit the doctor.

Government maternity centres do not have a wide enough coverage. For most deliveries, the midwives *(dais)* continue to provide service to the villagers. Upgradation of their skills by suitable training in government institutions has improved their service.

Sanitation is another important area of concern in the villages of Haryana. Open drains, poorly paved streets with poor drainage, cause stagnant pools which not only stink, but become breeding grounds for mosquitoes and other pests. Poor management of solid wastes especially dung heaps add to the unhygeinic environment. With the depletion of wastelands for defecation, human excreta is developing into another major problem. Apart from the unhygeinic aspect of defecation, the embarrassment of defecating in limited open spaces is becoming a human problem. Subsidized latrines are being encouraged, but the programme has not been followed up with the adequate persuasion required for such a programme.

Drinking water facilities are more or less satisfactory in the state. Tap water, handpumps, tubewells and wells are able to fulfil the requirements. However, for many, the drinking water facility is unable to cater to the requirement of bathing and washing. For the latter, villagers still depend on the village pond, where villagers not only bathe and wash, but also take their livestock for bathing and drinking water. These ponds thus become sources of skin infections.

Family planning is gradually being accepted in principle by the villagers. However, the concern for having the male child, and generally more than one male child, often leads to large families with 4-6 children. Contraceptives like the condom, oral pills, copper-Ts, IUCDs have still not been popularised. Family planning is still dependent largely on sterilization and that too on tubectomy. With Laparoscopic tubectomy, the operation has become easier, but the simpler vasectomy is still to get the acceptability that it deserves.

In village Silakhari, district Faridabad, the people are not at all satisfied with the health facilities. At least one member of every household has required hospitalisation in the last two years, for which the people have to go Ballabhgarh without proper facilites of transport. Also, the villagers complained that the poor villagers are not properly looked after in the civil hospital at Ballabhgarh, unless they grease the palms of the doctors. There is no qualified doctor in the village to take care of patients in case of emergency or in the night. Many of the villagers have listed providing proper health facilities in the village as the top priority for development in the village. [Gupta, 1994: Village Silakhari (Faridabad)]

COMMON DISEASES

There are no epidemics like Malaria, Cholera or Dysentery in village Shahpur, district Ambala. The infant mortality is 16 per cent, which is, as compared to the neighbouring village, on the lower side. With some addition of staff to the Sub-Health Centre, the infant mortality can be further reduced. [Anand, 1987: Village Shahpur (Ambala)]

Dysentery and Malaria are prevalent in village Rajpur, district Gurgaon. The Family Planning programme is a good success in the village. 75 per cent of the villagers have been operated upon. Women are more frequently operated upon than men because of the belief that the operation causes weakness.

Some families have a large size because of the desire for a male child.

The village does not have a primary health centre. The nearest dispensary is a kilometer away.

Immunization is not successful in the village. People are not even aware of it. It seems that medical teams have never visited them and spread awareness. [Gupta, 1992: Village Rajpur (Gurgaon)]

The common ailments that afflict these villagers in village Hirmathla, district Gurgaon are diarrhoea, T.B. and scabies. Because of poor hygienic and sanitary conditions like absence of drainage facilities, open toilets, diarrhoea spreads. The sub-soil water is brackish and leaves a salt film on the body if bathed in it. The protected water supply of the Public Health Engineering Department is not sufficient for the villagers to bathe regularly. Therefore attacks of scabies are common. [Ramsekhar, 1990: Village Hirmathla (Gurgaon)]

It has been observed that villagers in Kheri Dabdalan, district Kurukshetra do not fall ill very often or very easily because they live in an open atmosphere with plenty of sunshine and fresh air, unlike city dwellers where the air is extremely polluted. The villagers are hardy and their tough work in the fields makes them physically quite resistant. Obesity is rare in the village and thus the incidence of hypertension and cardiac problems is also very low. The usual type of cases reported are of cough due to excessive smoking of tobacco, digestive problems due to unhygeinic food and water, malaria, certain skin affections and general fever. [Kumar, 1986: Village Kheri Dabdalan (Kurukshetra)]

Most of the people from village Silakhari, district Faridabad, who can afford, get the deliveries at Ballabhgarh/Faridabad hospital. Amongst the poor, who form the majority in this village, the deliveries takes place usually at home. There are about 10 per cent deaths of children during deliveries though death of the mother is quite uncommon. Even the death of children is due to malnutrition of the pregnant mother and complications developed due to over exertion by the mother because of stress of household work. [Gupta, 1994: Village Silakhari (Faridabad)]

HEALTH FACILITIES

There is no PHC or sub-centre in Hirmathla, (it is a small village) district Gurgaon. There is also no qualified doctor in the village. Ghaseda, which is 2 km. away has a Primary Health Centre under which Hirmathla comes. There is a sub-centre at Rewasan, another small village at a distance of 3 km., where the multi-purpose health worker and Auxiliary Nurse-cum-Midwife are posted. Hirmathla comes under Rewasan sub-centre. There are a couple of registered medical practitioners in Ghaseda. A PHC is there is Nuh, which is the referral hospital for PHC, Ghaseda.

Villagers in Hirmathla contend that very rarely do the health staff visit the village. If they go to the PHC in Ghaseda, there are never any medicines, also the treatment is not proper. Therefore they go to the registered medical practitioners, who charge high fees. [Ramsekhar, 1990: Village Hirmathla (Gurgaon)]

Shahpur in district Ambala has a Sub-Health Centre which functions under the supervision of the Primary Health Centre located in Naggal. It was established in 1966 and has been functioning to the full satisfaction of the village. It is housed in a building which is the property of the village panchayat. There is one Lady Health Visitor, one Auxiliary Nurse, four Multipurpose Workers and two Field Workers.

Besides providing medical health facilities for most minor ailments and diseases of Shahpur village and to some of the neighbouring villages, the Sub-Health Centre cares for environmental nutrition, mother and child health, immunization from communicable diseases like malaria, small pox, cholera, polio etc. The centre maintains a record of births and deaths in the village and also serves as the family planning centre. People, particularly women, are educated in the need for keeping families small by the use of contraceptives and other birth-control measures.

A complete health record (family folders) of all the families residing in the village is maintained. It includes items like birth, death, illness, immunization and family planning of each family in the village. The staff is dedicated and the villagers are satisfied with their performance. But the medical staff needs to be increased for one doctor is clearly inadequate to meet the needs of such a large village as Shahpur. [Anand, 1987: Village Shahpur (Ambala)]

The PHC in the neighbouring village of Mangali Jhara and Singhram, district Hisar is inadequate. During the household survey nobody could recall ever being given a medicine from the PHC, though the doctor could prescribe medicines. Some medicine being out of stock for some time is understandable because of financial constraints, but it is hard to believe that all the medicines are out of stock all the time. My effort to cross-check the reality for myself as an ordinary person did not succeed, as the doctor in the PHC recognised me. But still it is hard to disbelieve everybody. [Rastogi, 1992: Village Mangali Jhara, Singhram (Hisar)]

There are three private medical practitioners in the village Dhauj, district Faridabad. Of these, two are Ayurveda graduates (B.A.M.S) and one is a Registered Medical Practitioner (R.M.P.). They charge fees varying between Rs. 10 and Rs. 30 depending upon the nature of the illness. There is also one midwife or *"dai"* who charges Rs. 100 alongwith a saree for every delivery she assists from rich families or if a son is born she charges more.

The story of the Dhauj PHC exemplifies government delays, inefficiency and apathy. The PHC was sanctioned many years ago. Construction was begun by the Health department in 1991. However, the PHC building was never completed due to delays and eventual paucity of funds. It stands even today as a ruin telling its own eloquent tale. The PHC consequently, is run by the compounder and a sister from one room in the Dhauj Rest House outside the village.

Medicines are available in the village from a chemist's shop. The common ailments are dysentery, flu and malaria. In case of any serious illness, the patient is taken to the Badshah Khan Government Hospital in Faridabad. [Misra, 1992: Village Dhauj (Faridabad)]

Villagers complained mainly about the lack of hospital facilities in the village Bhadana, district Sonepat, even though there is a PHC. The doctor is absent most of the time and the nurse and compounder look after the patients. As a whole the villagers do not have much faith in government doctors and they go to the private doctors in case of need. In case of emergency the patient is taken to the Civil Hospital at Sonepat. The villagers have no complaint about the lady health visitor and are generally satisfied about the immunisation work. There is no maternity centre in the village. The nurse and two Balmiki traditional dais help during child birth. Infant mortality is high. Almost every family has lost a child or two. Death due to road accidents occurs frequently. [Panigrahi, 1990: Village Bhadana (Sonepat)]

There is no PHC or dispensary in the village Barana, district Karnal. The nearest PHC is at Samana Bahu. A lady and a male health worker are supposed to visit the village at least once a week. They are supposed to provide medicines for common ailments and also vaccinate the new borns. They are supposed to advise serious patients to get themselves admitted at the PHC or the Civil Hospital at Karnal. There is a trained dai in the village for delivery purposes. She is supposed to receive Rs. 100 per delivery. No health worker had visited the village in the last one year. The children of the weaker sections are not vaccinated, while the others go to the PHC at Samana Bahu. The dai too does not receive remuneration for her services. Even the PHC at Samana Bahu is ill-equipped with medicines and vaccines and people have to procure these from the market. [Khemka, 1993: Village Barana (Karnal)]

There is a "Sastri" in the village Jhadsethli, district Faridabad who is reported to be an Ayurvedic doctor for curing mental illness. The Sastriji's house is used as a hospital for curing chronic mental patients. He is quite famous and patients from all over the country are said to come to him for treatment. The system adopted by the doctor, however is novel. He does not charge any fee at all from the patients. Instead, the villagers out of reverence for the doctor and the noble cause he is engaged in, tend to his needs and that of the hospital. [Prasad, 1990: Village Jhadsethli (Faridabad)]

Shanti came to village Makrani, district Bhiwani after her marriage. Her mother-in-law was the village midwife. Shanti recalls how in those days, delivering babies was a roughshod job. The umbilical cord was cut with a *"dati"* or *"khurpi"* or any other handy iron implement. She continued after her mother-in-law's death, then went to Dadri for a midwife's training course. She has a certificate, was given Rs. 300 and equipment, including a much needed pair of scissors. She now conducts deliveries accordingly, washes her hands with soap (no antiseptic) and warms water and uses whatever instruments she has. She has no fixed fees. Rs. 25 is what she tells everyone, but is compelled to take whatever people give her. Tetanus and other infections are surprisingly rare, but Shanti obviously cannot handle complicated or prolonged labour. For such cases, those who can afford, call a private doctor or get their women admitted in private maternity clinics in Dadri. [Vardhan, 1987: Village Makrani (Bhiwani)]

It is not surprising that due to inadequate staff in the Sub-Health Centre, there are a number of private medical practitioners in the village of Shahpur, district Ambala. There are eight registered allopath doctors. One of these doctors is popularly described as a "roving doctor", for he is always on his bicycle ready with the medical chest to visit families at their residence to attend to their ailments. Others too run their clinics. There is also a chemist shop. [Anand, 1987: Village Shahpur (Ambala)]

The Faridabad Complex Administration provides and maintains the civic amenities of village Jhadsethli, district Faridabad. Adequate sanitation facilities are provided with around 50 per cent of the households having septic latrines and the remaining having daily cleanable type of latrines. Sewage however is a problem in the village as most of the sewage is by open drain which is a health hazard. The drinking water supply to a part of the village is piped whereas the rest of the village depends on well water. There are a large number of handpumps. Water is also supplied for consumption from the village tanks.

The villagers are susceptable to attacks of Malaria and Gastroenterites. A dispensary is located in the village. A research and education unit of the All India Institute of Medical Sciences with a hospital wing is located about 4 km. from the village in Ballabhgarh. There is a trained *"Dai"* in the village. There are four private doctors who are registered medical practitioners. [Prasad, 1990: Village Jhadsethli (Faridabad)]

The village has a common well for the supply of drinking water, which is used by all the castes in village Theh Bahri, district Jind. Twenty three households, 15 belonging to Bhedkuts, 5 to Sansis, 2 to Brahmins and 1 to Balmiki have installed handpumps in their houses for drinking water. The piped water supply scheme covering four villages, namely Bangran, Bahri, Theh Bahri and Thal was started in 1985 with water works at Bangran. The source of water for the scheme is Bangran canal minor. It has 2 storage tanks, I overhead reservoir, 2 high level tanks, 4 filter beds and 2 clear water tanks. Domestic connections have not been given. In 1988, there were 6 public water taps provided at focal points in the village, which supply water for 5 hours a day from 6 a.m. to 8 a.m., 12 noon to 1 p.m. and 4 p.m. to 6 p.m. The scheme is maintained and operated by the Public Health Division of the Public Works Department, Jind. [Sharan, 1992: Village Theh Bahri (Jind)]

There has been no major epidemic in the last five years in village Pema Khera, district Gurgaon. However, incidence of Polio is very high. In a small village like this, with a population of only 2380, there are 50 victims of Polio. There is a sub-centre with an ANM, but she can attend only to minor ailments.

There is an Anganwadi Centre run under the Integrated Child Development Scheme. Run by an Anganwadi worker and a helper, the centre has 35 children in the age group 0-6. Apart from imparting informal education preparatory to admission in primary school, the centre also gives nutritional food to children, as well as to expecting nursing mothers. The centre also organizes vaccination camps, where all the children are immunized against various diseases.

Wells and handpumps are the source of drinking water in the

village. There is a separate well for Harijans in the village. As is the practice in most villages in the area, the village has a Jouhar (pond) which is used for bathing, washing animals etc. The Jouhar does not dry even in the summer. Of late it is also being used for fish rearing. [Prasad, 1986: Village Pema Khera (Gurgaon)]

SANITATION

The sanitary conditions are good when compared to other villages in Shahpur, district Ambala, but there is ample scope for improvement. The streets are pucca but not well kept and properly swept. Stagnant water pools are seen around the pucca road. The Harijan area is the worst in this respect. Here the roads are generally covered by earth, rather than brick. Sanitation is poor and the residents are very careless about in keeping the environment clean and hygienic. The panchayat is also remiss in its duties to this part of the village abadi.

The water supply is clean and ample. Pipe-water has now been made available to the village. The underground water is sweet, clean and germs free. [Anand, 1987: Village Shahpur (Ambala)]

Regarding sanitation, the people in village Dhauj, district Faridabad are in the habit of going to common wastelands or adjoining fields early in the morning to relieve themselves. Due to encroachments on these lands and population growth, the poorer sections and women now face embarrassment and difficulty in this regard. The State Government, as part of its Silver Jubilee Year Action Plan has initiated a programme of rural sanitation wherein individual and community latrines will be constructed at heavily subsidised rates. In Dhauj, about 250 individual latrines are being constructed at nominal rates of Rs. 300 for SC beneficiaries. Other beneficiaries will have to pay about Rs. 1200. The latrine is of a standard double pit prototype formulated by the Sulabh Sauchalaya International.

The main problems in adoption of these latrines by villagers are two-fold. Firstly, many are skeptical of the necessity for a latrine since they are accustomed to the age old practice of squatting in the outdoors. Secondly, to traditional villagers, the idea of having a latrine in the *aangan* or compound is anathema since they imagine the excreta will pollute the house.

The programme is a much needed initiative, but it needs to be pushed with greater vigour to make a difference to the sanitary habits and conditions of most villages. In Dhauj, it is common to see children squatting on roadsides and in lanes, converting the village into one filthy open toilet.

The system of wastes disposal is similar, with large garbage heaps along the road or in dumps. These wastes when matured into fertilizer are used by the person on whose land the dump exists. These dumps provide a fertile breeding ground for insects, rodents and mosquitoes. Misra, 1992: Village Dhauj (Faridabad)]

There are two Anganwadis in the village Bhankri, district Faridabad, each of which has one worker and one helper. There is one worker for a population of a thousand people. The *Anganwadis* are housed in rented accommodation.

Here the programme includes nutrition for bracing and lactating mothers and children between the ages of 3 months to one year and 6 months to 3 years. The children are given either 60 grams of Panjiri or 35 grams of peanuts and 17 grams of gud. The lactating mothers are given 100 grams of Panjiri or 55 grams of peanuts and 35 grams of gud. The ration timing is around 12 noon. The average number of children who go to the Anganwadi ranges between 13 to 15. Here the Anganwadi helper makes them pay, do P.T., learn poetry and teach them cleanliness.

The *Anganwadis* are beset with a number of problems. There is no furniture or seating place provided for the children, who have to sit down in the open in the hot sun. Moreover, the helpers in the *Anganwadis* at Bhankri had not received their salary since December 87 when they were appointed. [Sekhri, 1988: Village Bhankri (Faridabad)]

Table 4.29 : Anganwadis in Village Surera District Hisar

There are two Anganwadis in the village under the Integrated Child Development Scheme. These Anganwadis undertake to impart non-formal education provide supplementary nutrition conduct immunization, nutrition and health education.

The registration of children and mothers is as below:

	Scheduled Castes	*Others*	*Total*
Number of children in the age group:			
6 months to 3 years	46	140	186
3 years to 6 years	34	147	181
Number of pregnant mothers	6	12	18
Number of lactating mothers	2	18	20

The immunization work done upto date is as follows:

B.C.G.	57
D.P.T.	I—56 II—54 III—50
Polio	56
D.T.	55
T.T.I (Mothers)	12
T.T.I (Children)	52
Vitamin A solution	55

[Lal, 1984: Village Surera (Hisar)]

FAMILY WELFARE

Interviews of a wide cross-section of the villagers from Singhpura, district Rohtak revealed that they are not aware about the advantage of a small family. The lacuna lies in the health services available to the villagers and information regarding prophylactic methods of family planning. The villagers seemed unaware of any method except sterilization for family planning. That is absolutely unacceptable to the males, since they firmly believe that apart from other side effects, sterilization causes sexual impotency. The females are also afraid to undergo the operation since there is nobody to persuade them of the harmlessness of the operation. The trained dai has lost credibility because of her lack of knowledge and skill.

Only a few of the men interviewed were aware that other methods of family planning exist. Most of them had heard of oral contraceptive pills *"Mala-D"* and seen the advertisement on TV, yet not one of them actually knew the nature of these pills or the course. The men only occasionally use condoms and find it inconvenient. None of them had ever heard of the loop or copper-T. [Kundu, 1988: Village Singhpura (Rohtak)]

Garhpur Khalsa, district Karnal village has the distinction of having achieved 100 per cent family planning target in Haryana. The average size of the family is six members. There are only seven couples who have not got themselves operated because of various considerations like having only daughters, only one issue or no issue at all. The rest of the eligible couples have got themselves operated.

A very interesting feature of the family planning in this village is that males prefer to undergo vasectomy rather than women undergoing the ordeal of tubectomy. The reason for this was not very clear. The credit for achieving the 100 per cent family planning target goes to the village panchayat which could motivate everybody for this cause. [Chander, 1986: Village Garhpur Khalsa (Karnal)]

Local Household Remedies in Kheri Dabdalan, District Kurukshetra

For cough, the villagers take pure honey for the throat. They mix grind "kali mirch" in pure honey and lick it. This is useful both for cough and other respiratory problems. For fever, they take *"Tulsi ka Patta"* which is known to have febrifuge properties. Although the cases of Diabetes are rare, they use "Blackplum", which is known to sometimes cure Diabetes. [Kumar, 1986: Village Kheri Dabdalan (Kurukshetra)]

Most of the streets in the village Kheri Dabdalan, district Kurukshetra are paved with bricks, but the condition of the drainage is very poor, with the result that there occurs blockage of drains leading to very foul smell. The situation becomes acute during the rainy season, which results in increased incidence of malaria infestation. [Kumar, 1986: Village Kheri Dabdalan (Kurukshetra)]

Sanitary conditions in the village Ajitpura, district Bhiwani are very poor. Only 30% of the streets are paved with bricks. Proper slope and drains have not been provided and water from houses directly flows into the streets. It gets accumulated right in the middle of the streets in front of houses and stink. The problem becomes acute in the rainy season. The condition of kutcha streets is still worse. A complete development plan of the village was prepared in December 1985 with the help of the Junior Engineer of the Block Office. Paving of all the streets, proper drains and final disposal of sewage and construction of retaining wall around the pond was suggested to improve the sanitary conditions. The work was proposed to be taken up under NREP/RLEGP. [Dhillon, 1986: Village Ajitpura (Bhiwani)]

Some idea of the death and birth rates in village Santokh Majra, district Jind can be had by the reports maintained by the village chowkidar. The death reports mention the age, caste, sex and the cause of death. From 1980 to 1988, only six deaths of children below five years have been recorded, and the causes mentioned are illness, bad cold and tetanus. Four of the six are females who died before one year. On general inquiry, death of children by tetanus and even polio (but not very recently) was reported. The *Anganwadi* in the village is being run by an ex-nurse who has some idea of the various doses of vaccines to be given to the children. But the general insecurity and malnutrition coupled with the quest for sons means larger families. Cases of unnatural deaths are due to appendicitis, bad cold, T.B., diabetes, asthma, cancer, fever, tetanus, heart attack and one case of snake bite. Seven people over these years have been reported to have died of T.B., while eight of asthma. The total number of people who have reportedly died over the years are:

Year	*Deaths*
1980	8
1981	8
1982	11
1983	7
1984	7
1985	5
1986	6
1987	12
1988	11

Birth reports of three years, 1988, 1987 and 1986 were available. The total births were:

Year	*Births*	*Male*	*Female*
1988	16 (11)	11	5
1987	15 (12)	7	8
1986	18 (6)	10	8

The figures in brackets are the deaths in these years. Clearly the birth rate exceeds the death rate. Further the ratio of male: female population in Haryana of 1000:937 is also reflected in this village, in the greater number of males born, *vis-a-vis* females. The ages of mothers vary from 20 years to 40 years, which is a long reproductive span. [Jha, 1989: Village Santokh Majra (Jind)]

Family Planning in Kheri Dabdalan, District Kurukshetra

The response of the villagers towards family planning is favourable in the village and the government has little difficulty in persuading the people to adopt family planning. The villagers however do not like it when the village *patwari* or *Gram Sachiv* or health worker or some other government agency worker pulls an eligible case of sterilisation to achieve targets fixed for him. The villagers prefer to go silently for sterilisation without being hooked to some "promoter" who wants to put a particular case to his credit. Due to competition among the various departments for meeting their targets under family planning, certain persons demand money or pecuniary benefits to give them the credit of a promoter. In sterilisation tubectomy is preferred to vasectomy. Now the tubectomy is performed by Laparascopy which is more convenient. However, the use of contraceptive devices like IUCD, Nirodhs, Copper-T etc. have not been adopted by the villagers. [Kumar, 1986: Village Kheri Dabdalan (Kurukshetra)]

The family welfare services in village Mangali Jhara and Singhram, district Hisar are provided through the PHC located in a neighbouring village. Though contraceptives are distributed through the centre, yet sterilization is the commonly adopted family planning technique. Besides free medical and surgical services, transport and diet are arranged for sterilization cases. Cash incentive of Rs. 100 is offered. Though all the people are aware of the need for family planning, they will not have less than 4-5 children. Most of the sterilizations take place after the couple has produced about 4-5 children and thus only help the cause of medical officers and government officials in showing inflated achievement of targets. Everybody desires to have more than one male child and as such are yet to reconcile to the one male child. A person having three non-school going children is a very common sight so one can have the idea of interspacing. [Rastogi, 1992: Village Mangali Jhara, Singhram (Hisar)]

EDUCATION

According to the 1991 Census, percentage literacy in Haryana has been reported as 55.5 per cent against the national average of 52.1 per cent. Male literacy has been reported as 68 per cent and female literacy as 41 per cent. Literacy in Haryana is lower than in the neighbouring states of Himachal Pradesh and Punjab. A district wise analysis based on the number of literates and the total population (not population above a particular age group) shows that literacy levels are highest in Ambala, Rewari, Sonepat and

Rohtak (Table 4.31). Although in male literacy Rewari is highest, the proportionately higher female literacy level in Ambala puts the latter on top. The lowest performers are Kaithal, Sirsa, Jind and Hissar, in that order. In total literacy, Kaithal has only 34 per cent literacy compared to 55 per cent in Ambala. So far as female literacy is concerned Kaithal has only 23 per cent literacy, compared to 47 per cent in Ambala.

Table 4.30 : Literacy in Haryana as % of Total Population (1991)

District	*Male literacy*	*Female literacy*	*Total Literacy*
Ambala	63	47	55
Rewari	66	38	53
Sonepat	64	38	52
Rohtak	63	37	51
Yamunanagar	56	42	50
Kurukshetra	57	39	48
Faridabad	60	33	48
Mahendragarh	62	30	46
Karnal	54	35	45
Panipat	54	33	44
Bhiwani	57	28	44
Gurgaon	53	27	41
Hissar	50	26	39
Jind	49	24	38
Sirsa	47	28	38
Kaithal	44	23	34

Source: Data on Total Population, Sex-ratios, literate male and female derived from the *Statistical Handbook of Haryana,* 1991-92. % literates as proportion of total population derived from this data.

Despite rapid material progress in Haryana, literacy especially among women has lagged behind. Although the villages of the state have been well covered by an expanding network of primary schools, middle schools, high schools, balwadis and adult literacy centres, the lack of quality of education does not attract the down to earth, pragmatic villagers. The value of education has not been successfully popularised. At best, education is considered as a commodity to be consumed for the purpose of gaining qualifications to get jobs, especially government jobs. And when this education is unable to promise these jobs, its worth is questioned. With regard to education of girls in Haryana, it is a common refrain that what the girl practically needs to learn is management of household jobs, so as to be a successful wife and mother. With such a world view, especially when opportunities for female careers are extremely limited in rural areas, and when urban areas are already teeming with unemployed populations, it is very difficult to convince the earthy and commonsensical villager about the worth of the kind of education being imparted, in the schools of today.

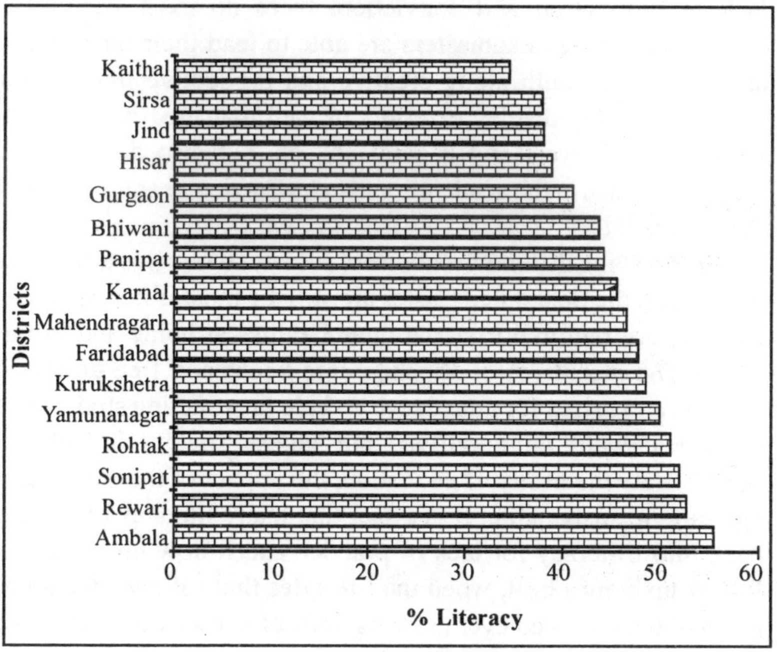

Fig. 4.1 : Total Literacy in Haryana as % of Total Population

The perception about the lack of adequate relevance of education is compounded by the low motivation and competencies of the teachers and administrators of education. The situation becomes worse when infrastructural facilites are also lacking. Although primary schools have sprung up in almost all the villages of Haryana, most of them do not have adequate accommodation and facilites for the growing number of students.

The low quality content, the indiscipline and lack of motivation of the teachers and the lack of facilites to engage the youth in productive and creative work, often makes the total environment of the schools indisciplined and meaningless. The village surveys repeatedly noted the complaints regarding lack of discipline, reflected most significantly in the rampant copying in examinations.

Within this general environment of inefficiency, cynicism, lack of motivation and conviction, there do exist islands of excellence. Some headmasters are able to lead their institutions and guide the youth along creative and productive lines. Such schools not only display exteriors of well managed institutions, with lawns, flowers and general upkeep, but also demonstrate their excellence in the academic and extra-curricular achievements of the students.

Observing different sections of society, it remains a fact that in villages, the Scheduled Castes are still the most illiterate. Their children are required to assist their families at home and in the fields. The incentives of stipends, free books and free uniforms for girls and prizes for attendance do help in attracting students of these backward communities, but unless society is able to demonstrate the utility of education, the impact of this education may not be sustainable. It is a fact that many literates often slip back into illiteracy for lack of practice and follow up. And this follow up comes best, when the lifestyles that follow education, demand the use of an ever growing body of knowledge which can be best acquired through the written word.

Maximum dropouts occur after Class V. Among the dropouts,

Scheduled Castes and girl students figure most prominently, followed by the Backward Classes. The demands on these children for assistance in the work place of the parent or at home compels them to dropouts. In addition, when the middle school or high school is not located in the student's village, many dropout, especially girls. Parents do not generally approve of the female child going out of the village to study.

However, since 1983, there has been a general upswing in the enrollment in primary schools, this increase appears to be sharper in the case of girls. General awareness on account of various factors seems to be responsible for this. From this trend it appears that the demand for good education is likely to grow.

To meet the growing demand of quality education, private schools are beginning to come up in the villages. With suitable support from the local bodies and the government, these could help in bringing competition into education, thereby raising the standards of even the government schools.

The District Primary Education Programme which has been launched in Haryana is likely to bridge the gaps that exist in infrastructure, teachers, syllabi and curriculum. The focus of the programme in attracting the girl child and the weaker sections may enhance enrollment further. As the need for education is propagated in the villages, the demand for relevant quality education is likely to increase. For this, the motivation and competence of the teachers is central. Alternatively, private schooling would come in to meet the demands. The way private clinics of Registered Medical Practitioners are beginning to gain preference over government dispensaries and health centres, the same kind of story may get replicated in the case of education.

LITERACY

The total number of literate persons in the village Khanna Majra, district Ambala was 360 out of the total of 556 people above the age of 14 years. Thus the village has a literacy rate of 64 per cent.

Literacy was highest 82 per cent among Khatris next came the Jat Sikhs with 78 per cent, then the backward classes with 62 per cent and the last were the Scheduled Castes with 53 per cent literacy.

A further breakup of literate people into different categories show that whereas there are 29 per cent people who are matric among the Khatris, their percentage among the Backward Class is 16 per cent and among the Jat Sikhs is 14 per cent. It is only 2 per cent among the Scheduled Castes. [Gulati, 1988: Village Khanna Majra (Ambala)]

The villagers of Santokh Majra, district Jind send their children to the village Middle School. Some well-off families, like Roys and Chauhans, send their children to study outside. The fact that the High School is at Rajound, which is 6 km. away, poses a problem for both boys and girls. Many of them have studied till Class X and then dropped out. The well-off speak about the problem of educating their children. The village school is certainly not their idea of education. About 20 to 25 boys and girls study outside the village after completing Middle School.

A survey conducted by the school authorities in 1988 reported that in this village, there are 107 children between the ages 6 to 11, of which 105 are registered in the school. In all there are 99 boys and 73 girls and 6 teachers in the school. The figures for literacy for 1981 were: Total literates 369, Males 219 and Females 150.

With 369 literates against a total population of 832, the literacy rate is much better than the average for the state (23%) or the district (13%). There are a few adults who have now forgotten to read or write. [Jha, 1989: Village Santokh Majra (Jind)]

Even though there is a high school and a primary school in village Bhadana, district Sonepat, the standard of education is not upto the mark. The schools are situated in the same compound and have adequate playing facility, staff etc. However, the quality of teaching is very poor as I perceived from my talks with some of the students of the schools. The teachers are least bothered either about the standard of education or students. Students are indisciplined and below expectation. Corruption and copying during examinations is rampant, connived by parents and teachers. The villagers are aware of it all, but accept it with a shrug. Parents send their children to get a pass certificate so that he qualifies for a job. It is a general perception of the villagers that degrees and jobs are bought and sold like vegetables, so there is no point of studying hard to pass exams. Some educated families send their children to either Delhi or Sonepat for better education. [Panigrahi, 1990: Village Bhadana (Sonepat)]

In village Silakhari, district, an important reason for villagers hesitation in sending their children to school is the scepticism developed by the villagers that, even if they study upto matric or even higher, they will have to do the same work, which they can do even without studying anything. They are not going to get government jobs. So the villagers relate education with the job only, not with the general development of the personality. Many of the villagers are illiterate. About 25 per cent of the villagers, mainly children of age upto 15, have studied upto primary level, but beyond that there are just 4 matriculates in the village, out of which one is doing good business in real estate. [Gupta, 1994: Village Silakhari (Faridabad)]

There is a high school and a private primary school in the village Telanwali, district Hisar. In the high school, there is also a primary wing. There are 213 students and 4 J.B.T. teachers in the primary wing. Above Class V there are 143 students and 7 teachers. The quality of education is bad. A private primary school has come up in the village. Panchayat has give Panchayat Bhawan building to the school for holding classes. The person who has started it is a B.Com. He started with 9 students last year, but now has 130 students on his roll. He has kept 3 other teachers and pays Rs. 500 per month to each of them. The school fee is Rs. 25 per student per month. Thus, landlords can send their children to this school. Although, their children are enrolled in the government school, they attend classes in the private school. Students from neighbouring villages, Kutiakhedi and Ghursal also come to this school. [Garg, 1993: Village Telanwali (Hisar)]

Table 4.31 : Growth in enrollment in Primary School, Makho Majra, district Karnal

	Scheduled Caste		*Backward Class*		*Total*	
Year	*Boys*	*Girls*	*Boys*	*Girls*	*Boys*	*Girls*
1959	3	0	8	3	14	3
1960	5	3	8	3	15	6
1961	4	5	10	3	18	11
1962	9	2	9	5	18	10
1963	5	6	7	3	14	10
1964	5	9	15	3	20	15
1965	-	-	12	3	19	6
1966	4	2	7	1	20	4
1967	4	2	5	0	16	5
1968	4	2	7	-	16	2
1969	3	2	8	-	15	2
1970	3	2	7	-	13	2
1971	3	2	10	3	15	6
1972	4	1	15	-	22	1
1973	3	3	16	-	24	4
1974	3	1	13	1	23	5
1975	9	7	24	11	40	19
1976	13	8	22	5	46	18
1977	13	12	26	4	56	26
1978	10	8	27	11	51	24
1979	5	5	31	12	47	20
1980	8	3	31	14	58	20
1981	9	9	22	12	52	28
1982	9	9	22	8	49	29
1983	7	9	19	12	36	25
1984	8	15	21	16	45	41
1985	13	17	16	16	41	45
1986	13	20	25	16	51	64
1987	19	23	25	19	61	64
1988	20	23	39	30	64	65
1989	30	29	29	30	74	91

[Khullar, 1990: Village Makho Majra (Karnal)]

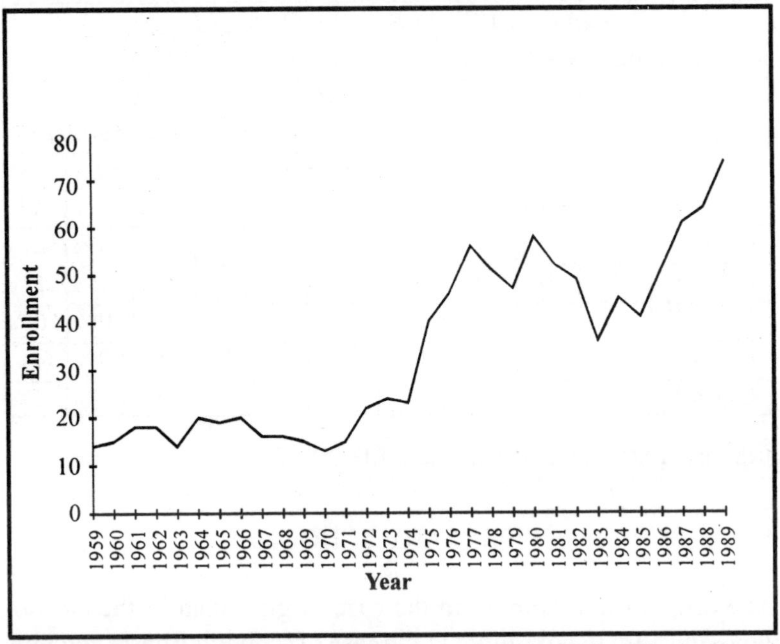

Fig. 4.2 : Enrollment of Boys in Primary School Makho Majra, District Karnal

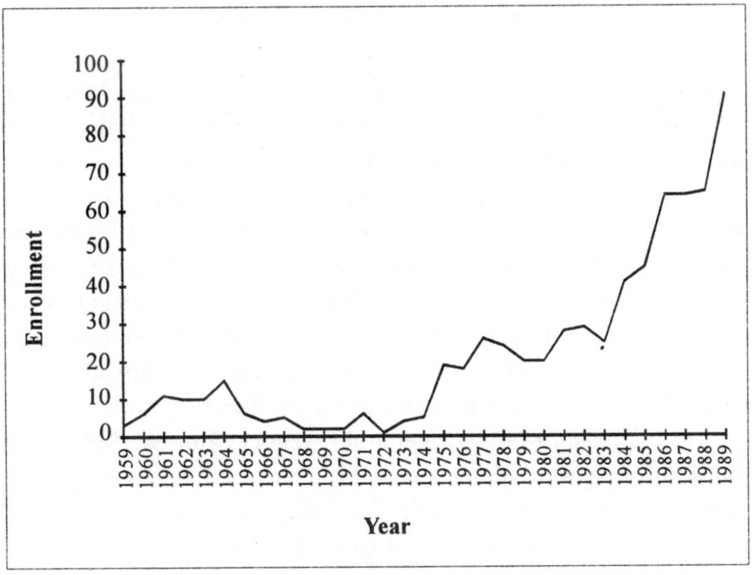

Fig. 4.3

Dropouts in Village Barana, District Karnal Dropouts between year 1991-92 and 1992-93											
	General		*Backward Class*		*S.C.*		*Dropouts in percentages*				
	Male	*Fe-male*	*Male*	*Fe-male*	*Male*	*Fe-male*	*To-tal*	*Fe-male*	*S.C.*	*To-tal*
Class I	0	0	0	0	6	5	11	29%	85%	32%
Class II	0	0	0	0	3	1	4	11%	57%	21%
Class III	0	0	0	0	1	1	2	20%	40%	10%
Class IV	0	0	0	0	1	0	1	0%	50%	6%
Class V	0	2	0	0	1	1	4	38%	67%	22%

[Khemka, 1993: Village Barana (Karnal)]

PRIMARY SCHOOL

The dropout rate is more in the case of girls than in the case of boys and among boys more in the case of scheduled caste students in Primary School, Ajitpura, district Bhiwani. In general, among boys the dropout rate is 2 per cent and among girls it is 10 per cent. Only 60 per cent of the girls take education upto fifth standard. Among the S.C., the dropout rate is around 12 per cent. Only half of the S.C. children who take admission in first standard complete studies upto fifth standard.

After fifth standard, girls normally stop going to school. Only in exceptional cases, they continue studies. Only one girl was found to be attending school in a high school of nearby village Manheru. The parents are not in favour of sending girls to other villages because of their conservative nature. When asked why they are not sending their daughters for middle or high school education, pat came the reply that they are to marry them also one day.

In the case of boys of general category, almost 100% to for middle/high school education in the nearby village. Some bright students continue their studies in colleges at Bhiwani. One of them recently passed the LL.B examination and is serving as a lawyer at Charkhi Dadri, a sub-division town of Bhiwani. There are two patwaris from this village who were appointed after matriculation. No scheduled caste candidate has been absorbed in government jobs as they do not fulfil the minimum educational qualifications. [Dhillon, 1986: Village Ajitpura (Bhiwani)]

There is one primary school in the village Surera, district Hisar. The school building has three rooms. The verandah is unsafe and requires immediate repairs. The rooms are insufficient. There should be at least five classrooms to house the 177 children. The children sit on the "*tats*" (mats). There is one tap in the school, but since the water supply comes in the morning and evening, hence running water is not available for drinking. A water carrier works part time and stores the water for the children. In the summer, many students bring their own water bottles to school. There is proper sanitation in the school and the school building is ideally located.

During the academic session 1985-86, there were 177 students in all, of which 127 were boys and 50 girls. On 31st March 1986 there were 100 girls and 50 boys of school going age who were not coming to the school. Out of this 150, about 50 children were likely to take admission in the academic year 1986-87. Girl's education is still neglected by the villagers, as the girls are kept busy in household jobs. The dropout rate in the school is low. Last year, only 8 students were continuously absent. Since education is free and the scheduled castes get free books, stipend etc., there is hardly any student who leaves school due to poverty.

The mid-day meal scheme sponsored by C.A.R.E. is being implemented in the school. Each student gets 80 gms. of porridge and 5 gms. of Soyabean Salad Oil. The students prepare the porridge themselves. This child nutrition programme also helps to some extent in attracting the children to the school. [Lal, 84: Village Surera (Hisar)]

There are 110 boys and 135 girls attending the Government Primary School in village Charow, district Karnal, 165 children who go daily to Karnal for education. Each and every child of school going age attends school in the village.

There are 74 children in Class I, 50 in Class II, 42 in Class III, 43 in Class IV and 36 in Class V. Although this indicates a significant dropout rate, some of it can be attributed to failures, some to those who opted to go to Karnal or Jundla. [Rao, 1987: Village Charow (Karnal)]

MIDDLE SCHOOL

Special classes in English and Mathematics for eighth class were taken for all the students by the teachers in the Middle School, Bajina, district Bhiwani. The headmaster was found very particular about the students. The result of the eighth class, the examination held by the Haryana Education Board was 90 per cent. This result was above the average result of the district as well as of the state. The headmaster was confident that the result will further improve during the session 1984-85. At least two students will get a position in the district.

All that the teaching staff is very good. All the sanctioned posts have been filled up. Besides one headmaster, there were two masters, six J.B.T. teachers, two teachers and one peon-cum-chowkidar. The discipline of the school and the cleanliness was quite appreciable. Attendance of all the students, class-wise was written on the attendance board with the signature of the class incharge. Details of the staff members with their joining dates etc., were displayed in the office of the headmaster in a nice way. Plantation of trees and flowers in the compound of the school was worth seeing. Seasonal vegetables are also grown in one side of the compound. A grassy lawn has also been maintained well in the school. Students are also trained in plantation work in their spare time. Such work is very helpful to make the students aware of the dignity of labour.

Attendance prizes are given to the Harijan students having attendance more than 70 per cent and whose family income is less than Rs. 6000 per year. During the year 1983-84, three girls and thirteen boys received Rs. 310 and Rs. 260 respectively, while the amount of Rs. 350 and Rs. 170 was given to 5 girls and 16 boys during the year 1984-85. Such steps are very helpful to make the Harijan students regular in attending classes. [Singh, 1985: Village Bajina (Ambala)]

PRIVATE SCHOOLS

The "Indian Public School" is a private venture in the realm of education in village Shahpur, district Ambala. This school which imparts education from "Nursery to V" is described by its management as "English School". It claims that the school is run on modern lines with English as the medium of instruction. It is housed in a small building which is rather small for its needs and provides a cramped environment to children. The surprise, however, is that such a school was in a village and is able to survive with enrollment adequate to meet the financial outlay of teachers, equipment and some financial gain to the management. It has over 100 children on its rolls.

There is also another *private-run tuition* group arrangement where girl students are trained for various examinations. [Anand, 1985: Village Shahpur (Ambala)]

There are three privately run schools in the village Dhauj, district Faridabad. These are:

- Islamic School, run by Maulana Mohammed Taiyab Qadri of the Madina Masjid a non-Meo Muslim who has migrated from Bihar and settled in Dhauj. This school is upto Class V and teaches only Urdu and Arabic. This school has a strength of about 175 students.
- Islamic Darool ul Uloom—run by Maulvi Haroon of the Jama Masjid of Dhauj. This is also upto Class V and again restricted to teaching Urdu and Arabic. This school has a strength of about 250 students.
- Hathras Public School—run by Subhash Chand Tyagi. This school imparts education upto Class V as per standard government syllabi and has a strength of about 150.

Among government schools, the Girls Primary School has a strength of 150 and the Boys Primary School of 230 students. It is noteworthy that enrollment in the private schools, especially the religious schools was greater than the government schools, and these schools were imparting no knowledge of secular affairs of the world and the nation. [Misra, 1992: Village Dhauj (Faridabad)]

As regards education of boys and girls at the primary level, their ratio has been worked out at 79 and 21 per cent respectively in village Nahla, district Hisar. At the middle stage, this ratio is 82 and 18 per cent and at high school level, the ratio is about the same as at the middle stage. However, in college, the girls of this village constitute only about 8 per cent of the total college going students. Thus, the number of girls getting education is much lower than boys. Moreover, a decreasing trend is observed as the level of education goes up. [Khandelwal, 1987: Village Nahla (Hisar)]

Female education presented a dismal picture in village Dhauj, district Faridabad. In large and growing families, young girls are employed to play surrogate mother-cum-housekeeper to siblings. This results in their very low enrollment and erratic attendance in school, even if they are enrolled. It was depressing to discover that a minuscule 5 per cent of the girls in the village were school going. The village men and the women themselves candidly admitted that in their view female education was completely useless. "A woman has to spend her life between the chulha and the children—of what use is reading and writing to her?", was the common statement, though the men did shamefacedly acknowledge that these social beliefs were outdated and needed change. [Misra, 1992: Village Dhauj (Faridabad)]

Educationally, the Harijans are more backward than the rest of the population in village Santokh Majra, district Jind. There is no Harijan boy who has studied beyond Class X. Harijan girls do not generally go to school, or dropout after class five or class six. [Jha, 1989: Village Santokh Majra (Jind)]

Surprisingly the Harijan girls are more in number in the school than the boys in primary school, Sullar, district Ambala. This is because the Harijan girls get scholarships. Some of the school teachers take personal interest, as a result of which the dropout rate seems to be less. Another reason is that the economic condition of the village is not so bad that they cannot send their children to school. During the last one year only 2 Scheduled Caste children and 1 another left the school. According to the villagers, one or two teachers personally visit them if their child stops going to school. [Nain, 1986: Village Sullar (Ambala)]

Incentives for Education, District Sirsa

The state government has over the years given incentives to the socially and economically weaker sections of the state's population. These include monetary benefits mostly and are specially designed to get the real needy to send their kids to school and make them a better and brighter future. The incentives are:

Scheduled Castes:

a) For > 60% attendance

Std. 6—8	stipend @ Rs. 15 per month
Std. 9—12	stipend @ Rs. 20 per month

b) For stationary

Std. 1—5	Rs. 20 per annum
Std. 6—8	Rs. 40 per annum
Std. 9—12	Rs. 60 per annum

Backward Castes:

Std. 9—12	stipend @ Rs. 20 per month

Girls: Free uniforms for all girls upto standard 12.

[Singh, 1993: Village Ganga (Sirsa)]

There is a government primary school in the village Makrani, district Bhiwani, which was established in 1962. The school has a staff of four teachers (including the headmaster) and a peon-cum-chowkidar. All the teachers are matriculates and have done the Junior Basic Teachers Training Course. The headmaster travels four kilometers every day from Ghasola, his native village, while the other three teachers, including Mrs. Rukmini Devi a lady teacher come from Dadri, the sub-divisional headquarter—11 km. away.

The standard of teaching is not good. The teachers, especially the headmaster do not teach the children properly. All the villagers were unanimous in condemning the headmaster. He is frequently absent and when he does make an appearance, a siesta in the sun occupies most of his time. The villagers strongly feel that the headmaster should be transferred, but add at the same time that his political connections are formidable. [Vardhan, 1987: Village Makrani (Bhiwani)]

PRIMARY SCHOOL

The government primary school in the village Makrani, district Bhiwani desperately needs another three rooms, one for each class. At present there are only two classrooms for 204 children, so the classes are held outside in the sun and most of the students are forced to sit on the ground. The village panchayat is in no position to contribute anything. However, all the villagers are ready to provide free labour, if the material for constructing the additional rooms is provided by the government.

Some basic furniture too is urgently needed. The blackboards are broken. In the name of teaching aids, all that the school has are a couple of science charts. There is no sports equipment at all in the school. So the children play Kho-kho and Kabaddi only. [Vardhan, 1987: Village Makrani (Bhiwani)]

For girls, the nearest Industrial Training Institute is located at Tohana, 35 km. away from the village Nahla, district Hisar imparting training in cutting and tailoring, embroidery, needle-work, weaving etc. For boys and rural artisans, there is one Rural Industries Development Centre at Fatehabad, 35 km. away. It imparts training in carpentry, weaving, shoe making, dye and calico printing etc.. For college education, students have to travel as far as 40 km. [Khandelwal, 1987: Village Nahla (Hisar)]

Thanks to the Christian influence, many Christian girls from the village have completed school (Class XII) and are eager to work as nurses, clerks etc. With an 8 per cent literacy rate, district Jind where rural women are most poorly educated. The careers available for boys are ITI trained technicians and clerks. There is also one doctor from the village. Out of the educated men, three undergraduates stay in the village. Roy's son does farming, Rajesh helps his father, the Sarpanch, in managing the affairs of the village and Chauhan's son who was a lecturer in Agra, now helps in farming. Rajesh tried to start an Adult Education Centre but it failed for lack of enthusiasm among the villagers. He tried to organize it in the Church, but the people said that this is a place of worship, not education. He helps in the school sometimes. [Jha, 1989: Village Santokh Majra (Jind)]

Village Mehrana, district Rohtak with a population of 4369 has a primary school and a High school. The children of the schools are neat and healthy. They attend school regularly, but sometimes Harijan and Backward Class children also work with their parents in the fields. The school going children spend a lot of time playing football and jogging. Jogging is a very popular sport among grown up males. One Kamlesh, from the village, had won the Gold Medal at the Nationals in wrestling. The average duration of school life is upto class eight. There are 1500 people who are eighth pass, 500 had schooling upto class ten, 30 upto class twelve, 10 persons are graduates, 5 postgraduates and one is doing Ph.D at Rohtak. Except for one, none have obtained a satisfactory career later on. One Mahavir is lecturer at Government College, Jind. One person has got admission to Haryana Agriculture University, Hisar, 7 persons had done polytechnic courses and one person is doing Bachelor of Engineering course at Bangalore.

The villagers, however, had a general complaint about the teachers in the school. The standard of teaching is not upto the mark. Copying is rampant in the examinations. [Joshi, 1991: Village Mehrana (Rohtak)]

ADULT EDUCATION

There is one Adult Education Teacher with about 8-10 students in the centre in village Charow, district Karnal. The literacy rate in the adults is around 70 per cent. This is far higher than the State or the All India Averages. [Rao, 1987: Village Charow (Karnal)]

One adult literacy centre has recently been started by Maulana Qadri of Madina Masjid in village Dhauj, district Faridabad. This has about 50 adult male students and classes are held in the evening for this centre. 100 Urdu literacy kits were obtained from the Jama Milia Islamia and given to Maulana Qadri, so that the small beginning made in the direction of literacy in the village is sustained and stimulated. [Misra, 1992: Village Dhauj (Faridabad)]

POVERTY ALLEVIATION PROGRAMMES

"People look forward to the government to help improve the conditions of their living and in turn, the government has to yield results, may be by extending grants only". (Kumar: 89: Hisar)

THE PROGRAMMES

In the last two decades a number of programmes were launched all over the country by the Government of India for alleviation of poverty in rural areas. The Integrated Rural Development Programme (IRDP), Rural Landless Employment Guarantee Programme (RLEGP), National Rural Employment Programme (NREP), Jawahar Rozgar Yojna (JRY), Training of Rural Youth for Self-employment (TRYSEM) and Development of Women and Children in Rural Areas (DWCRA) being the most prominent. IRDP in its present form was launched in 1978-79 in selected blocks all over the country. District Rural Development Agencies were set up in all the districts to implement IRDP, TRYSEM and DWCRA to begin with. Later other rural development programmes were also brought under the DRDA. The District Rural Development Agency is headed by the Deputy Commissioner as Chairman and a Senior scale IAS officer as Chief Executive Officer.

The employment generation and community works taken up in Haryana under NREP, RLEGP and JRY include the following:

- making of pucca roads
- gali construction
- johad repair
- installation of street lights
- construction of school buildings
- renovation of schools buildings
- residential plots and low-budget houses with sanitation facilities for the schedule castes
- smokeless chullhas
- gobar gas plants

Under IRDP loans have been distributed for income generating activities mainly for the following :

- Tubewell
- Buffalo unit
- Pair of bullocks
- Horse Tonga
- Sheep unit
- Camel unit
- Jhota Buggi
- Cycle rickshaw
- Kirana shop
- Motor mechanic shop
- Leather work
- Knitting machine
- Durree carpet making

Although the data base is inadequate, specific data relating to financing of different trades from villages of 9 districts of Haryana throws up the following picture:

Buffaloes	93
Pair of bullocks	30
Sheep Unit	3
Camels	5
Cycle shop	1
Cycle rickshaws	2
Horse Tonga	7
Jhota Buggi	8
Leather work	1
Knitting machine	1
Durree carpet	8
Motor mechanic shop	1
Shop	2
Tubewells	3
Total	165

Although the sample is small the picture that emerges is very clear. Animal Husbandry seems to be the most popular trade and within animal husbandry financing of buffaloes is by far the most attractive option. This is followed by the service sector in which transportation seems to be the most popular activity. In the above sample 17 cases have been financed for cycle rickshaws, horse tongas and jhota buggis (buffalo carts). Cottage industry like leather work, knitting machines and durree, carpet making is also popular. Financing of shops was not found to be very popular. This could be on account of the larger capital requirements for this trade.

General Observations on Poverty Alleviation Programmes

The village has been benefited by IRDP/ RLEGP/ NREP/ JRY/ TRYSEM/ DWCRA Programmes of the DRDA. A lot of work has been done by the employment generation programmes such as Gali constructiion, School building, Johad repair etc. Around 200 persons have got loans under IRDP so far and 90 persons are trained under IRDP. All the scheduled caste landless families are covered under IRDP in the village. Even though absolute poverty no longer exists in the village, the scheduled caste families are relatively poor and need constant help from the Government. (Panigrahi: 88: Sonepat)

A few development programmes were underway in the village. These included making of pucca roads, installation of street lights and renovation of school building. (Bajaj: 88: Hisar)

The Government has taken up a programme to provide schedule castes with residential plots and construct low-budget houses with subsidiary facilities of sanitatioin. (Prasad: 84: Gurgaon)

The village is benefitting from various government schemes like smokeless *chullhas,* gobar gas plants cooperative and IRDP loans.(Niwas:85:Ambala)

The Department of Agriculture had given subsidy for construction of individual biogas plants to 10 families during the last 5 years.

Excepting for the school building which was built 10 years back by the Education Department, no developmental activity seems to have taken place in this village. The streets of the village are narrow lanes with many ups and downs. There is no sewage and storm water drainage. As a result sullage water flows on the street.

STRENGTHS OF THE PROGRAMMES AS REPORTED BY THE PROBATIONERS

Assistance to the poor

...In a village like Khorma, where the people are poor but not down-trodden and are aware of modern life, IRDP has raised their standard of living. Those poor farmers who could not think of having their own tubewells, now own these because of minor irrigation assistance scheme and have really contributed to more production to themselves as also to the nation. Similarly the landless *'Harijans'* own buffaloes. Though it is doubtful whether the number of buffaloes and the quantity of milk yield has really increased after the launching of the IRDP in Khorma, there has not been any significant change in this respect, yet the impact of IRDP is that the buffaloes has changed hands and are now in possession of the poorer people and thereby have strengthened their household economics. (Kumar: 88: Narnaul)

...Not a single case has come to the notice where any household who is eligible for assistance under IRDP but have not been given any help so far. Atleast on paper, it appears only eligible households have been benefited under IRDP. (Rao: 85: Karnal)

Out of the 36 loans disbursed in the village so far, 30 are for pair of bullocks. All these 30 beneficiaries are either SC/Backward castes or small and marginal farmers. (Lal: 84: Hisar)

Of these assisted families almost all of them are from those living below poverty line mainly either SC or BC. (Chander: 84: Karnal)

...in the year 1982-83, a survey was conducted and 62 families were identified who are very poor and require assistance under IRD Programme. ... Now out of 62 families identified to be poor, 32 of them have been assisted ... The 17 families have been financed for the purchase of buffaloes. ... Six families were financed for the purpose of Horse tonga which they do not ply on the village route but on some other busy route.... One family has been financed for a sheep unit, one kirana shop has been financed and one family has been financed for doing leather work, repairing and manufacturing desi-footwears. (Kumar: 84: Kurukshetra)

...During the year 1983 a survey committee comprising of an official of the DRDA, a school teacher, a veterinary doctor and a bank official surveyed the village and drew up a list of 35 beneficiaries living below the poverty line to be assisted .....Of the 35 identified persons, 24 have been assisted by the DRDA in the year 1986. Nineteen have bought buffaloes and 5 bought camels. Of the 19 who have bought the buffaloes, 17 have bought the buffaloes from the village itself. Same is the case with the beneficiaries who have bought camels. All of them have bought the camels from the village itself. All of them are still in possession of the animals and they have not exchanged or sold them. (Vardhan: 85: Bhiwani)

...The SC people have rightly received the lion's share of the benefit. Only four families from Jats or Mahajans have received assistance. Only 5 small farmers have been benefited and no marginal famers exist in the village. (Kundu: 86: Rohtak)

Nature of assets

Under the IRDP around 29 families have been provided with income generating assets in the village. Mostly they have been advanced loans for purchasing either buffalo or cross bred cows or goats. (Chander: 84: Karnal)

During the year 1982, six people from the village were assisted under the IRDP. Five of these were given—loan for buffaloes and one for sheep. (Vardhan: 85: Bhiwani)

...The majority of beneficiaries have been given loans for purchase of buffaloes. Of the 15 beneficiaries, 10 received loans for the purchase of buffaloes. Two beneficiaries were assisted to purchase cycle rickshaws which they ply in Ambala Cantt. A lady received a knitting machine for producing knitware for sale. Another was assisted in setting up a shop and another in purchasing a *tonga*.....To my great satisfaction, I found everything in order. The buffaloes had not only been purchased in a genuine manner and under the supervision of the BDO and the veterinary doctor but also properly maintained after the purchase.

The Panchayat members as well as the local officials were satisfied with the implementation of the Programme and the disbursement of funds. The bank authorities were also hopeful of recovery. (Keshni Anand: 85: Ambala)

Three beneficiaries have received assistance for tubewells and have derived considerable benefit from it. (Mohapatra: 85: Rohtak)

In village Bhankri in the year 1981-82, 21 beneficiaries received loans for buying buffaloes under this scheme. In 1982-83 buffaloes were again preferred under this scheme by 16 beneficiaries. ......In 1983-84 there were only 5 beneficiaries and in 1985-86 there were 6 beneficiaries. For the first time in 1984-85 there was only one beneficiary who took loan for *Jhota Buggi,* in 86-87 there were five beneficiaries. (Rajni Sekhri: 86: Bhankri)

The survey revealed that against a sample of 96 households, 13 were assisted through DRDA under IRDP. Out of 13 households, four were assisted through the creation of asset under buffalo scheme, one got assistance under sheep, and seven households were assisted by providing Jhota Buggi. (Singh: 87: Karnal)

There are 40 IRDP beneficiaries. Out of the 40, 30 loans are given in the animal husbandry sector and 10 are given in the ISB sector. A cycle repair shop and a motor vehicle mechanic shop are being run with government assistance under IRDP in the village. The other 8 beneficiaries under ISB sector are being trained in TRYSEM in the training-cum-productioin centre (TPC) for the preparation of durrees or carpets. (Prasad: 88: Faridabad)

By and large, the assets given to the eligible households are still with them. But in those cases where they are not there, the reply was that they died due to illness etc.(Rao: 85: Karnal)

TRYSEM

DRDA is running 8 centres for imparting training to rural youth for self-employment in different trades like Mudha making, Blacksmithy, light engineering, carpet-cum-durri weaving, handloom and jute tat patti making. Mewat Development Agency, in collaboration with the Haryana Small Scale Industries and Export Corporation, the Haryana State Handloom and Handicrafts Corporation and the Haryana State Industrial Co-operative Federation, etc. is also having training centres for various trades *e.g.* Mudha making, carpet weaving, tat patti, handloom, leather tanning, blacksmithy, pottery and hosiery.

On completion of training, loans are arranged to enable the successful trainees to set up their own units. Tool bags are also given to the trainees at the conclusion of training by the DRDA under TRYSEM programme. About one thousand persons have been trained at various training-cum-productioin centres set up in different villages. (Rajni Sekhri :86: Gurgaon)

Community Assets

A few development programmes were underway in the village. These included making of pucca roads, installation of street lights and renovation of school building. (Bajaj: 88: Hisar)

The funds allotted under the JRY are being spent mainly on the pavement of streets and the village Panchayat is executing these works. Seven hundred and fifty feet of street have been brick-paved as on date. (Prasad: 88: Faridabad)

One street has already been paved with bricks. Another is being paved with it. ..... Two small bridges are being made and both are under the JRY and are executed by the Panchayat. .... In the highschool, earth work is being done to raise the level. All these are done courtesy JRY.

The most important thing with the JRY is that it ensures the involvement of the people through the Panchayat. In addition, it raises the expectation of the people in general in terms of development and which in turn means more pressure from the people on the development agencies and also, raises the accountability of the governmental apparatus. People look forward to the government to help improve the conditions of their living and in turn, the government has to yield results, may be by exetending grants only. (Kumar: 89: Hisar)

The village is benefitting from various government schemes like smokeless chullhas, gobar gas plants co-operative and IRDP loans.(Niwas:85:Ambala)

AREAS OF CONCERN

IRDP

The IRDP is not much effective due to the prevalence of many malpractices. (Lal: 84: Hisar)

There is no success story as yet.... During the survey, it was found that around 20 per cent of the beneficiaries have either never purchased their buffaloes or cows or have sold their assets.(Chander:84:Karnal)

But unfortunately unsatiable greed of officials working at the lower level has made mockery of the whole programme. Bank managers, veterinary surgeons do not act without getting their share. ... The awareness of the right to the subsidy is yet to come.(Prasad:84:Gurgaon)

While a simplistic overview of IRDP suggests that there is nothing wrong with the programme, everything does not seem to go right for this programme. Various reasons, some general, and some beneficiary-specific, have gone into upsetting some link or the other of this programme. The most crucial failure seems to be on the part of monitoring. (Prasad:88:Faridabad)

The index of co-operative loans for the purpose of seeds, implements and manure is very high in the village but 70% of the loanees are defaulters. Many of them have been put in judicial lock-ups for non-payment of loan money. ... It was found during the survey that not many people were forthcoming for taking loans because of this apprehension.

There are only three IRDP beneficiaries in the village and all of them have taken loan for buffaloes....The IRD Programme has had only a peripheral impact on the villagers. The three beneficiaries could not be inferred to have risen above the poverty line as a result of the programme. (Niwas:85:Ambala)

For the past 2-3 years no IRDP loans or any other kind of loans have been distributed in the village. The reason that most villagers gave was that since the village was politically not affiliated to the present government, no loans were given to them. But on inquiry, it was found that most of the villagers had taken one or the other kind of loan but had not repaid it and were defaulters. A consequence of waiving of loans policy. (Bajaj: 88: Hisar)

Nevertheless, after 31st March 1983 nobody in the village has received any help under this programme. Enquiry in the village revealed that when the officials visit the village many persons do fill up the form. But as the procedure involved in getting the loan is cumbersome the villagers have to run around a lot.

The bank requires surety for granting such big loans which is difficult for the beneficiary to arrange. Thus in many cases the applicants loose interest....Out of 33 beneficiaries who have received help under IRDP, 5 do not reside in the village. Three beneficiaries have received assistance for tubewells and have derived considerable benefit from it. (Mohapatra:85:Rohtak)

Out of the 16 beneficiaries in the current year 3 have been wrongly identified as per the survey and they were already above the poverty line with programme assistance provided to them. About 25 per cent of the beneficiaries did not possess the physical assets when contacted. ...This factor is enhanced on account of the family politics prevalent in village Bhankri. Rampant corruption at the lower level village functionaries and bank staff is another hurdle with which the villagers have to cope.(Rajni Sekhri: 86:Bhankri)

Everybody knows that nobody has sold or purchased the buffalo but nothing can be done about it since the beneficiary always gets the benefit of doubt.(Kundu:86:Rohtak)

A credit camp was organized in August 1989. Four applications were received from this village and all these applications were rejected. One of these was a defaulter because father of the applicant had taken loan from Chindalia Co-operative

Credit and Service Society. In the second application buffalo subsidy was taken in the year 1987-88. Third application was incomplete and on that ground it was rejected. The fourth applicant had already taken loan for horse cart earlier. ....In fact very few people apply for loan. Worse is that all the applications received for loan in the year 1989-90 got cancelled. It is clear that there is a lack of effort on the part of DRDA to identify the beneficiaries and help them under IRDP programme....It is felt that if the credit camp is well organized in letter and spirit and all the concerned field functionaries participate therein then the villagers will not face any problem. The reality however is that neither the field functionaries actively participate, nor they are committed to make the programme a success. Even all the beneficiaries are not available in the credit camp and those left out at that time, have to face many problems. (Kumar: 88: Narnaul)

Community Assets

Over a span of last 5 years the DRDA has taken up 43 houses for construction of smokeless chullahs. Only three of them were functioinal at the time of the survey. Most people have blocked the smoke pipes permanently. They complain that it consumes more fuel. More creative ones have dismantled the pipes and are using them as 'parnalas' *i.e.* as pipes to drain off water from the roof.

The Department of Agriculture had given subsidy for construction of individual biogas plants to 10 families during the last 5 years. None was found to be functional. One family was in the process of dismantling the plant during the survey. (Khullar: 88: Karnal)

Excepting for school building which was built 10 years back by the Education Deptt., no developmental activity seems to have taken place in this village. The streets of the village are narrow lanes with many ups and downs. There is no sewage and storm water drainage. As a result sullage water flows on the street. ... They are very reluctant to the idea of "Shramdan" or any other kind of voluntary effort providing village amenities. Under JRY 'Khol' were made at two places in the village for animals to drink water. (Ramsekhar:88:Gurgaon)

The Government has taken up a programme to provide scheduled castes with residential plots and construct low-budget houses with subsidiary facilities of sanitatioin. But some of the problems that have bogged down the programme are: (i) trouble in getting Panchayat land suitable for residential plots, (ii) lack of road facilities leading to the plots. (Prasad:84:Gurgaon)

IRDP

The observations of the probationers when aggregated reveal the broad truths of the poverty alleviation programmes in Haryana. It should be considered a substantial gain that the poor have been identified and programmes targetted at them. The fact that most probationers have reported that the beneficiaries of the programmes have been largely the poor, is also a significant gain. It has also been reported that as a result of IRDP, income generating assets have reached the poor. Moreover, in a state where animal husbandry and tertiary sectors are fast growing, the fact that most of the loans have been provided for these sectors, aligns the programme to the general developmental processes in the state.

Under TRYSEM, unemployed youth have received training in Mudha making, blacksmithy, light engineering, carpet-cum-durri weaving, handloom and jute tat patti making etc.. Other agencies like the Mewat Development Agency, in collaboration with the Haryana Small Scale Industries and Export Corporation, the Haryana State Handloom and Handicrafts Corporation and the Haryana State Industrial Co-operative Federation, etc. are also having training centres for various trades *e.g.* Mudha making, carpet weaving, *tat patti,* handloom, leather tanning, blacksmithy, pottery and hosiery. On completion of training arrangements for financing the trainees for setting up these trades is there.

On the negative side, malpractices, cumbersome procedures and non-repayment of loans seem to be the major weakness of the programme. Malpractices sometimes begin right at the identification process through loan application process and reach their peak at the time of disbursement. Not only is the machinery corrupt, but gradually the beneficiaries, in search of short term monetary gains go for the subsidy element of the loan, thereby sacrificing the income generating asset creation. This sacrifice puts the brakes on generation of additional income which results in non-repayment of loans. The atmosphere of loan waivers further vitiates this tendency of non-repayment of loans. The end result of this process is often quite bitter for the defaulter. Failure stories of this kind finally discredit the programme.

Community Assets

Employment generation programmes like NREP, RLEGP and JRY have been perceived by most of the probationers as primarily programmes for creation of community assets, rather than as programmes for employment generation. The assessment of these programmes is thus done not against the criteria of employment generation for the poor, but against the criteria of successful creation of community assets.

On the plus side it has been reported that pavement of streets, construction and repair of school buildings and street lighting works have been taken up with a fair degree of success. Success in bio-gas plants and smokeless chulhas has been limited. Many of the smokeless chulhas have been dismantled and their pipes used for alternate domestic purposes by the beneficiaries. Construction of low budget houses for the Scheduled Castes have has had to face constraints of availability of land and approach roads.

Though there is demand for civic amenities, especially for proper drainage in the villages, the voluntary effort required of the villagers is usually not forthcoming. There is dependence on the Government, but the latter is not having the wherewithal to plan and execute such works to the extent that they are required.

Impact of Poverty Alleviation Programmes

Taking into account the successes and failures of the programmes, it must be admitted that the impact of most of these programmes is very limited and that, primarily on account of the limited financial resources. During the Seventh Plan period (1985-1990) the total expenditure incurred on Rural Development in Haryana was Rs. 7148 lakhs[6]. This works out to an average of Rs.21000 per annum for the 6759 villages of Haryana. Within this meagre amount not only were the poor to be directly assisted by way of subsidies under the IRDP, but employment generating community works had also to be taken up. The limitations of the programme are obvious. Even for the subsequent years the outlays have not been impressive. In the Annual Plan for 1993-94, the approved outlay for Rural Development was Rs 1917 lakhs. This works out to an average of Rs 28,000 per annum for each village of Haryana. Wonders cannot be achieved with this level of investment. These programmes can only play a marginal, though an important role in providing some safety net for the poor, in the broad developmental dynamics of the state. So far as development of civic amenities of villages are concerned, these need a definite and independent focus and should not remain a byproduct of the poverty alleviation programmes.

NOTES

1. Director of Agriculture and Director of Land Records, Government of Haryana.
2. Agricultural Census (1985-86), Government of India.
3. Derived from Statistical Pocket Book of India (1992), Government of India and Statistical Handbook of Haryana (1991-92), Government of Haryana.
4. Derived from Gupta, D.P., "Agricultural Development in Haryana" (1985).
5. Statistical Pocket Book of India (1992), Government of India.
6. Statistical Handbook of Haryana (1991-92), Government of Haryana.

ANNEXURE A

Statement of Socio-Economic Surveys Conducted by IAS Probationers of the Haryana Cadre between 1983 and 1994

Year	*District*	*Village*	*Probationer*
1986	Ambala	Sullar	Navraj Nain
1987	Ambala	Bunga	Ram Niwas
1987	Ambala	Shahpur	Keshni Anand
1988	Ambala	Khanna Majra	Shashi Gulati
1989	Ambala	Ismailpur	Jyoti Arora
1985	Bhiwani	Bajina	Sarban Singh
1986	Bhiwani	Ajitpura	Sundeep S. Dhillon
1987	Bhiwani	Makrani	Vijay Vardhan
1988	Faridabad	Bhankri	Rajni Sekhri
1990	Faridabad	Jhadesethli	T.V.S.N. Prasad
1992	Faridabad	Dhauj	Sumita Mishra
1993	Faridabad	Palwali	Shrikant Walgad
1994	Faridabad	Silakhari	A.K. Gupta
1988	Gurgaon	Sukhrali	Surina Rajan
1988	Gurgaon	Gurgaon	Rajni Sekhri
1989	Gurgaon	Sukhrali	T.C. Gupta
1990	Gurgaon	Hirmathla	M. Ramsekhar
1992	Gurgaon	Rajpur	Ankuar Gupta
1993	Gurgaon	Bukharaka	Dr. G. Anupam
1986	Gurgaon	Pema Khera	S.S. Prasad
1985	Hisar	Agroha	Raj Rup Fulia
1987	Hisar	Nahla	K.K. Khandelwal
1990	Hisar	Mamupur	Tarun Bajaj
1991	Hisar	Bosti	Arun Kumar
1992	Hisar	Mangali J, Singhran	Anurag Rastogi
1986	Hisar	Surera	Roshan Lal
1993	Hisar	Telanwali	Vineet Garg
1989	Jind	Santokh Majra	A. Jha

Year	*District*	*Village*	*Probationer*
1992	Jind	Theh Bahri	A.M. Saran
1987	Karnal	Charow	P. Raghavendra Rao
1988	Karnal	Kunjpura	A. Nigam
1989	Karnal	Kachhwa	A. Singh
1990	Karnal	Makho Majra	R.K. Khullar
1991	Karnal	Dabri	Mahavir Singh
1993	Karnal	Barana	Ashok Khemka
1986	Karnal	Garhpur Khalso	R.P. Chander
1986	Kuruk-shetra	Kheri Dabdalan	Hardeep Kumar
1988	Mohinder-garh	Nasibpur	R.R. Jowel
1990	Mohinder-garh	Khorma	Anil Kumar
1991	Rewari	Khol	A. Chandra
1987	Rohtak	Untlodha	P.K. Mahapatra
1988	Rohtak	Singhpura	V.S. Kundu
1991	Rohtak	Mehrana	Vivek Joshi
1993	Rohtak	Mayna	Sandeep Garg
1992	Sirsa	Kheri	V. Raja Shekhar
1993	Sirsa	Ganga	Apoorva K. Singh
1989	Sonepat	Badkhalsa	Devender Singh
1990	Sonepat	Bhadana	B.K. Panigrahi
1993	Sonepat	Bhadana	Anil Malik

5

GUJARAT

C.N. Ray

Gujarat is one of the industrially developed state in India. It is situated between 20' N to and 24' N latitude. The tropic cancer passes through the Northern part of the state. It has also the longest sea coast among all the states. Upto 1959 Gujarat was part of Bombay state and only in 1960 it was bifurcated and became separate state. It accounts for about 5 per cent of total geographical area of India. The entire state is divided into three geographical regions. However, topographically it is divided into five parts and it also match with five popular regions: (i) Kachchh; (ii) Saurashtra; (iii) North Gujarat; (iv) Central Gujarat; and (v) South Gujarat. Agriculture is the main occupation in rural area as in other states in India. Till recently farmers continued to use old methods of farming. But rapid strides have been taken to make use of modern and more scientific modes of agriculture. However, the expected progress has not been made as rainfall is very irregular and at times scanty. Often cultivated crops wither away due to lack of rain. Various irrigation schemes have been implemented to ensure regular supply of water. Now, special emphasis is given for industrial development of the State.

Population

The population of the Gujarat State according to 1991 Census is 4.13 crore which constitute about 4.93 per cent total population of the country (excluding J & K). Gujarat ranks tenth in respect of population and ninth in respect of area. The density of population is 211 persons per sq.km. About 65.5 per cent of the total population are residing in rural areas. Thus, the urban population to total population in Gujarat is higher than that in the country (25.7). In repsect of urbanization it ranks fourth amongst the States in India. The proportion of SC and ST is 7.4 per cent and 14.9 per cent respectively. About 62.1 per cent of the SC and 91.9 per cent of ST population are residing in rural areas. The literacy rate of the state has increased from 36.94 per cent in 1981 to 48.64 per cent in 1991.

For a detailed analysis Gujarat can be divided into two regions:

1. The main land Gujarat consisting of 12 districts—the Dangs, Valsad, Surat, Bharuch, Vadodara, Panchmahal, Kheda, Ahmedabad, Mehsana, Gandhinagar, Sabarkantha and Banaskantha. This region was the part of the Bombay Presidency before independence, and of the Bombay State from 1947 to 1960.
2. The Peninsular Gujarat consist of Saurashtra and Kachchh regions, having Surendranagar, Bhavnagar, Jamnagar, Junagadh, Amreli, Rajkot and Kachchh districts. Nearly the whole of Saurashtra and Kachchh belonged to the Princely States. These states were integrated with the Indian Union in 1948. After their integration, Saurashtra and Kachchh formed separate B and C type state respectively of Indian Union. As a result of reorganization of the states both became a part of the Bombay State in 1956.

Land System and Agriculture

Before independence, the mainland and the Peninsular Gujarat had two different land tenure system. Ryotwari was dominant form of land tenure system in the former. Under this system, land was surveyed and revenue decided on the basis of survey and collected in cash by the State. The land was tilled by the individual who used to pay revenue to the state through intermediaries. Generally, the intermediaries belonged to Patidar or Anavil Brahmin castes. The *Zamindari system* was the dominant form of land tenure system in Saurashtra and Kachchh. The Rajputs were Girasdars, Bhayats, and Malgirasias, and had proprietary rights over their land.

The tenancy and Lands (Amendmend) Act of 1956 gave land to the tillers so that on a particular day (1st April, 1957) all tenants were deemed to have come in possession of the land they cultivated as tenants. Unlike the Zamindari Abolition Acts, the Tenancy Acts were not rigorously implemented as it adversely affected the Patidar landholders, who had considerable influence in rulling party and the administration. The Land Ceiling Act was introduced in 1960 and amended in 1974, which further lowered the ceiling limit. But the Act has largely remained on paper (Pathak, *et. al.,* 1979).

Farmers of Gujarat started producing commercial crops from the seventeenth century. The main cash crop was then cotton. Besides cotton, tobacco and groundnut also begun to be cultivated from the beginning of this century. During the last forty-five years, incentives for producing more and more cash crops are provided. The irrigated area increased more than four-fold from 1950 to 1981. Canals which watered only 3.4 per cent of the irrigated area in 1951-52 increased to 23 per cent in 1990. The number of oil engines, electric motors, pumps, tractors, etc., increased four to five times during the last two decades. The use of various types of chemical fertilisers also increased many times. Credit facilities provided to the farmers through co-operative societies and increased up considerably. They provide more than half of the financial needs of the cultivators.

The State Government has announced new agricultrual policy envisaging achievement of 4 per cent increase in production per year. Various incentives are being provided particularly to the small and marginal farmers belonging to scheduled caste and scheduled tribes. The policy provides for providing remunerative prices, high quality agricultural equipments, storage and marketing facilities, and promotion of exports of certain fruits, vegetables, etc. The state government has also undertaken projects to reclaim land and prevent salinity in coastal areas. It is also using Israeli technology for saline semi-arid areas. Agro-climatic plans are drawn emphasising watershed development. A drip irrigation programme of Israeli style has been taken up on a massive scale. Under this scheme every beneficiary farmers will have to share only 10 per cent of the cost of installation of necessary equipments in his farm. They are encouraged to form co-operative societies for adopting the new method of cultivation.

Caste and Agrarian Relation

The Brahmins and Baniyas belong to the higher castes. Roughly speaking, they consist 4 and 3 per cent respectively of the total population of the State. The Baniyas were absentee landlords before independence but now very few own land. The same is the case with the Brahmins except the Anavil Brahmins of Surat and Valsad districts (Breman, 1974; 1985).

The *Patidars* (Patels) earlier known as Kanabis, is the main landowning group in the whole state. The rich Patidar farmers in Gujarat held political and administrative power as revenue and police officers (Shah, non dated). A number of the Patidars of the upper stratum were active or were supporters of the freedom movement. They organized two important *'satyagrahas'*—Kheda in 1918 and Bardoli in 1928—to protect the interest of rich and middle loandowners (Shah, 1975). Their dominant position continued after independence. Since they do not have much stake in the *Zamindari system,* they played an important part in its abolition. In the mainland of the state they sabotaged the Tenancy Act as they were landholders. Later, they were also succeeded in making the land ceiling ineffective. They mobilised the middle and poor landholders against tenancy and land ceiling legislation.

The Rajputs, the Bareeyas and Kolis, if taken together, are popularly known as the Kshatriyas. They constitute roughly 30 per cent of the population in Gujarat. Traditionally, the Rajputs belong to the upper castes, whereas the Bareeyas and Kolis belong to low castes. Politically, however, they act as one caste, as all the three are against the *Patidars* for one reason or the another. After the abolition of *Zamindari* they lost their land to the tenant cultivators. Their power over villages also declined. The Rajputs blame the Patidars for their loss of power, as the latter have replaced the former. Also, the Rajput landlords were jealous of the remarkable economic prosperity of the *Patidars* (Ray, 1994).

Another group of rural poor is that of the schedule caste and constitute about 8 per cent of the total population of the state. The three-fourth of the rural SCs are landless agricultural labourers. They are scattered over the whole state, hence, numerically they do not constitute a group that is viable enough to confront the rural rich. Unlike the SCs, STs who constitute 14 per cent of the population are concentrated in a few districts of Gujarat. The major tribes are: Bhils, Dhodiyas, Gamits, Kunbia and Halpatis. They are also mainly agricultural labourers or cultivators owning less than one acre of land (Shah, Nd).

Thus, with the introduction of modern agricultural policies, traditional agrarian relations in rural Gujarat have undergone changes. Though share cropping and concealed tenancy exist, bonded labour system hardly exist in reality. Most of the castes are no longer homogeneous in the economic sphere. Economic stratification cuts across caste and vice-versa, leading to conflict. Conflict based on social and economic diffrentiation are of two types: (i) intra-class, inter-caste conflict, and (ii) inter-class conflict, having similar economic interests and belong to different castes. The members of the higher caste envy the neo-rich of the low and middle castes. The inter-class conflict is a conflict between conflicting economic interests.

Planning and Development

In Gujarat, the General Administration Department (GAD) act as Central Planning Authority. Its main function is to collect/compile proposals received from different sectors. The Secretary (Planning) in GAD is the Member Secretary of the State Planning Board which basically act as an advisory body. The planning organization is headed by the Chief Secretary who is assisted by a full time Secretary (Planning). The planning division is concerned with all the matters related to general principles of planning, policy formualtion, perspective, Five Year and Annual Plan preparation, implementation and monitoring.

The division is also responsible in co-ordinating the works of the Bureau of Economics and Statistics and Directorate of Evaluation. The set-up of planning machinery is divided as follows: (i) State Planning Board, (ii) Planning Division at the state level, (iii) District Planning Board at district level. Decentralised planning system have been introduced from the taluka level onward which has been identified as efficient model of local level planning and development.

RESEARCH PROBLEM AND GENERAL INFORMATION

Coverage

Within this brief historical background we will explain a set of village studies undertaken by the probationary officers of the Indian Administrative Service (IAS: 1983–1993 Batch), during their training at Lal Bahadur Shastri National Academy of Administration, Mussoorie. In total 39 village studies were undertaken which has covered 13 out of 19 districts of the state. These villages are distributed in all the five well known regions of Gujarat state. Details of the district wise villages are given in Table 5.1.

Objectives

These village studies were undertaken to understand the grassroot realities. It also sought to understand the prevailing socio-economic relationship. Special emphasis was, however, on understanding the state government's initiatives in the field of rural development.

Table 5.1 : Distribution of Villages

	Name of the District	*Name of the Village*	
1.	Kachchh	(a) Nagor, (c) Mota Asambiya, (e) Sumrasar, (g) Moti Rayam.	(b) Raidhanpur, (d) Loriya, (f) Jhura,
2.	Rajkot	(a) Vadla, (c) Vajdi Vad, (e) Lodhika.	(b) Kuvadava, (d) Navagadh,
3.	Junagadh	(a) Bharwala, (c) Sankola.	(b) Ranpur,
4.	Jamnagar	(a) Chela, (c) Danta,	(b) Falla, (d) Chela.
5.	Bhavnagar	(a) Ganeshgadh,	(b) Adhewada.
6.	Surendranagar	(a) Sankali,	(b) Karyani.
7.	Sabarkantha	(a) Matoda, (c) Dodivada.	(b) Derol,
8.	Panchmahal	(a) Paravadi, (c) Kanjari.	(b) Salia,
9.	Kheda	(a) Uttarsand,	(b) Tranja.
10.	Ahmedabad	(a) Transad.	
11.	Vadodara	(a) Timla, (c) Siswa.	(b) Kapuri,
12.	Bharuch	(a) Vavdi, (c) Zadeshwar.	(b) Sisodra,
13.	Valsad	(a) Marla.	

Method of Data Collection

1. Village level informations have been collected from Talati and Panchayat Office, District Census Handbook and various reports. It has helped them to prepare a detailed village profile.
2. In a limited number of cases a sort of primary survey was conducted. However, no systematic process was followed for sampling and data collection.

The entire exercise used a holistic approach mainly to

identify various components of rural socio-economic condition. It is also useful to identify problem and prospects of rural development. Informal discussions with officials as well as beneficiaries of various programmes helped to get an insight into planning and implementation of such programmes.

Population

Population growth is directly related to the cultural pattern and norms regarding family. Now, it is also related to the performance of various family planning (FP) programmes. At the district level FP target is set up every year and entire health administration struggle to achieve it. Results of the primary survey indicates that villagers are conscious about population problem. In some cases they themselves are keen to adopt modern techniques of family planning to restrict their number of children. Average number of children per family is about three. In some villages the rate of growth is quite high although people are conscious about FP. It is reported that people want more male child. If one has two sons and one daughter he may opt for FP but if it is reverse the couple will still try for one more son. The sex ratio is also biased in favour of males. This may be due to inadequate care of female children.

In some study villages the growth of population has been at a low rate but not because of low birth rate but primarily due to high rate of migration to the urban areas. In Bhal region, which is traditionally a backward region, seasonal migration is also a very common feature. A large number of people go out in November and return in June. The harsh unfavourable environment act as a push factor for migration.

Education

Educational facility in the form of primary schools are available in all the study villages and there is hardly any regional differences. However, literacy rate is not uniform and developed districts have higher literacy. General information regarding enrolment and dropouts are given only in few cases. But it is clear that enrolment rate is increasing in all the villages. Enrolment from the harijan households is also increasing. In Vadla and Lodhika of Rajkot district, it is reported that there are not many dropouts. But in Kapuri of the same district, it is noted that after completing primary education less than half continue in secondary level as there is no secondary school. It is more in case of girls. It is observed that rate of enrolment is not encouraging as far as harijans are concerned. It is also found that girls are particularly kept from going to the school as they are supposed to be helping hands in household chores and in looking after their younger siblings. Although there is hardly any cultural interaction, in the school the harijan children are not discriminated against and they mix freely with others.

In Uttarsanda of Kheda district it is found that in the primary school, attendance is more due to the Mid-day Meal Scheme. It is also observed that percentage of dropout and rate of failure is more in case of harijan students, than in the case of general category students. The rate of failure is more in class I and II in primary school and in Matric level of high school. In Sankli of Surendranagar, children of school going age who have dropped out due to non-availability of facility of further education in the village spend their time by doing household work and playing.

Literacy rate is growing in all the sample villages but the rate of growth is not uniform. In Kheda, some villages have achieved 95 per cent literacy, which may be a record in the entire state. Female literacy rate is much lower than the males, but due to literacy compaign the gap between male and female literacy has reduced to a great extent. However, this trend is observed only upto primary education. Sex ratio also varies from village to village but it is low in areas marked by high rate of out-migration. Sex ratio is much better in tribal dominated areas. Family size is decreasing in all the study villages and it is related to division of traditional joint family system. A sort of urban influence is mainly responsible for smaller family. Some researchers have observed that family size is more among upper caste and rich farmers in comparison to other socio-economic groups. It probably has a direct relation with asset and control over power structure as joint family reduces the chances of sub-division of asset and division within the community.

Major problems identified are:

(i) Enrolment rate among backward caste is not very satisfactory and no one is taking initiative to convince these households to send their children to school. Panchayat and other local level organizations can play an important role to ensure better enrolment while giving emphasis on girls.

(ii) Dropout rate is more in the beginning and at the end of primary education. This is so because in many villages facility for secondary education is not available. In some cases girls are not attending secondary classes because of distance and partly because of perception against women's education.

(iii) Mid-day Meal Scheme is acting as an incentive for better attendance. It is important as more children from economically backward sections are attending school to get some food. It also helps to reduce the problem of malnutrition among the school going children.

(iv) Facilities in the schools is adequate but quality of education is not explained properly. In some other studies researchers have raised questions regarding teaching quality and appropriate teaching method. It is a very important issue as enrolment and dropout is directly related to these factors.

(v) Liteacy rate has been increasing since 1961 but female literacy rate was much less than males till 1991. Literacy campaign in some districts has resulted in rapid increase from 1991 and the gap between male and female is reducing.

Prohibition

Upto 1994 Gujarat was the only state which prohibited sale, consumption, storage of any kind of intoxicant without permission or license. The effect is both positive and negative. The negative effect is illicit brewing of liquor which frequently results in the death tolls, locally known as *"Latha Kaand"*. (So, old addicts continue to drink whatever available in the nearby places). Prohibition has failed to have positive effect on economic condition of the labouring class. In fact women folk of the labour class complained that instead of saving on the surplus income men tended to use it up for drinking. These people are also forced to save as most of them become ill frequently and have to spend on medical assistance.

But in some villages like Bharwala of Junagadh districts prohibition has been fairly successful as most of the villagers are disciples of *"Parab Vavdi Guru"* a sect which among other things preaches prohibition. However, there is a very small number of addicts who buy liquor from the nearby village. Encountered with such grim reality one tends to feel that the law of prohibition has been reduced to a tragic farce. Villagers in some places alleged that the distillation of illicit liquor takes place with the collusion of the police. It appears that in the absence social education, prohibition will not have any positive impact on physical and economic well being of the people in rural Gujarat.

Social Habits

Television has become the major source of recreation and all the rich families own T.V sets. However, there are very few sets in Harijan and Tribal colonies. For those who do not posses T.V. sets it is common to watch it at a neighbours place on holidays and Sundays even children are totally mesmerised by the fascination of some popular T.V. serials.

In Kachchh villages people possess an extraordinary artistic sense, as evidence by the interior decoration of their houses and the paintings drawn on the walls of their houses. The clay work done by Rabaries on the walls decorated with design worked in clay and studded with tiny mirror pieces, show the innate artistic taste of this nomadic community. Walls are also decorated with photographs and pictures of gods and goddesses. The arrangement of wooden chests called *"patras"*, household utensils and other belongings in one of the interior rooms of the house are quite attractive and pleasing.

Children take part in modern sports like volley ball, street cricket besides traditional games like hide and seek, kabaddi, kho-kho, etc. Girls play various games which include dancing garbas, etc. Adults are fond of playing cards other than the ritual dancing Garba at the time of Navratri. Spending time in village square and discussing various socio-cultural issues is a part of social habit.

SOCIAL STRUCTURE AND SETTLEMENT

Social structure of the rural society usually explained in terms of social stratification which is caste based. Social stratification is also based on the principle of superiority and inferiority even in case of economic critieria like landholding. Many studies of rural development have clearly shown that benefits of development programmes goes to dominant caste, who have direct or indirect influence on decision making (Hirway, 1986). Social strucutre or the caste system can also be explained through settlement pattern, housing and infrastructure facilities.

Caste and Settlement

Settlement pattern in the study villages is caste based, *i.e.* Dabar Falia, Harijan Vasti, Vagharis Vasti, etc. Village Banjaras and migrants have their houses outside the main gramtal. Houses in hamlets are both temporary and permanent depending upon the financial condition of the residents. It is evident that economically dominant castes like Patels, Darbars live in pucca houses. It is also reported that facilities and amenities available in high caste areas are more than areas predominantly occupied by the lower caste families. Although the villages are electrified, low caste households use oil lamps or kerosene lanterns. It is happening as the cost of installing a metre and a point cost about Rs. 350, which is beyond the means of these people. In some districts electric connections have been provided under the *"Kutir Jyoti"* scheme.

In many villages Harijans live outside the main gramtal and are totally separated. Though the village in general is a continuous one and there is no formal division of settlements of other Hindus and Harijans, there is no intermixing of other Hindus' and Harijans' households within a single hamlet. In all the village study reports it is mentioned that Harijans are educationally, socially and economically backward and they are held in low esteem by the upper caste/class and have a paternalistic attitude towards them.

Members of the scheduled caste and tribes are not overtly treated as untouchables but they are discriminated against in very subtle manner. Higher caste usually say that they do not stop the harijans from entering temples but harijans themselves do not like to venture into these temples. Studies of different villages show that political independence and recent legislations are not enough to eradicate discrimination.

Housing

Housing condition varies from one geographical region to another and is directly related to caste, economic condition and local material. Villages in Panchmahal district, known as backward tribal district, most of the houses are *'kutcha'* built by the owners with the help of family members or relatives. In a normal house kitchen is in quite interior and no proper ventilation is provided. Walls are usually of mud and in the absence of adequate ventilation it looks rooms are dark. Roof is made of *'Naliya'* available in the local market. Trees available in the village or in nearby forest are also used extensively for rafters. In front of each house there is one big verandah which is used for sitting and meeting outsiders. As they build houses on their own land houses are spread over wide areas. Because of this a particular form of settlement exist which is totally different from villages in Central Gujarat, Saurashtra and South Gujarat. Some house were build under HUDCO's loan scheme for landless tribals. However, these houses are completely different from the traditional one. As a result they are not occupied by the beneficiaries.

Villages in Kachchh district reported to have both kutcha and pucca houses, kutcha houses are have mud walls covered with thatch or leaves. The pucca houses are built of stones and tiles. Many poor families also live in huts which is semi-permanent. Pucca houses are owned by upper caste families. Many harijans have been benefitted under *"Sau Chauras Vaar"* housing scheme. Few houses were built under IAY but these houses have not been occupied by the beneficiaries as they are reluctant on economic and cultural issues.

In Saurashtra villages stone is an important building material since stone quarries supply it cheaply. According to the 1981 Census in Junagadh district about 78 per cent of the houses in rural areas were built of stone as against 15 per cent in the state as a whole. As regards roofing material, 93 per cent of the dwellings have tiled roof which is either country tiles or Mangalore type. Flooring is done by earth covered with cow dung emulsion which is believed to possess certain antiseptic properties. It also help to keep the house cool during summer months.

There is no class based organization at the village level. This along with the settlement pattern has strengthened caste sentiments. Traditionally Patels, Brahmins and Kshatriyas controlling power in the village. With the introduction of Panchayati Raj low and middle castes started challenging the authority of high castes. In several villages they were elected in larger number than in the past, but only at few places they became Sarpanch. The party politics do operate at times but caste politics are more prominent. Most of the Sarpanchs and other panchayat leaders have party affiliation at the district level which determine the planning and implementation of various schemes. It is also used to get more benefit for the village. A Sarpanch having a greater clout is able to more allocations for his village.

Infrastructure

Water supply for drinking and domestic purposes is fairly good in the study villages. Bore wells and hand pumps are the two major sources. Overhead water tanks have been constructed by using funds under different schemes and villagers pay a small amount for water supply. Distribution network within the gramtal is not uniform and usually not available in Harijan hamlet. The approach roads suffer from similar problems. Funds are used for main approach road which usually cover the high caste areas. The sanitary conditions are not satisfactory as there is no internal drainage. Normally roads are used as drainage and it remain flooded during monsoon. In general it is observed that facilities and amenities available to high castes are relatively more than the same to low caste.

The situation is totally different in the tribal dominated villages. The case study of Timla in Chhota-Udepur taluka of Vadodara district can be used as best example. It is a tribal dominated village and located 27 km. away from taluka headquarters. The village is not directly connected by State Transport services and the nearest bus stand is 3 km. away. The village is deprived of most of the basic amenities. Electricity is available only to a small part of village, there is no water supply and other facilities are available only at a distance of 6 kms. The village is an ideal sample of a very backward village of the tribal area of Vadodara district.

Major Issues

1. As the social structure is caste based village settlement is also divided along the caste grouping. It is observed that higher caste groups live very close to the central part of the settlement where most of the village level facilities are available. Harijan and others are living away from the central part or outside the main settlement. They have no facilities like approach road, drinking water and electricity, etc. The situation is completely different in tribal dominated villages where settlement is smaller in size but not divided on the line of social background.
2. Caste based settlement structure has affected the implementation of some rural development schemes. Fund available for the entire village is used only for selected

areas and usually harijan settlements are neglected. This is also directly related to the village power structure which is normally dominated by the high caste groups. In some cases funds marked for harijan vas is actually utilized in areas where dominant castes are live.

3. Housing schemes like IAY and others have strengthened the caste based settlement. As these programmes are exclusively meant for SCs and STs, houses are constructed outside the main settlement, which goes against the principle of social integration. As government vested land is used for these housing schemes they are not suitable to be used for housing. There seems to an urgent need to have a mixed settlement pattern where all caste groups will be able to share common facilities. So caste based settlement and housing has been strengthened due to implementation of various government sponsored housing schemes in the absence of class based organization at the village level.
4. Diversity in house-form is observed along with regional character. The variation is from kutcha mud houses to pucca houses made of cement-concrete, linear as well as cluster form. In all these villages upper caste like Patels and Brahmins own better houses. These castes also having bigger houses where people living per room is very limited in compare to lower castes.
5. Party politics do operate at times but caste politics are more prominant. All the Sarpanchs belong to higher caste and they have party affiliation at the Taluka and District level. With the introduction of the Panchayati Raj some middle castes started challenging the authority of dominant caste but failed to acquire local leadership.

ECONOMIC ACTIVITIES AND AGRARIAN RELATION

Occupational Structure

Agriculture, horticulture and cattle rearing are the main income generating activities. In general it shows that about 85 per cent of the total households practice agriculture as the main occupation. There are few families whose main occupation is Animal Husbandry and they belong to the Bharvad caste. However, a good number of Bharvads have given up their traditional occupation. It is also true for other non- agricultural occupation like weaving, etc. In most of the sample villages there is hardly any activity worth mentioning in the secondary sector and very few are engaged in tertiary sector. Within the tertiary sector, service is the most important occupation in comparison to trade and business.

Secondary sector activities are limited only among 5 per cent of the total households. These households are mainly engaged in rural artisan work like carpentry, pottery, tailoring and weaving. A large number of households following traditional occupations like animal husbandry have left due to diminishing pasture land. Similarly, Vagris have been forced to give up cultivation and are becoming agricultural labourers. Another important feature is the large number of persons have their main occupation as tenant. This is due to the fact that some landed and landless people are share cropping.

Researchers have used several methods and framework to understand the rural society but these are based either on caste or class theory of stratification. Some researchers have also used "power" which controls the decision making at the local level. In the present context landholding and Panchayati Raj has been used to explain the village power structure and the agrarian relation. In all the sample villages a large number of households are landless and usually belong to lower caste. Patels are the main landholding community and also control the village panchayat and other local bodies. Among the landholding households there is inequality. In some villages only one community own more than half of agricultural land. Some communities like Bharvad, Suthar, Vaghris are usually landless and constitute the lowest strata of rural Gujarat. They have their traditional occupation but there is not enough scope of work due to several reasons.

Landholding

There is disparity in the ownership of land. Chela in Jamnagar is well documented which represent both the land system and landholding pattern in Saurashtra which was divided into many princely states. After independence several land reforms acts were enacted which gave right of ownership to the cultivators and tenants. In brief, the land reforms were implemented successfully in a very short span of four years. However, tenants were middle peasants and lower castes like Harijans position remained unchanged. In the new situation while the middle peasantry grew in importance and prosperity, especially with large schemes for promoting agriculture and rural infrastructure, the real poor and lower castes made little progress.

Primary survey in Chela shows that as many as 60 per cent of the families are landless. Amongst the 40 per cent who own land 80 per cent are big farmers who constitute only 9 per cent of the total households. The Mahajan caste alone own 1800 acres of land which is about 55 per cent of the entire land. Harijans also have a small share. The land was granted to Harijans by the government under land distribution programme to weaker section and some of them have been able to purchase plots from the migrant landowners.

In Central Gujarat, which was under the British rule, *Ryotwari system* was prevalent. "Village Transad of Ahmedabad District land is mainly held by caste hindus such as the Patels. Scheduled caste farmers consist of Vankars and Bhangis who possess very little land. These households are predominantly agricultural labourers working for rich farmers. Similar situation is also reported in Bharuch, Vadodara and other districts. All these cases simply show that land is still used as the main asset to consolidate the power of higher castes at the village level. It also indicates that even after the implementation of several laws, lower castes are usually land-poor and dependent upon upper caste for their employment".

Irrigation

Except in some parts of South Gujarat ground water is the main source of irrigation. Irrigation from the wells is the common practice. But all these wells are under private ownership. In Chela of Jamnagar district and also in many villages all over the state these wells are owned by the high caste and big farmers. Their wells are also pucca and equipped with pump sets, mostly electric motor or submersible pumps. This has resulted in the dependence of small and marginal farmers upon the big farmers for the use of well water, which is natural resource. In certain areas a farmer has to share his produce with the well owners, share is between 25 per cent to 35 per cent of the total output.

In Panchmahal, irrigation is the biggest problem for the entire region. Rains are the only hope for agricultural activities. There are neither perennial rivers, nor any irrigation project to augment water supply. The underground water level is declining and water problem becomes acute during the summer months in all the three study villages of Paravadi, Salia and Kanjari. Villagers desperately want irrigation facility for increasing the production and productivity. Lack of irrigation facility also results in large scale migration to cities for work either during lean season or for the whole year.

Irrigation facility can be increased, as lot of scope exists for it. People generally complain about the apathy of the government. They feel that farmers should get subsidy to deeper the existing wells. Then there is also a demand regarding deep bore well through which an area of 50 to 100 acres can be irrigated. If water is available then they can cultivate crops like wheat, maize, chana and vegetables, etc. So, to get more crops in winter, minor irrigation through well is the only answer for this region. In case of Ganeshgadh of Bhavnagar, which is in the Bhal region, no fresh water source is available. Even wells have only saline water. For irrigation purpose farmers have to depend exclusively on monsoon which itself is highly erratic and scanty. Two creeks exist very near to the village further worsening the already high level of salinity and alkalinity of the soil. Due to these reasons land has not been in much demand for agriculture. Similar situation exist in Kachchh villages. The first question which a Kachchhi living outside ask another one meeting, "How are the rains, this year?".

Agriculture and Cropping Pattern

In Central and South Gujarat villages, paddy and sugarcane are grown as rainfall is quite high and are also covered under several irrigation projects. These crops are not cultivated in North Gujarat, Saurashtra and Kachchh as farmers are dependent upon rainfall and wells for irrigating their field. Cropping pattern is also directly related to the quality of soil and rainfall. The South and Central Gujarat villages are more developed, irrigation facilities are available and mechanised implements are used. Chemical fertilizer like DAP and Urea are used in large quantity. It is normally bought from the outlets of co-operative society at the village level.

Normally farmers keep a reserve stock of the produce and use it for sowing in the next season. They also buy seeds from co-operatives, which supply improved variety. A very small number of farmers procure seeds from private agents. Introduction of improved and high yield varieties have increased the food crop as well as cash crop production in all the sample villages and there is hardly any regional differences.

Cropping pattern is changing all over the state because of changes in policy and development of infrastructure. In Panchmahal villages Maize and Jawar were the two important crops. Now farmers have started cultivating Paddy, Groundnut, etc., due to pricing mechanism and government encouragement. Improved implements such as iron plough, tractors and mechanical devices have become popular in this region due to government promotion. Similar results are also reported from Kachchh and Saurashtra villages. It indicates that villagers are struggling to survive by changing agricultural practices with active encouragement from the state government. It also indicates a very clear shift towards cash crops by using whatever irrigation facility available.

Agricultural operations are carried on both by family and hired labour. In case of hired labour wages are paid both in cash and kind. Daily wage labourers are paid upto maximum of Rs. 30 per day. In the normal situation labourers are paid less than the prescribed minimum wage of Rs. 32. Some labourers also work on annual contract usually known as *"Naukarnams"* and paid upto Rs. 3000 and also get food, shelter and pair of clothes. But nowhere people engaged as agriculture labourer are employed throughout the year. In Kachchh and North Gujarat it is less than 100 days a year while it is less than six months in remaining areas except in districts like Kheda and Surat. During the lean season labourers also engage in animal husbandry and homebased activities. Panchmahal village studies show that farmers cultivate their own land without hiring any labour. It also indicates that hiring of wage labourer is directly related to irrigation facility, intensity of cropping and overall level of development of that particular region.

Livestock

Cattle rearing is a subsidiary occupation in all the villages. Almost every family keeps cattle. The stock of existing livestock is directly related to pasture land availability which is usually owned by the government. These plots are under the control and maintenance of the village panchayat. People buy fodder in scarcity conditions but in normal situation leave them into open field for grazing. In drought prone areas cattle rearing is more prevalent due to limited agricultural activities. Milk production varies from place to place and is related to the type of cattle. Average milk yield per cow and buffalo varies from 4 to 18 litres in Loria, Sumarsar and Jhura of Kachchh district. Sankar, Kankrej and Thani breeds of cows and Sindhi breed of buffaloes are common in these villages. Villagers breed their own cattle and few purchase cattle from Banni of Bhuj. Price of a buffalo ranges from Rs. 3000 to 20,000 while that of a cow from Rs. 2000 to 6000.

In Junagadh district average milk yield is less in comparison to Kachchh. Milk yield of a cow is only about 3 litre and 5 litre in case of buffaloes. Here villagers buy their cattle from the weekly cattle market. The main cattle diseases are *'Kharva Mova'* and *'Gharsunda'*. In Kharva Mova, feet and mouth of cattle is infected and it required three to four months of treatment. Gharsunda is, however, a fatal disease in which the cattle has difficulty in breathing. Veterinary services are available and people are totally dependent on it.

In Panchmahal villages health standard of cattle is poor and result in low yield. Normally cows and buffaloes give two to three litres of milk per day. Cattles are affected by diseases like *"Zherbaj"*, *"Chakri"* and *"Ghadhsuntha"*. Veterinary facilities are available only in taluka headquarter. In Bharuch the present condition of cattle can at least be described as mediocre. The main reason is that farmers have not yet taken enough initiative to improve the quality of breed. Cross breeding centres are working in some villages but their performance is not very satisfactory as the coverage is less than 10 per cent.

Livestock ownership is an important issue and next only to land ownership. Primary data regarding ownership shows a positive co-relation between landholding and livestock ownership. It is also related to caste as reported in Chela of Jamnagar district. It is observed that some castes are traditionally engaged in livestock related activities and there is a need to introduce special programme for them.

Village Industries

In Kachchh villages non-agricultural activities in the form of village industry is very popular. Villages are known for handicrafts, tying and dyeing, embroidery work on cloth as well as leather, gold and silverware. Other crafts which deserve mention are making of blankets, lacquerware, clay toys and ivory work. Kachchhi works are known since long for its superior designs and exquisite workmanship. A lot of families earn their livelihood from crafts and cottage industries. Ahirs and Rabaries are famous for embroidery work. Normally women are engaged in these activities for 3-4 hours a day. People buy the raw material from Bhuj town and sell it either to private traders or to Handloom Corporation. But corporation has not been able to attract many households as they do not supply raw material at the village level. If corporation were to change its present policy and practice for wider coverage people engaged in these activities will definitely get more economic benefit.

In case of villages in Panchmahal district there is very limited scope for village industries. In the absence of non-agricultural activities people are totally dependent upon agriculture and livestock related activities. In Bharuch district there is hardly any industrial activity. Only a small number of women are engaged in spice grinding work. The spice powder is marketed through a co-operative. In Sankali of Surendranagar district there were weavers and kumbhars engaged in traditional non-agricultural activities. Now weavers have stopped weaving and kumbhars are engaged only when there is no agricultural work. Now all of them have become agricultural labourers. In Ganeshgadh of Bhavnagar district people are engaged in diamond polishing activity. A small number of beneficiaries of IRDP have also purchased these machines and work from home. Only in Vajdivad of Rajkot district are there formal industrial activities as the GIDC estate is situated in this area.

Major issues are :

(i) Traditional non-agricultural activities like weaving, pot making, basket making, etc., are becoming less popular because of several reasons.

(ii) Lack of non-agricultural activities resulted in increasing the pressure on land.

(iii) Role of co-operatives are very limited and private traders dominate the market. However, co-operatives can play a better role to encourage people in non-agricultural activities.

(iv) Special attention is to be given for the women engaged in home based activities and co-operatives can play an important role here.

GOVERNMENT PROGRAMMES

Development Administration

Administrative arrangement for the implementation of the IRDP is very different in Gujarat as compared to other states of India.

While in other states the Collector is the Chairman of DRDA, in Gujarat the Chief Executive of the Zila Panchayat, DDO is the Chairman. The DRDA is not under Zila Panchayats but the DDO is always under pressure from the panchayat members. The governing body of the DRDA also has a large number of politicians who bring considerable pressure on the DDO or the project director of DRDA. At the taluka level both executive and elected wings come together for planning and development.

Achievement of a target is an important measure of success not only for programmes but also for the staff that implement the programmes. Starting from the DDO to the VLWS all are keen to see that targets are achieved. Consequently there is more attention on target achievement than on helping the rural poor. All the DDOs and TDOs admitted that rural development programmes are basically target oriented and that they struggle hard to achieve them.

At the district level, the target for IRDP come from the state depending upon thc number of talukas/blocks. Talukawise allocation is not rigid and capable talukas are given higher targets and these are frequently revised in the meeting of the TDOs called by the DDO. The targets are revised as many as three or four times. The targets depend upon the taluka, the power and capability of the TDO, co-operation from the politicians, etc. Though it is usually believed that backward talukas should get a preference over others, in reality this is not done so. Sectorwise targets are never determined as there is no need. Information from the sample villages shows that there is a clear shift from agriculture and animal husbandry to ISB. It is happening as among other reason there are fewer procedural requirements. In case of agriculture or animal husbandry it involve other experts which is time consuming and target achievement is delayed.

The distribution of taluka target is not done according to any specific procedure. It is usually under the jurisdiction of the VLWS. However, at the taluka level targets are distributed for different groups of villages jointly by the TDO, extension officer of IRDP and VLWS. Some of the considerations kept in mind while fixing these targets are:

(i) Past performance of the village,

(ii) Infrastructure facilities in the village including approach road and the access of the village,
(iii) Availability of banks and other credit facilities,
(iv) Progressiveness of the people.

In short, it appears that targets are fixed in such a way that administration is able to tap the potential beneficiaries.

Attitude of the administrators can be explained in terms of their understanding of the problems of rural poor. It is observed that a majority believed that poor who are generally interested in improving their lot can always do so as large number of government programmes are designed to help them. Only thing these poor have to do is to approach the administrators. A small section, however, feel that poor are not seriously interested and there is no way to help them.

The third view is that the real poor can never get any significant benefit from the government programmes. The rural poor are a helpless lot at the lowest rung of society. They are so dependent upon richer sections that they are incapable of doing much for themselves. They will have to be helped out by some outside agencies. Unfortunately, there is no such agency and rural rich will not do anything that will go against their own established power. The administrators are also a part of the system in the sense that they are also trapped in the power structure and cannot afford to annoy the rural rich. As a result programmes are implemented exactly the way the rich want it.

Another factor that influences the mode of implementation is the influence of the Sarpanch and other village leaders. The VLWS, Talati and other staff accept the influence of local leaders not only because it does not clash with their objective of target achievement, but also because they cannot afford to displease the village leaders. Even higher level administrators are not free from their influence, exerted normally through taluka or zila panchayat leaders. This is reflected in the management of the development administration.

The role of the bank credit in meeting the credit requirements has been expanding over the years. Banks are expected to play an active role in rural development policies regarding their location and credits are formulated to meet this goal. A lead bank is fixed for every district to meet the credit requirements of the area. The lead bank is also expected to adopt a few villages in the district to do intensive work for eradication of poverty. To coordinate the functioning of banks and development administration District Level Consultancy Committees have been set up in all the district of Gujarat. But these committees have not done much in terms of bringing about desired coordination. Banks are following a cautious approach for lending and resulted in limited lending to the weaker sections.

There is also a tendency to lend for big items like oil engines, electric pumps, wells, etc., to a limited number of people to make the lending safe and also help them in showing high achievements. Banks always demand a guarantee or security though on paper they are told that they may not ask for it. Mutual or group guarantees are not accepted. Thus, unless a poor give guarantee he cannot even apply for a bank loan. An indebted person is never be considered for a bank loan. However, such a restriction is not necessary according to programme guidelines. Bankers also ask for recommendation or confirmation from the village leaders regarding honesty and repayment capacity of the borrowers before sanctioning loan to them. Studies revealed that villages are selected on the basis of their accessibility, for easy follow up, and relative prosperity of the people. Banks are also under pressure to sanction loan as directed by local leaders like MPs, MLAs and panchayat members.

Panchayat

Panchayat in Gujarat is quite powerful. In 1961 the Panchayat Act was passed. A number of functions were transferred including collection of land revenue. Sarpanch as the head of gram panchayat is directly elected and play a very important role. The Upa Sarpanch is elected by the members of the gram panchayat among themselves. To ensure participation of women and weaker section seats are reserved for women and scheduled caste and tribes. Talati, village level revenue official act as *Mantri* (Secretary).

Taluka Panchayat and Zila Parishad are not directly associated with implementation of the programmes like IRDP. It is the Gram Panhayat which plays the most important role. The panchayat is associated with these programmes in a number of ways. Sarpanch's signature is essential for various documents, he is expected to take initiativé for bringing new schemes to the village, to propagate them, and help VLWS in implementing them. The Sarpanch also influences beneficiary selection in a number of ways.

The Sarpanchs do not have clear understanding about the real constraints of the poor as they are preoccupied with their own interest. Through the panchayat a new elite group has emerged at the village level and use the panchayat to consolidate their power base. There is greater likelihood of the benefit flowing into the hands of non-poor and excluding the poor. As a result of all this some people have received benefit twice or thrice under the IRDP. It also indicates that benefit do not reach the persons for whom it is meant. Beneficiaries are also not very happy about assets provided to them. Sometimes, mainly in case of bullocks and buffaloes, assets are not worth of combined value of loan plus subsidy and results in paying more than the price of the assets by way of loan plus interest thereon.

Rural Development

In village Kapurai, district Baroda, village panchayat had received Rs. 1,02,000 under JRY. This was spent for digging the village pond and repairing link roads. Beneficiaries of other schemes are aware of various poverty alleviation programmes. In village Uttarsanda, district Kheda, about 326 households have received benefit under IRDP during 1980-89 period. A good number of beneficiaries have also received a second dose of loan and subsidy. The panchayat is particularly active in the JRY and construction of houses for rural poor under HUDCOs loan scheme. Under this housing scheme 57 new houses have been constructed. In Vajdi Vad of Rajkot IRDP has successfully helped the borrowers to earn their daily bread and villagers are grateful to the government. But no Harijan has received any benefit under these programmes.

In Vardi of Bharuch district 78 beneficiaries have received assets under IRDP since 1980. Majority of them, 62 beneficiaries, have received buffaloes but the milk yield is very low. However, they have shown a much higher survival rate than the buffaloes given by Scheduled Tribe Development Corporation in 1978. 45 beneficiaries have acquired assets in the secondary sector and it has helped the beneficiaries in augmenting their income. In comparison to the primary sector, secondary sector activities are more beneficial in this village. Under the TRYSEM, some youths were trained as wiremen and they have managed to improve their economic condition. A group of 15 women were also covered under DWCRA and they have started a unit to produce and sell pickles, papads and spices. In Loria, Sumrasar and Jhura of Kachchh district about 1000 families covered under different rural development programmes and about 50 per cent have received buffaloes. It is reported that the impact of these programmes has been excellent and about 50 per cent have crossed the poverty line. Similar results are also reported for Nagor and Raidhanpur village in the same district.

In Sankali of Surendranagar 20 families have been covered under IRDP. In general about 30 per cent have been able to generate additional income. However, 15 per cent have sold their asset and not paid the loan amount. In Vadla and Lodhika of Rajkot beneficiaries are from the scheduled caste and other poor families. But due to wrong identification of needs resulted in acquiring wrong asset. Loan for ISB is not adequate and hardly able to create assets for the beneficiaries and they remain poor. Similar situation is also observed in Kapuri as the assistance available is not sufficient to alleviate their poverty. The case of Kanjari of Panchmahal also shows the similar trend as beneficiaries failed to buy good quality buffaloes as only Rs. 4500 was available for each unit.

In general these studies reveal that rural poor want only two meals a day without any tension. They want some assurance and regularity of some minimum income which can assure their basic requirements of life. The poor are concerned mainly with generating regular income specially in lean season. Other expectation is to own land and cultivate it. Majority of the villagers expect the government help them in realising their dreams. People are optimistic about the future in the sense that they think they could improve their standard of living. But many families felt that situation will not improve and it may deteriorate. It appeared that high inflation, indebtness, helplessness and lack of faith in present system are the main reasons for these negative feelings.

Implementation of various rural development programmes have been undertaken by officials but people have a negative perception. A majority of people feels that officials are not very active nor helpful to them. The traditional bureaucratic style of functioning is still prevalent and the gap between the people and officials remain in the absence of any active initiative from the officials. As a result of it a large number of rural poor remain poor and non-participant. The case study of Ganeshgadh in Bhavnagar district show that there has been minimal impact of governmental programmes in peoples life primarily because not much work is done under governmental programmes.

MAIN FINDINGS AND CONCLUSIONS

Main Findings

(i) A rural area cannot be developed simply by establishing certain institutions in the hope that they will function optimally. Absence of alternative leadership facilitates monopolistic functioning of all the organizations like Panchayat, Co-operatives, Milk Co-operatives, etc. The paternalistic attitude of development agencies diminishes the sense of responsibility and self-confidence of the people.

(ii) There is disparity in the ownership of land. The skewed land ownership is also caused by the exclusive dependence on livestock by certain castes. In all the villages it is clear that big farmers and high caste own major part of land. Hardly any land in the village is held by the lower castes and small/marginal farmers.

(iii) There is a wide gap between the living conditions of the scheduled castes and affluent castes like Patels, Darbars at the other end. Domination by the high castes in almost every sphere of activity, be it political, economic or social, villages are normally seen in the context of village basically being a village of dominant caste only.

(iv) The skewed landownership pattern has resulted in the dependence of small/marginal farmers on the rich farmers for the irrigation. Small and marginal farmers pay a high price for the use of well water. Small farmers are also restricted to nearby well owners, and thus they are under the control of well owners.

(v) A considerable number of population were engaged in household industries but this sector has declined and most of the families engaged in traditional occupations have shifted to other activities like pretty business, agriculture, etc.

(vi) Development administration which implement schemes under special programmes for rural development tends to reach only a limited number of poor. As importance is given for achieving targets it has created a situation where schemes are implemented on the basis of ad-hoc considerations. There is no systematic approach in implementation, or even attempts to reach all the areas or the needy. It shows that planning component of the special programmes has been extremely weak.

(vii) Sarpanch and village leaders influence the implementation process to a great extent. Local level staff accept these influences as they cannot afford to displease the village leaders.

(viii) Rural development programmes have helped the rural poor to improve their economic condition where they are able to repay the loans regularly.

(ix) In many villages because of wrong identification of needs resulted in acquiring unwanted assets. People have failed to generate more income and in some cases even lost the asset.

(x) Loan amount both for buffaloes and ISB is not adequate to buy good asset. As a result beneficiaries have purchased inferior quality assets and resulted in indebtness.

In two cases SWOT analysis were undertaken to identify future possibilities. Results are given below:

1. Village: Transad, District: Ahmedabad.

Strengths

i. Location near Dholka, a taluka town.
ii. Diversified occupation.
iii. Fairly good health facilities.
iv. Awareness of the people.
v. Relatively better literacy rate.

Weakness

i. Disparities in landholdings and other assets.
ii. Wide social gap between castes.
iii. Absence of specialised economic activity on a large scale.

Opportunities

i. Potential for development of dairy farming.
ii. Specialised agricultural activity.
iii. Articulation of needs of the village by the MLA from Dholka.
iv. Harnessing manpower of the village in some productive activity.

Threats

i. Reaction to communal provocation in nearby places like Dholka.
ii. Vested interest of small group running the affairs of the village.

2. Village: Ganeshgadh, District: Bhavnagar

The village is in Bhal region and the area represent a peculiar situation where harsh geo-climatic conditions determine everything.

Strength

i. Higher ceiling limit and accordingly large holding units extremely favourable for salt manufacturing.
ii. Location near Bhavnagar which has been fast coming up as major diamond cutting centre.

Weakness

i. Harsh climatic condition.
ii. Lack of infrastructure.
iii. People's unwillingness to work as labourer in salt manufacturing.

Opportunities

i. Salt/alkali tolerant crop varieties which are drought resistant can be developed.
ii. Vast potential of salt manufacturing.
iii. Diamond cutting and polishing with the help of DRDA.
iv. With the repair of state highway it will improve communication with nearby urban centres.

Threats

i. Increasing salinity.
ii. Large scale migration.

The SWOT analysis shows that rural development strategy should take care of both the opportunities as well as threats at the regional level. Programmes sponsored by the central government is uniform but still regional opportunities can be used by participation of the target group.

APPENDIX I

	Author	*Village*	*District*
1.*	V. Thiruppugazh	Vajdi Vad	Rajkot
2.*	Arvind Kumar	Ganeshgadh	Bhavnagar
3.*	R.P. Gupta	Sankli	Surendranagar
4.	A.K. Rakesh	Zadeshwar	Bharuch
5.	Mukhesh Puri	Bharwala	Junagadh
6.	Sunayana Tomar	Kapuri	Vadodara
7.	Anita Karwal	Uttarsanda	Kheda
8.*	Sanjan Nandan	Chela	Jamnagar
9.	Manoj Agarwal	Sankrola	Junagadh
10.*	Syed Jawaid Haider	Timla	Vadodara
11.	Anju Singhal	Danta	Jamnagar
12.	A.V.K. Mall	Siswa	Vadodara
13.	J.P. Gupta	Sisodra	Bharuch
14.*	Jayanti Srinivasan	Transad	Ahmedabad
15.	S. Katikithala	Ranpur	Junagadh
16.	M.C. Nayak	Falla	Jamnagar
17.	Raj Gopal	Vavdi	Bharuch
18.	Jayant Parimal	Kanjari	Panchmahal
19.	A.K. Sharma	Salia	Panchmahal
20.*	Arun Solanki	Paravadi	Panchmahal
21.*	Pankaj Joshi	Loria	Kachchh Sumrasar Jhura
22.	Raj Kumar Mota	Asambiya	Kachchh
23.	Kamal Dayani	Nagor	Kachchh Raidhanpur
24.*	L. Chuaungo	Kuvadava	Rajkot
25.*	Vidyut B Swain	Vadla	Rajkot Ldhika
26.	G.P. Mahapatra	Karyani	Surendranagar
27.	Pankaj Kumar	Marla	Valsad
28.	I.P. Gautam	Aethewada	Bhavnagar
29.	Balaram Dikshit	Navagadh	Rajkot
30.	Sanjay Prasad	Tranja	Kheda
31.	Vipul Mitra Moti	Rayan	Kachchh
32.	Rajiv K. Gupta	Matoda	Sabarkanta Deyol Dodivada
33.	P.D. Vaghela	Chela	Jamnagar

* These reports are used extensively.

REFERENCES

Bhatt, Anil., (1970), *Caste and Political Mobilisation in Gujarat District,* in Rajni Kothari (ed.), Caste and Indian Politics, Delhi, Orient Longman.

Breman, Jan., (1974), *Patronage and Exploitation : Changing Agrarian Relations in South Gujarat,* India, London, University of California.

Breman, Jan., (1985), Of Peasant, Migration and Paupers : Rural Labour Circulation and Capitalist Production in Western India, Delhi, Oxford University Press.

Desai, M.B., (1971), *Tenancy Abolition and Emerging Pattern in Gujarat,* Baroda, M.S. University.

Dholakia, R.H.; and S. Iyengar., (1988), *Planning for Rural Development : Issues and Case Studies,* Bombay, Himalaya.

Dreze, J.P., (1990), "Poverty in India and IRDP Delusion", *EPW,* Vol 25 (39), pp. A95-A104.

Hirway, Indira., (1986), *Abolition of Poverty in India with Special Reference* to Target Group Approach in Gujarat, New Delhi, Vikas.

Hirway, Indira, (1986A), Wage Employment Programmes in Rural Development : *A Study of NREP in Gujarat,* New Delhi, Oxford and IBH.

Jain, S.C., (1983), *Impact of IRD,* Bardoli Taluka (Gujarat), South Gujarat University, Surat.

Jain, S.C., (1983), Impact of IRD, Uchchal Taluka, Surat (Gujarat), South Gujarat University, Surat.

Mehta, Dinesh., (1989), *Decentralised Planning in India : A Case Study of Ahmedabad in Gujarat State,* AIT, Bangkok.

Murthy, G.V.S.N., (1978), *"A Note on Poverty in Gujarat : 1977-78 to 1978-88",* Ahmedabad, SPIESR.

Pathak, D.N., *et al.,* Non dated, *"Dimension of Political Behaviour in Gujarat",* (Mimeo), Ahmedabad, Gujarat University.

Rao, V.M., (1987), "Changing Village Structure : Impact of Rural Development Programmes", *EPW,* Vol.22 (13), pp. A2-A5.

Ray, C.N., (1994), *Politics of Rural Development : The Case of Anti-poverty Programmes in West Bengal and Gujarat, Jaipur,* Rawat Publications.

Shah, Ganshyam., (1975), *Caste Association and Political Process in Gujarat,* Bombay, Popular Pub.

Shah, Ganshyam., (nd.), *Socio-economic Stratification of Politics in Rural Gujarat,* Paper presented in a Seminar, Ahmedabad, SPISER.

6

MAHARASHTRA

Harsh Mander and Ajay Sinha

Maharashtra : A State of Contrasts

The popular description of India as land of contrasts has special relevance to the state of Maharashtra, which paradoxically combines prodigious industrial development with agricultural stagnation, and the country's greatest urban wealth with pockets of abyssmal rural poverty. This paper attempts to utilise micro-village studies of Maharashtra prepared over several years by officer trainees of the Indian Administrative Service, to construct a small mosaic conditions in the Maharashtrian rural hinterland.

Contours of Geographical Boundary

The state of Maharashtra came into being on May, 1960 carved out of the much larger state of Bombay. The new political entity was formed on linguistic grounds, of regions dominated by Marathi speaking people, in contrast to the older province which also included Gujarati speaking areas. Geographically, the state of Maharashtra stretches east-west about 800 km and north-south 700 km, from Bombay to Gadchiroli and Dhule to Sindhudurg districts. It is situated in the western part of the Indian sub-continent, with a long narrow coastal strip of 8720 kms, stretching from Daman to Trekhol Creek and washed by the Arabian Sea. Running roughly parallel to this coast-line are the Sahyadris, popularly known as the Western Ghats.

Physiographic Divisions

The state can be divided into two major physiographic divisions, namely the coastal region known as the Konkan area and the Deccan plateau, built up mainly of nearly horizontal volcanic lava flows, described as the Deccan trap. The Deccan plateau has been carved out into three major river basins *viz.,* the Godavari, the Krishna and the Tapti basin. The Godavari basin comprises the Godavari basin proper and the Wainganga sub-basin. Its major tributaries are the Purna, Pravara, Sindphana and Manjra. The Krishna basin is divided into Krishna basin proper and the Bhima sub-basin. The Tapti basin has been carved out in the northern extremity of the Deccan plateau. The state falls into four broad regions : Vidharbha in East Maharashtra; Desh in the central plateau of the Deccan lying east of the Sahyadris; Marathwada; and Konkan, a narrow coastal strip west of the Sahyadris. A large part of the Deccan plateau falls in the rain shadow area, and is therefore chronically drought prone, whereas the other two areas, Marathwada and Konkan, benefit from high and assured rainfall.

Demographic Structure

Maharashtra is the third largest state in the country, both in terms of size and population. According to the 1991 census, its population is 84.63 crores, spread out over 307,607 square kilometers. The average density of population of 257 persons per square kilometers compares roughly with the national average of 267. However, there are sharp variations within the state from 13664 in Greater Bombay to only 41 in Gadchiroli (1981 Census). The population growth rate in the state during the 1981-91 decade was 25.73 per cent which was higher than that of India (23.51%). It was also higher as compared to that during the earlier decade, *i.e.* 1971-81 (24.54%) for the state. The proportion of urban population has been continuously increasing in the last three decades. It increased from 28.2 per cent in 1961 to 31.2 per cent in 1971 and from 35.0 per cent in 1981 to 38.7 per cent in 1991. The number of cities and towns also increased from 307 in 1981 to 336 in 1991. According to 1991 population census the rural population of the state was 61.3 per cent which was significantly lower than that of India (74.3%). During 1981-91 decade, the rural population of the state increased by 18.6 per cent to 4.84 crore. This growth rate in Maharashtra was less than that of India (19.7%).

The growth rate of rural population in the state in 1981-91 decade was slightly higher than that in earlier decade of 1971-81. The number of villages in the state increased from 41,833 in 1981 to 43,020 in 1991. The scheduled caste and the scheduled tribes population of Maharashtra as per 1991 population census were 87.6 lakhs and 73.2 lakhs respectively. They formed 11.1 per cent and 9.3 per cent respectively of the total population of the state in 1991. These proportions for all India figure were 16.3 per cent and 8.0 per cent respectively.

Industrial Development

Maharashtra is the leading industrial state in the country, with most of its industrial wealth concentrated in and around its cosmopolitan capital Bombay. Bombay's economy received a big thrust with the opening of the Suez Canal in 1869. Today, Bombay is indisputably the commercial, financial and industrial fulcrum of the country. This small island 22 kms long and 3 km wide contributes 33 per cent of income tax, 60 per cent of customs and 27 per cent of excise revenues of the central government. It accounts for almost 20 per cent of those employed in India's foreign trade. Almost a quarter of the country's industrial value is added in Maharashtra, the overwhelmingly greater part of in Bombay and also the Pune and Thane districts.

It has the largest number of units (15,163 out of 1.02 lakh units in the country) in the factory sector in 1987-88. These units provided on an average daily employment to 12.2 lakh persons in June 1989. Maharashtra also tops all other states in India in the production of minerals, textiles, sugar and other products such as chemicals, machinery, pharmaceutical, electronics equipment, etc. The state per capita income, at Rs. 7,997 is one and a half times the national average of 5,583 (Economic Survey of Maharashtra, 1993-94).

Even though Maharashtra has 9.3 per cent of population and 9.4 per cent of area of India, it boasts of 13.1 per cent of income at current prices. It accounts for 11.2 per cent of factories, 16.9 per cent of factory workers, 15.6 per cent of productive capital, 21.5 per cent of gross value of output and 22.2 per cent of value added by manufacture in the organized sector in India. It has nearly one-third of the joint stock companies and nearly 25 per cent of co-operative societies.

Agricultural Development

However, do all these buoyant and optimistic economic indicators reflect a correct and complete picture of the life and economic status of the Maharashtra's people? To what extent is the mammoth industrial wealth of the state genuinely a symptom of the economic and social well-being of the rural poor of Maharashtra?

The 1987-88 report states that as high as 29.2 per cent of the Maharashtra's population was subsisting below the poverty line. The picture becomes even more dismal when we look at agriculture, the mainstay for 61.27 per cent of the population which lives in the villages. In many standard indices of agricultural productivity, Maharashtra stands near the bottom of the national heap. For instance, against a national average yield of 1,574 kg per hectares for cereals, the figure for Maharashtra is mere 945; for foodgrains, Maharashtra's figure is 839 against a national average of 1,269; and for pulses 497 against 575. Amongst major crops the productivity of only sugarcane is higher than the national average in Maharashtra.

Although the average size of holdings in Maharashtra (2.65 hectares) was higher than the national average (1.68 hectares) in 1985-86, the income generated per hectares of gross cropped area (in 1984-85) was Rs. 3342 as against the all India average of Rs. 4646. The per hectare consumption of fertilisers in 1990-91 was Rs. 66.4 kgs in contrast to the all India average of 72.4 kgs. Despite extensive spread and impact of the co-operative movement, the state lags behind even in the production of milk. The per capita milk production in 1990-91 was 47.5 kgs as against national average of 63.7 kgs.

Sixty one per cent people engaged in agriculture contribute only 22 per cent to the state income, which is far below the national figure of 34 per cent, and is also low in relation to the proportion of the workforce engaged in agriculture.

The state suffers from chronic water scarcity, because poor natural endowments in the Deccan plateau are aggravated by stubbornly unsustainable water use patterns, both in industry and agriculture. In Maharashtra, a mere 11.8 per cent of gross cropped area is irrigated, as against a national average of 32.56 and even this is mostly squandered on highly water intensive crops like sugarcane.

Climatic Condition

The state has tropical climate. There are large variations in the rainfall among the different parts of the state on account of the topography and the distance from the monsoon tract. Maharashtra's average rainfall is 1200 mm. But out of 303 tehsils in the state, over 200 receive more than 750 mm of rainfall and 100 more than 1250 mm. Even the 100-odd tehsils that fall in the rain shadow region and are classified as drought prone get precipitation between 500 mm and 750 mm. This means that barring a handful of taluks, even the drought-prone area get rainfall of amount 500 mm or 20 inches. Regionally speaking, normal rainfall in Konkan is 3030 mm, in Central Maharashtra 950 mm; Marathwada 860 mm; and Vidarbha 1110 mm. The drought prone areas of the state are concentrated in the Pune, Nasik and Aurangabad revenue divisions. Excluding a few tehsils of Buldhana, the whole of Vidarbha is an assured rainfall region, so also the Marathwada districts of Parbhani and Nanded. Ninety-four tehsils of 14 districts were classified as drought-prone. Since the three-year drought of 1971-73, as many as 30,000 villages and settlements in Maharashtra were affected by drinking water famine year after year.

Infrastructural Network

Maharashtra also fares badly in its Infrastructural network, which has a bearing on rural areas. For example, the percentage of villages having a railway station within 5 kms distance in Maharashtra in 1977 was 12.82 as against the national average of 18.34. Hardly 7 per cent of village in Maharashtra came within 2 kms distance from a health centre while the national average was about 12. Only 24 per cent of village in Maharashtra were within 5 kms distance from a hospital as against over 35 village on all-India average. Maharashtra compares poorly even in respect of the per cent of location of village markets. In 1977 hardly 19 per cent of the villages in Maharashtra had weekly village fairs located within the respective villages, as against the national average of 27 per cent. However, the Maharashtra villages fared better with respect to credit co-operative and 80 per cent of the villages had such co-operative within 5 kms distance as against 61 per cent of the villages on all- India average.

Summing Up

The state of Maharashtra symbolises two images of development. At one hand it is a state with high industrial growth, rapid urbanization and substantial share in the economic development of the country; on the other hand, it is also a state where 29.2% of the people live below poverty line (1987-88 report); agricultural productivity is at nadir (compared to national average), and infrastructure at lowest ebb. It is at this backdrop, the present report is being conceived trying to garner further evidences from the villages as to what makes the Maharashtra a state of contrasts, by bringing out regional variations within the state.

METHODOLOGY

Between the Lines

There already abounds a wealth of micro-studies on rural Maharashtra, likewise, macro-issues have been widely analysed and debated both in official as well as scholarly literature.

This report differs insofar as it attempts to amalgamate and synthesise findings from a set of micro-village studies of Maharashtra, which are not the conventional research normally available in the literature studies. The basis for this report is instead the village study assignments prepared by officer trainees of the Indian Administrative Service between the period 1987-92.

These assignments constitute an important part of the district field training of the trainees, aimed at encouraging them to closely and critically observe, document and analyse the socio-economic reality of the countryside in the state to which they are allotted. For this they were required to base themselves for minimum of ten days and nights in a village selected by random sampling. The trainees were given prior training in the basics of statistical techniques and field research methodology.

The socio-economic study of each village consisted of two stages *viz.,* collection of data and analysis of data collected. After selecting the village based mainly on random sampling methods but also sometime on considerations of administrative convenience, data was collected at two levels. Data for the entire village was collected from existing official records available with the administration at district/ taluka/ block and village levels, and also by PRA/RRA technique. Sample study was also attempted based on a survey of roughly 10 per cent of the households, covering not less than 30 households.

For selection of samples, a complete list of households was obtained from the Gram Panchayat. Random sampling was used for selection of households to be interviewed. The last three census reports of 1971, 1981 and 1991 and the District Gazetteer were used for collecting supplementary relevant information. The records kept with various other departments like Zila Parishad, Agriculture Office, Agronomic Office, District Industries Centre, District Planning Office, Irrigation Department, etc., were also referred to for specific information relating to the village.

The assignments focused on various facets of rural life like Demography, Agriculture, Irrigation, Rural industries, Co-operatives, Animal husbandry, Rural Infrastructure, Rural

Leadership, Social life, etc. A SWOT analysis was also attempted to project the sustainability of the village. A review of the poverty alleviation and rural development programmes was also undertaken in these assignments. A study also included a profile of the poorest person in the village, and documentation of the experience of the poor of various facets of local governance.

Whereas the main objective of these studies has been to sensitise and educate the trainees about Indian social reality and to develop skills of empirical observation, documentation and analysis of social and economic issues, it was found that several of these reports contained interesting and valuable case study material and insights. There is no doubt that the studies lacked academic and methodological rigour. Yet, on the other hand, the trainees have greater access both to official documents and observational insights regarding governance of the kind not generally available to the conventional researcher. At the same time, the trainees have not been part of the government system long enough to let this cloud the clarity of their vision and the honesty of their observation.

Therefore, even while readily acknowledging the dilution of research rigour in the reports, it is still maintained that they contain invaluable and sometimes fresh insights into village reality as well as the micro-functioning of village level governance.

This report is based on 41 village assignments collected between 1987-92. The villages are spread across all the 4 regions of Maharashtra, namely, Western Maharashtra, Vidarbha, Marathwada and Konkan regions. The case study method has been attempted to project the status of the village of Maharashtra on various socio-economic indicators. A village is considered as an unit of study. As it is well known that regional variations are very acute in Maharashtra, an attempt is also made to understand the nature of these variations through this micro study.

List of Villages Covered

List of regional profile and name of villages and districts in brackets referred to during the course of this study is presented below:

Sl. No.	*Western Maharashtra Region*	*Vidarbha Region*	*Marathwada Region*	*Konkan Region*
1.	Dehne (Pune)	Wadholi (Chandrapur)	Phulambri (Aurangabad)	Hedavi (Ratnagiri)
2.	Ambe Chincholi (Solapur)	Kapustalni (Amravati)	Bhatkheda (Latur)	Chenna (Thane)
3.	Fursungi (Pune)	Korambi (Bhandara)	Falegaon (Parbhani)	Vangani (Thane)
4.	Amshi (Kolhapur)	Kawdas (Nagpur)	Ardhapur (Nanded)	Chandrapur (Thane)
5.	Kunjirwadi (Pune)	Nandgaon (Amravati)	Ambadi (Nanded)	Wavandhal (Raigarh)
6.	Kavathepiran (Sangli)	Sirso (Akola)	Kate Pimpalgaon (Aurangabad)	Karbude (Ratnagiri)
7.	Musti (Solapur)	Maualimd (Nagpur)	Mahalpimpri (Aurangabad)	Dapoli (Ratnagiri)
8.	Khochi (Kolhapur)	Dhapewada (Nagpur)	Pimpalgaon Mahadev (Nanded)	
9.	Mhaisal (Sangli)	Godhani (Nagpur)	Tidigaon (Aurangabad)	
10.	Banachiwadi (Kolhapur)	Bhendala (Gadchiroli)	Mugat (Nanded)	
11.	Ukoli (Kolhapur)	Baru (Amravati)	Sunegaon (Latur)	
12.	Kinhai (Satara)	Amadi (Nagpur)	Barad (Nanded)	
13.	Kolegaon (Solapur)			
14.	Anjaneri (Nasik)			
15.	Sitane (Nasik)			
16.	Sate (Pune)			
17.	Gavane (Dhule)			
18.	Jawalke (Ahmadnagar)			
19.	Salshingi (Jalgaon)			
20.	Pangaon (Solapur)			

Source : Village Study Assignments, LBSNAA, Mussoorie, 1987-92

STATUS OF LAND REFORMS

Land Reforms status in the villages can be understood under the following headings:

- Land Ceiling and Holding Patterns
- Land Tenancy
- Common Property Resources

Land Ceiling and Holding Patterns

Legal Status

Land ceiling on holdings of agricultural land in the form of Maharashtra Agricultural Lands (Ceiling on Holdings) Act came into force in 1961. The Act was amended in 1975 and some radical changes were introduced. The first change was that the ceiling was reduced to 54 acres of dry crop land or 36 acres of paddy land and it was lowered further to 18 acres for permanent or assured irrigation. Another change was the introduction of 'family unit' in place of a family. A special meaning was assigned to family unit, which included a spouse or spouses, minor sons and minor unmarried daughters. A provision was made to provide for a notional partition to ascertain shares of different family units, in a joint family property. Special posts of Tehsildars were created to function as chairpersons of the Surplus Land Determination Tribunals. Appearance by pleaders was not permitted. The period of appeal was reduced from 30 to 15 days.

In common with the rest of the country, the principal objective of imposing legal ceilings on land holdings has mainly been to ensure equity through distribution of surplus lands to the agricultural tenants, landless and marginal cultivators. The ceiling laws in Maharashtra contain elaborate provisions regarding total quantum of land that a person can hold. A person having land with assured irrigation facilities capable of yielding at least two crops in a year (class I) can hold 18 acres of land; land with assured irrigation for one crop has limit upto 27 acres; land with seasonal irrigation by flow has a limit of 36 acres; dry land in Bombay sub-urban districts has a ceiling of 36 acres; and a person possessing dry land not falling under any of the above categories can hold upto 54 acres. For each member in excess of five, one-fifth of the ceiling area upto a maximum of twice the ceiling area is the upper limit that a family unit can legally hold.

Reflections from Villages

In the 41 surveyed villages of Maharashtra, cases of landowners holding land in excess of the legal ceiling could not be captured, except in ***Chenna*** village (Thane district) where two farmers were found to have land excess to 54 acres. In fact there are various ways of circumventing and evading provisions of the Land Ceiling Act and as a result such cases mostly remain unnoticed.

Among stratagems adopted to evade ceilings, generally good quality land is shown as being of inferior quality by some of the big farmers, with the active connivance of village and taluk level functionaries, to retain the highest possible size of land holding. It is not difficult to change the relevant entries in the land records showing the category of land, from one having high ceiling limit to another category with a low ceiling limit, as it only requires an entry in the crop inspection form prepared by the village land records accountant or *talathi* annually.

The cases of ceiling surplus land are mostly found to be located in the hilly zone of the Maharashtra. Cases of *benami* transfer have also been reported which thwart or distort the implementation of the land ceiling laws. For instance, in ***Gavane*** village (Dhule District) several cases of *benami* transaction have been found and some of the cases are still pending in the courts. Just before the enactment of Land Ceiling Act of the state, most of the ceiling surplus lands were transferred illegally and thus during inspection very few cases were detected.

As per the account of Bandopadhya based on the Agricultural Census of 1970-71 (*EPW,* 1981, Vol. XXI, No. 25-26, June 21-28, 1986) 9.79 lakh hectares were estimated surplus in the state but upto October 1992, only 7.04 lakh acres were declared surplus which constituted 28.77 per cent of the estimated surplus. This shows the huge deficit between the estimated and declared surplus.

It was noticed in the study that the lands owned by a landholder which happened to be located in other districts remained undetected and hence could not be considered for determining surplus land. In Maharashtra, consolidation of land holdings has not been fully implemented and therefore fragmented land holdings are a common occurrence in most of the villages. As a result, the landholders having large dispersed land holdings in different districts or villages go unrecorded. Such concealed land holding is a practice among big landowners and is done generally in connivance with the local officials.

The Act also stipulates that the ceiling surplus land shall be distributed among the landless, SC, ST, and marginal farmers. In the present study, it is remarkable that the officer trainees could identify only in Ardhapur village (Nanded district) where under the Ceiling Acts of 1961 and 1975, 12 hectares of land was declared surplus of which 10 hectares was taken possession and was distributed among six beneficiaries. The gap between the land declared surplus and land taken possession is generally very large due to various factors. The big landowners whose lands were declared surplus went in for litigation. As a result, a large percentage of the lands initially assumed surplus were released to the landowners, mostly on the pretext of partition to near relatives like major sons, brothers, mothers etc. Most of such partitions were undertaken just before the cut off date in order to defeat the intent of the ceiling laws. The land released invariably belonged to big landowners.

The issue of distributing ceiling surplus land in the surveyed villages needs more microscopic study because of the fact that a large percentage of the people in the surveyed village were either landless or held holding which could not be treated as economically viable. The study showed that 44 people were landless in Wavandhal village (Raigad district) out of which 30 were scheduled tribes, 9 neo-Buddhists and only 5 were caste Hindus. It is clear that a person holding less than one acre of land can not generate enough food for a family having a minimum of 4 members, except through supplementary wage activities such as share-cropping and sub-tenancy. In Maharashtrian villages, the present study also showed that the percentage of people owning less than one acre of land was much larger. Secondly, these marginal landholders mostly belonged to the lower castes, SC and ST. For instance, in Jawalke village (Ahmadnagar district), SC/ST were found to be entirely deprived of land holdings. Similarly, in Kunjirwadi village (Pune district) 40 per cent of the villagers were landless and forced to work as agricultural labourers. In summary, the problem of implementing land ceiling laws is that most of the lands declared surplus have not been taken possession by the Government and secondly the lands which are in possession of the state are not equitably distributed among the poorest of the poor.

The second issue of Land Ceiling is the concept of land equity which theoretically denotes equal distribution of the land among the people. It also calls for reducing the disparity among the marginal, small and large farmers. The Act, however, directs that a person can not hold more than 54 acres of land. In the surveyed villages, two trends were noticed. In some of the villages the land holdings were negatively skewed and in the rest, the holdings were positively skewed. In the first case, the percentage of area owned by the marginal and small farmers was much greater than the area owned by the big landowners. For instance, in Ardhapur village (Nanded district), 60 per cent of the marginal and small farmers occupied almost 80 per cent of the area and the cases of big landowners was almost absent in the village. Similarly in Chandrapur village (Thane district), 111 landholders owned between 1-5 acres of land and in Chenna village (Thane district) more than 94 per cent of the farming household accounted for a maximum of 5 acre of operational holding and occupied almost 98 per cent of the area. In this pattern of land holding, the farmers do not get much scope to diversify their operations as the size of the holding is too small to undertake risk bearing activities; and secondly they tend to operate on other farmers' holdings as part time tenant or share cropper in order to sustain themselves. There are other cases also where they go for secondary and tertiary modes of occupation and work in EGS related schemes.

Another pattern of holding that was observed in some villages was one in which the land holdings were more positively skewed, in which most of the area lay in the hands of a few, but they have still managed to ostensibly stand below the ceiling limit, due to various circumvention as discussed above. In Falegaon village (Parbhani district), for instance, around 68 per cent of the land belonged to the medium and large farmers, who in turn constituted just 28 per cent of the population. Such pattern of holding was also observed in Gavane village (Dhule district) where 10 per cent of the people owned almost 85 per cent of the land.

Such hidden cases exist because most of these big landowners have either gone in for *benami* transactions or have failed to file returns and gone unnoticed. The present study, however, has indicated that cases of ceiling surplus land are there in a concealed form and secondly land holding pattern is mostly negatively skewed.

Land Tenancy

Legal Status

On 1st November 1956, tenancy on agricultural lands in Maharashtra were regulated by the following laws :

- Western Maharashtra—Bombay Tenancy and Agricultural Lands Act, 1950 as amended by the Tenancy Act, 1956.
- Marathwada—Hyderabad Tenancy and Agricultural Lands Act, 1950 as amended till 1954.
- Vidarbha—Berar Regulation of Agricultural Lease Act, 1951 which was subsequently incorporated in the Bombay Tenancy and Agricultural Lands (Vidarbha Region) Act, 1958.

The main provisions of the Bombay Tenancy and Agricultural

Lands Act, 1958 as amended from time to time were as follows:

(a) Maximum rent to be paid by a tenant was not to exceed 5 times the assessment or Rs. 20 per acre whichever was less.
(b) If tenancy was created after the tiller's day, the tenant was entitled to purchase the tenancy within one year.
(c) It was not necessary for the landlord to contribute towards cost of cultivation; rather the tenant was liable to pay the land revenue, irrigation cost, etc. All these together was not to exceed 1/6 of the produce.
(d) The landlord had the right to resume the land for personal cultivation for any other non-agricultural purposes before ownership was transferred to the tenant. After the termination, the tenant was to be left with not less than half the area leased to him.
(e) A tenant could surrender his interest of tenancy in favour of his landlord.
(f) On the tiller's day (1st April, 1957) every tenant was deemed to have purchased the land from his landlord subject to certain conditions.
(g) The purchase price to be paid by the tenant was fixed at 200 times the assessment for giving him the ownership rights.

The main provisions of the Bombay Tenancy and Agricultural Lands (Vidarbha region and Kachchh area) Act, 1958 were as follows:

(a) The rent to be paid by the tenant was fixed at 3 to 4 times of the land revenue.
(b) If a tenant is created by the landlord after 1st April, 1963, every tenant was entitled to purchase within one year of the commencement of the tenancy.
(c) There was also provision for a landlord to resume the land for personal cultivation before 15th February, 1961 subject to certain conditions.

(d) A tenant could terminate his or her tenancy by surrendering his or her interest in favour of the landlord in writing and verified before the Tehsildar.
(e) A tenant was entitled to purchase the land from his landlord.
(f) Ownership of land held by the tenants was legally transferred to them from the 'Tiller's Day' (1st April, 1961).
(g) Purchase price for ownership rights by the tenants was fixed at 7 to 10 times of the rent for occupancy tenant and 2 times of the rent for other tenants.

Hyderabad Tenancy and Agricultural Lands Act, 1950 have the following provisions:

(a) Maximum rent payable by a tenant was fixed 3 to 5 times the land revenue depending upon the wet or dry nature of the land.
(b) Every tenant had the right to purchase the land within one year from the commencement of tenancy.
(c) The land holder could resume the land for personal cultivation and terminate the tenancy by giving notice in writing before 31st December, 1958 and also give intimation to the Tehsildar before 31st March, 1959.
(d) The land holder could not terminate tenancy at least a month before the commencement of the year but the tenant could surrender his lands.
(e) The tenant was entitled to purchase the landlord's interest in land by payment of price which for the wet lands was the maximum of 6 times the rent and for dry lands 15 times the rent.
(f) The government had the right to declare from specified date the ownership of the lands to be vested in the tenants (protected, deemed protected and ordinary) and the tenant was declared as full owner of the lands.
(g) The Act was extended to the whole of Hyderabad area of the state of Maharashtra.

It was one of the earliest states in the country to declare a land to the tiller policy, by conferring occupancy and ownership rights to the tenant tiller in the early 50s itself. There was differential impact of the implementation in different regions of the state. It was most effective in the Konkan regions and least effective in Vidarbha region. On the whole, the implementation was relatively successful in the northern and western regions of Maharashtra. In the coastal region of western Maharashtra, 83 per cent of tenancy cases had been decided by 1970 and in the non-coastal region, 86 per cent of tenancy cases had been disposed of. In the coastal regions, tenants became legal owners of nearly 70 per cent of the leased land. Twenty per cent of the leased lands were reverted to the owners and in 10 per cent of the lands tenants continued as the owners, because they were of exempted categories like widows, minors or disabled people. The result was the reverse in non-coastal regions. The tenants became owners of only 24 per cent of the leased lands. The landlords got back nearly 56 per cent of the leased lands in respect of which tenancy was terminated. In the remaining 20 per cent of the leased lands, tenancies were continued because lands were under sugarcane farms, trust lands etc. where major provisions of tenancy laws were not applicable.

Status of Tenancy cases in the Villages

In the present study, the data suggests that today the incidence of concealed tenancy is not high in the state, but these findings are not definitive because in many cases is undoubtedly quite superficial. Of 41 villages surveyed, only 9 villages were recorded to have some form of tenancy in operation. It was found that though the tenancy laws forbid leasing and ensure that the tenant automatically become owners within a period of one year from the date of leasing, these laws were hardly implemented in such cases. In Kate Pimpalgaon village (Aurangabad district), some form of concealed tenancy was recorded by the officer trainees. Incidences of recorded tenancy was also observed in Karbude (Ratnagiri district), Wavandhal (Raigad district) and Jawalke village (Ahmadnagar district). These tenants were mostly those who were either landless or had small holdings and cultivated the lands of the big landowners. However, the incidence of unrecorded tenancy could not be captured during the survey. This might be due to the existence of concealed tenancy where oral agreement is made between the owner and tenant and therefore, goes unnoticed.

The study also showed that most of the tenants were at or below subsistence level and were drawn from among all the castes. The area operated by these tenants were also observed to be very low. For instance, in Wavandhal village (Raigad district), 12 tenants were found operating an area of 23.2 hectares. Similarly in Sirso village (Akola district), 7 tenants were found to be cultivating an area of 20 hectares.

The most common form of tenancy observed by the officer trainees was fixed cash rent, followed by a low incidence of share-cropping. In both these systems of tenancy, it was noticed that the terms of lease were greatly exploitative. The tenants were paying much higher rent or shares than the limit prescribed by the statute. In Kate Pimpalgaon village (Aurangabad district), it was observed that the rent is normally fixed at half of the produce, with the tenant bearing all the expenses of cultivation and landlord bearing the revenues payable on the land. Similarly in Wavandhal village (Raigad district), the rent was fixed half of the produce. In Nayakund and Amadi villages (Nagpur district), the *batai* system was observed. Under this system, the landowners and the tenant share the money required for seeds and labour. The crop is then shared between the landowner and the tenant or *bataidar* on a 50:50 basis. Such system was also observed in Sirso village (Akola district). The practice of share-cropping was recorded in Jawalke village (Ahmadnagar district). Here also the ratios are fixed at 50 per cent of produce and with equal share in cost of inputs.

The study showed that most of the tenants were working with the same landowner for relatively longer periods of time, reflecting at least some modicum of security. In some cases, the tenants were unaware of the provisions of the tenancy reforms laws. A tenant frequently continued to till the land for 3 years on the same field, and subsequently after the unwritten contract ceased the land was given to some other tenant by the land holder. Such cases were observed in Jawalke (Ahmadnagar district) and Ukoli (Kolhapur district) villages of Western Maharashtra region. In these cases, it was observed that the landowners deliberately misused the statute and intentionally broke the unwritten contract in order to avoid litigation.

The study reflects that although tenancy has been legally abolished from Maharashtra, it survives in some forms of concealed tenancy. And secondly, the rates fixed by the landlords are comparatively much higher than that prescribed in the statute. It continues to be a 'sellers' market' and the weak and unorganized tenant has no means to ensure that the landlord abides by the limits and conditions prescribed by the law.

Common Property Resources (CPR)

In villages, Government land includes cremation/burial grounds, land under roads, rivers and streams, pasture land, deorahati (land in the village on which the temples of the *Gram Devtas* is built), fallow land and gaothan or common grazing land. The Government lands are generally used for grazing, forestry, community/public purposes, assessed waste, homestead and cultivation. The cultivated lands are often encroached by the big landowners. However, the CPR- land is also distributed to the landless and the poor people.

The focus of the present study on Common Property Resources was limited to the amount of Government land available in the villages, the amount of land encroached by the people, the allotment of Government land to weaker sections for cultivation and homestead purposes and the evaluation of the overall assessment of the success of the redistribution programme of Government land in the villages. However, out of 41 villages covered, such information was available only for 7 villages.

As stated in the beginning, Government land in the villages is used for various purposes. As per the policy, the Government lands are also distributed to weaker sections of the society. However, no such cases were reported in the present study. Nevertheless, in Wadholi village (Chandrapur district) the

Government land has been allotted for residential purposes to 6 ex-servicemen. Each beneficiary is allotted a plot of size 10.8 metres. Some lands have also been distributed for community purposes. Like in village Bhatkheda (Latur district), the grazing land have been given for new residential settlements (*abadi*) and some part of the Government land has been sanctioned for primary health centres and schools.

However, one disturbing feature is the high incidence of encroachment on Government land. In the present study, 4 cases of land encroachment have been recorded. In Falegaon village (Parbhani district), 20 people who were reported to have encroached on the Government land. Similarly in Kawdas village (Nagpur district), 30.70 acres of Government land are in illegal possession of the big landowners.

The Government of Maharashtra in the past had allowed retention of possession and award of ownership rights over CPR lands which were illegally possessed by the small and marginal farmers and were used for the cultivation. Under this scheme, land upto 2 hectares were allotted to the people. Such cases were observed in Sunegaon (Latur district) and Pangaon (Solapur district) villages.

The present policy of the Government of Maharashtra to reserve a portion of the Government land for purpose of grazing is an important feature from the point of view of preserving one of the elements of common property resources for future generations. This policy is a step in the right direction because it was observed in the present context that in most of the villages, the grazing land were found to be depleting and as a result the reserved and protected forests were in danger. In Banachiwadi village (Kolhapur district), for instance, grazing land of the village has been converted into *gaothan* under the *gaothan* scheme of the Government. There is a need to protect the CPR for common use and make the village more sustainable.

Because of the paucity of data, the study could not comment on the extent of Government land allotted to the weaker section and the status of these allottees. But the trend shows that CPR in the villages are often misused and a large percentage of the CPR are illegally occupied by the big landowners. A comprehensive policy needs to be worked out for distribution of land for the purpose of cultivation and homestead for the genuinely landless, and a total management of CPR in the villages with a view to fulfil basic subsistence needs as also responsibility to unborn generations.

Concluding Remarks

The problems of implementing land ceiling laws in Maharashtra, as emerges from the study, is that cases continue to be trapped in prolonged litigation, a large part of the lands declared surplus have not been taken possession by the government, and the land which is in possession of the state are not judiciously distributed among the most eligible poorest of the poor.

Regarding land holding pattern, it was noticed that land holding was very skewed. With respect to tenancy it was observed that concealed tenancy is not that acute as reflected in other north Indian states. It must be stressed that this may be the result of superficial study, and not necessarily a genuine reflection of ground realities. The study also reflected that the tenants were living at or below subsistence level and were drawn from all the castes and operated a very small area of land. The most common form of tenancy recorded in the study was cash rent, followed by a low incidence of share cropping, and the tenants were paying much higher rent or share than the limits prescribed by the statute.

Regarding the common land, it can be commented that the CPR in the villages is more misused than the used and large percentage of it has been illegally occupied by the big landowners, by tacit complicity between rural elites and government functionaries.

AGRICULTURAL PRACTICES AND DEVELOPMENT PROGRAMMES

Low Yields in Land of Plenty

In the opening chapter of this report we dwelt at length on the paradox of the sectorally acutely skewed pattern of economic development in the state of Maharashtra, with commerce and industry far ahead of the rest of the country and agriculture among the worst laggards.

Around 58.54 per cent of the nearly 20 million hectares total land area of the state constitutes the net sown area. Of this around 70 per cent is under food crops while the balance is spread over oil seeds, cotton, other fibres, fodder crops and sugarcane. The trend is for a gradual reduction in the area under foodgrains, and its replacement by cash crops such as cotton and sugarcane. In the regions of Khandesh and Vidarbha, cotton is a traditional cash crops and Maharashtra ranks third among the states of India in cotton production.

Interestingly, there has been a visible shift from this traditional cash crop to the more lucrative but water intensive new cash crops. Maharashtra is today second in the production of sugarcane in the country and industrially supports a number of sugar mills which have been installed in the vicinity of sugar growing areas. The sugar lobby has come to dominate Maharashtrian politics.

Jowar, the staple food of the farmers in the state and a low rainfall low risk crop is the predominant foodgrain, comprising 5 million tonnes out of a total foodgrains production of 13.5 million tonnes. During 1994-95, the area under kharif *jowar* decreased by 13.9 per cent as compared to that of previous year, whereas the area under rice decreased by 1.2 per cent. The area under kharif cereals decreased by 3.4 per cent in the year 1994-95. In respect of the important cash crops of cotton and sugarcane, the area under cultivation of the former rose by 11.3 per cent, while that of the latter increased substantially by 50.6 per cent during 1994-95.

With regards to rabi crops, the area under rabi foodgrains decreased by 10.7 per cent in 1994-95 as compared to that of the earlier year. The area under rabi *jowar* and wheat decreased by 17.4 per cent and 8.4 per cent respectively. On the other hand, in the case of rabi pulses, the area is expected to increase by 9.2 per cent.

As stated earlier, agriculturally, Maharashtra is one of India's poorest regions. The soil, topography and climate in Maharashtra are not very favourable to high value crops. Adverse agricultural conditions also lead to relatively low yields of the important crops compared to that in several other regions of India. Nearly one-third of the area of the state falls in the rain shadow area where the rains are not very scanty but erratic. About one third area of the state is liable to crop failure due to the vagaries in the monsoon. Various factors *viz.,* variations in the aggregate precipitation, the day of onset of monsoon and cessation of the rainy season, the number of rainy days, and the frequency and duration of dry spells govern the crop response in a given season. The margin between the necessary rainfall needed for the normal growth of the crops and the normal rainfall is very narrow in the low rainfall area. Hence, the adverse effects of a small shortfall in rainfall or irregularities in rainfall precipitation have serious repercussions on farmers in this tract. The soil cover in this region being generally poor and scarce in moisture retention, longer dry spells result in failure of crop. In the areas with assured or high rainfall crop, failures are less frequent as there is a larger margin between the normal rainfall and the requisite rainfall for the crops grown, though the untimely nature of the rainfall does affect the yields.

Maharashtra's agriculture continues to be heavily dependent on monsoon. Less than 12 per cent of the gross cropped area is under irrigation. Since the Fifth Plan, roughly half of the plan investment in Maharashtra has been in the irrigation and power sectors. The state has invested nearly Rs. 6000 crores on creating major and medium surface storage and extending canals. According to the records of the International Commission on Large Dams, Maharashtra is the biggest builder, in the world, of large dams (more than 15 meters high). According to the Economic Survey of Maharashtra, 1993-95, the estimated net area irrigated in 1993-94 increased by 1.8 per cent to 25.14 lakh hectares from 24.70 lakh hectares in the earlier year. The estimated gross irrigated area in 1993-94 was 32.92 lakh hectares, showing an increase of 1.8 per cent over the previous year's area of 32.35 hectares. The percentage of gross irrigated area to gross cropped area in 1993-94 was 15.4 per cent. There is an indication that out of the total cultivable area of 182 lakh hectares in the state, about 84 lakh hectares

(46 per cent) can be brought under irrigation from all the sources, *i.e.* through water as well as through underground water resources. It is estimated that about three-fourth of the ultimate potential is through surface water resources. A number of major, medium and minor irrigation projects have been taken up by the state Government in the earlier two year plans to tap the above irrigation potential in the state. By the end of 1993-94, 21 major, 176 medium and about 1700 state sector minor irrigation projects have been completed. Another 37 major and 78 medium projects are under construction.

Maharashtra has potential and plenty of scope to grow various horticulture crops. The state Government has undertaken a programme to promote horticulture development through establishment of nurseries and granting of capital subsidy to small and marginal farmers and scheduled caste and tribe farmers. Under this programme, 135 horticulture nurseries have been established by the Government in the state to produce and supply planting materials of various fruit crops to the cultivators. The Government took an important discussion in 1991-91 to link up horticulture development with EGS, under which 100 per cent subsidy is made available to the farmers. Farmers having larger holdings are also covered under this programme and are allowed 100 per cent subsidy only on labour charges and 75 per cent subsidy on the cost of material. Under this programme, 0.80 lakh hectares of land was brought under fruit crops from April to December, 1994 benefiting 1.01 lakh farmers. The corresponding achievements during the earlier year were 1.03 lakh hectares of land 1.35 lakh beneficiaries. The area under fruit and vegetable crops has increased by more than 80 per cent in the period 1980-89. In 1988-89, this area was about 4.6 lakh hectares, out of which fruit crops alone accounted for 2.0 lakh hectares. Conventional foodgrains crops yield only Rs. 4 thousand to Rs. 9 thousand per hectare. On the other hand, horticulture crops have very high yield per hectare *viz.* Rs. 0.9 lakh (sweet orange), Rs. 1.40 lakh (banana), Rs. 1.83 lakh (mango) and Rs. 3.0 lakh (grapes).

Cropping Pattern

As seen earlier, the crop pattern varies considerably between different areas of the state according to the agro-climatic factors. In the heavy rainfall region of Konkan, paddy and *nanchni* are the major crops. Paddy is the major crop in Bhandara and Chandrapur. In Kolhapur district, paddy and sugarcane are the important crops. In Dhule, Jalgaon and Nasik districts, among the cereal crops grown, jowar, bajra and wheat are important. Cotton is the major commercial crop in Jalgaon and groundnut in Dhule district. Cultivation of sugarcane, grapes and onions in Nasik district and of bananas in Jalgaon district is another important feature of the cropping pattern. In the scarcity zone, sugarcane is an important irrigated crop. The greater proportion of area in this zone is devoted to the cultivation of cereals like jowar, bajra, pulses and some oil-seeds. In the assured rainfall region, jowar and cotton are the major crops grown and these are grown under dry conditions.

Konkan Region

In the Konkan region, as revealed from the study, cultivation is undertaken only in kharif season which stretches from June to October. Paddy is the only crop grown along with a few acres of land devoted to vegetable cultivation. The crops are exclusively dependent on monsoon. The first shower of rain in June helps the cultivators to proceed with the sowing of paddy for transplantation. Cultivation begins with the preparation of the soil for transplantation of the paddy seedling in the month of July. Harvesting of paddy commences in the last week of October and is continued till the end of November.

In Vangani village (Thane district), the villagers cultivate only in one season. The main crops grown are paddy, *nager* and *wari*. Few people go in for second crop (about 5 hectares) from Nov.-Dec. to April-May. The crops grown are *harbhara (channa)*, *moong dal* and *wal*. The common practice in the village is to manure the fields with the dung of cattle, sheep and goats, farm refuse and stable tiller.

The Japanese method of rain cultivation has been introduced in the Wavandhal Village (Raigad district). The cropping pattern of this village is almost similar to the overall district pattern. *Rab-manuring* is prevalent in this village. In this method, a plot in the rice field is chosen for the seedbed. About 3 to 4 *gunthas* of land is prepared for seedbed and is covered with rab which consists of this layer of brush wood, tree topping (called *that*), dung and grass and then fine earth is sprinkled on it and the rab is set on fire for the seedbed. This process is called rabbing, and it helps in loosening the soil and also checks growth of weed. On the '*rabbed*' seedbed, seeds are sown which grow vigorously only after one or two showers.

In village Hedavi (Ratnagiri district), rice is cropped during monsoon season. Also grown are *ware, nagali* and grass. In the rabi season, some fruit crops are cultivated.

Marathwada Region

Unlike the Konkan region where the crops are cultivated only in kharif season, the cultivation in the Aurangabad district of Marathwada region is more extensive and widespread. In Kate Pimpalgaon rainfall is fairly widespread between June and September. Crops grown during kharif season are *bajra*, *rung* and *tur*. In the rabi season also the people grow jowar, wheat, gram and safflower (*kardi*). The manure used in the village includes chemical fertilisers purchased from the local Co-operative Marketing Association. There is no seed farm in the village but there is extensive use of hybrids and improved varieties in the village, which is also purchased from the Multipurpose Co-operative Society. In Mahalpimpri village, depending upon the availability of water, the farmers take up rabi and kharif cropping. In the rabi season they cultivate *bajra*, cotton and *tur*. The farmers use both farmyard manure (biomass) as well as chemical manure. In Tidigaon village the major kharif crops sown include bajra (more than 50 per cent of the area), *mung, tur* and cotton. The other crops sown in very small area during kharif season are groundnut, *mut (noth)* and sunflower. The crops sown during rabi season are *jowar* (more than 50 per cent of the area), sugarcane, sunflower and some vegetables.

The villages of Nanded district have 3 cropping seasons. In Ardhapur village, the major crop grown in kharif season is jowar while the important cash crops are groundnut, oilseeds and sunflower. In Pimpalgaon Mahadev village, the crops grown during kharif season are kharif hybrid jowar, cotton paddy, *tur*, *moong* and oorad dal, sunflower and til oilseed. In the rabi season the people cultivate rabi *jowar*, wheat and gram. Some crops grown in between January and end of May are groundnut and sunflower. The annual crops are bananas and sugarcane. A similar pattern was observed in Mugat village where kharif and rabi crops were *jowar*, wheat (only in rabi season), cotton (only in kharif season), pulses and oilseeds. Oilseeds are also grown in summer season. Recently the Japanese method of paddy cultivation has been been introduced. The main features of this method are :

- Raising special nurseries for seedlings;
- Low seed-rate for seedlings;
- Heavy manuring of the crop, both in nurseries and in the field;
- Transplantation of fewer seedlings per bunch;
- Transplanting in rows; and
- Adequate inter culturing and proper weeding.

Ambadi village (Nanded district) is basically a kharif centred village although 50 hectares of land is under rabi crops. The crops grown in the kharif season are paddy, *jowar*, hybrid *jowar*, *tur*, soyabean and onion over 350.1 hectares of cultivated area. In the rabi season, the crops sown are wheat, *chana, dhana* and *jawar* and covers an area of 20.9 hectares of cultivated area.

In Falegaon village (Parbhani district), *jowar* and cotton are the main crops grown in the kharif and rabi seasons. The farmers are inclined to sow the summer groundnut in irrigated areas. In kharif season, *jowar* and *moong* while in the rabi season, *jowar* and wheat are also cultivated.

Similarly in Bhatkheda village (Latur district), cash crops like groundnuts, sesame and sunflower are taken up twice in the year. Under EGS linked horticulture, mango and *ber* trees have been taken up by the people. Some farmers have gone for social forestry. They have planted eucalyptus and *su-babool.*

Vidarbha Region

Double cropping is prevalent in this region. In Kawdas village (Nagpur district), cotton and *jowar* are two major kharif crops. Soyabean and *tur* are other important kharif crops. Of the total land under kharif crop, 50.22 per cent is used for cotton. This is followed by land under *jowar* (33.41 per cent), soyabean (8.36 per cent) and *tur* (4.24 per cent). Rabi crops are taken only on 7.6 hectares of land. Wheat and pea are the major rabi crops. The remaining rabi crops include brinjals, onions, tomatoes, palak, methi and coriander. Inputs like fertilisers, insecticides, improved seeds are supplied through the Kharedi Vikri Sahkari Sangh (Buying and Selling Co-operative Society).

In Kapustalni village (Amravati district) *chana* is taken as a double crop, immediately after *moong*. The major crops of the village are cotton, *jowar*, *tur* and *moong*. Mixed cropping is found here, *tur* is sown with hybrid *jowar* and *moong* with cotton. The main crops of Baru village of the same district in rabi season are gram and wheat. In kharif they grow *tur*, *sawar*, cotton and soyabean. A larger area has been set aside for soyabean cultivation because of good returns.

Rice and *jowar* are the main crops of Wadholi village (Chandrapur district). The farmers having small and marginal holdings go in for the same crops. Those having more than 10 acres go for comparatively better earning crops like sunflower and soyabean. Cash crops like sugarcane and cotton are totally absent.

The people of Sirso village (Akola district) have gone in for cash crops. 556 hectares of land (total 1017 hectares) is under cotton cultivation. Other crops grown are *jowar*, pulses, wheat, *kardi* and other fruits and vegetables. 32 hectares of land is sown twice.

Western Maharashtra Region

In Western Maharashtra, cropping pattern has shifted from food crops to cash crops and seasonally the farmers do cultivate in all the seasons. In Anjaneri village (Nasik district) the cultivation is limited to only kharif season. There has hardly been any change in the agricultural practices. Rice and *nagli* are two major crops grown here. The cultivation is more intensive in Sitane village of the same district. Out of a total of 740 hectares of land under cultivation, 560 hectares of land is under *jerayat* (rainfed) and 70 hectares is under irrigation. Under irrigated land, the crops sown are grapes, sugarcane, onion and vegetables. Rainfed land is mostly under *bajra*.

Similar pattern has also been observed in the villages of Dhule district. In Gavane village the major food crops grown are *jowar*, wheat, maize, *regi*, rice, and others and covers an area of 326 hectares. Similarly the cash crops cultivated are groundnut, other oils, cotton, fruits and vegetables, sugarcane and others, and these together cover an area of 94 hectares.

The main kharif crops of Kinhai village (Satara district) are kharif jowar, rajmah and bajra and covers an area of 613 hectares. Other kharif crops are groundnut, black gram, gram cowpea, paddy, sunflower and potato. Rabi crops are jowar and sugarcane. Sugarcane is the important cash crop of the village. The major horticultural crops are mango, coconut, papaya, grapes, pomegranates etc. The area under double cropping is 373 hectares.

In Dehne village (Pune), the major crops are paddy and oilseeds (groundnut) and subsidiary crops are gram, bajra and *nachre*. The area under single crop is 245 hectares and under double crop is 200 hectares. In Sate village of the same district most of the farmers cultivate only in the kharif season. The major crops grown are *jowar* and wheat. There has been no significant change from food crops to commercial crops except in case of a few big farmers who have introduced grape farming. Some farmers have started crop rotation.

Kharif crops grown in Jawalke village (Ahmadnagar district) are *bajra*, *tur*, *moong*, sunflower and groundnut and covers an area of 218 hectares. Rabi crops are *jowar*, wheat, gram fodder and grass. It covers an area of 1120 hectares. Sugarcane is also taken up in the rabi season and is cultivated in an area of 34.12 hectares. The cropping pattern of Ralegon Shindi of the same district has undergone a transformation mainly due to increase in irrigated area from 57 hectares in 1976 to 465 hectares at present. Earlier the main crops of the village used to be rabi *jowar*. Two crops could be grown in the few irrigated holdings in the village, *i.e. bajra* in kharif and *jowar* and wheat in the rabi season. Subsistence agriculture was the norm at that time. Now double cropping is practised on 254 hectares of land. A few of the richer peasants grow crops in all three seasons. Onion is now a major cash crop. Horticulture has also begun in the village. Important principal crops are *jowar*, *bajra*, wheat, maize, pulses, oilseed and cash crops are wheat, onion, pomegranate and sunflower.

In Salshingi (Jalgaon district) village both rabi and kharif crops are grown. The main kharif crops are hybrid *jowar*, *bajra*, *tur* (also sown in mixed cropping pattern), wheat, cotton and groundnut; other crops are sunflower, *erandi mathbi* and *chawli*. Cotton is predominantly grown as a cash crop. Rabi crops are rabi jowari (dadkar), gram and summer groundnut. In horticulture, banana is cultivated as a cash crop in an area of 37 hectares. Other crops are mausambi, lemon/orange, vegetables and pan (betel leaf). Banana is mostly cultivated in dry land.

In Kavathepiran village (Sangli district) tobacco is grown as a main cash crop in an area of 583.30 hectares. Other crops are kharif *jowar* (135.40 hectares), hybrid *jowar* (185.10 hectares), sugarcane (217.13 hectares). The village also has a good vegetable garden. In Mhaisal village area under the crops is completely lopsided in favour of sugarcane (2130 hectares). The area under the remaining two major crops is 120 hectares, with main crops being hybrid *jowar* and rabi wheat. The cropping pattern has shown a shift from food crops to non-food crops.

The cropping pattern of Banachiwadi village (Kolhapur district) showed that paddy was the main crop grown in an area of 117.87 hectares. Many other crops grown were nagali, nachani (rage), sugarcane etc. There was hardly any cash crop sown in the village.

The principal crops grown in Kolegaon village (Solapur district) are hybrid *jowar* (232.1 hectares), *jowar* (190.1 hectares), wheat (110.2 hectares), sunflower (40.8 hectares), *chana* (28.1 hectares) and *moong* (48 hectares). The other crops include *tur*, sugarcane and paddy. Out of the total cultivated area of 714.33 hectares, 658.22 hectares in under rabi crop while only 56.11 hectares is under Kharif crop. Almost all farmers grow just one crop in a year.

Status of Irrigation

Development of irrigation facilities in Maharashtra poses complex problems, because of the difficult terrain and meagre flow in rivers except during the monsoon season. Traditional irrigation in Maharashtra, barring the special case of small tank irrigation in the districts of Chandrapur and Bhandara in Vidarbha is almost entirely dependent on the construction of wells and small bunds across some stream or the lift schemes. The most notable *bhandara* schemes are in Nasik and Khandesh districts and co-operative lift irrigation schemes on river is fairly extensive in the Kolhapur district.

In this section of our paper, status of irrigation facilities in the villages as reported by the officer trainees, is being discussed.

Marathwada region

In ***Bhatkheda*** village (Latur district) of this region, the sources of irrigation are *bhandara*, wells and electric motors. The total land in the village is about 460.26 hectares out of which 100 acres is under irrigation. The village has two percolation tanks. The river Manjara also flows through the village and hence the general level of water in the wells is quite high. Various credit institutions have also contributed to the increased irrigation by providing loans for digging up of wells, drip irrigation, etc.

The Pimpalgaon Mahadev (Nanded district) is better equipped with irrigation facilities. Out of total cropped area of 1049 hectares, 224 hectares is under well irrigation, 81 hectares under lift irrigation and 121 hectares is under canal irrigation. Total unirrigated area in the village is about 630.96 hectares. Apart from well and lift irrigation sources, the major source of irrigation is canal water available from the Purna river project. The Purna river project has been in existence since last 22 years. There has been a major increase in the use of electric pump sets for irrigation purposes. In this village, the farmers have commercialised irrigation services. The rate is fixed at one-fourth of the total agricultural income of the cultivation 'purchasing' water.

In Tidigaon village (Aurangabad district), around 95 per cent of the total cultivable area is rainfed, and 5 per cent is under irrigation and is mainly used for growing sugarcane, wheat and vegetables. Among the different modes of irrigation used are 68 private wells, 4 community wells, and 4 percolation tanks constructed by the Government to re-charge the water table. In Mahalpimpri village only 175 hectares out of a total of 800 hectares of cultivable land is under irrigation and the source of irrigation is confined mainly to wells owned by farmers. Similarly in Kate Pimpalgaon village of the same district, 81 per cent of the total cultivated area is unirrigated and is mainly used for food crops. The 265 hectares of irrigated land yield vegetables (18 per cent of the total area). The ground water of the village is charged with the help of two rainfed percolation tanks. About 255 wells have been dug in the recent past to augment irrigation.

Vidarbha Region

In Vidarbha region, the Kawdas village (Nagpur district) because of its unfavourable geographical features, particularly its hilly tract, lacks irrigation facilities. Out of a total of 452.95 hectares of cultivable land, hardly 9.25 hectares (2 per cent) is under irrigation. The only source is irrigation well. The irrigation facilities in Nayakund village is quite limited. There is no canal or minor irrigation dam. The number of wells are 10 which irrigates 7 hectares of land.

In Amadi village (Nagpur district), around 14 hectares of

land is irrigated by the canal, 16 hectares by wells and 14 hectares by a minor irrigation dam. Therefore, around 44 hectares out of the total cultivable land of the village of 300 hectares is under irrigation.

In village Sirso (Akola district), of the total cultivated area of 985 hectares, only 32 hectares is under irrigation. The sources of irrigation are mainly confined to wells. Of a total of 45 wells, 17 wells are fitted with electric motors.

The scenario in Kapustalni village(Amravati district) does not look promising as far as irrigation is concerned. Most of the cultivation is rainfed and a few hectares of land is irrigated through wells, which number around 18. No other sources of irrigation is available in the village.

In Wadholi village (Chandrapur district), 83.78 hectares (10 per cent) of the total cultivable land of 848.21 hectares is under irrigation. In this area, the average annual rainfall is around 1147 mm and therefore the present cropping pattern does not require further irrigation facilities. However, irrigation potential is there, as the Walinganga river flows parallel in this village and can be used for irrigation.

Konkan Region

In Konkan region the agriculture is mostly dependent on monsoon. For instance in Chenna village (Thane district) of this region, irrigation facility is totally lacking. Though water is available in the river Chenna, it has not been utilised for irrigation purposes. Under the Jeevandhara scheme, 5 wells have been sanctioned to the tribal villagers. The land is at present totally rainfed. Similarly in Vangani village of the same district, most of the cultivable land is monsoon dependent. There is only one tank that is used for irrigation purposes. Under JRY, its capacity for storing rain water has been increased. This village needs new irrigation wells and *nullah bunding* so that double cropping can be promoted. The village Chandrapur is in command area of Surya project and it is hoped that in a few years, the village will be fully irrigated. At present, there are only three bore wells as the exclusive source of irrigation.

The village Wavandhal (Raigad district) again is entirely without irrigated land. Most of the community ponds, wells etc. are used for drinking and bathing purposes. No government initiatives have been taken up to improve irrigation facilities. At present, the cropping pattern is totally kharif based and no crops are grown in the rabi season.

Similarly in Hedavi village (Ratnagiri district), agriculture is totally rainfed and no irrigation facilities has been provided to the villagers. Karbudi village of the same district also projects the similar picture. A small stream that flows through the village is used for drinking, bathing and washing animals. There are 9 wells again unused for irrigation purposes.

Western Maharashtra Region

Compared to other regions, the villages of Western Maharashtra have better irrigation infrastructure. In Kochi village (Kolhapur district), 32.5 per cent of the total cultivable area is under irrigation. The major sources of irrigation are lifts on the Warana river and wells. The major area of irrigated land is under sugarcane.

The scenario in Salshingi village (Jalgaon district) is not so conducive for irrigated agriculture. Only 86.53 hectares of the total cultivable land of 932.22 hectares is under irrigation. However, there have been constant efforts to harness the ground water sources. A percolation tank was constructed in the village in 1967. Other sources of irrigation are 63 wells, 58 dugwells, and 14 functioning borewells (apart from 9 that have been abandoned). There are also 3 sprinkler systems, 2 drip irrigation systems and 76 pumpsets in the village. Despite the introduction of drip irrigation and sprinkler systems in the village, the rationalisation of cropping patterns by resorting to water economic crops and restrained need based irrigation has just not been taken up. Instead, the traditional methods of flood irrigation are still followed. In fact the dissemination of water conservation technologies has not been done properly by the extension wing of the Agricultural Department.

The Kavathepiran village (Sangli district) is situated near the banks of the Krishna river and therefore has enough river water for irrigation. Out of total 375.69 hectares of irrigated land, 93.37 hectares is irrigated through wells and 282.32 hectares from the river. Another village Mhaisal is also situated on the banks of the river Krishna and therefore has abundant water for irrigation purposes. There are 18 lift irrigation schemes, 274 wells and 1 percolation tank in the village for irrigation. The extent of wet lands under the irrigation schemes is 1148 hectares and under wells is about 300 hectares.

In Sitane village (Nasik district) out of the total 740 hectares of land under cultivation, 560 hectares is under *jerayat* (rainfed) and 70 hectares of land is under irrigation. The crops grown in irrigated lands are grapes, sugarcane, onions and vegetables. Rainfed land is mostly under *bajra*. All areas under grapes are watered by lift irrigation whereas vegetables depend more on well irrigation. Onions are under both well and lift irrigation. In village Anjaneri of the same district, out of total cultivable area (3012.95 hectares), 835.52 hectares is under irrigation. There are as many as 52 irrigation wells and a percolation tank. A minor irrigation project is under construction which will have 50 per cent dependability because it might go dry during the lean season. Under the Jeevandhara scheme, a few wells for SC/ST small farmers are also under construction. Pumpsets are being used for lifting water from the wells.

Irrigation in Gavane village (Dhule district) is limited to bore wells only. The area of land irrigated in this village is 35 hectares, out of which 19 hectares are under the kharif and 16 hectares under rabi crops.

Wells are the main source of irrigation in Musti village (Solapur district). There are 82 wells in the village of which 74 are useful for irrigation. There are 2 percolation tanks and 4 *bhandaras* which also support irrigation. Recently one lift irrigation has been installed by the government which has facilitated irrigation of rabi crops. The Zila Parishad has taken up 2 lift irrigation schemes in the village. The irrigation status of Kolegaon village of the same district is still worse. Out of the total 714.33 hectares of area under cultivation, only 18.23 hectares are irrigated. However, the *bhandara* or small dams built on the rivulet has improved the irrigation facilities and in future more area is expected to come under irrigation.

Around 118 hectares of total cultivable area (1375.42 hectares) is under irrigation in Jawalke village (Ahmadnagar district). Jawalke is declared a DPAP village and therefore watershed management has been given top priority. Under EGS, 57 *nalla bunds* and one percolation tank have been constructed. Several wells have also been constructed using land loans and subsidy provided by the Zila Parishad. Ralegaon Shindi lies in a drought prone area with an average rainfall of 350 to 500 mm annually. In 1976, one-tenth of the cultivated area of the village was irrigated by wells. The water conservation efforts made by renowned social worker Shri Anna Hazare have transformed the irrigation facilities available in the village. Groundwater has increased from a level of 50 feet in 1975 to 30 feet at present. The total area under irrigation is 465 hectares (total cultivable area 638 hec.) out of which 350 hectares is under well irrigation and 115 hectares under canal lift irrigation. There are 87 private wells and 8 community wells in the village. Each community well is jointly owned by 6 to 7 households, which share the water on a co-operative basis. Each community well irrigate an area of about 6-8 hectares. The village also has two co-operative irrigation societies which obtain water by lift from the Kinkadi canal. It irrigates 750 acres in three villages of this area, 300 acres lie in Ralegaon.

Concluding Remarks

As noted in the introductory chapter, the level of development in Maharashtra has remained confined to the industrial sector and agriculture is the neglected sector. The state also shows wide regional variations in cropping patterns. The study shows that in western Maharashtra, the villagers have shifted from food crops to more water intensive cash crops. This shift has led to the marginalisation of small farmers who lack both the economic resources and the risk bearing capacity to support such a cropping pattern. Secondly, this has led to the increasing commercialisation of agriculture. Unlike in other regions, the villagers of Konkan cultivate only during the kharif season. Other regions show agricultural operations in both major cropping seasons.

The agriculture in Maharashtra is of such low productivity most significantly because of the lack of irrigation facilities. Although Bhandara scheme and other minor irrigation projects have played an important role in some of the villages in providing irrigation facilities, the gross irrigated area in the state is much lower than the national average. The worst affected regions are Marathwada and Konkan regions which have been traditionally backward.

CO-OPERATIVE MOVEMENT

Brief Review

The co-operative movement in Maharashtra has played a significant role in the social and economic development of the state, particularly in the rural areas. Initially the movement was confined mainly to the field of agricultural credit. Later it rapidly spread to other fields like agro-processing, agro-marketing, rural industries, consumer stores, social services etc. There is generally a remarkable increase in the number of societies in all these fields. Many co-operative sugar factories have been organised by the cane growers.

The first co-operative factory was organised in 1950, soon after independence. A successful prototype already existed in the form of a private sugar factory owned and operated since 1934 by cane growers belonging to a minority peasant caste, the Saswad Males. By 1980, there were 60 co-operative sugar factories which produced nearly 90 per cent of the white sugar output in the state. These factories provided crop loans, guaranteed automatic repayment and also helped to establish ancillary organisations such as drip and lift irrigation, HYVs seeds, fertilisers, transportation, marketing etc. In short, these co-operative societies stand at the heart of an agro-industrial complex which is owned and managed by the village cane growers, with benefits accruing to those who grow half an acre of sugarcane or more.

The number of co-operative societies of all types taken together in the state increased by 5.7 per cent to 1,18,457 by the end of March, 1993, from 1,12,023 as on 30th June, 1992. There were 19,787 primary agricultural credit societies as on 31st March, 1993. These include Farmers Service Societies, Adivasi Co-operative Societies and Gramin Banks. The number of non-agricultural credit societies in the state was 13,653 as on 31st March, 1993 showing an increase of 7 per cent over the number as on 31st March, 1992.

Case Studies of Four Villages

Here, the case studies of four villages of western Maharashtra are being discussed where the co-operative movement has flourished.

In village Ralegaon Shindi (Ahmadnagar district), 9 co-operatives are functioning. The Sant Yadav Baba Tarun Mandal and Bhajan Mandali organise local festivals, collect funds for the same and attend to the numerous visitors. All villagers of 18 years and above are eligible for the membership of the Tarun Mandal. It also helps organise community marriages. The Mahila Mandal attends to the female visitors to the village. It organises festivals especially concerning women *viz.,* Haldi Kumkum and Makar Sankrati. The Mandal also conducts training classes like tailoring and embroidery. It had set up a Balwadi (which was later taken over by the Zila Parishad), a flour mill and a groundnut crushing machine. The most important co-operative in the village is the local credit co-operative called the Vikas Society. It is controlled by a few large landholders who have been members of Anna's Tarun Mandal. It gives annual crop loans to the tune of five to six lakhs every year. They have fixed rates for the amount to be loaned per acre for different crops. The rates vary for irrigated and rainfed lands. The village has nine member Panchayat. On Anna Saaheb Hazare's suggestion, 9 women were nominated as panchs.

In village Salshingi (Jalgaon district), apart from the credit societies known as Salshingi Vividh Karyakari Society, there are five other co-operative societies which are as follows:

- Dairy Society
- Crop Protection Society
- Salshingi Telbia Society
- Pajhar Talav Lift Irrigation Society (now defunct at the time of survey)
- A branch of the Bodwad Sahkari Mandi Samitee.

The Salshingi Multipurpose Co-operative Society was established in the year 1957 and registered in 1961. It has a total of 550 members of whom 450 are borrowing members and the rest of them are non-borrowing members. Its total share capital is Rs. 5,53,575. The multipurpose co-operative society works under the guidance, supervision and control of its executive committee which has 15 elected members. The society distributes agricultural and crop loans to its members. The norms are controlled by the Jalgaon District Central Co-operative Bank which is the open Co-operative Financing Banking Organisation in the district. The norms of credit limits are as follows :

i)	Dry Land Crops (jowar, bajra groundnut, sunflower and pulses etc.)	Rs. 1200 per acre
ii)	Cotton	Rs. 2500 per acre
iii)	Banana (irrigated)	Rs. 4000 per acre
iv)	Sugarcane (irrigated)	Rs. 4500 per acre

The interest rates (in Rs.) for different types of loans are as follows :

i) Upto 7.5 thousands—10 per cent
ii) 7.5 thousand to 15 thousand—11.5 per cent
iii) 15 thousand to 20 thousand—12 per cent
iv) 25 thousand and above—14 per cent

Kavethepiran village (Sangli district) has two *Co-operative Primary Milk Societies*, one *Agricultural Co-operative Credit Society* and one *Backward Class Welfare Co-operative Farming Society*. These societies are affiliated to District Central Bank and

District Societies. The Kavethepiran Vivid Karyakhari Sahakari Society is having nearly 1892 members and provides agricultural loans to the members. The society receives its funds from the District Co-operative Central Bank. The society also looks after the selling of controlled cloth and grains for the benefit of the members. Fertilisers are also sold to the members on credit basis.

The *Varna Co-operative Milk Society* has 441 members. The purchase price of milk is Rs. 3.90 per litre and selling price is Rs. 4.50 per litre. Based on SNF, the rates are fixed every month and the extra rate if any are given to the members as arrears. Advances of Rs. 4500—Rs. 5000 each are arranged through Banks for the members to buy new cows. The milk is collected by the Taluka Milk Society twice a day. The society in the past has given a bonus of 21 per cent to its workers and 10 per cent dividend to its members. The society has purchased cattle feed from the Sangli Co-operative Sugar Mill and supplied the same to their members.

The *Hanuman Co-operative Milk Society* has 235 members. The functioning and administration of this society is similar to the Varna Co-operative Milk Society. This society has organised exclusive veterinary facilities for its members. The society pays 50-75 per cent of the value of milk as advance to its members. Apart from these milk societies, there are two private milk vendors in this village. They collect nearly 200 litres per day and sell it to the Sangli market.

The *Navjeevan Samyuta Sahakari Sheti Society Ltd* is another co-operative society exclusively meant for the scheduled castes of the village. The society has 45 hectares of land and crops like jawar, black gram, sugarcane and wheat are cultivated. The society owns electric pumpsets, bullocks, mechanical agricultural implements like sprayers and pipe lines. The society also has godown storage facilities to store the grains. The society has been formed on the basis of Mahisal Co-operative Farming Society. It provide loans for cultivation and allied activities. This society is a good sign of joint farming and has a scope for development.

Dehne (Pune district) has several co-operative institutions such as Vividh Karyakari Sahakari Sanstha (Multipurpose

Co-operative Society) and Dudh Utpadak Sahakari Sanstha (Milk Producer's Co-operative Society). After Dehne was declared a tribal village, all co-operative institutions were merged into Dehne Adivasi Seva Sahakari Sanstha, established in 1977. It works for in villages with a total membership of 1929 out of which 1463 are tribals. In the foundation year, the share capital stood at Rs. 3165 and presently it has risen to Rs. 3,45,805. The *sanstha* has assisted agricultural production by sanctioning loans for purchasing milch animals. It is also an implementing agency for TSP. It runs fair price shops and supplies daily consumption articles. The *sanstha* has milk collection centres at villages Shergaon, Tokawade and Kharashi.

Another association known as Mahila Mandal started in the year 1985-86. At that time, it had 20 women members and were given a grant of Rs. 1000 by the government. The association took its proper shape after it was taken over by the Yuvak Seva Prabodhini. It has done fruitful work in the area of ICDS. It has also formed a *'Bhajan Mandali'*—a group which sings devotional songs and '*Harinam Saptah Mandal'*—a group which recites God's name in any auspicious occasion. These two groups maintains the cultural and religious fervour of the village. Recently, they have taken up the task of organising women living below poverty line.

Concluding Remarks

It would have been observed that all case studies are drawn from western Maharashtra, an accurate reflections of the mass regional variations in the development of co-operatives in particular and of Maharashtra in general. Above all, the case studies highlight the economic benefits to the members who have formed various kinds of livelihood co-operatives. The studies, however, lack sufficient detail for us to assess whether these benefits have uniform impact on various social and economic groups and gender.

POVERTY REDUCTION PROGRAMMES

Preview

The rural development programmes with a clear anti-poverty thrust broadly fall into two categories:

- Self-employment programmes; and
- Wage employment programmes.

As regards self-employment strategies, there are certain underlying stated or unstated presumptions behind the IRDP and TRYSEM. These are :

- that rural development strategies most importantly focus on each poor individual household and assist it to rise above poverty.
- the principal barrier to the large scale generation of self-employment opportunities among the rural poor is the absence of assets, resulting from the lack of access to credit. This is compounded by the absence of requisite skills;
- it is admitted that land is the paramount rural asset, which is the most powerful source of economic and social well-being in the rural context. However, in the background of the relative failure of land reforms to generate adequate surplus land for redistribution to all, or even a major section of the rural assetless, and the absence of political and administrative will for such thorough going structural reforms even in the future, a softer option is provided by IRDP.

For those with even a little land, additional resources to go with land, like bullocks, wells or pumps may be given. A second approach is to give moveable assets not directly related to land such as livestock or assistance to establish petty business or cottage industries. A third is to provide skills, such as masonry carpentry, blacksmithry, cobbling etc., followed by asset assistance, so that they can be self-employed.

Since the principle bottleneck to self-employment of the assetless rural poor is presumed to be absence of credit, it was believed that asset transfer to the poor mainly requires creating effective avenues of access to institutional credit. In order to reduce high repayment burdens, a part of the capital should be given as outright subsidy or grant, and the remainder as loan on low interest rate.

The other major category of rural development strategies for poverty alleviation are wage-employment programmes. These are programmes for providing supplementary wage employment to the rural poor on public works.

The experience of Maharashtra in alleviating poverty is interesting because it throws considerable light on the actual experience of the Employment Guarantee Scheme (EGS) is the only state in which it has been operational, from the early 1970s.

A recent article on "Alleviating Poverty: Maharashtra Employment Guarantee"* throws an interesting light on this issue. It initially highlights the vast variations and discrepancies in the overall regional development of Maharashtra. Although it has the second highest per capita State Development Project among Indian States in 1990-91, this figure hides enormous urban- rural contrasts and regional disparities. The 65 per cent of the labour force is dependent on agriculture, agricultural productivity is very low, rainfall and assured irrigation scant and droughts frequent. The incidence of poverty in Maharashtra declined significantly for all types of households between 1977-78 and 1983. In spite of the decline, the incidence of poverty for agricultural labour households was around 53 per cent in 1983. Their share in total poor households was the highest, around 54 per cent in 1983.

The approach of Maharashtra Government towards Poverty Alleviation Programmes (PAP) seems to be in two forms, *viz.*, general productivity raising programmes in agriculture and direct anti-poverty programmes with emphasis on employment. The direct anti-poverty programmes incorporate all the major self employment and wage employment strategies indicated in the introduction. However, it is the Employment Guarantee Scheme that is unique in the experience of Indian States. The main features of the EGS are as follows :

- Guarantee for wage employment in public works at district level.
- Eligibility of all adult persons in rural areas and 'C' class municipalities.
- Failure to meet guarantee entails payment of allowance of Rs. 2 per day.
- Wages on piece-rate: in theory seven hours work should yield minimum wages.
- Employment restricted to productive assets with emphasis on water conservation works.

This scheme is totally financed by the state government. In order to raise resources for the implementation of the scheme, the state government has levied special taxes and levies : (i) Tax on professions, traders, callings and employment; (ii) Additional tax on motor vehicles; (iii) Additional tax on sales tax; (iv) Special assessment on irrigated agricultural lands; (v) Surcharge of land revenue; and (vi) Tax on non-residential urban lands and buildings under Education Cess Act. Of the total resources required under EGS, 64 per cent were raised from professional tax and 30 per cent from additional tax on sales tax. It is clear that the programme involves a successful transfer of resources from the prosperous urban centres especially Bombay to the impoverished rural hinterland.

Highlights of PAP in the Villages

We will now look at micro-studies of the officer trainees to highlight the impact of various poverty alleviation and development programmes in rural Maharashtra.

Konkan Region

The studies of the officer trainees confirm firstly that beneficiaries under IRDP have been the SCs and STs. For instance in the Wavandhal village (Raigad district), 12 below poverty line families have been covered under the scheme in 1984-85; out of these, 9 were tribals. These beneficiaries were given bullock, bullock carts and cows. However, the impact of these services on the quality of life of the people is one issue to be further probed. In 1988-89, two beneficiaries and in 1989-90 only one beneficiary was covered under this scheme. Under the bio-gas development programme, 11 bio-gas plants have been obtained by beneficiaries. There is a need for community biogas plant linked with latrines to be introduced in this village. Under the National Rural Employment Programme (NREP), a Gram Panchayat office in 1984-85 and a 4 seat latrines were built in 1987-88. Under the Jawahar Rojgar Yojana (JRY), in 1989-90, one room Anganwadi building was constructed. Under the self employment scheme (TRYSEM), in 1979 and 1981, six and nine women respectively were given training in sewing.

In Chenna village (Thane district), 84 below poverty line families were covered (out of a total of 228 below poverty line families identified in the village) in 1988-89, and when assessment of the impact of IRDP on these beneficiaries was done, it was revealed that of 38 families who were assisted with goats, not even a single family owned the goats at the time of the survey. The report is silent about the status of these families, who either sold off the goats or could not afford to manage the assets adequately. Under NREP, various activities undertaken in the village were low cost housing for STs, compound wall of school building and village road construction. National Bio-gas Development Programme provided bio-gas plants to 12 families. But most of these plants have become defunct. This has happened partly because dung of cattle is not collected systematically. Integrated Child Development Services Scheme (ICDS) was started in this village only in 1983 and presently one Anganwadi is under operation. Under the Jeevandhara Scheme, 5 beneficiaries were identified out of which three wells have been completed.

In Karbude village (Ratnagiri district), under JRY, 2 school buildings and one road has been constructed. Under TRYSEM, tailoring training was given to four female beneficiaries. They were also distributed sewing machines. Two beneficiaries were trained in electric repairing. In Maharashtra, Employment Guarantee Scheme (EGS) has been linked also to Horticulture development. Under EGS Horticulture Scheme, any farmer having holdings up to 6 hectares, is entitled to get 100 per cent subsidy for Horticulture development. The farmer gets money for land levelling, excavation, plants, irrigation and maintenance. In this village, 20 families have taken the benefits under this scheme.

In Vangani village (Thane district), under the IRDP, out of 299 families below the poverty line, 198 have been assisted. Of these, 64 beneficiaries were SCs and 10 STs. Under the Jeevandhara Scheme, wells have been dug for SC persons having holdings of 3 acres and below. Assistance for training for self-employment for educated unemployed youth was extended to 10 persons for poultry, typing, video, dairy, tailoring and welding. Five bio-gas plants have been set up as against the target of 65. Under DWCRA, a Mahila Mandal for manufacturing *papad*, pickle and spices have been set up. Under TRYSEM, training has been provided for wiremen, tailoring and welding.

Marathwada Region

The IRDP scheme in Marathwada region has not been successful. For instance in Mahalpimpri village (Aurangabad district), 40 people were assisted with cows which were subsequently sold off or died. The beneficiaries have also not paid dues to the bank. A similar tale has been observed in Mugat village (Nanded district) where 49 beneficiaries were given assets for generating additional income, but the people could not afford to utilise the assistance and have remained below poverty line.

There is a need for stressing more on the demands of the people rather than the supply side. The assets so generated should match the actual felt needs as well as their own understanding of how the beneficiaries are going to manage the assets so generated.

Failure to do so often leads to assured scheme collapse. For instance, in Ambadi village (Nanded district), sheep and goat units were supplied to the beneficiaries, but later on it became non-viable because this area is short of animal fodder, therefore milch animal units have not been sustainable.

In Bhatkheda village (Latur district), two individuals were trained under the TRYSEM scheme. The EGS also provided employment to the unemployed. In past 2 years, various works like roads, percolation tanks etc. were undertaken under this scheme. In 1992-93, there were about 500 workers daily attending different EGS works in the village. During the drought year of 1991-92, the EGS labourers used to get extra half kilogram of wheat through the PDS. In the same year, a mobile PDS had started at the sites of EGS work. Around 36 beneficiaries have benefited from the bio-gas scheme. However, 18 of them have become non-functional. There are about 3 community latrines and 5 bio-gas plants operating on them. Seven out of 12 below poverty line households have been administered IRDP loans. The SC and ST beneficiaries have received loans for drip irrigation, pipelines, Jeevandhara wells, implements for harvesting crops, pesticides, electric motors etc.

In Ardhapur village (Nanded district), 90 per cent of those eligible have been aided through IRDP. Of them 30 per cent have managed to stay above the poverty line and the rest have maintained status quo. Under TRYSEM, about 20 village youths have been trained in various skills for self employment. The JRY has made a clear impact on building infrastructure in the village. Approach roads, a PHC building and the primary school have been built under this scheme. The *Samaj Mandir* has also been built out of the JRY funds. The EGS work has been utilised to give a percolation tank to the village. Also social forestry and village roads have been developed along with giving employment to the local unemployed persons. EGS works have also been utilised for soil and water conservation. There are 15 beneficiaries who have bio-gas plants. However, many of these plants have become defunct. Smokeless *chullahs* have also been given to many households. The concept of pit latrines as developed by Sulabha

Sauchalaya International is also being encouraged among the people.

In Ambadi village (Nanded district), 67 *Gharkuls* have been constructed under NREP. Under IRDP, 47 persons have been given loan, out of which only 2 persons have repaid the full loan and have been given second round of assistance. Sheep and goat units have helped the below poverty line families to improve their living standards. As this area is short of animal fodder, milch animal units have not proved to be viable. Four boys have received training under TRYSEM. Out of these 3 have started their own business and one could not start for want of loan. Under ICDS, this village has 7 Anganwadis. This village comes under Kinwat block and has an Integrated Tribal Development Project. Under this project, electric pumps and motors were supplied to the Kolam tribals for irrigation purposes and bullocks were supplied for ploughing. There are 13 Ashram schools in the taluka. These Ashram schools provide free boarding and lodging to tribal children.

In Mahalpimpri village (Aurangabad district), JRY has made a visible impact since its inception 3 years ago. Assets created so far are a room in the school building, a *Samaj Mandir* for the backward class and a drainage system. Under TRYSEM, 6 people were trained but have failed to utilise it for economic gains and have remained unemployed. Twenty hutments have been constructed for the people of backward and economically weaker sections under the Indira Awas Yojana. The Gram Panchayat has taken keen interest in Social Forestry and 10 acres have been included under this scheme. Based on Anna Saheb Hazare's model of Ralegaon Siddhi, the villagers are making efforts to bring Shram Shakti Dvara Gram Vikas Scheme to this village. It is a nodal programme wherein all schemes of rural development are brought to the village in an integrated fashion. The villagers contribute in the scheme by way of labour. It has been an extremely successful story in Ralegaon Siddhi.

In Tidigaon village (Aurangabad district), under IRDP, 54 persons were identified as below poverty line out of which 24 persons were provided assistance and this has substantially improved their economic situation. Five beneficiaries were provided assistance and technical know-how to install the bio-gas plants. The basic objective of this programme is to reduce the dependence on fuel wood and proper use of cow-dung cake. However, the programme has not proved successful as four of the bio-gas plants have become non-functional. Under the Revenue Huts programme of the Maharashtra Government, rural huts were constructed in the village for 14 identified beneficiaries. Under JRY, the Gram Panchayat was provided Rs. 32,000 in 1989-90 and Rs. 23,800 in 1990-91 to initiate the construction of a drainage system and school building. Besides these programmes, the people have also become receptive towards adult education.

Falegaon village (Parbhani district) has Vivid Karyakari Sahakari Society which provides loan to the farmers for seeds, fertilisers and pesticides. There is a milk co-operative society but there is no milk collection centre in the village. Hence, this society has become defunct. There are 13 community wells and 8 hands pumps. Under IAY, 8 houses were constructed in the year 1993-94 and were distributed to scheduled castes. IRDP has benefited 105 people. A teaching class centre is run through Social Welfare Department and 20 beneficiaries have availed of this service and are earning their wages. Social welfare department has distributed one electric engine, ploughs with bullocks to 5 person and a stitching machine. Eight STs have also benefited under Jeevandhara Scheme. Four beneficiaries have been distributed wells under Jawahar Vyapti Yojana. Under MADA and OTSDP, the ST beneficiaries have been provided financial assistance for construction of wells. A Jan Sikshari Vayakari Kendra is running in the village where the adults study in night. A Mangal Karyalaya, two rooms for a school, a village road and drain were constructed under JRY during the year 1993-94.

In Mugat village (Nanded district), under JRY, a few drains have been constructed. Under employment programmes, 50 families were given subsidy for construction of bio-gas plants but due to lack of maintenance, 40 plants have become disfunctional.

Vidarbha Region

In this region the information of only 3 villages are available. In Baru village (Amravati district), 12 persons have been provided goats, cows and bulls under the IRDP scheme. Two women have been provided with sewing machines. As for social forestry, the scheme has been taken up under JRY and 2450 trees of various fruits have been planted. Regarding bio-gas, 3 plants have been installed. A massive improvement has been done in the form of improved smokeless *chullahs* and till 1991, 102 such *chullahs* were installed. Under the Jeevandhara scheme, two wells have been built and under TSP six wells have been constructed.

In Kawdas village (Nagpur district), under the Minimum Needs Programme (MNP), 12 families were provided tiles (*kawelu*) for roofing. Janta saris-dhotis were distributed to 100 people below poverty line. Under IAY, 20 households were given houses for shelter. Social forestry scheme has not been implemented in Kawdas. Under the bio-gas scheme, although 32 plants were constructed, only 2 such plants were found to be functioning. The horticulture department has also implemented a scheme in which the beneficiaries are provided with all the expenses for planting and maintenance of mango, orange and other fruit saplings.

In Kapustalni village (Amravati district), all the major development programmes are under implementation. 125 families (out of 375 below poverty line families) have been assisted under the IRDP scheme. Under JRY, the Gram Panchayat took up nalla construction and village roads. Earlier latrines for scheduled castes were constructed. Other schemes like the SCP and the Zila Parishad Scheme for the benefit of the scheduled castes have also been implemented. IAY provided pucca houses to several houseless people. But the IRDP has failed as most of the beneficiaries have sold off their assets.

Western Maharashtra Region

Like in other regions, this region has also seen various developmental activities with mixed response. Social forestry scheme has been introduced in Dehne village (Pune district) since 1985-86. Around 2000 Nilgiri trees have been planted by the Gram Panchayat. Partially unemployed and landless villagers have been employed to nurture these plants. Some private landowners also have taken up social forestry scheme by planting fruit trees, bamboos and *subabul*. Government pays Rs. 8 per plant plus Rs. 5.40 per year for caretaking and watering. Under NREP, four works were sanctioned *viz.*, balwadi, public platform and school building, but none were completed. Under IRDP, till 1987-88, 42 families were assisted in primary, secondary and tertiary sectors. Tribals were the main beneficiaries. Under the *Gharkul* housing programme, by 1987-88, 13 houseless families were allotted huts. Four bio-gas plants were installed in 1988-89 in the village. Under the Land Development Scheme, 7 ploughs, 2 spray pumps and fertilisers were distributed to marginal and small farmers. A total of 38 farmers have received various benefits under this scheme by 1987-88. For economic upliftment of backward people, social welfare schemes have been implemented. Fifteen per cent of Panchayat funds have been statutory reserved for 'Social Welfare'. Training and Visit Scheme (TLV Scheme) started in this village in the year 1982-83. Under this, farmers are given training and guidance for cultivation of plant, use of hybrids, fertilisers, implements, etc. In kharif and rabi season, HYVs have been supplied to 147 farmers *via* village level workers (VLW) during years 1986-87 and 1987-88. Krishi Vigyan Mandal has been set up in the village. This Mandal has 11 members who are farmers. VLWs conduct the meetings of Krishi Vigyan Mandal to chalk out a proper crop pattern.

A number of rural development activities have been undertaken in the Musti village (Solapur district). Under the IRDP scheme, 14 beneficiaries were benefited. They were given the loans for milch animals, bullock carts, soap making etc. Under NREP, a canal was proposed to be built but due to paucity of funds, it remained incomplete. A road was constructed under EGS in which 37 labourers got employment. The government also constructed a percolation tank in the year 1982 under RLEGP scheme. Under JRY, 2 rooms for primary school, 10 bathrooms for backward class and a gutter was constructed.

In Kunjirwadi village (Pune district), 93 families have been covered under IRDP scheme. A total of 31 families have received their second dose of assistance. The beneficiaries were landless labourers (64) and marginal farmers (29). The loans have also been provided for milch animals, small business and industry. Three of the below poverty line beneficiaries were trained under TRYSEM.

The government sponsored development programmes started in Kochi village (Kolhapur district) in the year 1982-83 with the NREP. From 1985-86 to 1989-90, 60 families were assisted under IRDP, out of which 23 were SC beneficiaries.

In Mhaisal village (Sangli district), the total number of beneficiaries selected for IRDP loans were 783 out of which 510 were assisted till 1988-89. The subsidy limit per beneficiary is Rs. 3000 as the village is included under the non-DPAP area. Under NREP, various activities like construction of latrines, metal road, construction of gutter, houses for the poor were taken up. Under Jeevandhara, a subsidy of Rs. 23,000 was given for constructing wells. Work on social forestry was also undertaken in the village.

Comprehensive Watershed Development Programme (COWDEP) was started in the Ralegaon Shindi (Ahmadnagar district) village from 1983 onwards. Attempts were made to check the run-offs by afforestation, contour bunding, land shaping and grading, and nullah bunding. The plantation of fruit and fodder trees on five hectares area of Panchayat land by the social forestry department has proved to be an excellent measure. The Panchayat members allot management of the plantation by rotation to the village members who share the profits. A programme to increase the yield and quality of *ber* has been undertaken by crossing local species with improved varieties. Under EGS, forestry department implemented various activities and generated 17,500 mandays since 1987. Social Welfare Department executed various schemes like Harijan Chavdi repair, electric pumpset, community well, house construction, hostel building for backward class and Harijan basti toilets.

There were 241 below poverty line families in Kinhai village (Satara district) out of which 119 have received aid under IRDP. Under IAY, houses have been built for the homeless. Primary school and community hall buildings have been constructed under JRY scheme. For bio-gas plant, loan is given as per the unit cost of NABARD for various sizes of biogas plants. Subsidy is also given based on size and model.

The programme of IRDP started in Kavathipiran village (Sangli district) in the year 1978-79. In the year 1982-83 and till December 93, the loans were sanctioned for dairy development, rural artisans, supply of bullock carts, poultry etc.

In Sitane village (Nasik district), 86 people were assisted under IRDP till 1983. Three people were assisted under Jeevandhara. There are 22 *gharkools* built for SC/ST beneficiaries.

None of the below poverty line households in Salshingi village (Jalgaon district) have been covered under IRDP scheme. The major schemes which have been implemented in the village are JRY, TRYSEM, IAY, Jeevandhara, Janata Sari Dhoti, Vatap Yojana (Distribution of handloom sarees), Savitri Bai Phule Dattab Palab Yojana, Bio-gas plant and improved *chullha* scheme. Apart from these schemes, there are some beneficiary oriented (individual) schemes which are implemented by the Revenue department like Gaothan Extension Schemes and Indira Gandhi Vridha Shetkari Sahajya Yojana.

In Jawalke village (Ahmednagar district), 93 people have benefited under IRDP. Fodder Development Project have been taken up on a 2 hectares community plot with full finance by DRDA which will benefit 40 beneficiaries. Three SC below poverty line families have been given assistance under Jeevandhara. Eight houses have been constructed under Gharkul Yojana for landless. Under the JRY scheme, the villagers have opted for gutters. This village has been a major beneficiary of EGS during the last 10 years. A number of *nullah bunding* projects were taken up and completed during this period. Two percolation tanks were also completed. The EGS has been instrumental in providing employment to villagers in time of need and has also succeeded in developing essential infrastructure.

Concluding Remarks

The picture that seems to emerge is that IRDP in particular has been almost uniformly a failure. In most of the villages the people could not judiciously made use of the assets and as a result the desired impact could not be achieved. A pair of bullock asset proved to be a total failure invariably in all the villages.

The wage employment programmes have fared marginally better, insofar that they have yielded occasional useful community assets. There is no evidence of any sustained effort to plan and implement productive assets; nor does EGS appear to have provided any cast-iron guarantee against unemployment, nor any genuine social security net.

However, the community based development programmes like social forestry have attracted the people to take up such scheme in a big way. Again the scheme like gobar gas plant has been a failure because of the lack of maintenance. Regarding targetting of the beneficiaries, it can be said that there seems to be more regularity in selecting the beneficiaries as per the norms.

SWOT ANALYSIS

A region-wise SWOT (Strengths, Weaknesses, Opportunities and Threats) analysis is being attempted here in order to diagnose the problems and prospects existing in the villages and also examine the regional variations. The analysis could not cover Konkan region because the information of this region was inadequate.

Marathwada Region

Strengths

- Most of the villages have adequate infrastructure. Mugat (Nanded district) and Tidigaon Villages (Aurangabad district) are fully electrified.
- The Godavari flows through the Mugat village (Nanded district) and therefore there is abundant water for all the purposes.

- The EGS scheme has made available local employment to the rural people. This has partially reversed the migration process. Manpower, as a result, is readily available.
- Local leadership (e.g. Panchayati Raj) is completely ingrained in the village political reality.
- Falegaon (Parbhani district) is privileged to have PDCC branch and co-operative societies which offer short and long term agricultural loans.
- Community life in rural Maharashtra is very strong and therefore co-operatives may function efficiently.

Weaknesses

- ***Falegaon*** village (Parbhani district) is situated in hilly area and on a rough terrain and therefore geographical feature acts as a natural barrier. The area is very remote and hence tends to get neglected by all the departments. For irrigation, there is no water facility although large tracts of land are available for cultivation.
- ***Tidigaon*** village (Aurangabad district) lacks irrigation facilities as a result of which there is heavy dependence on monsoon.

Opportunities

- In village Falegaon (Parbhani district), large tracts of land are uncultivated and unirrigated and so there is possibility of increasing productivity by introducing irrigation facilities.
- Similarly in Mugat village (Nanded), out of a total of 2177 hectares of land under cultivation, only 125 hectares are irrigated whereas the rest of the land is dependent on the monsoon. Godavari river flows through the village and the farmers can use lift irrigation to pump the water from the river for irrigation purposes. The farmers can form smaller groups and install motors for lifting water.
- Another viable opportunity in Mugat village (Nanded district) is rural artisan based cottage industries in the

co-operative sector. Already there are families engaged in handicrafts but they are all functioning separately in isolation. These isolated families may be motivated to form a co-operative cottage industry which will be more economical and viable. It can use the latest implements and techniques for giving quality products and generate employment.

- In the same village there are 500 cows and 480 oxen. But due to the lack of any co-operative society in the village, the villagers have to go to Nanded to sell milk. The farmers can come together and get organised to form a milk co-operative society. The IRDP also may be integrated with this scheme which will also help in bringing below poverty line families above the poverty line.
- In village Tidigaon (Aurangabad district), there is the possibility of reducing the severity and impact of the shortage of water during bad monsoon years by laying down the water channel from the Godavari river which is around 40 kms away to the west. Though the cost of laying such channel would be high, the whole Vaijapur taluka is a declared Drought Prone Area, it can immensely benefit from construction of such a water channel. Besides mitigating the problem of irrigation and reducing the problem of over-dependence on rains, it will also remove many allied problems such as scarcity of fodder for cattle, etc.

Threats

- No apparent threat was found in the villages.

Vidarbha Region

Strengths

- Most of the villages were geographically located nearer to the district headquarters and therefore the communication networks were found to be well linked.

- Although average land holding was found to be small the people owned at least some piece of land for sustenance.
- Land reform measures appear to have been better implemented in the villages.
- Commercial crops have been taken up in a big way by the villagers.
- The villages are partially free from natural calamities like floods, cyclones, etc.
- Social/ political awareness have taken deep roots among the villagers.

Weaknesses

- There has been no revolutionary step in improving the productivity in agriculture. Irrigation facilities are wanting in most of the villages.
- Unlike in Western Maharashtra, the co-operative movement has not flourished in the villages of the Vidarbha region.

Opportunities

- In village Godhani (Nagpur district), there is a lot of scope for orange pulp marketing and other agro-based activities. EGS related horticulture also has high potential.
- The introduction of horticulture and allied agricultural industry especially in the co-operative sector can enhance the development of villages.
- Presence of large area of wasteland in village Godhani (Nagpur district) may be developed for agricultural purposes.
- Lands are fertile unlike in Western Maharashtra and adequate irrigation facilities would give boost to agricultural productivity.

Threats

- Growing communal tension because of socio-religious dynamics that has come to play recently.

Western Maharashtra Region

Strengths

- The Kolegaon village (Solapur district) being closer to taluka and district headquarters has better market penetration. The village is free from communal tensions. Rural infrastructure is in a better shape. It also receives better rainfall.
- Strengths of Gavane village (Dhule district) lie in 100 per cent electrification, its active elected panchayat and its peace loving people.
- Banachiwadi village (Kolhapur district) is also near to the state highway, panchayat samiti and tehsil headquarters and therefore has access to communication, banks, agricultural input supply centre, health centre etc. Success of the co-operative movement has created a positive impact in the quality of life of the people.
- Kinhai village (Satara district) is also near to taluka and district headquarter, river Vanganga flows besides the village, has adequate rural infrastructure and has a history of an active co-operative movement. *Rajmah* and sugarcane business has flourished since the last two decades. The village also boasts of having factories like MAFCO, sugar factory and tannery.

Weaknesses

- Kinhai village (Satara district) suffers from water problem during summers. Kolegaon village (Solapur district) is a DPAD taluka. Soil is not very fertile.
- Gavane village (Dhule district) also suffers from water scarcity, inadequate irrigation facilities and lack of transport services.
- Banachiwadi village (Kolhapur district) has hilly terrain, infertile lands, absence of water source for irrigation, poor water retentivity of soils, small holding sizes and

poor natural endowment. The village lacks a primary agricultural credit co-operative society.

Opportunities

- In Banachiwadi village (Kolhapur district), co-operative movement can be engineered in dairy and industrial sector. Water Conservation Programme launched in 92-93 by the state government would help the farmers in solving water crisis problem.
- Kinhai village (Satara district) has tremendous scope for agro-based industries. Area under sugarcane and *rajmah* may be increased to its full potential to enhance productivity.
- Kolegaon village (Solapur district) has scope for cottage based industries. But due to unavailability of raw materials and modern inputs the potential has not been fully utilised.
- Improved irrigation facilities will boost up agricultural production as the soil is very fertile and local labour is readily available.
- Due to lack of milk co-operatives, in a few villages like Gavane (Dhule district), the milk is either drained out or sold at a very low price. Such co-operatives would give maximum profits to the villagers and also help in instilling the concept of co-operation among the villagers.

Threats

- Kinhai village (Satara district) is an earthquake prone area. The people of Kinhai have been facing the threat of drought each year since last two decades. Pollution from nearby factories is also a major threat.
- The reduced tree cover and grazing land in Kolegaon village (Solapur district) is a major ecological threat. Due to the relocation of some project affected persons in this village, the original inhabitants have not accepted them and as a result this village has been caught in the web of group rivalry.

A PROFILE OF THE POOREST PERSON

Although sketching the profile of the poorest of the poor of a village is very subjective in nature, it serves primarily two objectives: it sensitises the officer trainees about the real conditions of the people living in the village and; secondly, also reflects the degree of poverty prevailing there. It is a direct confrontation with reality, so that the person sketching the profile may internalise the same and may do something constructive for this layer of the people. Given below is the sketch of a poorest of a poor person living in Kinhai village (district Satara).

> In a big village like Kinhai, it is a difficult task to ascertain as to who poorest person in the village is. I cannot say whether Kakka Appaji Jadhav is the *poorest* person or not but it can easily be said that he belongs to the poorest among poor category.
>
> He is around 50, son of Appaji Jadhav and works as a *mochi* or cobbler. During summers and monsoons he is able to earn anything between Rs. 10 or 20 per day. During winters, there are days when he is unable to earn anything. He is illiterate, has a half starved appearance and looks much older than 50 years (which he claims to be his real age). His wife, he says, is around 40 years of age and she does not keep good health. From the description he gave, it appears she is suffering from some respiratory problem. She used to work as an agricultural labourer but now is unable to undertake any activity due to health reasons. They have adopted a distant nephew. The son is 10 years of age and is studying in the Zila Parished School in class III.
>
> Kakkaji hails from Padsi village and was one among many brothers and sisters. His father was an agricultural labourer. He got married at a young age and then came to Kinhai with his wife in search of work. He tried his hand at several jobs and ultimately worked as an apprentice to a shoemaker. There he picked up his trade as a cobbler and took it up as full time occupation.
>
> Kakkaji's main problem is that he is feeble minded. He takes a long time to understand questions and is unable to express himself clearly. He has never approached any Governmental authority and neither has he heard of any schemes. He has a dull, vacant look in his eyes but when I asked him as to what he wanted most from life, his face lit up immediately and then he expressed his dream which all fathers have for their sons—I want my son to become a big man.

APPENDIX- II

INDICATORS OF INFRASTRUCTURE DEVELOPMENT

Sl. No.	*Particulars*	*Units*	*Maharashtra*	*All India*
1.	Road length per 1000 sq.kms area in 1987-88	Kms	673	561
2.	Motor vehicle per lakh population in 1990-91	Num.	3,174	2,226
3.	Railroute per lakh sq. km 1990-91	Kms	5,435	2,367
4.	Post office per lakh population in 1990-91	Num.	15	18
5.	Villages connected by all weather roads in 1987-88	Total villages	53	41
6.	Population served by each fair price shop in March 1991	Num.	221	2,124
7.	Banks per lakh population in March 1992	Num.	7.1	7.2
8.	Per capita bank deposits (March 1992)	Rupees	6733	2761
9.	Per capita bank advances (March 1992)	Rupees	4,202	1,648
10.	State's own tax revenue per capita 1991-92	Rupees	738	415
11.	State's own-tax revenue per capita 1991-92	Rupees	220	139
12.	Percentage of irrigation potential created to the ultimate irrigation potential upto 1991-92	Percentage	61.6	73.2
13.	Per capita consumption of Power (1990-91)	KWH	397	241
14.	Per capita consumption of Petroleum products (1990-91)	Kgs	120	65.2
15.	Per capita outlay on education (1992-93)	Rupees	254	232
16.	Hospitals and dispensaries per one thousand sq. kms (1989)	Numb.	36	12
17.	Beds in hospitals and dispensaries per lakh population (1989)	Numb.	121	74
18.	Per capita Development Expenditure (1991-92)	Rupees	1,086	870
19.	Per capita plan outlay VII Plan	Rupees	1717	1252
20.	Infrastructure Development Index (1990-91)	Points	111	100

Source : C.M.I.E Basic Statistics, Vol. 2, September 1988, 1990 and 1992.

IMPORTANT INDICATORS OF INDUSTRIAL DEVELOPMENT

Sl. No.	Particulars	Units	Maha-rashtra	All India	Bank of Maharashtra
1	Number of registered factories in 1987-88	Per-centage	14.78	100	1
2	Average daily employment in the factory sector	,,	15.15	100	1
3	Value of factory sector output 1987-88	,,	21.32	100	1
4	Per capita value added in the factory sector 1987-88	Rupees	793	336	1
5	Value of mineral production in 1999	Per-centage	36.55	100	1
6.	Production of mill cloth in 1989	"	38.00	100	1
7.	Production of sugar in 1990-91	,,	34.20	100	1

Source : C.M.I.E. Basic Statistics, Vol. 2, September 1992.

INSTITUTIONAL NETWORK (PERCENTAGE OF VILLAGES HAVING AMENITIES LOCATED WITHIN SPECIFIED DISTANCE, 1977)

Sl. No.	*Particulars*	*Maharashtra*	*All India*
1.	Railway Station	12.82	18.34
2.	Metalled Road	44.38	45.76
3	Bus Stop	46.40	40.26
4.	Post Office	46.20	53.24
5.	Primary School	93.23	90.12
6.	High School	31.76	20.92
7.	Health Centre	7.08	11.98
8.	Hospital	24.08	35.48
9.	Fertiliser Depot	36.31	43.89
10.	Seeds Store	37.75	40.33
11.	Agriculture Pump Repair	14.77	18.76
12.	Storage and Warehousing	29.96	20.72
13.	Veterinary Dispensary	45.54	45.19
14.	Credit Co-operative	79.78	60.75
15.	Bank	34.97	39.88
16.	Village Shandy	19.08	26.84

Source : Central Statistical Organisation, "Economic Census 1977", Government of India, New Delhi.

NUMBER, AREA AND AVERAGE SIZE OF OPERATIONAL HOLDINGS IN MAHARASHTRA

Sl. No.	*Size class Hectare*	*1970-71*	*1980-81*	*1985-86*	*1990-91*	*1970-71*	*1980-81*	*1985-86*	*1990-91*	*1970-71*	*1980-81*	*1985-86*	*1990-91*
1.	Below 0.5	6834	9914	12754	16672	1634	2630	3191	4119	0.24	0.27	0.25	0.25
2.	0.5-1.0	5585	9345	12126	16075	4142	7103	9125	12.057	0.74	0.76	0.75	0.75
3.	1.0-2.0	8743	15409	21026	27276	12842	23337	31346	39833	1.46	1.51	1.49	1.46
4.	2.0-3.0	6266	10275	12474	13969	15386	25363	30582	33689	2.46	2.47	2.45	2.41
5.	3.0-4.0	4606	6585	7069	7289	15920	22815	24622	25108	3.46	3.47	3.47	3.44
6.	4.0-5.0	3576	4601	4672	4469	15961	20556	20822	19864	4.46	4.47	4.46	4.44
7.	5.0-10.0	8715	9316	8496	7241	61213	63937	57800	48700	7.02	6.86	6.80	6.73
8.	10.0-20.0	4180	2819	2102	1530	56302	37213	27594	19749	13.47	13.20	13.13	12.91
9.	20.0 >	961	363	257	176	28394	10662	8440	6129	2955	29.37	32.84	34.82
10.	Total	49506	68625	81013	94697	211794	213616	213522	209248	4.28	3.11	2.64	2.21

Source : Statistical Tables on Agricultural Census, Commissioner of Agriculture, Maharashtra State, Pune

PERCENTAGE OF LITERACY IN EACH DISTRICT, 1991

Sl. No.	*District*	*Males*	*Females*	*Total*
1.	Greater Bombay	87.87	75.80	82.50
2.	Thane	77.56	60.28	69.54
3.	Raigad	75.94	52.20	63.95
4.	Ratnagari	76.64	51.61	62.70
5.	Sindhudurg	86.23	66.87	75.81
6.	Nasik	73.98	49.89	62.33
7.	Dhule	63.13	38.78	51.22
8.	Jalgaon	77.46	50.34	64.30
9.	Ahmadnagar	75.30	45.99	61.03
10.	Pune	81.56	59.77	71.05
11.	Satara	80.61	53.35	6.67
12.	Sangli	74.83	49.94	62.61
13.	Solapur	70.08	41.73	56.39
14	Kolhapur	80.33	53.08	6.94
15.	Aurangabad	72.93	39.64	6.98
16	Jalna	64.43	27.30	46.25
17	Parbhani	64.90	29.41	47.58
18.	Beed	66.34	32.34	49.82
19.	Nanded	64.38	30.96	48.17
20.	Osmanabad	68.39	39.16	54.27
21.	Latur	70.47	39.74	55.57
22.	Buldana	76.53	46.13	61.69
23.	Akola	77.63	53.28	65.83
24.	Amravati	78.40	61.13	70.06
25.	Yavatmal	70.45	44.81	57.96
26.	Wardha	78.33	61.02	69.95
27.	Nagpur	81.79	64.74	73.64
28.	Bhandara	78.82	50.44	64.69
29.	Chandrapur	71.30	46.81	59.41
30.	Gadchiroli	56.56	28.87	42.89
	Maharashtra State—1989	76.56	52.32	64.87
	Maharashtra State—1981	69.65	41.01	55.83
	India*— 1991	64.13	39.29	52.21

Source : Director of Census Operations, Maharashtra.
Registrar General and Census Commissioner for India.

Note: *Excluding Jammu and Kashmir

AREA AND DENSITY OF EACH DISTRICT, 1991

Sl. No.	District	Area in sq km	Density
1.	Greater Bombay	603	16,461
2.	Thane	9,558	549
3.	Raigad	7,152	255
4.	Ratnagiri	8,208	188
5.	Sindhudurg	5,207	160
6.	Nasik	15,530	248
7.	Dhule	13,150	193
8.	Jalgaon	11,765	271
9.	Ahmadnagar	17,048	198
10.	Pune	15,643	354
11.	Satara	10,480	234
12.	Sangli	8,572	258
13.	Solapur	14,895	217
14.	Kolhapur	7,685	389
15.	Aurangabad	10,107	219
16.	Jalna	7,718	177
17.	Parbhani	11,041	192
18.	Beed	10,693	170
19.	Nanded	10,528	221
20.	Osmanabad	7,569	169
21.	Latur	7,157	234
22.	Buldana	9,661	195
23.	Akola	10,574	209
24.	Amravati	12,210	180
25.	Yavatmal	13,582	153
26.	Wardha	6,309	169
27.	Nagpur	9,872	332
28.	Bhandara	9,321	226
29.	Chandrapur	11,443	155
30.	Gadchiroli	14,412	55
	Maharashtra State	3,07,713	257
	India*	32,87,263	267

Source: Director of Census Operations Maharashtra, Registrar General and Census Commissioner for India

Note: Figures are Provisional
*Excluding Jammu and Kashmir

LIVESTOCK POPULATION IN EACH DISTRICT OF MAHARASHTRA, 1987

(In thousand numbers)

Sl. No.	*District*	*Cattle*	*Buffa-loes*	*Sheep*	*Goats*	*Total Livesstock**	*Total Poultry*
1.	Greater Bombay	13	107	15	28	169	199
2.	Thane	550	214	2	196	976	1,427
3.	Raigad	503	162	1	150	821	1,359
4.	Ratnagiri	540	90	@	80	711	1,087
5.	Sindhudurg	284	123	@	76	486	808
6.	Nasik	914	175	252	531	1,902	1,382
7.	Dhule	718	145	136	393	1,415	790
8.	Jalgaon	683	296	37	434	1,470	487
9.	Ahmadnagar	991	124	310	759	2,208	1,646
10.	Pune	761	217	334	481	1,809	3,384
11.	Satara	458	294	365	321	1,449	1,785
12.	Sangli	301	298	229	270	1,107	2,204
13.	Solapur	509	204	281	594	1,606	1,376
14.	Kolhapur	272	477	146	173	1,075	931
15.	Aurangabad	530	76	93	356	1,073	325
16.	Jalna	447	63	52	248	822	199
17.	Parbhani	736	141	50	382	1,325	289
18.	Beed	614	158	190	369	1,344	458
19.	Nanded	706	195	53	352	1,352	334
20.	Osmanabad	343	109	45	220	725	230
21.	Latur	404	166	48	181	811	192
22.	Buldana	579	115	85	325	1,118	253
23.	Akola	605	113	20	316	1,075	276
24.	Amravati	587	107	25	295	1,031	292
25.	Yavatmal	798	122	10	421	1,368	616
26.	Wardha	424	51424	7	178	667	155
27.	Nagpur	700	83	21	303	1,121	434
28.	Bhandara	746	150	3	296	1,213	673
29.	Chandrapur	711	103	52	270	1,146	649
30.	Gadchiroli	556	80	13	197	880	600
31.	Maharashtra State	16,983	4,755	2,873	9,195	34,255	24,839

Source: Quinquenniel 14th Livestock Census, 1987.

Note: *Excludes Dogs

@Less than five hundred

Details may not add up to the totals due to rounding

APPENDIX III

LIST OF VILLAGE STUDY REPORTS

Sl. No	Name of Office Trainees	Village Covered	District	Batch
	MARATHWADA REGION			
1.	Om Prakesh	Bhatkheda	Latur	1992
2.	Alka Tewari	Mahalpimpri	Aurangabad	1990
3.	BaldevSingh	Tidigaon	Aurangabad	1989
4.	SamirKumar Biswas	Mugat	Nanded	1990
5.	Vimlendra Sharan	Ardhapur	Nanded	1992
6.	Kishore Gajbhije	Ambadi	Nanded	1987
7.	Devara Rajgopal	Falegaon	Parbhani	1992
8.	Arvind Singh	Kate Pimpalgaon	Aurangabad	1988
9.	Amitabh Joshi	Pimpalgaon Mahadev	Nanded	1988
	VIDARBHA REGION			
10.	Milind Mhaiskar	Wadholi	Chandrapur	
11.	Deepak Kapoor	Baru	Amravati	1991
12.	Anand M.Limaye	Kapustalni	Amravati	1989
13.	L.V.Nilesh	Bhendala	Gadchiroli	1991
14.	B.P.Shrimali	Sirso	Akola	1992
15.	Manisha Patankar	Godhani	Nagpur	
16.	Nitin Gadre	Nayakund and Amadi	Nagpur	1989
17.	S.A.Tagade	Kawdas	Nagpur	1991
18.	R.A.Rajeev	Dhapewada	Nagpur	1987
	KONKAN REGION			
19	Anil Diggikar	Karbude	Ratnagiri	1990
20	Krishna Swaroop Vasta	Hedavi	Ratnagiri	1987
21	Rajiv Jalota	Wavandhal	Raigad	1988
22.	Rajesh Agarwal	Chandrapur	Thane	1989

Sl. No	*Name of Office Trainees*	*Village Covered*	*District*	*Batch*
23.	Veera Rana	Vangani	Thane	1988
24.	Naresh Kumar	Chenna	Thane	1987
	WESTERN MAHARASHTRA			
25	Aswani Kumar	Mhaisal	Sangli	1987
26.	M. Ramaswamy	Kavathepiran	Sangli	
27.	Anoop Kumar	Salshingi	Jalgaon	1990
28.	M.D. Pathak	Banachiwadi	Kolhapur	1991
29.	Vijay Kumar Gautam	Kochi	Kolhapur	1987
30.	Nand Kumar	Ukoli	Kolhapur	989
31.	Sanjay Sethi	Kolegan	Solapur	1992
32.	Rajesh Kumar	Musti	Solapur	1988
33.	S.V.R. Srinivas	Gavane	Dhule	1991
34.	-	Sitane	Nasik	1989
35.	Iqbal Singh Chahel	Anjaneri	Nasik	1989
36.	Nitin Kareer	Kunjinwadi	Pune	1988
37.	Avinash Dharmadhikari	Dehne	Pune	1986
38.	Seema Sharma	Kinhai	Satara	
39.	Arun Kumar Tiwari	Sate	Pune	1990
40.	Apurva Chandra	Jawalke	Ahmadnagar	1988
41.	Meeta Rajiv Lochan	Ralegaon Shindi	Ahmadnagar	1990

SELECT BIBLIOGRAPHY

Annual Season and Crop Report, Maharashtra State, 1979-80, Government of Maharashtra, Bombay.

Appu, P.S., *Land Reforms in India : A Survey of Policy, Legislation and Implementation,* 1995, Land Reforms Unit, LBS NAA (Government of India), Mussoorie, U.P.

Attwood, D.W., Israel, M. Wagle, N.K., (Ed.), *City, Countryside and Society in Maharashtra,* South Asian Studies Papers No. 2, University of Toronto, 1988, Centre for South Asian Studies.

Attwood, D.W., Baviskar, B.S., *Who Shares? Co-operatives and Rural Development,* 1988, Oxford University Press, Delhi.

Bahadur, K.P., *The Castes, Tribes and Culture of India, Vol. III,* Western Maharashtra and Gujarat, 1981, Ess Publications, New Delhi.

Brahme, Sulabha, *Drought in Maharashtra 1972 : A Case for irrigation Planning,* Gokhale Institute of Politics and Economics, 1983, Orient Longman Limited, Pune.

Census of India 1991, Series—14, Maharashtra, Paper—2 of 1991, Provisional Population Totals, Bombay.

Detailed Statements of outlays Provided for District Level Schemes in the Annual Plan, 1990-91, Government of Maharashtra, Planning Department, Bombay.

Economic Survey of Maharashtra 1994-95, Directorate of Economics and Statistics, Planning Department, Government of Maharashtra, Bombay.

Economic Survey of Maharashtra 1993-94, Directorate of Economics and Statistics, Government of Maharashtra, Bombay.

Encyclopaedia of India, Maharashtra, 1992, Rima Publishing House, New Delhi.

Gadgil, Gangadhar, Deshpande, A.A., (Ed.), *Maharashtra: Problems, Potential and Prospects,* 1988, Somaiya Publications Private Ltd., Bombay.

Ghate, Rucha, S., *Forest Policy and Tribal Development : A Study of Maharashtra,* 1992, Concept Publishing Company, New Delhi.

Growth of Industries in Maharashtra, A Statistical Projection, Bombay.

Handbook of Basic Statistics of Maharashtra State, 1993 Government of Maharashtra, Bombay.

Inamdar, N.R., *Educational Administration in the Zila Parishads in Maharashtra,* 1974, Popular Prakashan, Bombay.

Kudi, U.L., *Impact of Communalism on the Working Class and Peasantry (A Case Study of Maharashtra),* 1986, Daya Publishing House, Delhi.

Murugkar, Lata., *Dalit Panther Movement in Maharashtra,* 1991, Popular Prakashan, Bombay.

Murkuti, S.R., *Socio-Cultural Study of Scheduled Tribes : The Pardhans of Maharashtra, 1990,* Concept Publishing Company, New Delhi.

Portrait of Maharashtra, The Director of Publicity, Government of Maharashtra, Aug. 1970, Government Central Press, Bombay.

Punekar, S.D., Golwalkar, Alka R., *Rural Change in Maharashtra : An Analytical Study of Change in six village of Konkan,* 1973, Popular Prakashan, Bombay.

Selected Indicators for Districts in Maharashtra and States in India, 1983-84, Government of Maharashtra, Bombay.

Second Maharashtra By 2005 : A Study in Futurology, Tata Economic Consultancy Services, 1977, Popular Prakashan, Bombay.

Season and Crop Reports, Maharashtra Report, 1980-81 Government of Maharashtra, Bombay.

Southern Economist, Vol. 32. No. 19. February 1, 1994, Bombay.

INDEX